MULTIDIMENSIONAL
HUMAN BEHAVIOR
IN THE COMPLEX
SOCIAL ENVIRONMENT

MULTIDIMENSIONAL HUMAN BEHAVIOR IN THE COMPLEX SOCIAL ENVIRONMENT

DECOLONIZING THEORIES FOR SOCIAL WORK PRACTICE

Edited by

Jemel P. Aguilar
Ph.D., LCSW, M.P.H.

and

Elisabeth Counselman-Carpenter
Ph.D., LCSW

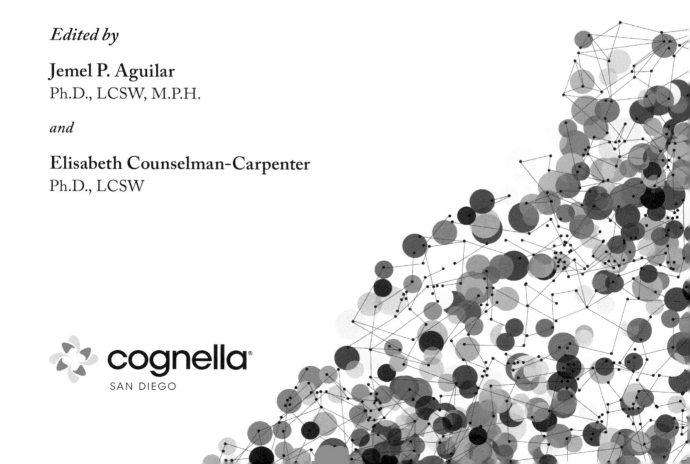

cognella®

SAN DIEGO

Bassim Hamadeh, CEO and Publisher
Amy Smith, Senior Project Editor
Alia Bales, Production Manager
Jess Estrella, Senior Graphic Designer
Kylie Bartolome, Licensing Coordinator
Kim Scott/Bumpy Design, Interior Designer
Stephanie Adams, Senior Marketing Program Manager
Natalie Piccotti, Director of Marketing
Kassie Graves, Senior Vice President, Editorial
Jamie Giganti, Director of Academic Publishing

Cover image Copyright © 2020 iStockphoto LP/naqiewei.

Printed in the United States of America.

3970 Sorrento Valley Blvd., Ste. 500, San Diego, CA 92121

Brief Contents

Detailed Contents

ACTIVE LEARNING

This book has interactive activities available to complement your reading.

Your instructor may have customized the selection of activities available for your unique course. Please check with your professor to verify whether your class will access this content through the Cognella Active Learning portal (http://active. cognella.com) or through your home learning management system.

Preface

This book came to be for the simplest of reasons: we could not find a book that helped us investigate the vast number of situations that arise when examining human behavior. Challenges in traditional HBSE courses are many: students focus on behaviors to the exclusion of contextual and environmental influences, while some of the larger social dimensions like economics, politics, and policies are viewed as overwhelming and distal factors outside of a professions scope of practice. . The theories students need to understand can be challenging and applying theories to practice encompasses another level of thinking and skills that many times are omitted from textbooks. Indeed, 'traditional 'theories are developed using populations and situations that differ from social worker's contemporary clientele and social problems. we seek to introduce students to look at the big picture. What are the societal forces that contextualize human behavior? How do theorists help us understand this bigger picture, and can we bring this knowledge into social work practice?

Yet looming beyond the challenge of teaching theory and applying it to practice is the theoretical canon, which is the underpinning of most HSBE courses and books for those courses. "Traditional" theory is written from the perspective of, and typically focuses on, white, cisgender, straight, middle- and upper-middle class, able-bodied males. Populations with multiple, marginalized identities are regulated to the sidelines of a chapter or the diversity of these populations are contained in one 30 page chapter.

We have developed this book, then, to address what we have perceived and which many of our colleagues have as well as a barrier to helping students understanding human behavior in the social environment e. First, rather than jumping right into human behavior from infancy and continuing throughout the lifespan, our book begins in Part I with a brief discussion of the fundamental context for human behavior and development. Therein we decolonize the structure of human behavior in the social environment textbooks through the book's content and structure, as well the geopolitical milieu. The context of human development, thus, shapes all other aspects of the life course and provides context for the discussion of the lifespan in Part II.

While 'traditional' theories are not given short shrift, a wider theoretical perspective that focuses on the widespread diversity of people with multiple marginalized identities is examined. For example, chapters that examine Piaget and Vygotsky's formulation of cognitive development over the life course will also include research describing the cognitive development of children with multiple identities who are also influenced by speaking both English and another language, familial responsibilities, and navigating interactions in communities and schools. Moreover, each chapter integrates the latest knowledge from neuroscience related to populations with multiple identities and their influence on human development. Finally, chapters are linked to social work practice by framing how knowledge about populations with multiple marginalized identities, human development, and neuroscience can assist social workers in engagement, assessment, intervention, and evaluation processes that maintain the dignity and worth of populations, starts where clients are in their help-seeking process, and support social workers to address social problems.

Features

- **Context as applied to human development** helps students understand the connections between context and stages of human development

- **Theory** is presented throughout the text, providing better insight into understanding the situations and populations of people with multiple social identities

- **Focus on multiple social identities throughout** the entire book helps redress some underexamined areas of development

- **Explicit focus on the practical application of theories** takes the student away from "what is going to be on the text" thinking into "how i can apply this knowledge in my work"

Pedagogical Elements

- Chapters begin with **Learning Objectives** that help students understand the focus of the chapter

- **Case studies/vignettes** in each chapter (many of which are directly from the lives of the chapter author or their student) engage the student and provide a real-world perspective, aiding in understanding theory in practice

- **Reflection Questions** appear in most chapters, challenging students to think critically about key concepts and theories

- **Theory ↔Practice boxes** throughout the text examine and demonstrate the ways that classical and contemporary theory inform practice

Acknowledgments

We wish to acknowledge and thank our students throughout the years, who have challenged and inspired us to put together a book that would support their learning and that of their successors. We also thank our reviewers, whose insights and suggestions we had always considered even when we weren't able to consistently follow them Finally, we thank the staff at Cognella, from Kassie Graves, Vice President of Editorial, Amy Smith, Senior Project Editor, Alia Bales, Production Manager, and Jess Estrella, Senior Graphic Designer.

—Jemel Aguilar

I would like to acknowledge and thank the contributing authors for their work, vulnerability, and commitment to transforming and decolonizing how future generations of students conceptualize human development. I would also like to thank all of my colleagues at Adelphi University for their support, the interim administrative leadership team of the School of Social Work, Provost Chris Storm, and President Christine Riordan. On a personal note, I would like to thank my professional mentors for their continued guidance and wisdom, especially J. S., B. A. D., and R. B. Thank you to Peter Labella for his contributions, and deep thanks to Kassie Graves and the entire Cognella team for their leadership and commitment to this text.

I would also like to acknowledge my ancestors, who paved the way for me to position myself in this context to do this work: I hope that this project continues to honor your dreams and sacrifices, especially my late parents Terry Dankel Counselman and Richard Counselman. Mahalo to my hānai family, especially Joyce W., Anne G., and Elizabeth M., who supported me through this entire project; my biological Dad, Tom; and to my family—my partner, Diane, and my children of heart and body: Colin, Brady, Matthew, and Talia for their love and unwavering support during the long hours devoted to this project.

—Beth Counselman Carpenter
March 2023

PART I

The Contexts of Human Development

The diversity of approaches to teaching and learning human behavior in the social environment sometimes obscures the practice-based realities that social workers face. A lifespan perspective is a linear approach to understanding how people grow and change prenatally until their death. The lifespan perspective occurs alongside and within a social context and environment that adds nuance to human development, making a linear developmental perspective dynamic and complex.

Part I introduces the complexity and contextual backdrop shaping aspects of human development. In Chapter 1, Jemel Aguilar introduces how context and environment influence human development, given the multiple social identities of people and populations. Systems and complexity theories are foundational to understanding human development's dynamic and complex nature in the social environment. Three classic systems theories are discussed, and basic concepts are highlighted to set the stage for examining complexity theory. In Chapter 2, Soma Sen examines globalization's effects on social work contexts and the importance of understanding economic influences on human development, the social environment, and social opportunities. Sen focuses on the work of Marx and Gramsci while introducing key economic concepts for social workers.

Part I sets the stage for the subsequent chapters that strive to move social workers beyond Eurocentric views of human development that cluster many populations with marginalized social identities in with White, middle-class, heterosexist, and cisgendered theories. These two chapters also infuse how institutional and social hierarchies, multiple social identities, social domination, and subordination create structures, systems, and interpersonal interactions that negatively and positively influence development. Chapters 1 and 2 also provide basic guidance on moving from theoretical knowledge to social work practice, which is an added feature to help social workers practice human behavior in the social environment.

CHAPTER 1

Context in Interaction with Human Development Across the Lifespan

JEMEL P. AGUILAR

1. Explain the difference between a client system's social context and social environment.

2. Apply the concept of social context and environment to client systems to identify the factors influencing development in the social context and the social environment.

3. Analyze the potentially positive and negative influences of factors in the social context and social environment on client systems.

4. Evaluate contextual and environmental risk and protective factors for a client system's developmental outcomes.

5. Create a multilevel, biopsychosocial-economic-spiritual assessment for a client system.

Introduction

Immediate and **distal** surroundings shape human development throughout the lifespan by providing or limiting opportunities, resources, and **iatrogenic** influences. This bold assertion has further qualifications in that (a) aspects of the immediate and distal surroundings might be visible or invisible to the person experiencing them or to an assessing observer, (b) the positive and negative influence of surroundings are interactive, cumulative, and sometimes contradictory to absolutist assumptions, and (c) human development is adaptive and ever-changing across the lifespan. In this chapter, the relationship between human development and contexts is explained along with the asserted qualifications to illustrate potential variations in development. This chapter, therefore, sets the stage for social workers to think about the social environment, social context, and interactions among people. Also, the chapter examines how systems theories, systems thinking, and systems perspectives inform social work engagement, assessment, intervention, and evaluation.

This chapter is just the beginning of a lifelong journey in thinking and conceptualizing the environment, context, and personal interactions such that social workers can effectively engage, assess, intervene, and evaluate client systems, policy initiatives, and organizational settings. The material in this chapter and its application to social work thinking positions readers on the long road toward continually achieving the following Council on Social Work Education competencies:

- Demonstrate ethical and professional behavior.

- Engage diversity and difference in practice.

- Advance human rights and social, economic, and environmental justice.

- Engage in practice-informed research and research-informed practice.

- Assess individuals, families, groups, organizations, and communities.

- Intervene with individuals, families, groups, organizations, and communities.

- Evaluate practice with individuals, families, groups, organizations, and communities.

By the end of this chapter (and even this text), readers will not be competent in these areas but will have a foundation to build competence upon throughout one's careers. The following aims mark the end goal and measure one's understanding of the content described in this chapter.

CASE STUDY

Alex watches the news each morning. CNN reporters describe the wars happening around the world, the spread of COVID-19 variants, arguments for and against mask and vaccination mandates, new songs released by famous artists, and policies allowing citizens of one country and preventing citizens of another country from migrating to the United States of America. After the news, Alex prepares for today's history test and hopes that the night of spaced repetition and concept mapping is sufficient for passing the history test. These strategies seemed very different from rote memorization that Alex used in the past, and many YouTubers spoke highly of these methods because the British medical student Alex follows used these techniques to excel in medical school. In contrast, a Stanford doctoral student who studies education explained in considerable detail concept mapping as a study method. "Here goes," Alex thinks as the front door of the apartment complex slams shut.

Alex walks down the sidewalk toward the bus stop, stepping around some litter. Alex hears muffled talking swirling around but focuses on the links between concepts found in the history text. "The international criminal court is linked to crimes against humanity, of which genocide is an example. Crimes against humanity also include systematic torture and systematic rape." Alex stops at the corner before looking both ways and then crossing the street to the bus stop.

At the bus stop, Alex talks with Jenny about the history test, studying, and potential questions that Mrs. Mimble might ask, adding, "She's such a tough grader." As Alex and Jenny walk off the bus, Jenny says "bye" and runs over to a group of friends, quickly joining the conversation. Alex continues walking into the high school, only to be stopped by the line waiting for security to allow students to pass through the doorway. Entering school has changed a lot over the years as more and more school shootings happen across the United States of America. The spread of school shootings contrasts with students on TikTok from around the world discussing their school challenges. unlike the active shooter drills, debates over the validity of school shootings by some segments of conservative media, and the growing debates about teachers carrying guns in schools. Further contrasting problems include the contemporary debates about sexual orientation and gender identity discussions in school settings, whether parents should decide if their child must wear a mask, and the violence laid against school board members by frustrated parents.

Alex walks through the door and heads toward the history classroom to settle before the test. Alex sits next to Katia, whose eyes are puffy and red. Katia looks at Alex and says, "we've been trying to reach my family in Ukraine and Russia all night. I am not ready for this test and really don't care right now." Katia starts to cry. Mrs. Mimble walks into the classroom and greets the students: "Hi everyone, can you turn off your phones, take off your watches and put them in your pockets, and those with glasses, please put them in front of you on your desk so I can check them before we start the test." Mrs. Mimble starts to walk around the classroom as she continues to give instructions: "You will have the whole class time to complete the test …" she leans over the looks through a student's glasses to check if they are smart glasses, and once you are done, close the booklet and sit quietly until everyone is done. Do not take out your phone or watch until I give everyone permission." Mrs. Mimble checks another student's glasses and says, "Taking out your phone or watch will result in automatic failure of the test."

Alex listens to Mrs. Mimble. Alex's heart starts to race faster and faster as Mrs. Mimble moves around the classroom. The spaced repetition and concept mapping exercises pass through Alex's mind faster and faster—too fast to be a last-minute review. Alex's hands start to shake. Alex's right leg starts to move up and down. Next, Alex gets up and leaves the classroom to get some air as Alex's chest has tightened. Is this an asthma attack? Mrs. Mimble says, "Alex, where are you going?"

It Is Nature, Nurture, and the Environment That Interact

At one point and time in history, and maybe even in our personal lives, Western societies viewed the actions of others as either coming from their innate selves—nature—or from their upbringing—nurture. Assertions about the "natural basis" for behaviors are linked to mystical, temperamental, or essentialist explanations for a person's behavior. For example, behaviors now described as part of the spectrum of schizophrenia were once related to demon possession, random mood swings, or who an [insert cultural group] are in reality (Kurtz, 2016). In contrast, nurture-based assertions are used to explain illicit substance use, criminal behavior, and even escaping poverty. For example, nurture-based claims take the form of arguments about substance use or criminal behavior as resulting from poor parenting or the destruction of the "nuclear family" as an explanation for social problems, some of which have always existed in many societies and throughout history. In the social science literature and professional disciplines like social work, the nature versus nurture debate raged on until finally losing its foothold in the minds of practitioners thereby making way for a more nuanced understanding of nature and nurture in which nature and nurture interact and are also shaped by elements surrounding a person, group, family, or society. This new understanding of human behavior was based on an interactionist framework, which argued that multiple forces are at play to explain a person's behavior or the outcomes in a context. This interactionist framework includes the environment—which encompasses families, communities, and societies—as well as biological, physiological, and neuroscientific knowledge. This interactionist framework spread across many disciplines' orientations to human behavior and became a dominant framework for understanding people and their behaviors (Ramage & Shipp, 2009).

Many scholars agree that human beings are complex and interact with biological, social, cognitive, emotional, historical, and situational factors—among other things—to inform the behaviors seen by others and the meanings for behaviors observed by others. As practitioners dedicated to helping people contend with their circumstances, social workers practicing with individuals, families, groups, or societies must (a) parse factors leading to observed behaviors, (b) develop hypotheses about the source and meaning of behaviors, and (c) then implement interventions to change adaptive mechanisms to the multiple, interacting factors producing observed behaviors (Strom-Gottfried et al., 2016).

It is this charge that requires social work practitioners to:

- Approach individuals, families, groups, and societies with an understanding that what is presented to the social worker during the interaction might be a signal of their distress or emotional disorganization.

- See beyond the behaviors and presentation to what is underneath.

- Evaluate the potential multilevel and interacting influences leading to the behaviors seen.

- Implement effective and respectful new ways to interact with the personal and social world.

- Determine whether suggestions and recommendations are leading to our projected outcomes while having minimal "side effects" that might compound the stressors in a person's or group of people's lives.

The number of tasks, level of knowledge needed, mental and emotional discipline, technical skills, artistry, creativity, and patience needed to be an effective social worker might seem daunting at first glance. As a first practice tip, viewing these skills as tools to be developed over decades instead of years and through practiced education instead of trial and error because our mistakes can influence client systems' access to life-sustaining food, clothing, and shelter, as well as mental or physical health.

Systems Theories and Perspectives

There are many different systems theories and perspectives, as well as many different systems theorists (Ramage & Shipp, 2009). While these thinkers and their ideas differ, the elements or concepts are similar. They, therefore, allow others to group a set of theories under the umbrella of systems theory while also respecting the individual contributions of systems thinking to different areas of the social and biological sciences (Ramage & Shipp, 2009; Wilson, 1963).

The intent of systems theorists was the make sense of the world in much the same way that people in the past did who attributed behavior to nature, nurture, or mysticism, but systems theorists embraced the complexity of the world, the transactions that occurred, and the interactions that led to a range of outcomes captured by the concept of multifinality. **Multifinality** suggests that given a similar starting point, multiple pathways can lead to different outcomes. There will be more on multifinality later in this chapter, but for now, understanding that more than one outcome exists given a similar starting place can help understand the intricacies that systems theorists were grappling with and what might have influenced the growing diversity of systems theories.

During their scientific careers, systems theorists were grappling with questions about the multiple outcomes they observed in their social world. To provide a contemporary and somewhat culturally myopic example, a systems theorist might ask how two Latino-African American boys reared by a single out-of-work father, growing up economically poor in a housing project in the Bronx that is encased by drug use, drug selling, and gang violence, and both of whom walk to the same school end up in different places in life. One becomes a prominent oncologist while the other becomes convicted for a wire fraud conspiracy. Given the similarity of their circumstances, some might argue that one boy had grit—the drive to persevere—while the other fell prey to the neighborhood. Yet, those explanations lack consideration of subsequent questions, such as why one had grit and the other did not. Systems theorists systematically observed people to answer these questions rather than enter the proverbial rabbit hole of off-the-cuff explanations for these two boys. As a result of disciplined observation, testing, and interpretation, systems theorists explored relationships between concepts that led to many of the systems theories written about and discussed today, as well as insight into human behavior and new scientific and practice pathways to follow.

While we have been talking about systems theories, we have not defined them and their representative parts so the systems theories can be differentiated from other types of theories. Four components that determine systems theories from other theories in the social, political, economic, and biological sciences include an emphasis on the (a) whole and parts, (b) relationships, (c) boundaries, and (d) the theory to practice relationships (Ramage & Shipp, 2009). Systems theories focus on the whole and its parts, as in the person and their environments. Returning to the Latino-African American boys example above, to begin to understand these boys, a social worker must consider each boy and each environment, including his school, home, housing project, street community, school, classroom, and many other countless physical and social environments that each boy passes through in their lives. Despite living in the same setting and even apartment, the boys might view the environments differently, thereby experiencing and understanding their settings and contexts in ways that differ among the boys and across their life stages.

In addition to the environments for each boy, we must consider that each boy is an amalgamation of biological, cognitive, emotional, and physiological systems also influencing and are influenced by multiple contexts and environments. In essence, various systems exist in transactions and relation to each other, better described by relationships, the second component that is vital to understanding systems. We must identify the whole and its parts and then examine the relationships between the whole and its features.

Returning to the Latino-African American boys example, the parts of their lives include the housing project that is located in and related to the portion of the city block, which is also found in a neighborhood that is also a part of the section of a city, which is also part of a city. Many features can continue to be identified and their linkage to other elements until we arrive at the global community. Each of these parts separately and in combination have relationships that influence the actions, beliefs, emotions, and physiological responses of each part and their combinations. Consequently, the parts and their combinations can influence movement toward the outcomes that we indicated earlier. It is in examining the parts and their relationships that systems theorists begin to embrace the complexity of human development because the number of parts interact in differing ways and produce a variety of outcomes (Ramage & Shipp, 2009).

After identifying the elements and the relationships, it becomes necessary to identify the boundaries that separate the parts and inspire the need for a relationship. **Boundaries** identify the components included in and outside the system. A simple explanation of boundaries can be drawn from looking at social cliques in that members within a social clique recognize in-group members and out-group members. In high school settings, for example, jocks can identify each other by their relationship to sports teams, the apparel worn, or their position on the team. Non-jocks can also identify themselves as outside of the jock clique given their nonmembership, lack of official team apparel, or team position. In this example, team membership, team apparel, and place on the team are boundaries separating jocks and non-jocks. But, as is the case in contemporary society, some people will wear team apparel to signify their affiliation with a team, but this act does not position the person on the team. In essence, wearing a New York Wolves football jersey during a practice and a game does not make me a player or a part of the team despite my attempt to align with the group (see https://www.newyorkwolves.com/). Returning to boundaries, boundaries can also exist within seemingly wholes, in that jocks can be further separated by athletic talent, position in the team hierarchy, role in the success or failure of the team, or many other attributes. Attributes, therefore, allow for further segregation of the whole, parts, and their relationships by pointing to the boundaries within and between systems. Despite the athletic prowess of all the women football players, Tara Thomas and Clarissa Tullis are the 2022 Offensive Players of the Year, Jamie Robinson and Nhandi Brown are the 2022 Defensive Players of the Year, and Jesse Felker and Allison Cahill are the 2022 Most Valuable Players of Year, which separates these professionals from all the others in their respective leagues.

With these basic components, many systems theorists formed and expanded upon the work of other theorists, and the social work discipline tied systems theory to the work of Mary Richmond. Delving into all the systems theorists and their relationship to social work is beyond the scope of this chapter. Therefore, three prominent theorists are discussed to explore how systems theories and thinking shape the subsequent chapters and the use of theories in social work practice.

Urie Bronfenbrenner

Urie Bronfenbrenner (1979) is a well-known systems thinker whose conceptualization of the ecology of human development influenced social workers' approach to social work practice, policy, and research. Bronfenbrenner outlined a systems theory that he asserts is a new perspective contrasting the nature versus nurture debate. Bronfenbrenner argues that human development results from interactions between the developing person and their environment. Bronfenbrenner's conception of the environment outlines nested structures, each inside the other, that starts with the social context closest to the developing person, followed by surrounding environments that are more distant than the immediate social context. For the Latino-African American boys discussed earlier, the people in their housing project whom they interact with frequently are in the immediate social context. The residents of that housing complex are surrounded by a local neighborhood that is also surrounded by a more extensive section of a city, which is surrounded by the city. In the words of Bronfenbrenner, the boys are nested within the housing project, that is nested within the local neighborhood, that is nested within the more extensive section of the city, that is nested within a municipality. Each of these nested structures influences the boys' development, and the boys affect their context and environment in reciprocal ways.

Identifying the nested structures then warrants consideration of the relations among the nested structures, or the relationship between the boys and their housing project, the housing project and the local community, the local community and the city, as well as countless other combinations, including the boys and their city. Examining how these relationships influence development can proceed by a social worker asking the following questions: Does the housing project have areas for physical and social development, or are children in the housing project regulated to only the inside of their home because of parental concerns about children's social safety and exposure to drug use or violence? This examination or search for understanding warrants additional theories, frameworks, models, and research knowledge to be imported into the analysis, thereby adding greater depth and nuance to the potential relationships between a person and their environment. For example, the market fluctuations (Chapter 2), intergenerational transmission of trauma (Chapter 3), or challenges to adulthood in this context (Chapter 8) shape system relationships and boundaries. Understanding these structures and their relations also requires a consideration of how they positively and negatively influence development instead of searching for positive or negative influences. For example, the contexts that both boys navigate in their lives might differentially interact with the genetically transmitted historical trauma, yielding different expressions of the trauma. To deepen an examination of the relationships between systems, it is necessary to add additional concepts Bronfenbrenner (1979) outlines for his theory, including role, active engagement, ecological transitions, molar activity, content, elements, and development-in-context, that expand on the ways in which the individual, social context, and social environment interact in relation to each other and produce reciprocal effects.

Roles are any one society's or culture's interaction patterns interacting that govern social interactions, establish expectations for behaviors, and create social positions for members of that society. In a classroom environment, the roles for the teacher and the student are established through family interactions as children are taught to attend to the rules put forth by adults and then extended or challenged in early learning environments such as Head Start or prekindergarten. Over time, student–teacher interactions accumulate and govern how students and teachers might interact during class or other learning-based interactions. This explanation does not necessarily suggest a positive relationship between school systems and students or education or learning and students (see Chapter 5) but instead acknowledges that interactions occur and the meanings of the relationships between these systems varies from child to child.

Returning to the two Latino-African American boys to help further illustrate this concept, the boys will enter their schools in the role of student that accompanies a set of behaviors imposed onto the boys by the school and might be familiar or foreign to the two boys. Each boy will attend school systems with an understanding of the relationship between them as a system, adults as a system, and the school as a system that will influence the boys' interpretation of the expected behaviors for each system (see Chapter 7 for historical examples). The term "might" acknowledges the diversity of ways that teachers and students choose to act in school settings, implement and maintain rules, and the contexts surrounding and shaping school structures. As teachers and students interact over time, these interactions facilitate developmental processes for the teacher and student in that they *might* develop new ways of interacting, different understandings of each party's roles in the environment, new meanings for behaviors or situations, and behavioral changes stemming from elements outside the teacher–student interaction (Chapters 7–9 expand on the adult side of this interaction). How the teachers and the boys enact the expectations in the school setting produces additional behaviors, emotions, cognitions, and roles that symbolize **molar activity**—indicator of change that builds upon itself over time and has meaning and intent). For the two boys, interactions with teachers in Head Start or pre-K programs or with parents and adults become molar activities for future social interactions regardless of the setting. Like learning from caregiver–child attachment interactions, the boys learn about social processes like asking for help, appropriate ways to speak with adults, how adults interact with children, including different types of children, and how interpersonal power is used in social interactions (see Chapter 4 for information on attachment). Information from the larger social environment, social context, or comments from others surrounding the boys can also inform molar activity in that, for example, the widespread exposure to news about the murder of George Floyd, Ahmaud Arbery, and many other African American or Black-presenting men along with the marches by White supremacists in Virginia might influence the two boys' understanding of the world around them, including their school environment, teachers, and the potential opportunities or barriers that lay ahead of them (see Chapter 2 for larger system influences on human development). Molar activities such as these can then shape future social development and lead to changes in behavior to adapt to perceptions of dangerousness or unexpected outcomes of system interactions.

Niklas Luhmann

Niklas Luhmann studied Talcott Parsons's systems theory concerning social environments and, in particular, societies. Luhmann (2013) found that Parsons's view focused on actions, and it was unable to explain why, in American society, some populations flourished while others did not. Linking this notion about the differences in outcomes given similar circumstances, Luhmann, in essence, questions whether Parsons could explain multifinality, or why the two boys in the example above had different results. Additionally, Luhmann argued that despite some systems theorists' focus on the stability of systems—in that the work of a system is to return to **homeostasis**, a balanced state—Luhmann suggested that stability ignores the reality of changes and adaptation in systems. In essence, systems are more flexible than some systems theorists proposed. Finally, Luhmann argued that many applications of systems theory focused on structural elements and components such as societies and their influence on individuals and less on individuals' influence on societies. Comparing Bronfenbrenner's (1979) outline of systems theory to Luhmann's, it is obvious that Bronfenbrenner starts with the individual and moves outward, which Luhmann would critique as limited. Luhmann's formulation of systems theory, consequently, sought to develop a more flexible systems theory that explains disparities in societies while also providing guidance for systems theories' application to practice.

Luhmann's (2013) systems theory suggests that the application of systems theory can be viewed from the perspective of the individual toward elements surrounding the individual as in school, family, neighborhood, community, state, and society). Conversely, Luhmann suggested that systems theory can be applied to situations from the perspective of larger elements, such as organizations or communities. Luhmann's assertion about the multiple viewpoints or perspectives of systems provided many disciplines with a means to begin to understand how these sets of theories can be employed in various occupations like social work that focuses on many different types of client systems such as individual children, intergenerational families, community groups, or social services agencies. Thus, Luhmann offers practitioners more flexible guidance for linking systems theory to application or practice environments. Luhmann also suggests that the meaning of interactions between elements of a system is a vital aspect of understanding the interactions. Bringing back the example of the two boys from earlier, each boy living in a housing project might have different meanings that inform the way the boys understand their relationship with the others in the housing project, the housing project itself, and other facets of their social context. Thus, for one boy, the meaning he attaches to the housing project might encourage him to align less with others in the housing project and more with others outside the housing project (see Chapter 6 for insights into identity and meaning). Alternatively, the boy might view the housing project in a way that aligns him with others in the housing project and less with teachers and administrators in the school environment, thereby resulting in his focus on the housing project and its residents versus the school and its faculty. In each case, the meanings drawn from interaction shape how each boy sees his context and subsequent behavior. In Luhmann's conceptualization of systems theory and its brief application to the example of the two boys, practitioners might target the meaning of the interaction between the housing project and each boy and how these meanings are communicated.

Luhmann (2013) asserts that communication provides theorists insights into the meaning of the interactions between elements of a system and how identities are shaped as a result of the interactions between parts of a system. For example, a social worker in a Boys & Girls Club after-school project might listen to how each boy describes and discusses their perspective of the housing project and their interactions with their neighbors. One boy might describe staying inside his apartment because "people are always getting in trouble, and I don't want to get in trouble," while the other states, "A lot of the older boys have cool stuff that I want, like the latest sneakers, lots of money, games, and cool phones." In the first statement, the boy indicates that the element of his apartment suggests a sense of safety from the outside world and that his housing project includes many people involved in something he is trying to avoid. His identity consists of an element of not getting into trouble or being around people that do. In contrast, the other boy's statement indicates that he admires the material items he sees others have. He is around older boys, and his identity includes a need to be part of a group with resources. He wants things that might be unaffordable to him at this point.

While examples of the two boys stem from the boys' perspective, Luhmann's (2013) interpretation of the systems theory can be applied from the perspective of the Boys & Girls Club. The Boys & Girls Club might develop an after-school program to help children and adolescents develop soft skills like problem-solving, study habits, and distress tolerance to influence the relationship between children and the crime in their neighborhoods. For the Boys & Girls Club, the presence of an illicit economy near families with little access to affordable after-school services might mean that families of color and low-income families will be trapped in the cycle of incarceration and poverty (see Chapter 2 for insight into geopolitical influences on development).

The perspective on the interaction between the illicit economy and families in these environments can be communicated to stakeholders, practitioners, and many others through the program's mission and vision statements. Thus, elements larger than individuals also develop meanings from the interactions of components and then communicate those meanings to others like individuals do in social interactions. Therefore, Luhmann's (2013) formulation of a systems theory adds meaning, influences on identity development, and communication while also making explicit assumptions about transitioning theory to practice. Also, Luhmann challenges applied systems thinking from the individual's perspective toward the environment, while others have applied these sets of theories and concepts from the environment to the individual.

Gregory Bateson

Gregory Bateson was an anthropologist who applied ethnographic research methods while living with and studying various cultures, including the Iatmul tribes in Papua New Guinea and families in Bali. His perspective influences the theories and concepts that he produced in his work as a White, highly educated, and Westernized heterosexual man and the lived experiences of observing and participating in the daily lives of people he studied. Based on this reflexive observation of his position concerning the knowledge he produced and the people he observed, Bateson (2002) developed and discussed the fallacy of misplaced concreteness that argues for different ways of viewing the world and interpreting others. Bateson seemed to understand that the observer's approach to a situation and the theories that guide their observation inform assumptions about the proposed "work" that needs to be addressed. Invoking or acknowledging the influence of the observer on the observed, Bateson articulates **ethos**, which is identified as "conventional emotions" linked with "normative behavior." A society's ethos can be interrupted by rituals or revolutions in society, whereby conventional emotions or normative behaviors are transgressed or disrupted. Linking ethos and Bateson's ideas about the role of the observer suggests that observers might interrupt rituals or initiate revolutions to disrupt everyday conventions in society, as described in the literature on the colonization of societies (see also Chapter 3). Alternatively, an observer can view the actions of society and interpret the social world from the observer's ethos, whereby the observed society is viewed and interpreted negatively or positively compared to the observer's societal beliefs.

Ethos, ritual, observation, and the observed can be applied to interactions using the example of the two boys discussed in this chapter. As the boys enter their home schools, they interact with adults who might have cultural backgrounds or childhood educational experiences that are different than their own; these adults might also view the expected behaviors or ethos of the school environment in ways that are informed by their adult expectations and job roles. Thus, adult observers might interpret students' behavior or emotional control from the expectations that are more relevant to other adults or to people of a particular cultural, socioeconomic, political, or social location (see Chapters 5, 6, and 8). Adults around these two boys might also interpret the boys' behaviors or emotional reactions positively or negatively based on how they align with the adult staff members' ethos. So, one boy that sits still in the class directing his attention to the teacher at the head of the class, raising his hand to participate in the lesson, and following all the rituals the teacher has set up for the classroom would, from the perspective of Bateson's (2002) conceptualization, be viewed as a "good student and child." In contrast, the boy who moves in his seat and tracks the events in the classroom and the outside world might be viewed by this teacher as uninvolved with the lesson. Periodically, answers questions without raising his and continually being told to "raise his hand" because this is the expected behavior in the classroom, the teacher views this boy as "a bad student and child." These interpretations fall prey to what Bateson characterized as the **fallacy of misplaced concreteness**—describing a system according to the qualities of one situation. In the boys' housing complex, for example, these same behaviors might have different meanings, and the tracking of the events in one's context might be adaptive and create safety, whereas focused attention on one situation demonstrated by the "good" student might be maladaptive in the housing complex setting because its opens up the opportunity for victimization. In essence, observing the boys' behaviors in different contexts changes the meaning and usefulness of the behavior. Bateson applies this fallacy to some observers' use of a singular event or way to describe whole cultural groups, as is found in many stereotypes and prejudices, thereby tying this fallacy to the concept of ethos and his arguments about the observer–observed relationship. For the boys, teachers that view one boy as good and the other as bad based on their behavior in school are falling prey to this fallacy and stereotyping these boys.

Bateson's systems theorizing extended into many areas, including thinking systems and the ways that the mind and nature are related. Cybernetics, as he called it, explores the ways that the systems in the world engage in competition and dependency with other systems and consequently influence (a) how people think and (b) the thinking systems developing from relationships between the world and the mind. Bateson's focus on cybernetics spawned many research studies, debates, associations, and journals outside of his work on systems theory. Bateson's focus on cybernetics also explored how adaptive changes occur, which he postulated were the outgrowth of **feedback loops**: the information given back to a system about its stability, behavior, emotions, or other facets or variables in or interacting with the system. In response to this "feedback," systems were able to adapt and adjust their course, known as "self-correcting." Harkening back to the boys in the classroom, teachers' responses to their behavior in the classroom and neighborhood residents' responses to their behavior in the housing complex are both sources of feedback that might differ or contradict.

Self-correcting as an adaptive response to feedback, however, is not always the outcome of feedback. Feedback was one of many sources of interaction between systems. It could spawn other ways of adapting, such as changing the relationship between systems, ignoring feedback, or overcompensating for the feedback provided in ways that destabilize the system. Applied to the boys' classroom example in this chapter, the boy that sits in his seat and raises his hand to answer questions posed by the teacher might receive feedback about his behavior through grades, mentoring relationships offered by his adult teachers, and opportunities to explore new environments because of his academic achievement. This same boy might also receive feedback from others in his neighborhood or family that complements or detracts from the feedback in his school. In contrast, the other boy that attends to the events in the classroom will also receive feedback about his behavior, such as laughter from others in the classroom including the teacher, a mentoring relationship with a teaching staff when asked to leave the classroom, inattention from educational support personnel such as guidance counselors and school social workers because of the feedback these groups are receiving from the systems they interact within their personal and professional lives, as well as the feedback the boy receives currently or had received in the past about his behavior from their neighborhood and families. While individuals providing feedback might assume that the feedback or even punishments are more likely to lead to behavior changes, some boys might filter the feedback to maintain a sense of themselves (see Chapter 5 for further elaboration). Known as **autopoiesis**, filtering information such as feedback is a mechanism for self-regulation and self-organization. Thus, feedback to systems can be manifold as well as conflicting or congruent, or confusing, which challenges the simple classification of feedback as positive or negative. Hence, a teacher might believe they are giving the boy some positive feedback, he might interpret the feedback as negative and filter it out. Feedback might also not be necessarily attended to because of its relationship to the self-system. The outcropping of feedback for this boy might be divisions—known as **schismogenesis**—in that the feedback communicated to the boy begins to fracture his relationship with school personnel, the school environment, or learning in general while bonding him to others in different environments than these settings. Given the multidimensional and multilevel influences on human development, critically separating features in systems can help to organize one's conceptualization of an organization, person, family, or community.

Social Context and Social Environment: Differences in Concept and Influence

The systems theorists presented are but three of many theorists that contributed to systems theory and its concepts as well as applied this manner of thinking to the problems facing diverse disciplines. It is neither the intention to review all systems theorists nor is it feasible to within the number of pages set out for this chapter, but instead, systems theorists and theories presented introduce the ideas of the theorists so that readers develop a beginning familiarity with the concepts and models of thinking embedded in this area of theorizing.

Bronfenbrenner, Luhmann, and Bateson attempted to analyze and explain what they saw in the world around them, including both the consistencies in thought and action as well as the contradictions between what was said and what was observed. For example, Bateson participated in a war effort that included attempts to draw civilians away from military efforts and toward the American side of the conflict. These observations about the use of language to upend the relationships of elements within systems like a country informed his conceptualization of schismogenesis, which describes creating divisions within a system leading to destabilization of that system. Luhmann, on the other hand, observed how people within a social system might listen to ecological communication and engage in autopoiesis, filtering out some information while attending to other bits of information. Autopoiesis in contemporary family arguments such as "hearing what you want to hear" are claims laid by a family member against another person. While Bronfenbrenner, like Bateson, was also informed by war efforts and the contradictory thoughts presented to observers and those living through these events, he focused on other aspects of systems interactions like boundaries. The theorists' backgrounds inform many aspects of the theory aside from Bateson's assertion about the role of the observer in interpreting what they observed but also suggests that each of these theorists was focusing on the instability in interactions within systems and systems themselves as well as the inherent uncertainty in systems. While the instability and uncertainty of systems will be discussed in the next section, these notions of instability and uncertainty fall under the umbrella of complexity theory that can challenge the notion that systems are simple relationships that exist in homeo-static relations (Johnson, 2009). Thus, the next few sections start by distinguishing between social context and social environment to begin to outline the potential sources of instability, uncertainty, and observer influence.

Social Context

Systems can be viewed as nested layers, wherein some layers abut each other while others are mediated by layers and thus are more distal from each other. For example, a school is a system that abuts two other systems: the neighborhood system and the school district system. The school district system mediates the relationship between school systems and the state department of the education system. In this example, from the view of the school system, some systems, like the district and local neighborhood, are proximal to the school system, while others are more distal, such as the state department of education and even the federal department of education. Thus, the school system has an immediate social context that is a specific setting where social interactions take place, communication and meanings are exchanged, interpretations of social interactions occur, boundaries exist, feedback loops are created or maintained, and roles are assigned to elements of system components, such as people or groups. Social contexts are the site of many interactions, meaning-making, culture-building, and what practitioners enter into when engaging with client systems and conducting assessments. Thus, elements of a system and the system itself can develop an ethos that is specific to the system and be different from or con-tradict the settings surrounding the system, such as a neighborhood. This idea about intra-system interactions and intersystem interactions gives rise to the complex nature of systems and the potential for instability and uncertainty. To gather a fuller understanding of complexity and complexity theory, it is necessary to explore the social environment and its role within systems.

Social Environment

In contrast to the social context that emphasizes immediate interactions, the social environ-ment is a larger *set of systems* that encapsulate social contexts.

Elements of the social environment include, for example, social groups; communities; workplaces; policies; social movements; cultural systems individually and collectively based on gender identities, ethnic heritage, language, physical abilities, and disabilities; political systems; and social capital. Systems within the social environment influence social contexts in ways that are congruent with not only ideologies in the social context but also in ways that are incongru-ent with social contexts. Returning to the two boys example in this chapter, the larger social environment might present messages based on the notion that "all *men* are created equal," yet these messages might conflict with the boys' observations about the available resources in the school and their local community in contrast to the resources presented on television shows or documentaries about schooling and schools. Elements of school systems might also observe the differences in the messages in the social environment about the value of education yet observe in their social contexts behaviors or policies that undermined the ability to educate students in

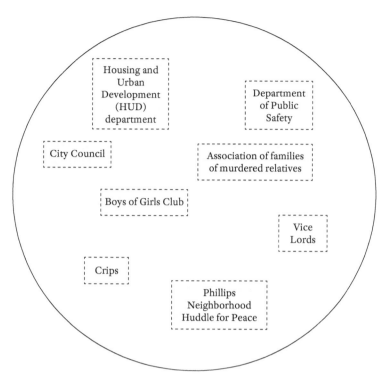

FIGURE 1.1

ways that reflect the policy mandates implemented in larger systems in the social environment (Lagana-Riordan & Aguilar, 2009). For example, teachers in the school system might hear messages about the value of education but recognize the limited funding and resources available to their school in comparison to a neighboring school in a wealthier part of the city. Some teachers might engage in autopoiesis—filtering of information—to avoid schmiogenesis, the creation of a schism in a system. Still other teachers might interpret these actions as the fault of the students and parents in the area—another form of autopoiesis—and consequently consider the funding differences as feedback on the neighborhood families behaviors and social value.

These contradictions are captured in Bateson's notion of the double bind in which a system or an element of a system either in the social context or social environment receives two conflicting messages. The conflicts can include emotional and behavioral differences that are presented in a way that prevents a system from clarifying which message is accurate, indicates power differences between systems or elements in the system, and communicates that punishment can occur if the system or element of the system fails to achieve the unclear goal.

An interpersonal example of double bind communication occurs when a person emotionally communicates anger toward another person while also portraying a "frozen smile," an attempt to hide one's answer and present friendliness. A structural example is a policy initiative designed to alleviate a social problem but lacks funding to support the implementation of the policy initiative and sustain the changes over time.

Integrating the Social Context and Social Environment: The Birth of Complexity

Some might quip that viewing society as a nested and interacting set of systems is complicated. Systems theorists are more likely to suggest that systems, including societies and people, are complex. The difference between complicated and complex is more than just semantics, because complexity points to the outcome of interacting systems, while complicated is better understood as an opinion about the intricacies and paucity of simplicity in systems. Scholars developed complexity theory, which was imported into the social sciences to examine interacting systems that can lead to the multifinality in outcomes. **Complexity theory** also includes the role of instability and uncertainty that contrasts with the assumption that systems are typically homeostatic.

Complexity science brings much insight into system behaviors and the outcomes associated with interacting systems. Applying complexity theory to systems thereby embraces the surprises emerging from interactions among elements in the systems as well as how systems are influenced by past experiences, adapt, and the deficits derived from assuming systems are closed. Assuming that systems are closed often inhibits any examination of how the social context and social environment influence the system. For example, if a social worker views or assumes that the family system of the two boys is closed, then this view and assumption prevents the social worker from believing they have any influence on the family system, implies the environment did not shape the family as it developed, and suggests the past experiences are not sources of information and instigators of family adaptation. Essentially, the social worker is starting from a deficit position instead of a place that considers every system's ability to adapt and change.

Before delving into the important views about change and adaptation, it is important to outline the key principles of complexity theory that also guide the application of complexity theory to social work practice.

KEY PRINCIPLES OF COMPLEXITY THEORY

- Systems contain a collection of agents and objects.
- Objects and agents have and are affected by memory and feedback.
- Objects and agents adapt based on many things, including history and meaning.
- Systems are open and influenced by contexts and environments.
- Systems evolve such that interactions influence adaptation.
- Systems will demonstrate emergent phenomena that can be surprising and extreme.
- A controller is not necessary for emergent phenomena to occur within systems.
- Systems can demonstrate a mix of order and disorder.

In complexity theory, facets of systems can be organized into agents and objects. **Agents** can include individuals such as each boy in the example throughout this chapter. Agents can exist in networks as well as be proximally or distally linked to one another. Thus, there are many agents in the boys' life such as the teachers, their neighbors in the housing projects, the storekeepers, and young people that have the resources that one of the boys admires. **Objects** are an additional aspect of systems and include the "things" such as the housing project, the reputation of the area, the social capital of residents or gangs, the school, and the school system. Agents and objects interact as evident throughout the descriptions of the boys' daily environment and give rise to experiences that provide feedback to both agents and objects while also creating memories. The boys, for example, traverse their housing projects on their way to school.

The boys are each an agent, and the housing project and school are objects in the system. Interactions between the agents and objects produce experiences, such as a sense of admiration or danger, that inform the meanings that each boy attributes to their person and environment interaction while also accumulating a history of experiences that will inform future behaviors, emotions, cognitions, and interpretations. Some of these ideas are explored in the subsequent chapters on identity development and those that interrogate contextual influences on development, but at this point it is important to understand that memories and reputations gathered through interactions inform not only current behaviors, emotions, and thoughts but also future ones. Thus, agents, objects, and memories are important components of a complex system.

A system's history, whether it is the developmental history of each boy or the social history of the neighborhood or school, facilitates adaptation and strategies for change. Adaptation and strategies for change, therefore, are developed and informed by the experiences and interactions that each boy had with other agents or objects in their environment and the meanings that these boys developed from these experiences and interactions. As a more illustrative example, the boy that views others in his neighborhood as a source of trouble adapts to this situation by changing his behaviors, which might involve spending more time outside, while the boy that admires the material goods of older people in this neighborhood might change his behaviors to mimic those that he observes. In each situation, the boys are engaging in a process of interacting with agents and objects over time and then adapting to both the systems around them and adopting strategies that are based on history and interactions. This explanation can be extended to interactions with systems in the school, such as the teachers, in that teachers will discuss their interactions and experiences with the boys, the children from their housing projects, and even the parents that form the history, memories, and feedback to this system as they communicate their experiences and expectations to other agents in that system.

Given the interactions explained above, it is clear that the school and each of the boys are open systems that are receiving information and influences from their context and environment while simultaneously communicating information and influencing their environment. This notion of simultaneous influence and communication between systems is a part of complexity theory's position that systems are open and evolve as interactions, agents, objects, and experiences change. The evolution of systems includes the physiological and biological changes that the boys will undergo through their lifespan, as well as changes in their understanding of the world around them. The evolution will include everchanging attempts to adapt to the world as it changes; For the boys, this world might be just their neighborhood, housing complex, and school. Similar evolutionary processes exist for the objects in the environment as well. For example, with the onset of the COVID-19 pandemic and the requirement to move to online learning, members of the school staff evolved their skill set to include online learning and, in some cases, preliminary technology troubleshooting to help their students with minor technological problems. The pandemic, a system that results from the interaction of two other systems—viruses and social proximity—interacted with the daily lives of another system—people—and caused a surprising change in how people interacted, worked, and learned. Complexity theorists would suggest that some emergent phenomena are surprising and extreme; therefore, pandemics, family conflicts, and revolutions are always a possibility when multiple systems interact.

In contrast to the assumptions of other systems theorists, complexity theorists suggest the phenomena arise without the influence of a guiding force. Essentially, pandemics will occur even without someone developing a pathogen to wipe out humanity as the plot of many sci-fi movies suggests. Emergent phenomena occur without a central guiding force. Given the room for surprises in complexity theory, not all systems are completely in disarray or completely ordered. In contrast to the either-or assumption of complete disarray or order, complex systems can demonstrate both disarray and order. Hence, the objects in the boys' neighborhood can be in disarray, indicated by the presence of condemned or poorly maintained housing, the absence of food stores with healthy foods, significant crime rates, and an illicit economy, while also including a close-knit community with multiple generations of families that have lived in the neighborhood. While some outside of the system might view the neighborhood as bad, the notion of badness does not capture the complexity of the neighborhood system and the strengths within that neighborhood that help people flourish. Hence, judging the neighborhood based on aspects of it could lead to the fallacy of misplaced concreteness that was discussed earlier.

The components of complexity theory and the brief application of this theory to the example of the boys now require a deeper exploration of applying this theory to practice situations. Additionally, an explanation of how other non-systems theories can be coupled with complexity theory to deepen an understanding of client systems and explain phenomena outside the scope of complexity theory. The next section moves into the integration of theories and then the application to social work practice with client systems that might be individuals, families, neighborhoods, groups, or communities.

Integration and Application

The importance of understanding theories lies in their use in practice situations. In general, applying theories to practice involves adapting the concepts to the practice situation, interpreting the data from the application, and then developing explanatory hypotheses to be used to guide decision making. In the following section, complexity theory and theories described in subsequent chapters are applied to the case study of Alex presented at the beginning of this chapter and to answer the question, what might have potentially influenced Alex's decision to leave the classroom?

Assumptions

Reading the case of Alex might lead some to assume that Alex left because of a panic attack because of the anxiety of the ongoing test. While this assumption might, on its face, seem accurate, the assumed outcome does not explain why Alex did not self-regulate since this is not the first test Alex completed and there was no indication that Alex was concerned about the test or grade. Moreover, there is considerable information about the situation that we are not given, such as Alex's demographic factors—age, gender, sexual orientation, living situation, socioeconomic status, and health or mental health status. Some readers might have assumed Alex's gender because of contextual clues, but as described in subsequent chapters like Chapter 7–9, the fluidity of gender identity and expression warrants careful consideration and evidence. Moving from assuming to inferring involves making use of theories to fill in the blanks to guide what might be potential answers, given the information available from the client system and explanatory theories.

The Complexity of Alex

Alex is an agent that passes through several systems like the community system, the neighborhood system, and the school system. These systems contain important objects, such as the home, community, and a school. Alex's interactions with these objects is one that encompasses meanings and histories that might direct Alex's behavior and flow over into the systems that occupy these objects. For example, Alex interacts with a school system that contains many subsystems, like the history classroom, teachers, school staff, and other schools across the United States of America. School systems interact with educational systems, federal or state or local government systems, and community systems. Interactions between, for instance, community systems and school systems resulted in *Brown v. Board of Education*, violence against school board members because of mask mandates and initiatives during the early days of the COVID-19 pandemic, and No Child Left Behind legislation. Hence, the relationship between school systems and some community systems is positive, for others its tenuous, and for another group it is negative. These relationships might be even more complex because Alex's community might have a negative relationship with the school system, while Alex has a positive relationship with the school.

Alex's relationship to the local community is also influenced by the relationship between that local community and the larger social environment, including the geographic allyship and conflicts. While Russia's unjust invasion of Ukraine could be over 4,000 miles away from Alex's community, for some members the invasion and subsequent war is a phone call, email, telegram post, or Zoom call away. These interactions encompass a metric distance, but also the emotional proximity presented by Katia is crying in the classroom, making both the metric and emotional distances a potential double bind for Alex. Aspects of the multiple meanings in the messages sent by individuals are discussed in the chapter on adolescence and identity, yet these exposures to worlds outside one's immediate social contexts provide a window to other shaded identities.

Alex has several other relationships that influence Alex's interpretation of the school system, the housing system, and other systems that can be identified through an assessment. Understanding and interpreting the relationships and systems involves using other theories like those found in chapters of this text, to add insights into the analysis but also to consider additional factors that might influence the interpretation of the system or relationship. For example, many communities with marginalized identities or social locations might have intergenerational legacies of violence and abuse that lead to intergenerational transmission of trauma and subsequent differences in physiological, psychological, and social behaviors. These physiological, psychological, and social behaviors might then be interpreted by others based on a fallacy of misplaced concreteness. Moreover, as evident in all the chapters, people simultaneously hold multiple identities or social locations that are embody privileged and marginalized in contexts, like Alex's ability to peruse YouTube videos for study habit videos, which indicates access to a computer and internet, while also being a student a lesser powered position compared to that of teachers and school staff. Thus, Alex holds multiple identities that guide Alex's position in the world but also influence Alex's interpretation of the systems and relationships in Alex's life.

Thus, while it might seem that Alex's decision to leave the classroom is because of a panic attack, other interpretations might include (a) information overload given all the situations Alex is exposed to along the walk to the classroom; (b) a side effect from albuterol, a rescue inhaler; or (c) the meaning of the test, given Alex's future aspirations. Examining the multiple systems that Alex moves through highlights the multiple factors that can lead to information overload, while the symptoms observed can be from a rescue inhaler for a condition that might not be reported in the case study, and given we are unsure of Alex's demographic characteristics, that concerns could be about passing the class, college acceptance, or team supports—among other things. Essentially, this cursory view of the complexity of Alex suggests that we cannot assume a simple observation is the correct "cause" of a behavior, because there might be many potential outcomes.

Conclusion

Complexity and systems theory overlap in many concepts, including:

- Systems are multileveled.
- Systems consist of other systems.
- The parts of systems are as important as the whole.
- Systems are self-regulating and self-organizing.

Applying this framework to social work practice suggests that clients are systems that can be easily described as client systems with social groups memberships and multiple identities.

Social workers, therefore, use complexity theory to gather information about client systems at several phases, like engagement, assessment, intervention, and evaluation. Other theories discussed in this text, including those about identity development, historical trauma, market economies, multiple marginalized identities, and social isolation, must also be understood and then coupled with complexity theory to deepen explanations of complex systems. For example, a school social worker assessing students might gather information about their current classroom behaviors, family environment, neighborhood context, and academic achievement to explore why a presenting problem exists. While some might examine the data about their students in a linear fashion, others might organize the data using Bronfenbrenner's systems theory to separate the data into micro, mezzo, and macro factors.

Social workers viewing this data from complexity theory would focus on understanding (a) the client as a system that consists of subsystems and (b) the mechanisms the system uses to self-regulate and organize. Focusing on the interactions between agents and objects, the relationships between agents and objects, as well as exploration of the meanings derived from interactions can start to illuminate potential actions that can develop from these interactions. But complexity alone is not enough, because other theories of development provide additional insights into facets of development that can also deepen the assessment and highlight areas of intervention. For the two boys discussed in this chapter, observing their behavior in the classroom through the lens of complexity theory requires identifying the agents and actions in the setting but also the agents and objects that mentally enter the classroom through the minds of the boys. These mental representations can include housing community members with the latest sneakers and electronics that are admired by one or both of the boys, the heroes and heroines that the boys view on television, the lives of the actors and characters on their favorite television show, and the ideals that the school presents to the boys. Social workers can also examine how the economics of the local community shape the housing and employment opportunities for residents in public housing complexes, structures generational development, and impinges the developmental risk and protective factors that shape the boys' daily lives. The market economies of the local communities directly influence school district budgets but also the additional businesses in the area that support aspects of the school through services like package delivery and office supplies. Shifts in these business services can positively or negatively influence financial and then social resources available to school staff and students, which then shapes the educational opportunities that students are afforded.

Similarly, changes in the social, economic, and psychological needs of students and their families because of histories of violence, untreated traumatic reactions, and exposure to contemporary violence (either through news reports about events around the world, social media outlets, or witnessing these events in the communities) can influence the two boys, the school staff, community residents, and the multiple systems that these systems navigate through in their daily lives. Violence or reports of violence can be heaped upon the histories of violence exposure, results in social or physical isolation later in life, or product maladaptive ways of coping that impair social judgment but also set trajectories with legal, medical, and psychological consequences that endure well past the immediate days and weeks of the initial event.

For example, if the boys hear about a shooting of a teenager in their neighborhood, this event might also occur during the time in which news outlets are reporting school shootings and violence against men of color. Each event exists at one point in time, yet the effects of these events can extend to years or decades after throughout the biological, social, and psychological development of the boys.

Because both complexity and systems theories emphasize interactions and relationships through assertions such as (a) systems communicate, (b) systems are provided feedback, and (c) meanings are embedded in systems interactions, social workers must also explore the data and observations for these interactions and relationships. Thus, after examining the structure of the client systems, social work practitioners can explore types and qualities of communication between systems, including verbal, nonverbal, and implied forms of communication. It is important to note that there are many ways that communication is expressed that go beyond verbal statements. Sometimes, as Bateson (2002) noted, communication can be unclear and contradictory, as in a double bind message. To illustrate, some simultaneous and various forms of communication can be found in political systems that might enact legislation that, on its face, suggests an attempt to improve education for all children and adolescents in the United States of America. The legislation is a form of written communication that structures how funding mechanisms can be distributed to state school systems; the legislation is also a form of symbolic communication in that it might claim to equally distribute funding according to schools while implicitly focus on the multiple identities of dominant social groups—that is, White, middle- to upper-class families with at-home learning materials, such as computers and private study spaces that are quiet. Other forms of communication might also be embedded in this legislation and, as indicated in the Key Principles of Complexity Theory textbox, all are important, given that the parts of systems—which include communication—are as important as the whole.

Because communication between systems exists, it is important to note that communication is not always recognized, received, or accepted. Consequently, how communication is recognized, received, and accepted can influence the meanings created from all the forms of communication. This notion of the complexity of communication between systems is illustrated in studies of domestic violence, child maltreatment, family interactions, politics, and organizations. Thus, during communicative interactions, systems might filter out information that challenges the system despite the communication providing feedback about the system, the interaction between systems, or the outcomes of system interactions. If the boys discussed in this chapter, for example, complete a reading comprehension test and one boy received high marks while the other boy did not, then the boys can integrate the grade feedback in different ways that influence their self-system. The boy with high marks might interpret losing 3 points as an indication of failure, while the boy that received low marks might interpret this feedback as an indication that he is "not good at school" and in turn filter out this feedback and focus on "the teacher does not like me." Both of these responses to the feedback involve processes of controlling one's self-system, like filtering information, self-regulation, and self-organization. Therefore, during the assessment or intervention phase of practice, a social worker working with each boy can explore the boy's interpretation of the grade feedback, the meanings the boy's attribute to the scores, how the feedback might have destabilized the self-system, and the system-level adaptations resulting from the feedback. This aspect of exploration with the boys elucidates the inner workings of boys self-system and integrates many key components of the complexity of receiving the grade, including objects and agents adapt based on many things, including history and meaning; objects and agents have and are affected by memory and feedback; and systems will demonstrate emergent phenomena that can be surprising and extreme. As is evident in the paragraphs above, applying this area of knowledge to social work practice involves understanding of concepts such as communication and how that plays out during interactions between systems to give meaning to feedback.

To deepen an examination of the interactions between systems, the meanings developed, and the emergent phenomena, social work practitioners can integrate other theories into their analysis to guide their understanding of the elements influencing a system and identify *potential* outcomes or processes. In exploring the response to the grading feedback, social work practitioners can integrate that concept of self-protection, from theories of the Self, that delves into real or perceived threats to one's self-concept (Tangney & Leary, 2012). In essence, the boys might interpret their grades as a threat to their view of themselves as capable individuals, thus filtering out potential areas of growth in favor of protecting the sense of self. Other concepts from theories of the Self, like possible selves, can also be integrated to the analysis and form the potential basis for interventions into the meanings and filtering of feedback and communication. Hence, the flexibility of an integrated complexity and systems theory enables social work practitioners to add many other theories to an understanding of interactions between systems to better explain the relationships between systems and inform interventions and evaluations.

So how can a social work practitioner explain the different outcomes of the boys in the example throughout the chapter? To start, social workers can use ecomapping and genograms to identify the structure and client system's views of the interactions between agents and objects in the social context and environment. *Ecomaps* and *genograms* are graphical depictions of complex systems that demonstrate the structure and interactions from the perspective of the reporting system.

Social work practitioners can also create ecomaps or genograms for different time points in the evolution of a system. For example, a social work practitioner exploring the evolution and outcomes of a policy initiative can create an ecomap for the objects and agents that lead to the creation of the policy initiative, another illustrating when the policy initiative was implemented, and then at points of change and at the current iteration of the policy. Similarly, social work practitioners working with children or families can also construct ecomaps or genograms at different developmental time points to identify the history of the client system as well as the changes in interaction over time. Formulating ecomaps and genograms of client systems allows social workers to apply complexity theory, particularly identifying agents and objects, interactions that fuel memories, emergent phenomena, and areas of order and disorder in and across system interactions.

Applying the interpretative aspects of complexity theory for systems involves examining the interactions and feedback that systems engage in while also attending to what is said and not said but expected. This aspect of applying complexity theory to client systems engages social work practitioners' creativity, comparing verbal and nonverbal communication and creating practice-related hypotheses about the acknowledged and unacknowledged problems facing client systems.

KEY TERMS

- Distal: an anatomical term that indicates something is located away from the center or specific point of attachment.

- Iatrogenic: an adjective that describes illness or harm caused by the process of medical treatment.

- Multifinality: suggests that given a similar starting point, multiple pathways can lead to different outcomes.

- Boundaries: identify the components included in and outside the system.

- Roles: any one society's or culture's interaction patterns that govern social interactions, establish expectations for behaviors, and create social positions for members of that society (e.g., teacher and student).

- Molar activity: an indicator of change (i.e., behavior) that builds upon itself over time and has meaning and intent.

- Homeostasis: a balanced state.

- Ethos: conventional emotions associated with normative behavior.

- Fallacy of misplaced concreteness: occurs when an abstract belief is mistaken for being concrete.

- Feedback loops: the information given back to a system about its stability, behavior, emotions, or other facets or variables in or interacting with the system.

- Autopoiesis: a mechanism that allows for self-regulation and self-organization. In this context, the individual filters information to maintain a sense of themselves.

- Schismogenesis: literally means "creation of division." In this context, it refers to the individual's fractured relationship to various systems.

- Complexity theory: examines interacting systems that can lead to the multifinality in outcomes, including the role of instability and uncertainty that contrasts with the assumption that systems are typically homeostatic.

- Agents: individuals who can exist in networks as well as be proximally or distally linked to one another (e.g., teachers, friends, neighbors, etc.).

- Objects: are an additional aspect of systems and include the "things" in an individual's environment (e.g.,. neighborhood, school, etc.).

REFERENCES

Bateson, G. (2002). *Mind and nature: A necessary unity*. Hampton Press.

Bronfenbrenner, U. (1979). *The ecology of human development: Experiments by nature and design*. Harvard University Press.

Council on Social Work Education. (2022). *2022 Education Policy and Accreditation Standards for baccalaureate and master's social work programs*. https://www.cswe.org/accreditation/standards/2022-epas/

Johnson, N. (2009). *Simply complexity: A clear guide to complexity theory*. Oneworld Publications.

Kurtz, M. M. (2016). *Schizophrenia and its treatment: Where is the progress?* Oxford University Press.

Lagana-Riordan, C., & Aguilar, J. P. (2009). What's missing from No Child Left Behind? A policy analysis from a social work perspective. *Children and Schools, 31*(3), 135–144. https://doi.org/10.1093/cs/31.3.135

Luhmann, N. (2013). *Introduction to systems theory* (D. Baecker, Ed.; P. Gilgen, Trans.). Wiley.

Ramage, M., & Shipp, K. (2009). *Systems thinkers* (1st ed.). Springer.

Strom-Gottfried, K., Hepworth, D. H., Dewberry Rooney, G., & Rooney, R. H. (2016). *Empowerment Series: Direct social work practice: Theory and skills*. Cengage Learning.

Tangney, J. P., & Leary, M. R. (Eds.). (2012). *Handbook of self and identity* (2nd ed.). Guilford Publications.

Wilson, J. (1963). *Thinking with concepts*. Cambridge University Press.

CHAPTER 2

Geopolitical and Economic Influences on Human and Social Development

SOMA SEN

Introduction

The contexts of social work as a profession have changed with globalization. Social workers are being increasingly asked to work with clients and communities who have been impacted by global forces and are finding that the classical models of human development fall short of an analytical model. Due to the primacy of Western thoughts in the knowledge-making process because of colonialism and globalization, many Western-centric social scientific theories have metastasized as the "truth," and social work as a profession is no exception. In fact, historically the social work profession has overtly harmed many communities of color and continues to do so by unquestioningly utilizing frameworks that legitimize Western hegemony. With these issues as a backdrop, this chapter will do the following:

LEARNING OBJECTIVES
1. Understand the ways in which social work promotes global economic and social justice. (Competency 2)
2. Consider how geopolitical circumstances create social injustices. (Competency 3)
3. Understand the basic concepts of market economy and how economic systems work. (Competencies 6 and 7)

- Introduce basic concepts of market economy and how economic systems work. It will explore neoliberalism and how the profit motives of transnational corporations and developed countries have historically destroyed communities of the Global South and other Indigenous cultures—and continue to do so.

- Introduce theoretical frameworks of Karl Marx to understand the economies of geo-politics and of Antonio Gramsci to understand hegemony, enabling social workers to question the primacy of Eurocentric values in the knowledge-making process of our profession.

- Offer an alternative, integrated framework for assessing human development.

- Provide a framework for social work practice based on critical theory that aligns with social work's values of enhancement of people's well-being, promotion of social justice, and empowerment of oppressed populations while blending micro and macro practice.

To illustrate this, let's consider these two case studies.

FERHANA'S STORY: DREAMING OF GOING TO BED WITHOUT BEING HUNGRY

At 10 years old, Ferhana lived in a tent settlement in Balkh, Afghanistan, after her family was displaced by conflict. When COVID-19 hit, Ferhana's parents struggled to find work and afford food. The entire family, including Ferhana's four siblings, survived off tea and bread. While Ferhana's father would sell things he found to buy biscuits for the family, some days he did not find anything, and the family went hungry. For 5 months, the family could not buy a single piece of meat, vegetable, or fruit. As COVID-19 continued to spread across Afghanistan, Ferhana grew more scared.

SALIM'S STORY: FIGHTING TO SURVIVE THE WINTER IN A REFUGEE CAMP

Amid a bitter winter, Salim, age 2, tries to stay warm at a refugee camp near the Syrian border. With temperatures nearing subzero, Salim will face this brutal winter in a snow-covered tent with only the clothes on his back to keep warm. The cold days are long, but the nights are always longer for Salim. When the sun goes down, the temperature drops, and he can feel the freezing air against his cheeks. He shivers to keep his body warm, but with no blanket, he has nothing to protect him from the cold air breezing through the tent. He is one of many children fighting to survive the winter in a refugee camp, and as the conditions turn treacherous, he is in desperate need of warm clothes, blankets, and food. Children are the most vulnerable in refugee camps because they are taken away from their homes, schools, friends, and families and are forced to start new lives in strange environments.

These two examples highlight why in the current milieu of globalization, the social work profession can no longer limit itself to its nation/state boundaries. It is quite possible that a social worker in the United States might be working with a 10-year-old girl like Ferhana or a 2-year-old boy like Salim through various refugee resettlement programs. Considering such global connectedness, it is imperative that social work educators and professionals not only incorporate a geopolitical understanding of global social injustice into social work but also rethink the efficacy of current theoretical frameworks for working with diverse groups of clients from around the world.

The Council on Social Work Education (CSWE, n.d.) website states that "social workers share a commitment to advocating for social and economic justice for all members of the community" (What Is Social Work? section). Additionally, increasing economic globalization and its widespread influence requires social workers to conceptualize many domestic social problems within the larger global context. The changing global economy, coupled with geopolitical shifts, calls for trained and sensitized practitioners at the international dimensions of practice. CSWE's Council on Global Issues (CGSI) guiding principles of international social work assume that social, political, and economic forces that are global in character underlie the dynamics of human rights and social injustice found in local communities. Within the profession, a comprehensive agreement exists that geopolitical forces contribute to and sustain local and global social inequalities. Despite this, social work professionals are skeptical, particularly of the Eurocentric approach that focuses on behavior modification, which puts the onus of change on the individual (Ferguson & Lavalette, 2006). Individual-level behavior modification contradicts the social work profession's systems framework that argues for an ecological examination of social problems. The ecological framing assumes social problems and their solutions lie at the juncture of multiple systems and in the space between the individual and the structural; this is known as the **person-in-environment fit**.

Surprisingly, most schools of social work across the country and the profession itself continue to endorse and use "classical" theorists like Erikson, Piaget, and Kohlberg to assess human behavior despite understanding the deficits of these frameworks for social workers' visions of professional practice. So how does the professional adapt these classical theories that assume the epigenesis and universality of development yet are limited in their analytical power when understanding diverse human experiences? Drawing on geopolitical events and Ferhana and Salim as examples, a social worker using the classical models of human development would assume that these children would develop similarly to same-age children growing up in the quiet suburbs of the United States, which ignores Ferhana's and Salim's significant and ongoing material, economic, emotional, social, and physical losses, as well as their peers' stability and material, economic, emotional, social, and physical continuities. Despite the decontextualization of human development proffered by classical theorists, the social work profession understands that context matters greatly in all aspects of human development and social life.

There is break in logic here. We haven't established the idea of decontextualization of classical theorist. So how can we make the statement "Despite the decontextualization ..."?

In spite of this general understanding, there is a growing skepticism in the profession that social work, particularly the Eurocentric approach, focuses primarily on behavior modification, putting the onus of change on the individual (Ferguson & Lavalette, 2006). This is in direct contradiction to the social work profession's person-in-environment framework, which argues for an ecological examination of social problems—one that assumes that social problems and their solutions lie at the juncture of the micro level and the macro level, or the individual and the structural, respectively. In fact, most schools of social work across the country and the profession itself continue to use classical theorists like Erikson, Piaget, or Kohlberg to assess human behavior despite the understanding that these frameworks, with their assumptions of epigenesis and universality of development, are limited in their analytical power to understand diverse human experiences.

For example, drawing on current geopolitical events and the case examples of Ferhana and Salim, a social worker utilizing the classical models of human development would assume that these two children, who have witnessed and experienced more loss and destruction than children growing up in the quiet suburbs of the United States, would be developmentally similar to others their age.

THEORY ↔ PRACTICE

Assessments gather data from several domains of a client system, including employment history, living situation, medical status and history, and developmental history. At this point in the interview, helping professionals strive to create a case formulation that links theories of human behavior with the client system's experiences, practice wisdom, and client system's sense of itself.

To apply the theoretical information in this chapter, the following questions can guide the helping professional:

- In what ways are the client system's' history of internal migration or between-country migration influenced by geopolitical forces?

- Are family members of the client system located in other countries and dependent upon the client system for emotional or social resources? How might this influence the development of the client system or family?

One of the main critiques of the traditional developmental theories follow from the critiques of the **modern paradigm** within which these theories are embedded. The belief in the monolithic metanarrative and the reliance on objective truth are perhaps the greatest drawbacks of theories that fall under this paradigm and its positivistic antecedence. These frameworks are decontextualized and reductionist and fail to capture the complexity of human experience. A social worker who does not understand the global forces that played a critical role in moderating these children's age-related developmental tasks will generally do more harm than good.

It is, however, not the intention of this chapter to engage in an involved critical analysis of the traditional or classical theories of human development but rather to argue for an alternative framework that addresses the limitations of the classical theories and provides social workers with a more integrated perspective that includes both the micro and the macro dimensions for engaging, assessing, and intervening with individuals, group, and communities. Thus, the purposes of this chapter are to:

- Understand how geopolitical circumstances create global social injustices.

- Present an alternative framework for understanding human development that considers such global contexts as an essential variable of the analytical model.

- Suggest a critical practice framework.

To understand the antecedents of global injustices, one needs to understand concepts such as capitalism, neoliberalism/neocolonialism, free market, and laissez-faire, or "the invisible hand." One also needs to understand the pernicious impacts of capitalism through alienation and exploitation of labor. Such understanding requires some foundation knowledge on the market economy. It is also critical to recognize that the profit motive of the Western world, or Global North, is the underlying factor of many of the atrocities of the world, including wars, climate shifts, and global poverty—to name a few (Prigoff, 2000). In fact, Chomsky (1999) argued that the development of economic and political policies that support private power acts essentially as a social hierarchy that places the drive for profit over the wider needs of the population.

Economics and Social Work: A Crucial but Neglected Relationship

All social work programs in the United States require students to take courses in social policy so that social workers understand both how policies affect their clients as well as how their own practice is guided by these policies. Another impetus behind such a requirement, presumably, is to provide students with tools to critically review policies and advocate for new policies or policy changes that would enhance their clients' well-being. However, a lack of knowledge base in economics prevents these courses from achieving the goals set by them. According to Page (2022), three principle factors play a role in ignoring the natural connection between these two streams of disciplines, and these are (a) social work's mistrust of economics over the questions of poverty in 19th-century England; (b) social work's search for its uniqueness weakened its ties to social science disciplines, including economics; and (c) social workers often deal with individuals whose plight in life is often connected to their economic marginalization (p. 48).

Microeconomics and Macroeconomics

In the field of economics, the rules and principles of two categories of economics, micro and macro, govern economies of all sizes. The field of **microeconomics** is concerned with the study of product markets, consumer behavior, individual labor markets, and the theory of firms. **Macroeconomics,** on the other hand, is the study of the whole economy. It looks at "aggregate" variables, such as aggregate demand and aggregate supply, the national level of employment/unemployment, supply output, and inflation.

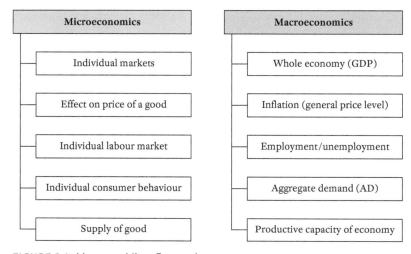

FIGURE 2.1 Macro vs. Micro Economics

To understand the global economic patterns, global poverty, and the related injustices, macroeconomics is useful since it deals with monetary/fiscal policy; reasons for inflation and unemployment; economic growth; international trade and globalization; reasons for differences in living standards and economic growth between countries; and government borrowing.

While the following description of the relevant concepts is presented from a microeconomic point of view, the same principles work at the aggregate level. This idea is familiar to the field of social work, where many of the same principles work at all levels: micro, mezzo, and macro. I chose to describe these concepts at the micro level for ease of understanding.

Perfect Competition

Perfect competition is a highly simplified concept of how markets operate in an idealized state. The following conditions must hold for a market to be perfectly competitive:

1. *small buyers and sellers*: The market will have many buyers and sellers, and they will each be too small relative to the market so that the behavior of any one of them does not impact the overall market price.

2. *homogeneous product*: The goods sold by one firm in a certain market are identical to the goods sold by another firm in that market.

3. *perfect information*: All buyers and sellers know everything there is to know about any factors that affect their decision to buy and sell in a market.

4. *free entry and exit*: The buyers and sellers are free to enter or exit a market, and there are no barriers that would prevent them from doing so.

While it is true that very few markets in the real world might meet all these conditions, the idea of a perfectly competitive market is so widely used to create social policies that any policy analysis requires an understanding of this concept. Take, for example, the debate over setting the minimum wage. The minimum wage policy is a measure to alleviate poverty, and social work, with its values of equity, can easily get behind these laws. However, the opponents of such measures often argue that a minimum wage increases the unemployment of unskilled laborers. In order to advocate effectively for their clients, social workers must understand this tension. In addition, an understanding of the market is also essential in under-market failures, which are often the reason for government interventions—another reason for social workers to have a basic understanding of the **free market** that follows the assumptions of perfect competition.

 THEORY ↔ PRACTICE

Client systems might take part in different aspects of the labor market as employees or managers, for example. During the assessment phase, social work professionals can ask client systems:

- How, if at all, have wages or employment changed over time? Does the pace of wage or employment changes mirror the cost-of-living changes?

- What is their average travel time to employment sites? In what ways might the length of travel time create additional demands on the economic status of the client system (e.g., purchasing meals during the workday or not eating during the workday to save money)?

Then, considering the larger client systems (e.g., groups, neighborhoods, or communities), begin to determine or theorize:

- In what markets might the demand for local jobs outpace the supply of local skilled workers?

- How might the competition between local skilled workers create social divisions in the labor market?

- In an identified market, what might be a government intervention to address the inequities in that market?

Markets

Now let us consider the markets themselves and the players in these markets. While each of these markets can be considered for a single consumer, firm, and investor, in here the consideration is at an aggregate, or macro, level. The players in these marketplaces are **consumers,** or the buyers of goods, the **firms,** or the sellers of such goods; **laborers**, who are key to the production process; and the **investors or capitalists,** who invest in the firms that produce the goods. Three important prices are decided in these markets: **commodity prices, labor prices (i.e., wages), and price of capital (investments), or rate of interest**. The three specific markets we will consider here are the **product or commodity market, labor market,** and **capital market**.

In any of these markets, there are two important relationships to be considered: **demand** and **supply**. Both demand and supply represent the relationship between any of these prices and the quantity of the commodity, labor, or capital/investment, all else remaining the same. In other words, this means that price is the only factor that impacts the quantity. In addition, this relationship in any given market is determined over a period of time, thus giving us the demand and supply curves rather than a static point.

In the case of demand, typically, the relationship between price and quantity is inverse. Therefore, as the price of a commodity increases, the demand for it decreases, and vice versa. This general relation is called the **law of demand**. Even if a few individuals continue to buy the same amount as the price goes up, enough individuals in the market stop buying or buy lower quantities so that the law holds for the market as a whole.

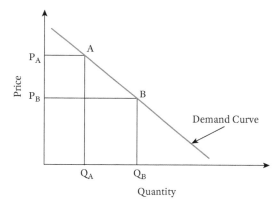

FIGURE 2.2 Demand Curve

As can be seen from the above figure, QA (lower quantity) is bought at a higher price P_A, and a Q_B (higher quantity) is bought at P_B (lower price).

In the case of supply, on the other hand, typically, the relationship between the price and the quantity is positive. In other words, as the price increases, the quantity supplied in any specific market increases. This general relation is called the **law of supply**. Just as in the case of the law of demand, the actions of a few individuals do not impact this relationship for the market as a whole.

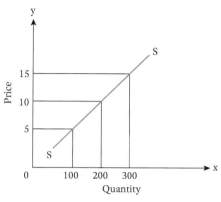

FIGURE 2.3 Supply Curve

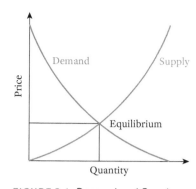

FIGURE 2.4 Demand and Supply
Curves and Equilibrium Price and
Quantity

From the above figure we can see that as price goes up, the quantity supplied increases.

However, the demand and supply curves are not to be considered in isolation. But in fact, it is the price at which the demand and supply curves intersect that determines the equilibrium price and quantity in a given market. At this price, the quantity in demand is exactly equal to the quantity supplied.

An important point to note is that the equilibrium price and quantity in any given market are not static. As price changes, the demand and supply also change. For example, if price goes up, the demand will go down. However, as demand goes down, the market adjusts and the supply also goes down. This dance between supply and demand ensues until an equilibrium price and quantity are reached, which may be the same or different from the previous ones.

Product or Commodity Market

The primary players in a **product or commodity market** are consumers who buy the goods and firms that sell the goods. Both buyers and sellers are driven by certain motives. The consumers are driven by the desire to maximize their utility and satisfaction from products, given their income constraint. The firms, on the other hand, are driven by the desire to maximize their profits while minimizing their production cost. Let us take the market for cotton shirts for example.

TABLE 2.1 Hypothetical Market Demand for Cotton Shirts

Market demand quantity	Price	Market supply quantity
50,000	$100	150,000
75,000	$75	125,000
100,000	$50	100,000
125,000	$25	75,000

The market equilibrium is where supply and demand intersect. Therefore, in this case, equilibrium price is $50 and the equilibrium quantity is 100,000 cotton shirts.

Labor Market

The demand and supply of labor are determined in the **labor market**. The participants in the labor market are **workers** and **firms**. Workers supply labor to firms in exchange for **wages (labor price)**. Firms **demand** labor from workers in exchange for wages. The laws of demand and supply elaborated above also apply here. As the price for labor increases, the demand for labor decreases, and vice versa. On the supply side, as the wages increase, more people are willing to enter the work force. Let us continue with the example of the cotton shirt industry.

TABLE 2.2 Hypothetical Demand and Supply for Shares in the Cotton Shirt Industry

Labor demand quantity	Annual salary	Labor supply quantity
50,000	$36,000	150,000
75,000	$30,000	125,000
100,000	$24,000	100,000
125,000	$20,000	75,000

These numbers indicate that the 100,000 individuals are willing to work at $24,000 annual salary in the cotton shirt industry. However, this relationship is not straightforward, since firms are driven by profit motive, which in turn forms the impetus behind keeping the production cost low; labor cost forms a significant portion of production cost.

It is also important to note that a firm's demand for labor is determined by the output, or production. If the demand for cotton shirts increases, the firm(s) manufacturing cotton shirts will demand more labor and will need to hire more workers. On the other hand, if the demand for cotton shirts falls, the firm(s) will demand less labor and will reduce its work force. However, in the situation where the demand for cotton shirts increases and the manufacturing firm(s) s find the equilibrium salary of $24,000 per annum too high, firms might employ a variety of methods to keep the production cost low by employing a **peripheral labor force** or by shifting the production process to parts of the world where labor is cheap. I will discuss the social justice impact of these strategies of cost fraying in the next section.

Capital Market

The final market we will consider in this chapter is the **capital market**. This is the marketplace where capitalists decide whether or not they want to invest in a market or buy bonds and shares. Just as the other markets, the laws of demand and supply hold for this market as well. The price of investment is the rate of interest. A low rate of interest is conducive to investing, whereas a higher rate of interest is conducive to selling the shares and stocks. So, in our example of the cotton shirt industry, when the interest rate is low, investors are willing to invest more capital in the industry, thereby leading to its expansion.

TABLE 2.3 Hypothetical Demand and Supply for Shares in the Cotton Shirt Industry

Demand quantity of shares	Annual interest rates (%)	Supply quantity of shares
10,000	5	4,000
8,000	6	5,000
6,000	7	6,000
5,000	8	8,000

The equilibrium rate of interest and quantity of shares are 6,000 shares of the cotton shirt industry at 6% annual rate of interest.

THEORY ↔ PRACTICE

Rental or mortgages are a significant aspect of home budgets and therefore can burden client systems. Considering those client systems that social workers professionally interact with must rent in an area, they are subject to the supply of rental housing in that area. They must also contend with the rental market demands.

1. Using community data, determine the number of available housing units in a neighborhood for a given price point (affordable rent).

2. Using community data, determine the number of rental units available at that given price point (affordable rent).

3. Determine if there is a gap in the supply and demand of affordable units. Next, identify how client systems have navigated or adjusted to meet these gaps.

4. Determine the ways that the neighborhood collectively adjusted to the gap.

5. Determine the interventions that the city, state, or federal institutions use to redress.

The Rise of Industrial Capitalism

Prior to the Industrial Revolution, in the West a vast majority of people lived under the social structure of European feudalism. Tradition guided the feudal relationships in which the peasants farmed their lands and offered a part of their produce to their feudal lords who in turn provided military protection. Production of goods was for self-sufficiency and was produced primarily for their own use and not for trade. The onset of the Industrial Revolution of the late 18th century, however, brought about new ways of manufacturing in Great Britain, Europe, and North America. This era was characterized by "the transformation of productivity by division of labor, factories, and technology. ... It contributed to the rise of the idea of society most crucially through two notions: the division of labor and the market" (Calhoun et al., 2002, p. 8).

Adam Smith (1776/1977), a Scottish philosopher, established the importance of both in his book *The Wealth of Nations*. According to him, the division of labor was a social process and one that was integral for increasing productivity. The concept of division of labor was that instead of one individual person with skills and craftsmanship producing a commodity, the entire production process would be divided into many discrete processes and laborers would be trained to be specialists in each. To continue with our cotton shirt example, instead of one tailor producing one shirt, the production process might include someone who cuts the cloth, someone who sews the collars, someone who sews the arms, someone who sews the body of the shirt, and some who assembles these various parts to make the shirt. As individuals, they each may be less skilled than the person who could produce the entire shirt by themselves, but together they could produce more shirts. This made for economic efficiency in two ways: by increased productivity and by lowering the cost of labor since the individual laborers were less skilled and could be paid less. This also demonstrated that disparate individuals with disparate jobs were interdependent in society. Another important aspect of this production process was the presence of an entrepreneur or capitalist who owned the means and factors of production. Smith (1776/1977) argued that government was not the only way to organize society and that, in fact, the market was equally capable of organizing society. Smith concluded that individuals act rationally and collectively to produce and purchase goods and services that society requires. He called this mechanism of self-regulation of the markets "*the invisible hand.*" Smith was the founder of classical economics whose key doctrine is that a laissez-faire attitude by the government toward a marketplace leads to the greatest number of goods for the greatest number of people and results in economic growth. It must be remembered that Smith was writing at a time when monarchies were the social order, and in his emphasis on the market, he was illustrating how relationships among ordinary people arranged by the forces of the market (rather than by the laws of the kings and governments) could provide a social structure.

The Industrial Revolution

The Industrial Revolution, by greatly increasing the output of goods made by machines rather than people, coincided with the advent of **capitalism**. For example, in the textile-manufacturing industry, mechanized cotton spinning increased the output of a worker by a factor of about 1,000, due to the application of spinning jenny, water frame, spinning mule, and other inventions. The power loom increased the output of a worker by a factor of over 40. The cotton gin increased the productivity of removing seed from cotton by a factor of 50. These resulted in huge profits, and the owners of the production houses then further invested this money in expanding factories and production.

This led to the rise of **capitalism**, an economic system in which the factors of production are privately-owned and money is invested in business ventures to make a profit. In capitalism, private enterprise controls the factors of production, which include land, labor, and capital. Private companies control and deploy a mix of these factors at levels that seek to maximize profit and efficiency. Some of the most important aspects of a capitalist system are **private property, private control of the factors of production, accumulation of capital, and competition.** Put simply, a capitalist system is controlled by market forces. The underlying assumption is that to achieve equilibrium and full employment, the market should be left alone to operate, without any government interventions. Such a laissez-faire attitude also assumes that there is perfect competition. Perfect competition assumes free entry and exit into the market. If we continue with our example from the cotton shirt industry, the capitalist in such an industry owns and controls the land on which the factory stands, the machinery that is used in the production process, and the labor that produces the shirts. The market for cotton shirts will determine the equilibrium quantity and price. The equilibrium market price and quality from our example is $50 and 100,000 shirts.

In a perfectly competitive market where there are many buyers and sellers, the capitalist only controls their production process. The capitalist, driven by the profit motive, would try to minimize the cost of production. However, according to the invisible hand, the labor market, which is driven by the demand and supply of labor, will set the labor cost, or the wages. So, if such a capitalist cannot control the wages and still wants to make profits, they would go to cheaper sources of labor and seek out new markets for their goods. Herein lies the exploitative nature of capitalism and the fallacy of the assumption of perfect competition. I would argue that the assumption of perfect competition is an ideal state and does not consider racism, sexism, and other forms of marginalization that create barriers to entry and barriers to perfect information, thereby debunking the myth of the market being fair.

Karl Marx and Critiques of Capitalism

One of the loudest critiques of capitalism was from Karl Marx (1818–1883), a German philosopher. While his work was informed by the 19th-century textile or mine workers, his analytical framework remains pertinent today and, in fact, has been successfully utilized by social scientists and scholars alike to understand social ills. In this chapter, I will also draw upon Marxian concepts to understand global social problems. Where Adam Smith saw social harmony and growth resulting from capitalism, Marx saw the exploitation of labor and class struggle. According to him, the actual economic fact is as follows:

> The worker becomes all the poorer the more wealth he produces, the more his production increases in power and range. The worker becomes an even cheaper commodity the more commodities he creates. With the *increasing value* of the world of things proceeds in direct proportion the *devaluation* of the world of men. (Marx & Engels, 1978, p. 71)

Marx put forward what has been called a "historical materialist" theory of human nature and development. Marx's theory of historical materialism seeks to explain human history and development based on the material conditions underlying all human existence. For Marx, the most important of all human activities is the activity of production by means of labor. In order for human beings to continue to survive, it is essential that they can produce (and reproduce) the material possessions/requirements of life. In fact, for him, how those material goods are produced is the key to understanding society. According to Marx, economics is the fundamental structure on which lies culture, politics, religion, and morality, which he called "superstructures."

A few important concepts crucial in understanding Marxian analysis of society are a **commodity, commodity fetishism, alienation of labor, and exploitation of labor**.

To understand these concepts, we need to understand Marx's nature of "commodity." According to Marx, any **commodity** has two values: use-value and exchange value. An "external object, a thing which through its qualities satisfies human needs of whatever kind" is then exchanged for something else (Marx 1977, p. 125). Thus, "he who satisfies his own need with the product of his own labor admittedly creates use-values, but not commodities. In order to produce the latter, he must not only produce use-values but use-values for others, social use-values" (Marx, 1977, p. 131). This he refers to as "exchange value." This commodity can have various exchange values, depending on the commodity it is being exchanged with. According to Marx, money takes the form of that equivalence; however, money hides the real equivalent behind the exchange: labor. The more labor it takes to produce a product, the greater its value. Therefore, Marx (1977) concludes, "As exchange-values, all commodities are merely definite quantities of congealed labour-time" (p. 130). For example, when we look at a cotton shirt, we can describe certain physical things about it. We can describe its color, the softness of the material, the cut of the shirt, and how it fits us; however, we can say nothing about the labor that produced it, how it was made, and the working conditions under which it was made. It tells us nothing about the social relations among the cotton farmer, the weaver, the tailor, and everyone else involved. Thus, in a capitalist society, social relations are between commodities and not between people, and commodities and money are seen as the embodiment of all human labor. This leads to the alienation of labor and a related concept of commodity fetishism.

Let us consider the idea of **commodity fetishism** first. Once a commodity appears in the market and is associated with a monetary value, it is fetishized to have some intrinsic and magical quality of its own. The value of the commodity comes from the commodity itself rather than the labor that produced it. Such magical qualities are enhanced through the sponsorship of celebrities and elite athletes. A case in point is Nike Air Jordans. These shoes took on a magical quality and perhaps the belief that shoes would make the wearer a superstar, thus obfuscating the labor time that went into its production.

Alienation of labor is intrinsic to a capitalist system. Such an alienation happens in four ways:

- alienation from the product: The product does not belong to the laborer, but rather to the capitalist.

- alienation from the process: The division of labor deskills the laborer and forces them to do the same task over and over as a cog in the wheel.

- alienation from species being: The deskilling of labor means that they are no longer able to plan long term and merely follows orders.

- alienation from each other: The division of labor makes the workers work in isolation and pits one against the other.

Finally, we need to understand the **exploitation of labor**. According to Marx (1977), all working-class people are exploited. He argued that the ultimate source of profit and driving force behind capitalism is the unpaid labor of workers, which he called "surplus labor." Marx defines *labor power* as a worker's ability to work. The capitalist buys, in addition to all other raw materials, machinery and labor power of workers. Working-class people who do not own the means of production and sell commodities have one commodity that they can sell, and that is their labor power. This they sell to the capitalist in increments in exchange of wages. They then use their wages to buy commodities necessary for life (e.g., food, clothing, housing, education, health care, etc.) at a given standard of living. The important point to understand here is that the cost of wages is independent of the actual value produced by the workers during the labor process.

For example, a laborer in our cotton shirt industry makes approximately $104/day (based on the equilibrium wage of $24,000 per annum). Let us say that this laborer can earn $100 worth of goods needed for sustenance in 4 hours. If it was a matter of fair pay for fair work, the laborer should be able to go home after 4 hours. However, since the capitalist is paying them for the workday, they still need to put in 4 more hours to earn that wage. The value created by the additional 4 hours that is embodied in the product is what Marx refers to as "surplus value." So, when this surplus value is sold in the market, the capitalist gets all the proceeds. Herein lies the exploitation of labor and the secret source of capitalists' profit. Thus, the greater the surplus value, the greater the profit, and since wages are determined by the cost of living, the lower the cost of living, the greater the surplus value of labor. Therefore, it is in the interest of capitalists to move the production processes to countries where cost of labor power and cost of living are cheap. This is the root of colonialism and neoliberalism that will be discussed in the next section.

THEORY ↔ PRACTICE

Commodity fetishism might not, on its face, directly relate to the rental market. The magical quality of commodities, however, impinges upon the finances of client systems. To that end, helping professionals moving from the assessment to the intervention phase can explore a client system's commodity fetishism by asking:

- What commodities are "must haves," and what adjustments have the client systems engaged in to obtain these commodities?

- What social, psychological, or economic meanings do these commodities have for the client systems in their social worlds? What does it mean to be without these commodities?

Helping professionals can then move from assessment to intervention by exploring how, like some client systems, laborers creating these commodities are alienated from the commodity and the purchasers. Helping professionals can therefore ask:

- How does your part of the work or tasks connect to the final product for the company? How vital is your task to the company?

- In your everyday life, when do you think about your work as relevant to the company's operation?

- How might the client systems change their relationship with their work in the company?

Geopolitics of Social Justice

While it may be tempting to question the relevance of a 19th-century philosopher and revolutionary in understanding global social problems and the world economy of the 21st century, Marx's theory of labor still continues to provide useful insight in understanding how context matters, particularly in the social work discipline. A good starting point is to understand how global inequalities have risen with globalization. Increasingly, international production, trade and investments are organized by global value chains (**GVCs**) where the different stages of the production process are located across different countries. Globalization motivates companies to restructure their operations (including design, production, marketing, and distribution) internationally through outsourcing and offshoring of activities. This is a way that the transnational corporations have shifted industrial manufacture from Europe and North America to South America, Asia, and other developing countries. In their pursuit of profit maximization and driven by the desire to increase accumulation of surplus value of labor, these corporations have sought out sources of cheap labor and cheap raw material. As a result, low-income countries have experienced significant economic growth as a result of being integrated into global production networks, and many have transitioned from being a low to a middle-income country. However, this seemingly positive outcome obfuscates a dire truth. According to Sumner (2016), more than 70% of the world's poor live on less that $2.50 a day and reside in middle-income countries of the Global South. This is because labor power in global value chains is extremely precarious, where laborers are compensated with low wages and work under deplorable conditions for long work hours. This enables capitalists to extract even more surplus value from a labor pool that is considered easily replaceable and cheap. In the following paragraphs I will describe the condition of labor in the 21st century and how we got there.

Colonialism as a Precursor

This condition of labor and social injustices needs to be understood in the context of colonialism. In fact, the new global economy, I will argue, is a less subtle and covert progeny of

European colonialism carried out most notably by England, Spain, Portugal, France, and the Netherlands. *Colonialism* can be defined as roughly 500 years of European dominance and exploitation of people and resources of countries, such as South and Central America, Southeast Asia, the Caribbean, India, and Africa, that now constitute the "Global South," previously referred to as the "Third World." Just as was the case under colonialism, under the current "neocolonialism" or "neoliberalism," which encompasses policies and practices guiding production, labor, trade, and moneys, resources continue to flow from the Global South to the Global North.

India is a good example of how colonialism led to the current conditions and social injustices. The story of India is reflected in the stories and fates of all the countries of the Global South. India, rich in spices and natural resources, has been a part of mercantilist fantasy since the 15th century. Trading rivalry among the Portuguese, the Dutch, the French, and the English led to the establishment of trading posts in India by all of them in the early 17th century. However, none was as enduring as the British. By the mid 19th century, the British had established direct and indirect control over almost the whole of India, and in fact, India was so valuable to England that it came to be known as "the jewel in the British crown" (Mehta, 2005).

The British colonialism agenda had one goal (i.e., movement of commodities and resources from India to England and the exploitation of Indigenous people for labor and social marginalization). Under the British Raj, as the British rule was referred to, policy of commercialization of agriculture, farmers were forced to produce cash crops such as opium, tea, coffee, sugar, jute, and indigo, instead of food crops such as rice and wheat that ensured sustainability. Indian peasants were forced to grow these cash crops that spoiled the fertility of the land, and no other crop could be grown on it. The condition of the farmers, in a country that was rural, continued to deteriorate. Not only were the farmers forced to produce cash crops but they were also charged exorbitant taxes on their lands. The farmers thus had to constantly borrow from moneylenders to pay the British government, and many of them lost their lands to these greedy moneylenders for not being able to pay back their debt, thus going from landed farmers to being landless laborers farming for others.

Farmers were forced to produce cotton and other cash crops, and the raw cotton was exported to Manchester, where cotton garments were made and then sold back in the Indian market at exorbitant prices. India became a source of raw material to feed the demands of the Industrial Revolution in Britain, which had made the production process so efficient that an ever-increasing need for raw cotton was needed. In addition to the agricultural sector, the British also destroyed the other interdependent domestic and small-scale cottage industries, such as the handloom and other Indigenous crafts. The British Raj levied a high level of taxes on these industries to support the Industrial Revolution in Britain (Maddison, 1971). The high taxes translated into prices too high for the Indian market, thus resulting in large-scale unemployment of craftsmen. The British, on the other hand, took full advantage of buying these commodities at a comparatively lower price in the Indian market and trading them at a much higher price in the markets outside India. This is just one example of exploitation that characterized British rule in India. We can easily see Marx's concepts of labor exploitation and the creation of surplus value that are hallmarks of the capitalist system at work.

> Over the time the British system worked on destructing the Indian economic system and as result the India's share to world GDP came down to around 4% in 1947 AD from more than 22% in 1600 AD when East India Company arrived in India. The misery of Indian agriculture sectors which was started by the British still continue even after 72 years of independence and the contribution of agriculture in GDP has come down to 14.46% in 2018–19 from around 50% at the time of independence but still half of Indian family are dependent on agriculture for their livelihood. (Upadhyaya, 2019, p. 5)

It is important to note that colonial domination was rationalized by the belief in the superiority of the Europeans over the Indigenous populations, and the British Raj was no exception. "At its worst, this rationale, which was racist as well as ethnocentric, was used to justify slave trade and genocide. In less severe variations, Europeans envisioned themselves as civilizing their subjects, who, we should note, were virtually always not white" (Polack, 2004, p. 282). Following this justification, the British Raj destroyed India, her people, her industries, and her culture in five different ways:

- draining its wealth through the process described above

- starving Indians, such as in the case of Bengal famine between 1943 and 1944, which claimed over four million lives and is said to have been engineered as part of an unsympathetic and ruthless economic agenda of the British

- creating a class of Indians called the "Babus," who are Indians in blood and color but English in all other senses (opinions, morals, and intellect) and could serve as a go-between for the British imperialists and the masses they ruled

- constructing infrastructure such as the railway for the benefit of the British but with policies such as "dogs and Indians not allowed" that prohibited Indians from riding first class

- using the "divide and conquer" tactic of pitting Indians against Indians, most notably along religious lines

Debt Crisis of the Global South

It was not until 1947 and World War II, when Great Britain was fighting war at different fronts, that India finally gained her independence from 200 years of British rule. However, the India that the British left behind was a mere skeleton of herself, bereft of a strong economy, burdened with a dithering infrastructure, and a country divided into India and Pakistan. Around the same time, other colonies around the world were experiencing similar fates. In addition, for many of the previous colonies, the power vacuum created by the retreat of the colonizers saw an increase in military coups, dictators, and undemocratically elected governments who continued to perpetuate class inequities.

One of the antecedents of such inequities was the "debt crisis of the Global South," whose origins can be traced back to the time right after postcolonial independence. This was a time when investors from the Global North, including the World Bank and the International Monetary Funds (IMF), both international lending agencies, set out to alleviate global poverty by promoting international trade, high employment, and sustainable economic growth. These institutions started providing capital for infrastructure development in the newly decolonized countries to develop hydroelectric dams, highways, or power plants. Unfortunately, most of these developmental projects really benefitted the corporations of the Global North that profited through the running of these projects, rather than the local communities. In addition, these developmental grants were given as **tied aids**, which meant that the borrowing country could not use the funds at their discretion but were forced to use them for the projects that they were earmarked for. Highways and dams were built that ran through rural communities and agricultural lands, thus decimating farmlands and destroying the livelihoods of many. Such projects ultimately displaced a significant number of low-income people and drove them more deeply into poverty. During the decade between 1985 and 1995, an average of 10 million people were displaced annually because of such projects (Moussa, 2000).

During the 1970s, the Organization of Petroleum Exporting Countries (OPEC) made immense profits from their oil exports by limiting the quantity exported, particularly to the Global North, thus greatly increasing the price of oil. If we think back to our supply and demand curves and commodity pricing, we will see that demand for oil remained the same, but the supply decreased—triggering automatic price increases. At the same time, the profits made by the OPEC members were invested in the Western commercial banking sector. Thus, the northern bankers were left to deal with two tasks:

- Find ways to continue to pay for the highly priced oil to maintain the quality of life in Europe and North America.

- Find ways to invest the petrol dollars.

They had to find borrowers to invest in, and the developing countries that needed infrastructure development were considered a sensible and safe option by the banks. This led the World Bank and IMF to give out loans in haste to the developing countries so that they could pay their oil debts with the interest collected on these developmental loans and invest the oil money. During this time, debts totaling to ultimately hundreds of millions of dollars were given out. Unfortunately, in their hastiness, these northern bankers failed to assess not only the viability of the projects and their relevance to local communities but also how these loans would be paid back (Chomsky, 1999). Many of these large-scale projects did not always adequately help the local communities, and the funds were often usurped by the wealthy elite or the northern corporations that controlled the projects. A case in point is the Philippines's Bataan Nuclear Power Station, which was built during the corrupt government era of the Marcos by Westinghouse for $2.8 billion dollars, 11 times the original estimate. However, this power station was never used because it is situated over an earthquake zone (Polack, 2004). In addition to the fact that these developmental projects did not really help in poverty alleviation, in order to upkeep the debt and interest payments the borrowing countries resorted to producing commodities for export to Northern-based transnational corporations rather than for sustenance. Thus, money continued to flow from the Global South to the Global North. This issue of debt of the Global South took prominence in August 1982 when Mexico declared that it could no longer meet the repayments on its external debt, and many other countries in the Global South followed suit. Three factors played a key role in precipitating the international debt crisis of the 1980s. First, there was a second oil-price hike in 1979. This resulted in an economic recession in the Global North and thus stunted growth. As a result, it further strained the ability of the countries in the Global North to balance their coffers. The banks, again in order to cover the cost, then offered further loans to those countries so that they could satisfy those pressures. Second, in order to control inflation, the United Kingdom and North America increased the interest rate with the hopes that this would curtail investment and slow down the economy. If we recall from the information on capital markets, the higher the rate of interest, the lesser the investment. However, as the economic growth slowed in the West, it multiplied the problems for the developing world. The rise in global interest rates meant the borrowing countries of the Global South now not only had to pay more interest on their borrowed capital but were also facing a shrinking market for their exports, which in the past had been an option to finance their debit payment. Third, this reduced demand led to a reduced price of commodities produced and sold by the Global South, and the countries started defaulting on their payments (Hurt, 2018).

Structural Adjustment Policies and Global Debt

The Global North and its financial institutions responded to this crisis through **structural adjustment programs (SAPs)** to restructure the debt. These policies set parameters for countries that are required to reform various macroeconomic and fiscal policies in order to be able to continue to participate in the global economy. These policies were characterized by trade and financial **liberalization, deregulation, and privatization**. The rationale presented was that, collectively, these macro policy changes would ensure that the borrowing countries are able to service their debts and create a climate for economic growth. However, such programs came at high cost, both in terms of people and natural resources, to the point that instead of alleviating the plight of those living in poverty in the Global South, it is them who are shouldering most of the debt burden, thereby increasing social and economic inequities in these countries (Hajrow & Joyce, 2009).

During the 1990s, neoliberalism, or market liberalism, became the dominant view of development rooted in the notions of "free market" enterprise (Clarke, 2005). The term **neoliberalism** broadly refers to the postcolonial sociopolitical and -economic arrangements that underscore market relations, reduce the role of the government and public sector, and stress individual responsibility (Boas & Gans-Morse, 2009). SAPs are a direct policy result of neoliberalism, which aims to reduce the expenditure of the government and reduce the rate at which the government intervenes in the economy (Simon, 2002). SAPs promoted international trade and liberalization. Thus, the SAPs regularly required cutbacks in the borrowing country's government spending on health, education, and other social services to meet the interest payments on their debts. They have been forced to privatize **public goods** such as roadways, utilities, and water. In most cases, these functions that typically belonged to the country's government have been bought off by private companies, often by transnational corporations, whose primary interest has been profit.

Although touted as poverty-alleviating developmental policies by the World Bank and IMF, there are several criticisms of SAPs. In fact, critics of these policies view SAPs as modern tools for colonization, couched in the language of development. The creators of these austerity measures clearly understood that "debt is an efficient tool. It ensures access to other peoples' raw materials and infrastructure on the cheapest possible terms" (George, 1990, p. 143). I will present three ways in which SAPs achieved modern-day colonization, or **neocolonialism**. Firstly, SAPs by their nature are a direct threat to the sovereignty of nations, given the fact that outside organizations such as the World Bank and the IMF are dictating a nation's economic and social policies. Secondly, through the requirements of privatization and minimization of governments' role in controlling internal economy, pathways are created for multinational companies to infiltrate these economies and extract their resources, thereby replacing the goal of public prosperity with the goal of private accumulation. Finally, SAPs have wreaked havoc on Indigenous cultures. Kinship-based societies, for example, operate under the rule that collective group resources are not to serve individual purposes. In fact, gender roles and obligations, familial relations, lineage, and household organization are crucial to the functioning of such societies. Thus, SAPs' focus on the primacy of the free market in organizing social structures and their emphasis on individuality are in direct contradiction to the ways of life for many collective societies of the Global South. In fact, instead of these SAPs actually helping the Global South or the developing countries to get out of debt, they have pushed these countries further into poverty. In 1988, the low-income countries of the world sent about $50 billion to the high-income countries, and the cumulative total of these transfers since 1984 is nearly $120 billion (United Nations Conference on Trade and Development, 1988). The problem became so pervasive that the "debt of the Global South rose to over $2 trillion by the end of 1999, with 47 of the poorest countries of the world owing 422 billion of that sum" (Polack, 2004, p. 284).

Even though the World Bank and IMF have reversed some of this money flow, the trend set by the SAPs continues today so much so that even prior to the pandemic, many low- and middle-income countries were in a vulnerable position, with slowing economic growth and public and external debt at elevated levels. However, the pandemic exacerbated this issue further. Developing countries currently have about $11 trillion in external debt, of which about $3.9 trillion in debt service was due in 2020 (Kharas, 2020). According to Jones (2022), reporting for Debt Justice, which is a part of a global movement on breaking the debt chain, developing country debt payments increased 120% between 2010 and 2021, reaching their highest level since 2001. Average government external debt payments represented 14.3% of government revenue in 2021, more than double the 6.8% recorded in 2010. In addition, the COVID-19 pandemic has caused unemployment in the Global South to soar. Millions of jobs were lost, with just sub-Saharan Africa accounting for 22 million of those. Export-reliant economies of the developing world have experienced severe blows from the pandemic resulting from broken supply chains and surging oil and gas prices. Such problems are being further aggravated by the current war in Ukraine. Given that Russia and Ukraine are the first and fifth largest wheat-producing countries, respectively, this war could easily result in global food shortages.

To deal with pandemic-related crises, many low- and middle-income countries have been forced to access expensive short-term loans from the IMF, China, or private lenders. In fact, some of the world's richest banks have made a fortune over the last year, profiting during the pandemic while funds are being drained from the lowest income countries in the world. According to the Debt Justice website (n.d.), without any regulations to curtail them, these banks can charge exorbitant rates of interest and could potentially make up to 250% from servicing the debts of these counties. This is only possible in a free-market economy with minimal government interventions. And as the time for repayment looms large, we are once again seeing a retraction of spending on education, health care, or climate change (Malloch-Brown, 2022). As Polack (2004) aptly states, "Debt has functioned as a mechanism by which money, commodities, and resources have tended to flow in one direction—toward the wealthy countries and peoples of the northern hemisphere" (p. 284). This is not too different from the situations during colonialism. In fact, Kate Roworth (2012) states that approximately the wealthiest 10% of the world's population is responsible for the excessive resource consumption and the production processes of the companies producing the goods and services that they buy. Some additional markers of global inequities include the fact that 57% of global income is in the hands of just 10% of people; 50% of global carbon emissions are generated by 11% of people; and 33% of the world's sustainable nitrogen budget is consumed by meat production for the EU market, which constitutes only 7% of the world's population (Roworth, 2012).

Exploitation of Labor in the 21st Century

This legacy of colonialism and the consequent debt of the Global South created a perfect opportunity for further exploitation of labor in the 21st century. On April 24, 2013, Bangladesh and the world witnessed one of the worst impacts of labor exploitation when the Rana Plaza in the industrial district of the capital city of Dhaka collapsed, killing 1,133 and wounding 2,500 garment workers. This not only highlighted the concept of labor as a global commodity but also brought into sharp focus a fundamental fact about capitalism: Its health and survival depend upon extreme exploitation of labor in low-wage countries with minimal laws protect-ing the labor, where transnational corporation driven solely by profit motives have relocated their production processes. It also underscored Marx's concepts of alienation of labor and commodity fetishism that characterize a capitalist society. In fact, the garment industry is the quintessential example of the kind of export-oriented industrial capitalism that has trapped much of the Global South. In addition, in their desperate need to finance burgeoning debt, the developing countries have "loosened environmental standards, taxes, tariffs, and other regulations to attract buyers for local resources and commodities" (Polack, 2004, p. 284). This includes the implementation of trade agreements such as the creation of Free Trade Zones (FTZ), North American Free Trade Agreements (NAFTA), and General Agreement on Tariffs and Trades (GATT). Interestingly, these agreements were also designed to reduce global poverty by increasing the participation and integration of developing countries in world markets. But in fact, the results have been the opposite, resulting once again in asymmetric economic benefits by providing the Global North–based transnational corporations with cheap sources of raw materials and labor resulting once again in the money moving from the **Global South** to **Global North**. These liberalized trade zones operate under minimum government interventions, particularly in terms of minimum wages, working hours, and use of child labor, thus greatly benefiting the transnational corporations.

The abject poverty and modern-day slavery that have resulted from such labor exploitation have also resulted in related global patterns, such as immigration (documented or undocu-mented), an increase in crime, ethnic hatred, and civil wars that have further devastated the Global South. In addition, many of the wars that are being fought around the globe are to protect the financial interests of the West. One also cannot not ignore the ramifications of the impact of the unbridled greed of capitalism, and in fact, many scholars and policymakers also point to adverse implications of free trade for the natural environment. In the context of trade liberalization, scholars often talk about a concept called **international environmental burden**, which basically refers to the idea that the environmental impact of the production of commodities takes place outside the country where consumption takes place (Kolcavaa et al., 2019). Unfortunately, it is those living in poverty with a very little safety net that bear the burden of climate change. Prigoff (2000) beautifully summarizes what has been presented in this chapter thus far as follows:

> At this point in world history of critical problem ... corporate and financial insti-tutions have gained control of the decision making ... and are using that power to promote their own self-interest, which are detrimental to the interests of community and humanity in general. (p. 225).

While Prigoff wrote the above more than 2 decades ago, unfortunately, the broad spectrum of global economic issues has only gotten worse. The social work profession, with its founda-tions in social justice and human rights, is in the forefront of dealing with global crises of our times, which include food insecurity, refugee crisis arising out of the fact 80 million people were displaced from their homes, climate change, and child labor and trafficking—with Asia alone accounting for as many as 8 million children who are being forced into begging and child labor because parents cannot afford to buy enough food (World Vision, 2020). Thus, social workers will be increasingly called upon to work with clients like Ferhana and Salim, whose lives have been upended by the geopolitical situation in the Middle East; and it is crucial that they be armed with theoretical frameworks that do justice to both the context and the individual. In the next section, I will present an alternative framework for human development and practice.

THEORY ↔ PRACTICE

- How would you define social justice for your clients?

- Consider one form of social injustice you see impacting your client(s), and connect it to a current geopolitical situation.

Alternative Model of Human Development and Critical Practice

One cannot ignore the ubiquitous nature of traditional or classical theories of human development, such as those by Erikson, Piaget, Kohlberg, in social work education and practice. As stated earlier, such frameworks, widely utilized to engage, assess, and intervene with diverse population groups, all have foundation in the Western philosophical traditions and are particularly rooted in modernity. These theories, therefore, are mired with the assumptions that in essence make them reductionist, deterministic, and decontextualized. They involve a high level of abstraction from reality that is actually much more complex; they are narrow in their application in that they are focused on one universal norm set by the West; and they put the onus of change squarely on the shoulders of the individual, thereby upholding "individualism," a Western value. Thus, such frameworks are ultimately limited in their analytical power when applied uncritically to non-Western population groups.

Even though we live in a much more integrated and global society, the primacy of Western thoughts, spread through colonialism, in the knowledge-making process cannot be ignored. Therefore, a critical question to ask as social workers is why our profession that celebrates diversity and difference in people continues to use these traditional frameworks despite their obvious limitations. I would argue that the answer lies in the concept of hegemony. With this in mind, in this section, I will (a) present basic ideas on how hegemony works so that social workers can start to question the Eurocentrism that we unwittingly continue to uphold; (b) offer a counterhegemonic framework for understanding human development; and (c) present tenets of critical practice that is based on critical theory, which allows social workers to take a questioning and skeptical existing social orders and hegemonic points of view, particularly in the context of our profession and engage in reflective practice that overcomes the false dichotomy between micro and macropractice that plagues our profession.

Antonio Gramsci and the Theory of Hegemony

Antonio Gramsci, the general secretary of the Italian Communist Party, suffered a long and miserable confinement when arrested by the Fascist State in 1926. During his imprisonment, which ultimately resulted in his death in 1937, Gramsci presented to the world one of his most significant contributions to 20th-century Marxist thoughts: the theory of **hegemony**. The basic premise of the theory is that human beings are not ruled by force alone but also by ideas (Bates, 1975).

The term "hegemony" has its root in the Greek term *hēgemonia,* meaning "the dominance of one group over another." It is particularly used to refer to the dominance of one of the ideas over others and the process by which such ideas become common sense, thereby preventing any alternative points of views from emerging. The associated term *hegemon*, therefore, is used to describe the group or class of people that possess the hegemonic power to disseminate the hegemonic ideas (Rosamond, 2020).

Antonio Gramsci, a Marxist philosopher, was interested in the question of how capitalism, a hegemony, has survived in both advanced capitalist and non-Western societies. While in the latter, such supremacy, he had observed, could be attained through domination and coercion, in this section we are more interested in how perpetuation of class rules under capitalism has survived in Western capitalist societies since this process sheds light on why social workers continue to accept Eurocentric frameworks as "common sense." According to Gramsci, this has been achieved primarily through consensual means via intellectual and moral leadership. Social work education often provides that leadership, albeit inadvertently. To counter hegemony, one must recognize that the social work profession, guided by social work education and research, is placed within the hegemonic neoliberal framework. The very fact that more often than not we put the onus of change on the individual and pay lip service to understanding that individual behaviors are reflections of larger social issue created by inequality, poverty, punitive social policies, and so on is a prime example of how our profession functions as a hegemon. Thus, following Bourdieu's (2003) recommendation that "the intellectual world must engage in a permanent critique of all the abuses of power or authority committed in the name of intellectual authority," it is imperative that in the social work educational sphere and profession, powerful norm-makers be continuously and critically self-reflective (p. 19).

Garrett (2018) provides a great example of a neoliberal idea of "productive labor" and how social workers, not acquainted with hegemony, might inadvertently be guided by such ideas in their practice. Neoliberalism that is heavily influenced by free market capitalism propagates the view that individuals are most valuable when they are contributing to the economy, not when they are financially dependent on others. A social worker who ascribes to this common sense might therefore suggest that a client is ethically compelled to seek out employment and thus dissuade them from engaging in activities that might support the community rather than the individuals. Such a solution might in fact be detrimental to a client coming from a more collectivist culture. Another example of neoliberal hegemony at work is the increase in retirement age. Modern trends in population aging are in fact leading to increased and unsustainable strain on health and social services. A social worker not versed in hegemony will perhaps support such a policy, for instance, but one who is seeking out counterhegemonic solutions might question the neoliberal discourses on productivity and look for alternative solutions that are not rooted in economic productivity.

I would argue that another way social workers tend to uphold Eurocentric hegemonic ideas is through the continued use of traditional developmental theories. Almost 2 decades ago, Qin and Comstock (2005) urged social workers to critically assess the traditional developmental theories for their very rootedness in Western, Eurocentric thoughts and focus on individualism to reach full human potential. In the next section, I will present a counterhegemonic framework that considers a combination of both macro- and micro-level factors impacting human development and offer a critical framework of practice that has roots in critical theory that values social justice and empowerment of oppressed populations (Moya Salas et al., 2010).

An Integrative Model of Human Development

The integrative model presented here is based on the theoretical framework for development of minority children in the United States proposed by García Coll et al. (1996). García Coll

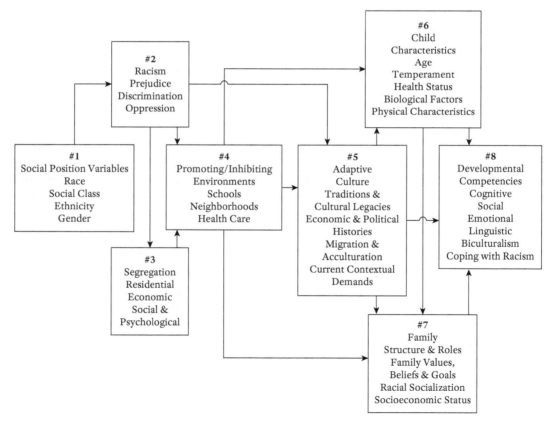

FIGURE 2.5 Integrative model for the study of developmental competencies in minority children

and colleagues (1996) opine that "developing more inclusive models requires the rigorous specification and integration of contextual influences far beyond what has been done to date in either ecological theory or transactional theory" (p. 1894). According to the authors, "The lack of attention to issues of race, ethnicity, and culture in developmental science has resulted in a literature on minority children and their families that concentrates on explaining developmental deviations in comparison to white middle-class populations rather than examining normative developmental processes and outcomes" (García Coll et al., 1996, p. 1894).

The model proposed by García Coll et al. (1996) has eight interconnected constructs and begins with the preeminence of social position factors (alternatively referred to as "**positionality/ intersectionality**") including race, social class, ethnicity, and gender. Through processes of racism, classism, sexism, and so on, society uses these variables to stratify and assign individuals in the social hierarchy that pertains to children of color. Effects of such stratification are then felt by these children through multifaceted segregation in the forms of residential, economic, social, and psychological. These factors then create conditions that uniquely impact the developmental trajectory of a minority child. These "nonshared" experiences with mainstream populations define the unique pathways of development for these children. The model further hypothesizes that such segregations ultimately impact the various environments of children of color, such as school, health care, or neighborhood, which might both promote and inhibit their development. In response to such inhibiting and promoting environments, adaptive cultures are created that are defined by sets of goals, values, and attitudes that differ from the dominant culture. Such adaptive culture, therefore, evolves from a combination of both historical forces and current demands. Thus, both inhibiting/promoting environments and the adaptive culture directly influence family processes, including the day-to-day interactions and experiences as well as the children's biological, constitutional, and psychological characteristics. The model suggests that children are not simply passive recipients of their experience; rather, they influence their family processes and contribute to their own socialization. As a result, minority children's developmental competencies emerge as a direct function of individual contributions of adaptive culture, family processes, and the child's own characteristics operating through the interactions among these systems of influence.

While García Coll and colleagues' (1996) model was originally developed to consider the unique developmental trajectories of children from historically marginalized communities, the model's versatility in engaging, assessing, and intervening with population groups whose disenfranchisement has roots in the geopolitical impacts of capitalism discussed in this chapter is undeniable. It can also be easily adapted to understand the developmental competencies at any stage of human development. Another strength of this model is that it does not reject traditional developmental theories but in fact recognizes that such models "may nevertheless have a heuristic value in guiding the study of the normative developmental process in children of color" (García Coll et al., 1996, p. 1893) and "incorporates and expands current formulations of mainstream developmental theoretical frameworks, as well as culturally different/ diverse models, builds upon an already knowledge base" (García Coll et al., 1996, p. 1895). In fact, the traditional developmental theories can be used to evaluate Factor 8, displayed in the right-most box, which presents the various developmental competencies of the child. The rest of the factors (1–7) can then be explored as context to better understand the developmental trajectory of the minority child.

Let us take, for example, the 10-year-old Ferhana and 2-year-old Salim from the beginning of the chapter. According to Erik Erikson (1963), Ferhana is navigating the syntonic and dystonic forces of **industry versus inferiority (school age)**, whereas Salim's developmental struggle lies in resolving the contention caused by **autonomy versus shame and doubt (toddler)**. Contrary to the linear perspective that Erikson takes, what this integrative model does is that it allows us to consider all other factors, including their social position variables and how they are assigned to a certain social stratum defined perhaps by their refugee status, poverty, loss of homeland, and the psychological and social segregations that result from being in refugee camps as a result. It also helps us understand how adaptive family cultures develop in direct response to war and other larger macro forces of neoliberalism and neocolonialism. Finally, this model can help us understand the unique developmental competencies of Ferhana and Salim that are impacted by a culmination of all these proximal and distal factors.

THEORY ↔ PRACTICE

- What are some common sense ideas that we take for granted in social work practice?

- How are these ideas upholding Eurocentric hegemony?

- Having identified these ideas, how do you plan to rectify them?

- Applying García Coll et al.'s (1996) model to one of your clients, what assessment questions would you ask to determine the client's developmental competency?

Critical Social Work Practice

So far in this chapter, I have presented certain basic economic concepts to help profit motives and labor exploitation under capitalism. I have also discussed how global economic inequities have their historical base in colonialism and how these continue to be perpetuated through values and policies of **neocolonialism**. I have argued for the importance of understanding hegemony so social workers can critically question our theories and practices. To that end, I have also offered a counterhegemonic framework of human development that addresses many of the critiques of traditional developmental theories. In the next and final section, I will argue for a **critical practice** framework that encompasses all the points discussed in this chapter. As such, such a practice model allows social workers to take a skeptical stance toward current theories and practice by questioning social work hegemony; it helps practitioners analyze power imbalances in society by considering historical and geopolitical contexts and recognizing that local problems have global antecedents; and it urges social workers to be self-reflective and understand how their own social position impacts their client populations and their work with clients—and finally take actions to promote change.

I will briefly introduce **critical theory**, which forms the foundation of critical practice. The origins of the school of thought known as critical theory date back to the 1920s and 1930s with the social philosophers Theodor Adorno and Max Horkheimer (Held, 1980). Horkheimer promoted the idea that the foundation of knowledge in social sciences was reflexivity. *Reflexivity* meant questioning and analyzing the existing social order and the way power was distributed to understand and explain the human condition (Moya Salas et al., 2010).

The general tenets of critical theory are that by focusing on the power and domination within a social structure, one can become more conscious of the need for change and in turn work toward that change. It posits that by reflecting on the individual places we hold in the societal structure as determined by our sex, gender, and sexual orientation, we can take a conscious part in the empowerment process of the self and others. The key components of critical theory are (a) examining historical and geopolitical context, (b) considering power distribution, (c) engaging in self-reflection, (d) practicing nonjudgmental inquiry, (e) acknowledging value, and (f) realizing that from greater awareness comes action.

Given these tenets, I would argue that a critical practice framework informed by critical theory is an excellent framework for understanding human development. Critical practice includes three main areas that incorporate the above six tenets, and these are (a) being aware of the historical and geopolitical context, (b) being aware of the practitioner's own positionality and values (self-reflection), and (c) engaging in respectful partnership with clients and communities. When intervening from such a framework, a practitioner does not view all human development as a universal process and treat all humans as a monolithic group but recognizes the complexities of personhood created by the intersectionality of race, class, gender, or sexual orientation while considering larger structural force,s such as geopolitics, capitalism, or globalization, as context.

In addition, current practice knowledge suggests personal and social changes are enhanced when micro and macro practice occur simultaneously. Rather than being dichotomous, they are interconnected and must be unified. Meaningful, effective social work practice entails assisting individuals in getting their needs met and in altering conditions that create oppression. Thus, the goal of critical practice is to assist individuals in seeing their oppression so they might engage in collective action that transforms society. Working with individuals and families entails providing resources, skill building, and/or therapy for consumers to deal with the consequences of oppression. It also requires facilitating a connection between private issues and structures of domination. Vodde and Gallant (2002) note, "Unless we are able to adequately connect the problems of clients in oppressed groups to the roots of their oppression and the clients to each other, fundamental change will not occur" (p. 440). Herein lies the power of critical social work practice. Thus, working with Ferhana and Salim, a critical practitioner could not only use a counterhegemonic, integrated framework, such as the García Coll et al. (1996) model, but could also act through consciousness raising. Moya Salas and colleagues (2010) offer some guidelines for critical practice that align perfectly with the material covered in this chapter.

According to them, first and foremost, such practice begins with a commitment to recognize how the personal and political are connected and consequently integrate social care with the elimination of oppression. More specifically, to engage in critical practice, social workers must consider the following interrelated yet distinct dimensions (Moya Salas et al., 2010):

- *historical and cultural context*: What events preceded the issue of concern? Include an assessment of events affecting the individual, events within the relevant settings, and societal events that are related to the client's social location, or positionality.

- *power distribution*: What is the power position of the client? Which social groups have more power than the client? How does the practitioner's power compare to the client's power? What effect might such a power difference have on the client–practitioner relationship? What kind of privileges does the client have or not have? In what ways do these privileges translate into power or lack of power? How does a client's intersectionality influence the client's situation?

- *self-reflection*: What are the practitioner's own values, beliefs, and experiences related to the issue the client is experiencing? How does their social location, or positionality, contribute to your values and beliefs? How might their intersectional identity affect their interactions with their client?

- *nonjudgmental inquiry*: In what ways is a practitioner being judgmental? What ideas do they have regarding what is appropriate or what is right or wrong for their client? Do they consider all viewpoints (particularly the client's) in good faith? How do they ensure that they are truly interested in the client's well-being and interest and not in other vested interests? How do they ensure they have the intellectual humility to accept errors in their inquiry?

- *values*: How do they acknowledge others' values? Can they differentiate between what is important to their client and what is important to them, and can they be clear about the differences between their and the client's values? How do they negotiate differences between these disparate values?

- *action*: What steps can be taken to improve the client's well-being and address social change? How do they engage the client in developing a plan for action that addresses both the personal and political situation? How do they ensure that a respectful partnership exists between them and their client? How do they ensure that this action leads to changes in the client's context? How do they enhance their client's awareness of how the current social order perpetuates the situation?

Thus, any social worker working with Ferhanna and Salim could use such a framework to guide their practice with them. While the integrative model of human development provides a specific tool to understand the developmental milestones of these two children, the critical practice modality provides a practice perspective that allows practitioners to question neoliberal policies that contribute to the social conditions for Salim and Farhana; it allows them to critique social constructs such as "refugee" "middle eastern," and the like and question the hegemonic ideals behind them; and finally, through critical self-reflection, consciousness-raising, and advocacy, it allows them to bring about true change in society so that children like Ferhana and Salim can enjoy a fairer and more equitable world.

THEORY ↔ PRACTICE

In planning interventions, helping professionals can now examine a client system's positionality as it influences potential targets to address problems in their lives. To that end, helping professionals can explore the following with client systems:

- For the rental market example, what events preceded the search for a new apartment? Include an assessment of events affecting the individual, events within the relevant settings, and societal events that are related to the client's social location, or positionality.

- What aspects of the problem does the client believe they have the power to change? Consider affordable rent, collective efforts to address the supply and demand, changes to their beliefs about commodities, or their relationship to employment.

- What is the helping professional's beliefs about their role in the global economic market, the geopolitical and economic change process, and multilevel interventions?

- How does the client system view the development of a plan for action that addresses both the personal and political situation?

- What does the client view as the strengths and weaknesses of developing a respectful partnership to change problems?

- Based on experience, what obstacles have gotten in the way of engaging in change over time? Consider the geopolitical, economic, social, psychological, and material obstacles.

CONCLUSION

In the current milieu of globalization, social workers are increasingly called upon to work with clients whose lives have been upended by the impact of neoliberal policies, unfairness of the market economy, and socially irresponsible capitalism. It is therefore imperative that we train social work students to understand that local problems have global antecedents. To that end, this chapter covered some basic concepts of economics so that readers can understand the roles of market and industrial capitalism in creating global inequities. The chapter presented Marx's concepts of alienation of labor and surplus value of labor as a context for comprehending labor exploitation in the 21st century. In this chapter, I also argued that one of the ways neoliberalism continues to thrive is through the process of hegemony. In the social work education system and profession, one of the ways we succumb to hegemony is through the use of traditional human development models despite their limitations. Thus, it is crucial that social workers familiarize themselves with Gramsci's theory of hegemony so that they can critically evaluate their own knowledge base and the efficacy of traditional practice models in their work with diverse client populations. Finally, I presented an integrative model of human development and offered some implications for practice that provide a pathway that is away from the typical dichotomous nature of our profession. Plenty of scholars have written about the dichotomous foundations of social work. According to Moya Salas et al. (2010):

> Most schools of social work and textbooks delineate separate curricula for micro and macro practice, reinforcing this dichotomy for students learning to become social workers. Today, with our emphasis on environment, it is likely not an intentional preference or slight of either form of practice. Rather, it seems to reflect the difficulty in teaching social work practice and its multifaceted approaches. (p. 92)

Both the counterhegemonic human development model and the critical practice framework equip social workers to move away from the false micro-macro dichotomy since both models strive to achieve the goals of examining power in the social order, analyzing historical context, and raising awareness through self-reflection.

Having established the theoretical and economic contexts that undergird social work and its aim to include traditionally marginalized communities, the next section of the book will consider marginalized people through the lifespan.

KEY TERMS

- Person-in-environment fit: refers to the idea that social problems and their solutions lie at the juncture of multiple systems and in the space between the individual and the structural.

- Microeconomics: the study of product markets, consumer behavior, individual labor markets, and the theory of firms.

- Macroeconomics: the study of the whole economy. It looks at "aggregate" variables, such as aggregate demand and aggregate supply, the national level of employment/unemployment, supply output, and inflation.

- Perfect competition: highly simplified concept of how markets operate in an idealized state. The necessary conditions are having small buyers and sellers, a homogenous product, perfect information, and free entry and exit.

- Free market: a market characterized by minimal government interventions.

- Consumers: buyers of goods.

- Firms: sellers of goods.

- Laborers: vital in the production of goods.

- Investors/capitalists: invest in the firms that make goods.

- Law of demand: states that as the price of commodity increases, the demand for it decreases and vice versa.

- Law of supply: as the price increases, the quantity supplied in any specific market increases.

- Product or commodity market: a market in which the consumers are driven by the desire to maximize their utility and satisfaction from products, given their income constraint, and the firms are driven by the desire to maximize their profits while minimizing their production cost.

- Labor market: determines the supply and demand for employment. The participants in the labor market are **workers** (supply labor in exchange for wages) and **firms (demand labor in exchange for wages)**. As the price for labor increases, the demand for labor decreases and vice versa

- Peripheral labor force: includes employees who are temporary or perform tasks that can be outsourced.

- Capital market: marketplace where capitalists decide whether or not they want to invest in a market or buy bonds and shares.

- Capitalism: an economic system in which the factors of production are privately-owned and money is invested in business ventures to make a profit.

- Commodity: an economic good, usually a resource, that has two values: use value and exchange value.

- Commodity fetishism: refers to how once a commodity appears in the market and is associated with a monetary value, it is fetishized to have some intrinsic and magical quality of its own. The value of the commodity comes from the commodity itself rather than the labor that produced it.

- Alienation of labor: refers to the process whereby a worker is made to feel foreign to the products they create, which occurs through alienation from the product; alienation from the process; alienation from species being; and alienation from each other.

- Exploitation of labor: refers to the Marxian concept that all working-class people are exploited. He argued that the ultimate source of profit and driving force behind capitalism is the unpaid labor of workers, which he called "surplus labor."

- Global value chains (GVCs): production chain created by the fact that the different stages of the production process are located across different countries. Globalization motivates companies to restructure their operations (including design, production, marketing, and distribution) internationally through outsourcing and offshoring of activities.

- Tied aids: funds that are only to be used for the projects that they were earmarked for.

- **Structural adjustment programs** (SAPs): policies that set parameters for countries that are required to reform various macroeconomic and fiscal policies in order to be able to continue to participate in the global economy. These policies were characterized by trade and financial **liberalization, deregulation, and privatization**.

- **Neoliberalism:** broadly refers to the postcolonial socio-political and economic arrangements that underscore market relations, reduces the role of the government and public sector, and stresses individual responsibility (Boas & Morse, 2009).

- **International environmental burden**: refers to the idea that the environmental impact of the production of commodities takes place outside the country where consumption takes place (Kolcavaa et al., 2019).

- **Hegemony**: theory that postulates that human beings are not ruled by force alone, but also by ideas (Bates, 1975).

- Critical theory: theory that postulates that by focusing on the power and domination within a social structure, one can become more conscious of the need for change and in turn work toward that change. It posits that by reflecting on the individual places we hold in the societal structure as determined by our sex, gender, and sexual orientation, we can take a conscious part in the empowerment process of the self and others.

REFERENCES

Bates, T. R. (1975). Gramsci and the theory of hegemony. *Journal of the History of Ideas*, *36*(2), 2351–2366. https://doi.org/10.2307/2708933

Boas, T.C., and Gans-Morse, J. (2009). Neoliberalism: From New Liberal Philosophy to Anti-Liberal Slogan. *Studies in Compariative International Development*, 44, 137-161. https://doi.org/10.1007/s12116-009-9040-5

Bourdieu, P. (2003). *Firing back: Against the tyranny of the market*. Verso.

Calhoun, C., Gerteis, J., Moody, J., Paff, S., Schimdt, K., & Virk, I. (2002). *Classical sociological theory*. John Wiley & Sons.

Chomsky, N. (1999). *Profit over people: Neoliberalism and global order*. Seven Stories Press.

Council on Social Work Education. (n.d.). *Discover social work*. https://www.cswe.org/students/discover-social-work/

Debt Justice. (n.d.). *Global South debt*. https://debtjustice.org.uk/campaigns/no-new-debt-trap

Erikson, E. H. (1963). *Childhood and society* (2nd ed.). Norton.

Ferguson, I., & Lavalette, M. (2006). Globalization and global justice: Towards a social work of resistance. *International Social Work, 49*(3), 309–318. https://doi.org/10.1177/0020872806063401

García Coll, C., Lamberty, G., Jenkins, R., McAdoo, H. P., Crnic, K., Wasik, B. H., Vázquez García, H. (1996). An integrative model for the study of developmental competencies in minority children. *Child Development, 67*(5), 1891–1914.

Garrett, P. M. (2018). *Social work and social theory: Making connections* (2nd ed.). Policy Press.

George, S. (1990). *A fate worse than debt.* Grove Weidenfeld.

Hajro, Z., & Joyce, J. P. (2009). A true test: Do IMF programs hurt the poor? *Applied Economics, 41*(3), 295–306. https://doi.org/10.1080/00036840601007229

Held, D. (1980). *Introduction to critical theory: Horkheimer to Habermas.* University of California Press.

Hurt, S. R. (2018). Third world debt. In *Britannica.com dictionary.* Retrieved April 5, 2022, from https://www.britannica.com/topic/Third-World-debt

Jones, T. (2022, January 23). *Growing global debt crisis to worsen with interest rate rises.* Debt Justice. https://debtjustice.org.uk/press-release/growing-debt-crisis-to-worsen-with-interest-rate-rises

Kharas, H. (2020, April 13). *What to do about the coming debt crisis in developing countries?* Brookings. https://www.brookings.edu/blog/future-development/2020/04/13/what-to-do-about-the-coming-debt-crisis-in-developing-countries.

Kolcavaa, D., Nguyenb, Q., & Bernauera, T. (2019). Does trade liberalization lead to environmental burden shifting in the global economy? *Ecological Economics, 163*, 98–112. https://doiorg/10.1016/j.ecolecon.2019.05.006

Maddison, A. (1971/2010). *Class structure and economic growth: India and Pakistan since the Moguls.* Routledge.

Malloch-Brown, M. (2022, March 16). The Global South's looming debt crisis—and how to stop it. *Foreign Policy.* https://foreignpolicy.com/2022/03/16/global-south-sovereign-debt-crisis-covid-economy-imf-reform.

Marx, K. (1977). *Capital: A critique of political economy* (Vol. 1; B. Fowkes, Trans.). Vintage Books.

Mehta, I. (2005). *Advanced study in the history of modern India: Vol. 1. 1707–1813.* Sterling Publishers.

Moussa, H. (2000, May). *The interconnections of globalization and migration with racism and colonialism: Tracing complicity* [Paper presentation]. The Canadian Ecumenical Jubilee Initiative's Vision and Practice of Jubilee Conference, Toronto, Ontario, Canada.

Moya Salas, L., Sen, S., & Segal, E. (2010). Critical theory: Pathway from dichotomous to integrated social work practice. *Families in Society: The Journal of Contemporary Social Services, 91*(1), 91–96. https://doi.org/10.1606/1044-3894.3961

Page, A. N. (1977). Economics and social work: A neglected relationship. *Social Work, 22*(1), 48–53. https://doi.org/10.1093/sw/22.1.48

Polack, R. (2004). Social justice and the global economy: New challenges for social work in the 21st century. *Social Work, 49*(2), 281–290. https://doi.org/10.1093/sw/49.2.281

Prigoff, A. (2000). *Economics for social workers: Social outcomes of economic globalization with strategies for community action.* Wadsworth.

Qin, D., & Comstock, D. L. (2005). Traditional models of development: Appreciating context and relationship. In D. Comstock (Ed.), *Diversity and development: Critical contexts that shape our lives and relationships* (pp. 1–23). Cengage Learning.

Rosamond, B. (2020, May 6). *Hegemony. In Britannica.com dictionary.* Retrieved April 5, 2022, from https://www.britannica.com/topic/hegemony

Roworth, K. (2012). *A safe and just space for humanity: Can we live without the doughnut?* Oxfam. https://www-cdn.oxfam.org/s3fs-public/file_attachments/dp-a-safe-and-just-space-for-humanity-130212-en_5.pdf

Simon, D. (2002). Neoliberalism, structural adjustment, and poverty reduction strategies. In V. Desai & R. B. Potter (Eds.), *The companion to development studies* (pp. 86–92). Hodder Education Publishers.

Smith, A. (1977). *The Wealth of Nation.* University of Chicago Press. (Original work published 1776)

Sumner, A. (2016). *Global poverty: Deprivation, distribution, and development since the Cold War.* Oxford University Press.

Tucker, R. (1978). *The Marx-Engels reader.* Norton and Company.

United Nations Conference on Trade and Development. (1988). *Trade and development report, 1988.* https://doi.org/10.18356/d8fdb701-en

Upadhyaya, R. (2019). *Devastating impact of British rule on Indian agriculture. Social Science Research Network.* https://doi.org/10.2139/ssrn.3442594

Vodde, R., & Gallant, J. P. (2002). Bridging the gap between micro and macro practice: Large scale change and a unified model of narrative-deconstructive practice. *Journal of Social Work Education,* 38(3), 439–458. https://doi.org/10.1080/10437797.2002.10779109

World Vision. (2020, July 7). *As families' incomes plummet, millions of children go hungry, forced to work or beg.* https://www.worldvision.org/about-us/media-center/as-families-incomes-plummet-millions-of-children-go-hungry-forced-to-work-or-beg

CREDITS

Understanding Marginalized Identities Through the Lifespan

In contrast to traditional human behavior in the social environment (HBSE) textbooks that add a diversity section within a chapter, Part II examines aspects of the lifespan from the explicit standpoint that all people have multiple social identities. Thus, a vital aspect of these chapters is that people hold ethnic, class-based, gendered, economic, physical, mental, and many other identities simultaneously and in all contexts. The social context and environment, along with the viewpoint of others in social interaction, order these identities as part of social interactions. This interactive process marries the social context, social environment, and human development to produce the complexity that social workers experience in their practice settings. These chapters review dominant human development theories that have been classically taught in HBSE courses and challenge students to think beyond these linear perspectives that are exclusive and often no longer relevant to the clients we serve today.

In Chapter 3, Elisabeth Counselman-Carpenter looks at historical trauma and explores the birth of a family and how new generations developed. The chapter considers how the process of adding children to a family system, the pregnancy, adoption, kinship care, and birthing experience, can carry vestiges of the traumas of colonialization, subjugation, and erasure. In Chapter 4, Tanika Eaves and Melissa Mendez discuss infancy to toddlerhood and explore the creation of marginalized identities from the legacy of slavery and the contemporary traumas associated with family separation at the borders. In Chapter 5, Laura Quiros and Elisabeth Counselman-Carpenter look at the challenges of becoming oneself in marginalized communities as an early adolescent and in the midst of family crises. Classical theories, such as those by Piaget, Erickson, and Bronfenbrenner, are examined, and their strengths and weaknesses are assessed. In Chapter 6, Amelia Ortega and Jamali Moses confront the issues of hierarchies and identity development from late adolescence to young adulthood. They examine the role of schools in helping young adults heal from trauma and the school-to-prison pipeline.

In Chapter 7, starting with the problems faced by young adults, Autumn Asher Black-Deer, Braveheart Gilliani, and Flora Cohen examine the markers delineating young adults' development. They detail cultural differences in how young adulthood is experienced and focus on the divide between individualist and collectivist cultures. In Chapter 8, Gio Iacono and Lisa Werkmeister Rozas survey middle adulthood through queer theory, the matrix of coloniality, critical race theory, and critical realism and contrast these theories with traditional theories of human development and attachment. In Chapter 9, Mayra Lopez-Humphreys, Rose M. Perez, and Beverly Araujo explore middle adulthood through the lens of some critically affirming frameworks, including liberation psychology, relational cultural theory, intersectionality, and strengths-based perspectives.

In Chapter 10, Christine Holmes delves into problems older adults face, such as social isolation and loneliness. She details the risk factors associated with personal and structural social disconnection. In Chapter 11, Pablo Arrazia closes the text in the final chapter by discussing what makes a "good death," the end-of-life experience, and conceptualizing death and dying. Each of these chapters brings a different perspective to human behavior in the social environment by starting with the complexity in social work and guiding readers in applying the theories to social work practice.

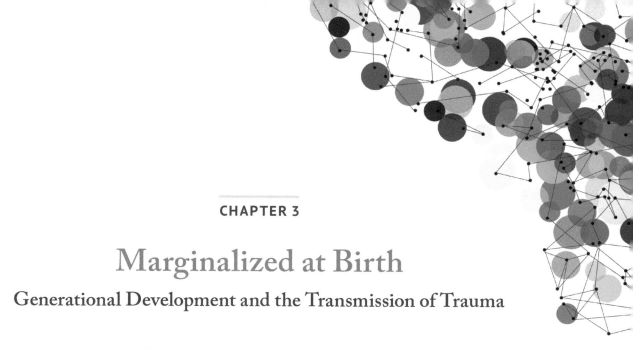

CHAPTER 3

Marginalized at Birth

Generational Development and the Transmission of Trauma

ELISABETH COUNSELMAN-CARPENTER

Introduction

Historically in human behavior and the social environment (HBSE) literature, families have been viewed through a Western, often medical model, lens through which the foundational beliefs of the United States emphasize individualism, freedom, and autonomy (Barton & Bishop, 2014; Bermudez et al., 2017). Traditional theories of development do not highlight the critical importance of communal culture, ancestral ties, and intergenerational relational processes, nor do they often acknowledge the way trauma is passed down through generations (McCubbin and Moniz., 2015 McGregor et al., 2003). These elements are imprinted on us from birth and need to be accounted for. In this chapter, we will examinethe building and development of a family in a more inclusive way. Please note that throughout this chapter the terms "folx" and "womxn" will be used. Both terms are meant to be wholly inclusive of all identities, those already known and those yet to be identified and claimed.

> **LEARNING OBJECTIVES**
>
> 1. Recognize and identify historically oppressive ways of defining a family and explore more inclusive definitions of families and intergenerational relationships (Competencies 1 & 3).
>
> 2. Develop an understanding of cultural and historical trauma (Competency 3).
>
> 3. Expand the ability to critically analyze generational development through an intersectional lens (Competencies 1, 3, 6 & 7).
>
> 4. Understand how one's positionality may bias the assessment process of generational development (Competency 1).

OPENING VIGNETTES

You are a social work intern in your first placement a family service agency that provides outpatient substance use and clinical services, adoption and foster care services, and community outreach. You have been assigned your first solo intake by your supervisor, and the notes from the clinical coordinator are brief and difficult to read. Ty is identified as 24 years old, 21 weeks biologically pregnant, and referred by the local emergency room for "stress reduction and anxiety management" after being checked for preterm labor. When Ty sits in your office, they are tearful and angry, stating that they don't want to talk about stress and don't understand why they were referred for therapy.

Sam, age 50, and their spouse Alex, age 61, have been referred to your agency for couples therapy. They are expecting their first child together, and the stress of this experience has led to an increase in fighting, tension, and irritability. Sam recently quit their job, and Alex is feeling pressured to financially support their family. They both report increased interpersonal tension, Alex reports symptoms of insomnia, and upon entering your office, they sit on opposite sides of the couch. Sam immediately appears tearful, while Alex struggles to make eye contact with you.

In reading these brief vignettes, please write down answers to the following questions: Where would you start with each of these clients? What made you think to start there? What are your automatic assumptions about each of these clients? What are you thinking about who they might be and the stories that they bring to your first session? What is important for you to ask about during this first meeting? What might you wonder about but not be ready to explore? How would your identities impact this first meeting in each of these sessions?

Culture and Trauma

All people come from populations that have rich traditions that structure interactions in social settings, delineate appropriate and inappropriate behavior, as well as outline the histories of that particular culture and future trajectories of younger members in the cultural group. While events such as wars, acculturation, or choices based on survival might have physically, and even emotionally, separated a person and their culture, cultures are resilient and are carried through the body and spirit in the history of a person. To understand culture, it is important to differentiate between social groups and cultural groups. **Social groups** are identified through interdependence, structure, self-categorization, or social identity (Stangor, 2015). **Cultural groups**, in contrast, are smaller segments of a population that share a social identity and different degrees of cultural norms, practices, and ideologies. Social groups can include multiple cultural groups. For example, a White social group can include people from Italian, Swiss, Polish, and Jewish cultural groups. The myth of "culturelessness" can allow **disparate cultural groups** to join **dominant social groups** and then participate in a singular narrative that creates **subordinated social groups** (Sidanius, 1993). These subordinated social groups also include cultural groups that, like dominant social groups, include multiple cultural subgroups.

THEORY ↔ PRACTICE

When assessing generational development, helping professionals can begin by identifying the social groups that client systems are a part of or associated with. To that end, helping professionals can explore the following with client systems:

- Some people, for example, might identify as part of a White social group. Yet previous generations have geographic ties to Poland, Germany, Canada, and Russia as well as Judaism and the queer community. How might client systems you are interested in working with describe their social backgrounds?

  - In what ways might multiple social groups combine to create an individual client system?

- How might the client system use multiple social groups to explain their understanding of family and family relationships?

- How might client systems use multiple social groups to explain their understanding of social relationships?

- In contrast to social groups, client systems are a part of smaller segments of a population that share identities, norms, practices, and ideologies. For example, a client system might be connected to the following cultural groups: LGBTQIA folx, Holocaust survivors, Canadian Indigenous people, Ashkenazi Jews, or expatriates. How might client systems describe their multiple cultural backgrounds' influence on family and generational development?

- How might these views of social and cultural groups' influence coincide with or conflict with a client system's perspectives on generational development?

- What rituals, myths, legends, and traditions might a client system identify as important during the generational process?

- What rituals, myths, legends, and traditions might a client system have lost in a colonialization process?

These divisions of social groups can then give rise to policies of violence and violent actions that punish a subordinated social group because of their nondominant status, which can include social identities, religious ideologies and practices, cultural norms, practices, and sources of knowledge. Over time, both dominant and subordinated social groups continue to develop histories that contain narratives about heroes, villains, legends, belief systems, and many other important themes that are vital to the soul of a culture and a testament to each social group's struggles and successes.

It is important to note the differences in descriptors: *dominant social groups* versus *dominant culture*. The dominant social group is a collection of different cultures under the banner of an ideology yet creates a dominant culture that attempts to control, limit, and/or erase the unique features of the subordinated social groups.

The ideology of dominance includes a constructed history that becomes instructive about the dominant social group's ancestry and justifications of subordinating others, and creates an implicit legacy for future generations with a warning about what could happen if dominant social groups do not attend to potential threats posed by subordinated social or cultural groups (Sidanius, 1990). The narratives and histories of dominant social groups then become the "history" of a nation, and the subordinated social group's perspective of history becomes viewed as cultural advocacy, which then justifies the dominant group's skepticism of the narrative. In a pointed history of the United States, Roxanne Dunbar-Ortiz (2014) describes a teaching exercise where students draw the America as it would be in 1783. In explaining the results of that exercise, Dunbar-Ortiz (2014) writes:

> What became independent in 1783 were the thirteen British colonies hugging the Atlantic shore. When called on this, students are embarrassed because they know better. I assure them they are not alone. I call this a Rorschach test of unconscious manifest destiny embedded in the minds of nearly everyone in the United States and around the world. This test reflects the seeming inevitability of U.S. extent and power, its destiny, with an implication that the continent had previously been *terra nullius*, a land without people. (p. 2)

The Context of Cultural Trauma

Alexander (2004) defines **cultural trauma** as "when members of a collectivity feel they have been subjected to a horrendous event that leaves indelible marks upon their group consciousness, marking their memories forever and changing their future identity in fundamental and irrevocable ways" (p. 1). The social science interpretation of culture, history, and cultural history has been primarily focused on psychological and social aspects of a culture's past. Neuroscience, however, has lent further insight into the intergenerational transmission of cultural histories and their presence in subsequent generations' biological inheritance and adaptations. It is important, therefore, to understand the starting point for human development in the social environment from a scientific view that contrasts with other ways of viewing the genesis of human development. Much foundational literature in HBSE starts with biology, which may suggest conception as the starting point of human development. Yet research in the biological and neurosciences now demonstrates that the cultural histories of famines, natural disasters, economic surpluses, and human-made and -induced violence becomes encoded into the person's cellular and neurological register and is then transmitted to subsequent generations that have never been exposed to the index event. In short, human development starts well before biological conception and is shaped by cultural history.

Groups that prospered and were less likely to contend with famines, for example, also transmit biological and neurological reactions or adaptations to surpluses. Many experiences become encoded in biological facets of a person and then transmitted to future generations. In essence, previous generations' experiences have an influence on present and future biological situations.

Understanding that a culture's past influences future generations' psychological, social, and biological futures is the starting point for conceptualizing cultural trauma. Next, it is important to consider cultural histories. For some cultural groups, cultural traumas are woven into their histories and have become significant turning points in the culture's framework about how they understand the world, the meaning of being a person from that culture, and the biological or neurological influences on subsequent generational development.

Cultural trauma shapes many aspects of subsequent biological, emotional, social, and cognitive trajectories of future people of that culture. Before delving into cultural trauma and other associated concepts that are relevant to human development and the social environment, it is important to understand the context of cultural trauma as well as aspects of cultural trauma so that practitioners can differentiate cultural trauma from its related terms when applying this concept to practice with social groups. We will now move into discussing cultural trauma.

In efforts to expand regional and international power, some countries established colonies in other regions or countries, which involved subjugating the local populations with the intention of supplanting the local culture with the colonists' culture. This meant that the beliefs, norms, behaviors, style of dress, and systems of interaction of the colonists' culture were forced upon the local population. Colonists presumed that their cultural systems and symbols were "better than" the cultural systems and symbols of the local peoples and began the process of devaluing, diminishing, and extinguishing local cultural systems and symbols in order to enhance and spread colonists' cultural systems and symbols. This displacement of local cultural systems and replacement with a foreign and sometimes contradictory value system gave rise to intrapersonal, interpersonal, and social group conflicts between colonists and local people, within local communities, and within families (Dunbar-Ortiz, 2014). It is important to note that this process was not a *cultural shift*, but *colonization* that led to forms of violence against local communities that we now describe as structural violence, systemic violence, genocide, hate crimes, domestic violence, and sexual assault.

The devaluing, diminishing, and extinguishing of local cultural systems and symbols was just as violent as the actual acts of violence taking place and severely damaged and/or extinguished the aspects of culture that are life-sustaining to individuals, families, and communities. In this context, cultural trauma is preceded by a social group's attempt to replace another group's cultural system and symbols through destruction. The implicit or explicit devaluing, diminishing, and extinguishing of cultural systems and symbols establishes an equally implicit or explicit hierarchical system of social relationships. In all, the process and ideology of devaluing, then diminishing, and eventually extinguishing a local culture, its cultural systems and symbols, and supplanting it with a foreign and sometimes contradictory value system with the colonial culture engenders the opportunity for violence and conflict.

There are some history texts that document aspects of the traumas experienced by Indigenous peoples in what is now North America or what is also known as the Global North[1] through forced relocation and forced colonization, the experiences of Africans and future African Americans because of the American slave system and then other legalized forms of slavery (e.g., Jim Crow laws), the systematic killing of Jewish and Romani peoples among countless other cultural groups during the Nazi Holocaust, and the Cambodian Genocide during Pol Pot's regime. At times, scholars position these historical narratives as a mechanism for the archetypes of the "hero" versus the "villain," which then implicitly reinforces a dominant cultural narrative. By this reinforcement, there is little to no acknowledgment that illuminates the complex and traumatic nature of the past or contextualizes the present (Loewen, 2005). These important events are not isolated incidents but a part of a network of ideologies that attempted to destroy cultural systems and the people associated with them.

Historical Trauma

In contrast to **cultural trauma,** **historical trauma** focuses on the contemporary psychological outcomes of historical behaviors that Brave Heart and DeBruyn (1998) describes as "massive cumulative group trauma across generations" (p. 2). In addition to the list of events and experiences that are the impetus for traumatic reactions across generations, Brave Heart adds genocide, "ethnic" cleansing, forced acculturation, persistent discrimination, and daily reminders of the devasting history of one's cultural community to the causes of historical trauma.

In discussing the transition from individual(s) to family, we challenge the readers to not think of these growing units as those that are "at risk." We do not want to endorse a Western medical model lens of deficit-based assessment, despite the significant role that cultural, intergenerational, and relational trauma might play in many cultural communities' experiences, but we want to encourage the readers to focus on underlying factors of resilience within individuals and communities while contemplating the ways in which assessment frameworks that highlight the eight core values of trauma-informed principles, including safety, trustworthiness, empowerment, collaboration, culture, holism, compassion, and reciprocity (see Chamberlain et al., 2019), might be used to continue to enhance and amplify healing.

THEORY ↔ PRACTICE

When assessing cultural trauma, helping professionals can begin by identifying the intergenerational transmission of cultural trauma and its effects on contemporary customs. To that end, helping professionals can explore the following with client systems:

- How and from whom has the client system learned about their own culture and identity? How has this knowledge influenced their day-to-day interactions and beliefs about the world?

---

1   "Global North" is a term that includes 57 economically advantaged countries found in North America, Europe, Australia, and East Asia (Collins English Dictionary, n.d.; Graml et al., 2021; Redmond & Martin, 2021).

- What cultural buffers (e.g., pride in one's cultural background, involvement with cultural elders or mentors, etc.) are used in times of distress or joy?

- How and in what ways do a client system's cultural histories influence their perspectives on building a family?

- How do client systems' cultural groups manage grief and loss? How might a client system participate in these grief and loss processes?

- How might cultural beliefs and processes regarding grief and loss contrast with Western medically based ideologies about grief and loss?

Generational Development Defined and Interrogated

"Generational development" is the term that we will be using throughout this chapter to discuss how people become a family and how people engage in the parenting system. We use the term "system" intentionally, as the experience of parenting is often regulated by external and institutional factors grounded in the value system of the Global North. The term "generation is a structural term that typically refers to the designation of parent–child relationship as well as a chronological period of approximately 20–30 years that describes the birth of an infant, the infant's chronological and emotional development from child to adulthood, which then leads to a potential period where the adult might then lead the next generation into child rearing or to the experience of "having children" (Bermudez et al., 2017). **Generational development** is meant to be used as a term that includes one or more people that are considering or finding themselves contributing to the next generation, which includes intentional or unintentional pregnancy, fostering to adopt, formal or informal adoption, kinship care, and traumatic or forced pregnancy and includes the influences of involuntary infertility, miscarriage, stillbirth, donor parents, and those who identify as childless by choice. Hence, there are many ways people participate in the development of generations.

The term "family" is emotionally loaded, complex, and has multiple definitions, particularly based on the speaker's positionality. Traditionally in social work and behavioral health literature, the term "parent–child relationship" is often used, but the authors of this text agree that the word "family" as it is often discussed in social work texts is foundationally problematic and limiting. How we historically have been taught about families has been rooted in the beliefs of the Global North and a long history of colonization and White supremacy (Bermudez et al., 2017). For example, Braithwaite (2010) defines *families* as a unit comprised of long-term, supportive commitments that may also include legal, coresidential, economic, or emotional ties, in addition to the possibility of biological relationships. Certain "types" of families and family structures have historically been privileged in the Global North, such as the term "nuclear family" that has been widely upheld as the "standard" of family and which is thought to comprise of married heterosexual parents and their biological children in an economically self-sufficient unit. Couples that are childless by choice or involuntarily childless are often considered "simply" couples rather than families, and we would argue in this chapter that the experience of family is not based on the existence of children.

Another expression used to describe an ideological definition of family is the **standard North American family (SNAF)**, centered in gendered, dyadic, heterosexual couples focused on parenting (Smith, 1993; Bermudez et al., 2017). Families that "appear" different when measured against the SNAF lens are then typically identified as the root of social problems (Coontz, 2000; Walker, 2009) and are subsequently referred to as "nontraditional," "alternative," or "diverse" when viewed through this lens of cultural imperialism. Even the linguistics around these families are othering and suggest nonnormativeness, such as "families of choice" or "fictive kin," which refers to a transactional approach in which friends fulfill roles of family members or consider themselves voluntary members of a family and are often tied to queer folx, elders, incarcerated individuals, or individuals experiencing homelessness (Davis et al., 2011; Hull & Ortyl, 2019). Even the actual existence of fictive kin as a phenomenon has been questioned. Nelson (2014) found in an extensive review that although designating nonbiological kin is common or meaningful in socially marginalized populations, it is mostly assumed by others/outsiders rather than demonstrated empirically when measured (Hull & Ortyl, 2019). The SNAF focus has rendered the multidimensional aspects of families outside this narrow illusion-based definition nearly invisible. Uttal's (2009) framework of interfluentiality, which more explicitly connects family ties to communities, is a more nuanced view. Uttal states that when we deconstruct social ideologies and expand our perspective to include historical information, it broadens the ecological model and deepens our understanding of family life.

TABLE 3.1 Definitions of Family

Historically privileged definitions of family	Inclusive definitions of family	Questioned definitions of family
Nuclear family: comprised of married heterosexual parents and their biological children in an economically self-sufficient unit.	Braithwaite's (2010) definition: a unit comprised of long-term, supportive commitments that may also include legal, coresidential, economic, or emotional ties, in addition to the possibility of biological relationships	Fictive kin: no actual blood relationship between members but all the benefits of kinship.
Standard North American family (SNAF): Centered in gendered, dyadic, heterosexual couples focused on parenting.	Uttal's (2009) notion of influentiality: A bidirectional framework in which families and communities are relational, interdependent, complex, and dynamic.	Families of choice: not always supported in the research; transactional in nature; a commitment of chosen relationships of intimacy, care, and support.

In fact, historical research of the Great North points to familial structures and functions that have long looked very different from the SNAF and challenge the myths perpetuated in family studies by theorists such as Talcott Parsons (Uttal, 2009). Some examples that challenge the SNAF are generations of Indigenous communities both in Canada and United States that include household membership complexities and multiple caregiver involvement. These kinship conventions, which often include different words and names for familial relationships, have consistently contrasted with "traditional" structural Euro-Canadian familial notions (Tam et al., 2017b; Uttal, 2009). There is also a long-documented history in many communities of what has been termed as the "functionally extended family." In the functionally extended family, the quality of relationships is determined by family processes (recognizing the pattern of engagement) rather than simply by recognized family structure (who has been identified as the head/heads of household and/or generational leaders and their offspring), and this has been well documented. Functionally extended families also include the multiple members of adoptive and stepfamilies and the diversity of roles that many different members may play as part of this family.

Adoptive families, stepfamilies, and extended families, in terms of processes, do not differ from what has been historically recognized as "biological family" (Georgas et al., 2007). It is important to also consider who recognizes what defines a family. This is particularly salient when looking at queer families. For example, mythically, it is believed that the right to be with one's family is protected as per international human rights conventions, such as International Convention on the Rights of the Child (1989) and the Universal Declaration of Human Rights (1948). This, however, does not extend to queer families in many countries. As of 2022 in the United States, for example, 11 states allow state-licensed child welfare agencies the ability to refuse foster or adoptive placement of children with queer caregivers based on religious beliefs (Movement Advancement Project, n.d.). Historically, it was not even until 1979 that the first gay couple was allowed to adopt a child in the United States (Resolution on Sexual Orientation and Marriage, 2011), and only 27 countries currently allow for same-sex couples to adopt. An even smaller number of countries allow those with other queer identities to adopt children. In recent years, more countries have actually moved to ban same-sex adoption, such as Hungary in 2020 and Poland in 2021, due to culturally conservative trends within those nations. On the continent of Africa, South Africa is the only country to permit same-sex adoption (Movement Advancement Project, n.d.). Unfortunately, what constitutes a family is often highly regulated by political, religious, and legal influences along with the beliefs of who may be in charge of a designated country, state, territory, or nation at that particular point in time.

THEORY ↔ PRACTICE

The following questions are offered as a multilayered lens through which to assess gestation and generational development, which includes intentionality, access to care, chronology and length of gestation, the role of loss, and the role of legal rights and recognition of family status.

In terms of provider views and values of family: Where does this family receive their health care (if they have access to it)? How do the identities and values of this system intersect or diverge from the values of those receiving care? How does the family value institutional and formal health care versus community or spiritually-based health care?

In terms of access to care: Does this family have access to care that relates to and support their positionality and identities? How difficult or easy is it for this family to obtain care, have physical access to care and economic support for care? Are there indigenous or ancestral practices that can support the addition of this generation and can they be accessed by the family?

In terms of intentionality: For folx who become biologically pregnant, was this an intended pregnancy, was it an unintended pregnancy, and was this pregnancy the result of sexual assault or violence? Was this an intended adoption or kinship care, or did it happen suddenly and as a result of an emergency, crisis, or loss?

In terms of chronology: How long was this family engaged in generational development? Was there an extended period of time during which the family (which may be a family of one) was trying to build itself through the pregnancy experience, adoption, or kinship care? Or did generational development happen suddenly, such as through emergency foster care?

In terms of loss: How much loss has this family experienced prior to the gestational period? Has there been the loss of homeland, family of origin, or culture of origin, and what has their relationship been to historical trauma? Has there been loss such as infertility, miscarriage, stillbirth, terminated parental rights, failed adoption, ruptured foster care relationships, incarceration of a family member, involuntary or voluntary separations between caregivers and children, or denial of rights allowing the family to grow?

In terms of legal rights: Is this family legally recognized in the state or country in which they reside or in their country of origin? Are all intended caregivers of a child legally recognized and protected in word, in court, and on legal documents?

Family Formation

There are many paths to the creation of a family, and the beginnings of these paths are forged often well before a child arrives to be raised by their caregivers. As stated earlier, there are many outside structural forces that have opinions on what "makes a family" and who gets to say they are parents or not. The process of family formation is exceedingly complex, which we hope this chapter reflects, but for folx in transition or who identify as transgender, regardless of country, there are even more layers related to parental rights, particularly for those who are unmarried and coparenting or in domestic partnerships. In the United States, individual states have different regulatory laws related to surrogacy, adoption, and recognized legal parenthood for transgender parents as well as for those who use assisted reproductive technologies (ARTs), which can lead to what are known as "complicated parentage challenges" (Justia, 2022). Complicated parentage challenges—where there is neither clear precedent nor a federal guideline—fall outside of the myth of the SNAF and can lead to prolonged and contested legal battles about who "should" parent. Most states do not have state case law on record to determine the relationship between a parent's transition, parent's gender identity, and the "best interest of the child"; sadly, both the states of Nevada and Kentucky have terminated parental rights of a parent based on gender identity and related to their transition experience (Justia, 2022).

When working with transgender folx who are on the journey of generational development, understanding the path to parenthood and the legal challenges, related expenses, and nuances for future custody is crucial in terms of comprehensive assessment and service provision. When generational development involves the use of ARTs such as intrauterine insemination (IUI), a form of fertility treatment that involves placing sperm inside a woman's uterus close to the fallopian tubes in order to increase the chances of conceiving; in vitro fertilization (IVF), an even more complex form of fertility treatment; surrogacy, in which a person with a uterus carries a fertilized egg through the gestational process; or the process of adoption, the emotional and financial costs can be enormous and include experiences of loss, high levels of fear and anxiety, a sense of shame, emotional fatigue, and feelings of failure (Domar et al., 2012; Rich & Domar, 2016). The financial costs of ARTs can also be astronomical. While there are limited grants available for people using assisted reproduction, the cost of the processes is significant, with conservative estimates ranging around $16,000 for an IVF fresh cycle and pregnancy-associated medical costs for a single birth to be around $27,000 (Crawford et al., 2016). Financial stress while struggling with infertility increases the emotional pressure on those trying to conceive and lowers the odds for conception efforts to be successful. Adoption also comes with unique financial pressures that may differ from generational development that occurs through spontaneous pregnancy. While adoption through the foster care system can cost nearly nothing (the nuances of the foster care adoption will be addressed later in this chapter), independent private agency adoption can range from $15,000–$45,000 within the United States and upwards of $50,000 for intercountry adoption (Child Welfare Information Gateway, 2022). From the Second World War through 2004, approximately one million children were adopted through intercountry adoption, but that number has declined significantly since the early 2000s (Rotabi & Bunkers, 2011). Intercountry adoption, once known as "international adoption," initially had a blank slate approach in which adopted children were encouraged to assimilate into the culture of their newly adopted country of residence (Richards, 2018). However, the 1993 Hague Convention on Intercountry Adoption established precedent that intercountry-adopted children be provided with a genealogical heritage, including knowledge about their country of origin; family history; biological connections; and stories, which becomes the responsibility of the adoptive parent(s) (Richards, 2018). Intercountry adoption involves nuanced complexities related to how constructs around race, culture, and belonging are facilitated, particularly by intercountry adoptive parents, and there has been polarizing debates about the overall practice of intercountry adoption (Bartholet & Smolin, 2012; Juffer & Tieman, 2012; Richards, 2018). Understanding the simultaneous financial and emotional costs, gains, anticipation, and loss through the generational development journey that includes ARTs, adoption, and/or through intercountry adoption as a family grows is critical for holistic assessment and understanding of foundational family dynamics.

For families created through kinship care, foster care, and adoption, there are other nuanced considerations to consider when considering generational development. Adoption, like gestational pregnancy, can include a period of anticipation in which the caregiver(s) prepare for, plan, and imagine their child. However, during the period of anticipation of being paired with an adoptive child, there is not necessarily an end date that is known, and the anticipatory period can linger for years. This period can also include experiences of fear, particularly related to the risk of losing a wanted child, rejection during the adoption assessment process, termination of the process, and a general feeling of loss of control (Eriksson, 2016). For those who serve as foster parents, it is important to understand the disenfranchised grief that may occur when children are "placed out," reunified with other family members, or a foster care placement fails (Lynes & Sitoe, 2019). Foster care is particularly complex when "placement cessation," as it is sometimes known, occurs. **Placement cessation** is when a foster care placement is terminated, both expected and unexpected. When this occurs, it presents as a unique paradoxical situation in which caregivers are encouraged to deeply invest and care for a child while recognizing that loss is probable and potentially expected and emotionally painful (Bick & Dozier, 2013; Dozier et al., 2007). Unfortunately, placement cessation often occurs abruptly and without warning. When exploring family development that transitions from foster care to adoption, it is also important to understand the context in which foster parents prepare would-be adoptive parent(s) for their transition for the child to be in their home. Assessing and understanding the dynamic between prospective adopters and current foster carers has been shown to have a significant impact about the success or failure of an adoptive placement (Browning, 2015; Lewis, 2018; Neil, Beek, et al., 2018; Neil, Young, et al., 2018). Transitioning between foster care and adoption has been identified as an emotionally complex task for both children and caregivers in which both loss and a new relationship that needs to be nurtured are experienced simultaneously. Blackmore and Burns (2020) and Lewis (2018) highlight the lack of research surrounding the perceptions of adopters and how they experience the transition of their child into adoption, but overall transitioning into adoptive parenthood can involve higher levels of stress, lingering legal complications, and grappling with the adjustment to a child who may possess characteristics that were unexpected by the adoptive caregivers (Goldberg et al., 2012; Moyer & Goldberg, 2017).

Kinship care, or the experience of child placement with family or friends of a child, has its own nuanced experiences related to human development. Kinship care providers are often grandparents, aunts, uncles, or family friends with whom children are placed upon removal from their original caregivers, typically through the child welfare system, and may be temporary or permanent depending on the circumstances. Kinship care has been found to have improved attachment outcomes for children and fewer behavioral and improved mental health outcomes for children as compared to general foster care placement. At the same time, kinship care providers have been found to experience higher levels of stress and higher levels of disadvantage than stranger foster care providers (Vasileva & Petermann, 2018, Winokur et al., 2018). This can be attributed to higher levels of hostility from birth parents, greater challenge with the children placed, or fewer support services provided to kinship carers (Farmer, 2009). Kinship care providers also experience higher levels of interpersonal stress, including lone responsibility of care, living with a chronic illness or disability, and more significant financial hardship (Farmer, 2009).

For those who experience biological pregnancy, the impact of cultural imperialism cannot be understated. Many folx with marginalized social identities may experience both barriers and facilitators to medical care or might avoid seeking care due to a long history of negative experiences with the health care system. Issues around seeking health care may include more difficulty accessing care, particularly for those identified as undocumented residents; experiences related to microaggressions, discrimination, and actual acts of physical or verbal aggression during a health care appointment; and, in general, receiving lower standards of care.

While it is beyond the scope of any one chapter to discuss the multilayered needs of queer families and their generational development, it is important to highlight some of the unique aspects that come with queer family planning. Decision making around having a child in a queer family differs significantly from cisgender generational development. The first decision is whether or not a queer couple or those within a queer relationship recognizing each other as a family decide to remain childless or consider having a child together. There are many routes to adding a child to a family, but these routes are heavily governed by finances, such as the cost of fertility treatments and ART, adoption state laws that can deny a queer family's right to adopt and foster, and multiple emotionally complex decisions, such as who should serve as the gestational carrier (Malmquist et al., 2021). Gender identity also plays a significant role in generational development, as nonbinary individuals, transgender men, and butch lesbians may find carrying a pregnancy creates an emotional dissonance that conflicts with their gender identity (Ross et al., 2012, Malmquist, 2021). Also, the birth-giving experience plays a significant role in parenting for many years after the actual birth (Malmquist, 2021). Having inclusive medical care that highlights the multifaceted nature of queer pregnancy and birthing is critically important but not always easily accessible due to a lack of health insurance, transportation, and adequate training of health care providers.

Understanding the context in which a pregnancy occurs is critical in assessment of all folx, including transgender and nonbinary men. Light et al. (2018) have found that transmasculine men and those assigned female at birth who identify as men have the same unintended pregnancy rates as comparable to the entire U.S. general population, even when taking testosterone therapy. As the emotional experience of carrying an unanticipated pregnancy can evoke a myriad of emotions, clinicians should not assume the emotional significance of a pregnancy unless clarified directly by the client.

THEORY ↔ PRACTICE

As client systems and helping professionals move from assessment to intervention phases, determining prior attempts to address problems can reveal the plethora of supports that client systems tap into before accessing helping services. Thus, helping professionals can explore:

- What Western forms of support were sought or might be used during the gestational period?

- What cultural forms of support were sought or might be used during the gestational period?

Prenatal Care

In the Western medical model, care for a person who is biologically pregnant is known as **prenatal care (PNC)**, with routine PNC considered a form of preventative health care service. PNC, particularly when it starts in early gestation, is an opportunity for identifying and addressing risk factors. It also can provide emotional support and psychoeducation of the pregnant person, which has been shown to improve both maternal and neonatal outcome (Gadson et al., 2017; Johnson, 2020; Shah et al., 2018). Typically, prenatal care should start during the first trimester of pregnancy, and while in 2018, it was documented that 77.5% percent of women received care during this time, it has been well established that folx from socially marginalized groups are less likely to receive adequate PNC, such as not receiving care during the first trimester of pregnancy or being less likely to attend perinatal classes, and may not receive PNC at all (Gadson et al., 2017; Green, 2018, Martin et al., 2019). It is also well documented that Black women, when compared to White women receiving PNC, are twice as likely to deliver a premature baby, are 3–4 times more likely to die of a pregnancy-related cause, and are twice as likely to have their baby die in the first year (Creanga et al., 2017; Mage et al., 2019; Mohamed et al., 2014; Petersen et al., 2019). Similarly, North American Indigenous women also experience twice as high maternal morbidity and mortality as compared to non-Hispanic White women, especially in rural settings (Johnson, 2020; Kozhimannil et al., 2020) and in general experience more difficulty with access to PNC, inconsistent care, and difficulty with communication styles of medical providers during PNC (Carter et al., 2021; Johnson, 2020).

Other challenges during the prenatal period relate to women who also carry a *DSM-V* psychiatric diagnosis. Many challenges at the intersection of prenatal care and psychiatric treatment involve (a) significant knowledge gaps by medical and behavioral health providers, (b) limited reproductive safety data for women living with bipolar disorder and on mood-stabilizing medication (Viguera et al., 2007), (c) that most psychosocial interventions for pregnant women with marginalized social identities are tested on White subjects (Ponting et al., 2020); and (d) providers have limited knowledge as to risk and protective factors related to recurrence of symptoms (Viguera et al., 2007). It is generally accepted that pregnancy can simultaneously be an exciting yet stressful time, which includes the impact that prenatal maternal emotional distress may have negative outcomes on pregnancy, and for womxn of color, added stress of being separated from their families of origin, lack of familiarity with the medical system in the country they have immigrated to, and increased financial and cultural stressors (Ayon et al., 2018; Ponting et al., 2020; Valencia-Garcia et al.2012, Wu et al., 2020). In general, Black and Latina womxn are found to experience higher rates of depression and anxiety as compared to White womxn (Ponting et al., 2020). Also, formal antenatal diagnoses of depression and other psychiatric diagnostic categories carry with them increased levels of stigma, and diagnoses are often undetected and undertreated during pregnancy (Mughal et al., 2022) due to misinterpreted symptoms and inadequate screening for all womxn (Leftkovics et al., 2014). Womxn who carry psychiatric diagnoses such as posttraumatic stress disorder are also at risk for relapse of the illness due to discontinuation of maintenance medication. Presence of psychiatric symptoms other than depression are often overlooked because typical prenatal care only screens for depression (Kim et al., 2014). Due to historical and systemic oppression, there may also often be limited self-reporting of the need for support services during pregnancy related to fear of reports to child protective services (Kim et al., 2043).

Recommendations for more inclusive prenatal care include (a) the use of home visiting programs during pregnancy and infancy, particularly for families that have been identified as low-income "at-risk" families with limited access to care; engaging tribal or community elders in program development; as well as the use of community-based participatory research to assess the success and challenges of such programs (Barlow et al., 2006; Butts & Rich, 2013). It is imperative to work toward destigmatizing help-seeking as part of the PNC journey, particularly for those who experience the intersection of pregnancy and a behavioral health diagnosis. There is a need for the use of more nuanced instruments that capture the emotional complexity of the gestational journey to identify womxn who may need additional support during this period. Formal research related to more inclusive forms of prenatal care for marginalized populations remain conflicting in terms of findings and clinical recommendations. The work of Darling et al. (2021), who conducted a systematic review of programs targeting populations with low rates of PNC attendance, found that none of the interventions to increase attendance at PNC appointments had improved clinical outcomes for folx with historically marginalized identities. Conversely, Ickovics and colleagues (2007) found that group prenatal care (GNC), particularly for Black women, improved outcomes significantly, including up to a 45% reduction in preterm labor. Another form of inclusive PNC is at-home visitation, and Barlow et al. (2006) reported success in the at-home visitation model of prenatal care demonstrating improved outcomes for North American Indigenous women. Overall, there remain significant challenges in theory about health disparities during pregnancy, including the lack of research that moves outside of the Black–White dichotomy and looks at multiple marginalized racial groups that also include Asian/Native Hawaiian women, Indigenous women, and non-Black Hispanic/Latina women (Almeida et al., 2018; Johnson, 2020).

THEORY ↔ PRACTICE

- As client systems and helping professionals engage in the intervention phase, helping professionals can explore the following: How might client systems view prenatal care, including the frequency of appointments, the types of tests and procedures, invasiveness, and accessibility?

- What prior prenatal experiences might client systems have with cultural and Western medical care?

- How might the body of the person gestationally carrying be regulated by external forces, including governmental laws, historical traumas, and access to health care?

- How might historical forces influence pregnancy—whether it is a physical or emotional pregnancy—in the present day?

The Birth Experience

The birth experience for those experiencing gestational parenthood has been found to be a highly individual experience and is influenced in many ways: the birther's identities, their prior experiences, and their present-day context. It been identified, as well, as a time in which the intersection of gendered racism and trauma may powerfully intersect (Malmquist, 2021; Markin & Coleman, 2023. Racism within health care settings and structural racism perpetuated by health care providers has been well-documented (Crear-Perry et al., 2020; Hariharan et al., 2021; Hardeman et al., 2018). Research demonstrates that people of color, as well as transgender and nonbinary people, experience significantly higher rates of discrimination, mistreatment, poorer quality of care, and outright aggression as compared to the overall population in the United States (Markin & Coleman, 2021; Moseson et al., 2020) in all health care settings. Birth centers, as well as gestationally related centers (abortion centers and practices providing contraceptive and reproductive care), are usually highly gendered environments. Training physicians and nurses in transgender care during their educational experience remains shockingly low, with more than half of accredited programs providing no LGBTQIA+ trainings and 30% or less of doctors being comfortable with caring for transgender patients (Moseson et al., 2020), yet nearly 12% of people between the ages of 18 and 35 identify as transgender, gender expansive, nonbinary, agender, genderfluid, or genderqueer (Gay and Lesbian Alliance Against Defamation, 2017). Similarly, antiracist curriculum and praxis within medical schools remains in its early stages and is often hampered by using only White, male, and cisgender patients for clinical demonstrations, case studies, and medical illustrations, and often those teaching medical school courses, even across specialties, are White identified (Hariharan et al., 2021; Hardeman et al., 2018).

There are multiple layers of the generational development experience that can evoke reactions linked to trauma and compound the effects of what is discussed earlier in this chapter as either cultural or historical trauma. These include, but are not exclusive to, removal of a placed child in a foster care or adoptive experience, if a child is temporarily removed from their birth parent, the experience of a stillbirth, and medical trauma during the child-birthing process. The traumas and losses that may occur during this time will be magnified by historical trauma and intergenerational losses of one's ancestors and their homeland. As discussed earlier in the chapter, cultural trauma highlights the impact created by extremely adverse life events that have such an impact that they can be "passed down" in a nongenomic but epigenetic way from gestational carrier to fetus in a way that affects fetal DNA (Yehuda et al., 2014). If the gestational carrier is experiencing higher levels of psychological stress, this has been shown to have a physical impact on the infant, including lower birth weight and lower birth size (Brown, 2020). Large-scale events, such as the 9/11 terrorist attacks in the United States, regardless of the states lived in, have been found to impact both interuterine growth on the fetus during the first trimester and lead to a higher risk of future health problems for the fetus postnatally (Brown, 2020). Similarly, the impact carries through not just the infant–parent bond of that generation but passes down to future generations. Studies related to the impact of the Holocaust and the cruelty inflicted during the residential school system in the Greater North for Indigenous populations demonstrates the impact that proximal stressors have on collective well-being. While the goal of this chapter is to focus on the developing family and the role that historical and cultural trauma play in early attachment patterns, as Conching and Thayter (2019) state, it is important to understand the "biological pathways through which historical trauma actually impacts health," particularly around biological pregnancy and family development, and the role that epigenetics plays in how "a collective trauma experienced by one generation can negatively impact the well-being of future generations" (p. 74). While the impact of the COVID-19 pandemic is in its own infancy of study, early research demonstrates that those experiencing pregnancy during the pandemic experienced higher rates of depression and anxiety (Berthelot et al., 2020).

Understanding the circumstances during which the gestational carrier has lived, particularly during the earlier weeks of gestation, should be a key aspect of inclusive and holistic assessment, as well as developing an understanding of any cultural and personal history at the ancestral level, including the absence of knowing one's ancestral history due to genocide, whitewashing, or paucity of documentation related to slavery and human trafficking. It is also key to understand the role that the gestational carrier's adverse childhood experiences may play, through behavioral mechanisms, in the experience of attaching to the child that may arrive through pregnancy, foster care, kinship care, or adoption (this will be explored much more deeply in the next chapter). Hoke and McDade (2015) provide a framework of "biosocial inheritance" that identifies "the process whereby social adversity in one generation is transmitted to the next through reinforcing biological and social mechanisms that impair health, exacerbating social and health disparities" that helps deepen understanding of this type of transmissible socioemotional experience (p. 187).

THEORY ↔ PRACTICE

As client systems and helping professionals engage in the intervention phase, helping professionals can use a genogram to depict major historical events of the past three to four generations, thereby documenting intergenerational collective and individual trauma. Following this, helping professionals can then explore the following with the client system:

- Where has biosocial inheritance occurred, and where might it manifest with this client?

- What might be the client system's expectations around the birthing process?

- What supports are in place if the birthing process does not meet these expectations?

- What are the support people's birthing expectations? How might they align with the client system's expectations and hopes?

The Birthing Process

For people who create a family through gestational parenthood and the experience of physically going through childbirth, there are several risk factors related to trauma that are important to identify and understand. In general, trauma, both medical and emotional, during the childbirth process has been identified as a worldwide and universal phenomenon for gestational parents; global prevalence from traumatic childbirth experience is estimated between 9% and 44% of all births (de Graaf et al., 2018). Postnatally, approximately 24%–30% report posttraumatic stress symptoms at the 6 weeks postpartum mark (Czarnocka & Slade, 2000; Soet et al., 2003). This can also be compounded by another contributing factor, known as the fear of childbirth (FOC), which has been identified as a health issue of concern and which impacts about 14% percent of those who are assigned female at birth, a similar number of their male partners, and is just beginning to be studied in transgender and nonbinary gestational carriers (Malmquist, 2021). As Malmquist (2021) states, in relation to FOC, "negative expectations lead to negative experiences," and it is important for social workers to explore, understand, and attempt to ameliorate the multiple barriers and opportunities for negative experiences in health care settings during the childbirth process for all folx with marginalized identities (p. 272).

Repeated studies have found that, in general, for those assigned female at birth and identifying as womxn, overall, 1 in 6 women reported one or more types of mistreatments during the childbirth experiences (Ertel et al., 2012; McLemore et al., 2018; Vedam et al., 2019), 26.9% of low-income women of color reported mistreatment, while Indigenous women, Asian women, Latina women, and Black women reported nearly double the amount of mistreatment behavior. Mistreatment behavior includes being shouted at or ignored by doctors, nurses, and midwives, scolded by birth professionals, and having requests refused or not responded to within a timely fashion. Even when socioeconomic status is controlled for, women of color typically experience more microaggressions, active aggressions, invisibility, and silencing during the birth process, which can compound negative experiences during the childbirth process (Markin & Coleman, 2021). Systemic and institutional racism and cisheterosexism can inherently complicate and increase risk factors for those who are giving birth and have the capacity to enhance the impact of medical trauma during the birthing process.

While this chapter has focused significantly on the intersection between trauma and historically socially marginalized identities, it is important to highlight work that also seeks to implement models that perpetuate factors of resilience. Becoming a parent through generational development has also been shown to be an opportunity for healing (Chamberlain et al., 2019), as a strengths-based perspective can create positive reinforcement that supports caregivers and infants. It is critically important for perinatal care providers and those involved systemically in providing care to developing families to have frequent, comprehensive, and system-based contact with future parents, with a focus on engaging the community as a whole and recognized elders within that community in particular while understanding the role that complex trauma may play (Chamberlain et al., 2019). Holistic assessment during this period should include an assessment and evaluation of access to community support and identification of and communication with relevant community elders. **Community-based participatory action research**, which is a form of collaborative research that involves all stakeholders, including participants, throughout the entire research process (see Healthy City, 2011), and strengths-based assessment are both needed to challenge the deficit-based lens that remains present in understanding generational development and the emotional implications of this period in life.

Case Studies

At the beginning of this chapter, you learned a bit about two different cases. We will now discuss each of these cases.

Sam and Alex: Case Prologue

Sam and Alex met at work and married about 15 years ago. They began trying to get biologically pregnant about 2 years into their marriage. After a year without conceiving successfully, they went to a fertility specialist and began the ART process. After extensive testing, they began IUI, and eventually IVF. After 3 years of ART, with tight finances, they stopped trying to become biologically pregnant. Sam took a job that provided significant financial gain but required a lot of travel. Although they had initially agreed that they did not want to pursue adoption, Alex eventually broached the idea, and Sam quickly agreed. They decided they wanted to add a baby to their family, as opposed to an older child, and ruled out both the foster care and domestic adoption experience. It took a few years of full-time employment to both pay off the debts incurred by the ART process and to save up to start the process of international adoption.

Sam states that they is exhausted by working so hard for so long to pay for the expenses of having a child in their family. They states that they is experiencing some ambivalence about the upcoming trip to Korea to meet their child. They states that while they feels that quitting their job is the best thing to do to build attachment with their new daughter, they will miss the support of thei coworkers, the challenges that their job brings, and the financial support of two incomes. Alex is initially reluctant to speak with you. They gives off vibes of being incredibly angry, and it is only after they harshly whispers to Sam, "We're not even supposed to be here anyway" that you think to dig more deeply. You press him to share why they seems so upset at this initial appointment.

You find out that their adoption coordinator has strongly encouraged them not to pursue therapy, as any outside psychological support must be documented, typically in medical insurance records as an explanation of benefits (EOB) in their adoption file and is shared with the birth and foster families abroad. There is significant stigma in receiving mental health services within intercountry adoption—with the erroneous belief that being in treatment means there are problems at home or behavioral health weakness, which then would cause a birth parent to reject choosing that adoptive family. Alex is worried that even though they have not reported this intake session to the adoption coordinator that the EOB will reveal the appointment and the planned trip will fall through, and they will lose their chance to bring their daughter home. They also eventually reveals that they had initially hoped to retire at 62, but with only one income, they realizes they will need to work for at least another decade and worries that ageism in their company will cause them to lose their job.

Sam and Alex: Points to Consider

Alex has valid concerns about ageism in theirindustry, financial pressure, and the possibility that engaging in therapy can impact their ability to successfully adopt. It may be that by trying to get help, they are doing harm to the 13-year journey they have been on to add a child to their family.

In addition to the excitement of adding a child to their family, Sam is also struggling with grief and loss related to their professional identity and the loss of both a support system and financial support.

It does not appear, initially, that either Sam or Alex has had the time or space to process the grief and exhaustion of trying to build their family for nearly 13 years. ART is not only expensive but can be invasive and traumatic. It will be important for you to assess for the presence of any medical trauma and grief related to these experiences.

Sam and Alex: Case Epilogue

You decide to process the pros and cons of staying in therapy throughout the 5-month period that precedes their trip to Korea. Eventually, both Alex and Sam agree that they are concerned that jeopardizing a successful adoption is a stress that outweighs the benefits of therapy. Sometimes, therapy is the problem, not the answer, and this case highlights tremendous structural flaws in the generational development process. You realize that you will never be able to build a therapeutic alliance with folx who cannot trust this process, and you cannot assure them that this process will do more good than harm. You provide some psychoeducation about grief and loss related to infertility and ART, normalize the feeling of ambivalence before the arrival of a child, encourage Sam to follow up with her primary care physician should the insomnia occur, and provide resources for individual and family therapy for when they return from Korea.

Ty: Case Prologue

Considering yourself in the same role as the opening vignette, you have been assigned to conduct an intake with a new client named Ty. Ty is identified as 24 years old, 21 weeks pregnant, and referred by the local emergency room for "stress reduction and anxiety management" after being checked for preterm labor. When Ty sits in your office, they are tearful and angry, stating that they don't want to talk about stress and don't understand why they were referred for therapy.

Ty is initially clear in stating that she does not want to engage with "this process." You find out that during her trip to the emergency department, multiple nurses repeatedly asked her what substances she might have been taking and made a point of asking to do both a urine and blood toxicology screen. Ty felt humiliated. When the hospital social worker came by, she immediately began asking Ty about her safety at home. Only at the prompting of her partner did she agree to come to the appointment made by the discharge clinician. Ty reports that ever since discharge 4 days ago, she has felt both panicky and shaky. She has been unable to keep much food down and has had to call out sick to work for the past 2 days. Ty reveals that one of the nurses mentioned that should she go into labor now, it was unlikely that the baby would survive, and she has been perseverating on this idea. She has been unable to sleep and is plagued by nightmares where she wakes up in a pool of blood. After sharing her concerns with you, she asks what she should do next.

Ty: Points to Consider

While we are behavioral health providers, we are not medical providers. Some of the symptoms that Ty is reporting may relate to possible medical conditions that could become life threatening to them or their child. We cannot make an assessment or assumption about her mental health until her physical health is addressed first. The very first step in this case is advocating for Ty to immediately find inclusive and supportive health care, particularly prenatal care. This is something that should happen during this session with Ty and will require the social worker to use the skills of advocacy, case planning, and resource provision.

Although it may be your natural impulse to reassure Ty that everything is okay, we cannot actually guarantee or predict that. What we can tell Ty is that we will support them through this process to the best of our ability and assure them that we will be a companion to them through the next steps of being seen by a doctor. The impact of the humiliation Ty experienced at the last appointment cannot be underestimated, and you may need to actually go with Ty back to the ER or call their doctor together to get their concerns taken seriously.

Once Ty is medically assessed, you can consider what may be going on in terms of stress, or even acute stress disorder symptoms based on what happened at the ER. Although it can be a very exciting time, pregnancy is also a time of role change. Psychoeducation around ambivalence related to biological pregnancy, role change within one's generation and family structure, and the evolving family processes are all part of therapeutic work with Ty. Taking a developmental history—doing a genogram in which pregnancy histories, birth histories, and any related loss or trauma—should be part of the work to understand how the emotions related to this experience may be manifesting.

Ty: Case Epilogue

Ty was immediately referred for medical care. Time during the intake session was used to contact their primary care physician, and their partner. It was determined that Ty should return to the ER, but their doctor felt waiting until that evening was safe. Ty was able to then return to the ER with her partner, who helped advocate for Ty. A list of questions was prepared for Ty to ask during the ER visit, which they saved on their phone. Ty was admitted for observation.

Initially, there was no follow-up from Ty, but approximately a year later, Ty did return to the agency. Ty was placed on a medical bed rest and spent 3 months in the hospital before their child was delivered at 27 weeks, and premature. The baby spent 5 weeks in the neonatal intensive care unit and was discharged home with medical support. Ty had had to take an unpaid leave from work for 6 months and ended up losing the position. Both Ty and the baby had been deemed in good health, but at this point, Ty was plagued by nightmares of being in the hospital and moments where doctors thought the baby would not survive, and Ty was struggling to attach to the infant. Ty was accepted both into individual therapy and a parent–baby bonding support group where they were able to begin to process the medical trauma from the prior year.

CONCLUSION

This chapter on generational development explores (a) how families are built and created and (b) the influences of cultural subjugation and historical trauma that may be passed through generations. In this chapter, I sought to challenge the idea of the standard North American family and offer insight into the multitudes of ways that families develop. The chapter opened with a discussion of how the ideology of dominance influences social groups and consideration of how membership of different social groups influences the birth of a family. Understanding the birth of a family requires a deep look into the role that cultural, historical, and intergenerational trauma carries through from generation to generation. This includes looking at historically significant events such as plagues, famines, war, genocide, natural disaster, terrorism and a global pandemic and understanding how the neurobiology of an entire population may be shaped during the occurrence of these events. We also looked at the ways in which cultural subjugation influences communities and carries over to the next generation and the myth of culturelessness within the context of colonization.

As this chapter explored the different ways individuals become members of a family, it discussed the ways in which family development looks for folx with marginalized identities, such as queer folx, and the role that assistive reproductive technology may play in helping a family grow, and an oft-neglected subject in discussions about families: childless by choice families. This chapter also explores the development of kinship and adoptive families through community and formal and informal kinship care and the role and influence the foster care system plays in building a family. Finally, this chapter discusses the multitudes of influences and the ways in which trauma may be perpetrated through both the prenatal period and birthing process and the ways in which behavioral health professionals can deepen their assessment during this uniquely vulnerable time for expectant families.

I have also offered a reflective framework through which social workers can consider inclusive assessment of growing families. Hopefully this chapter has challenged the way in which the reader thinks about the word "family" and provides alternative ways of considering the creation of a family and how to assess, engage, and intervene when working with growing families.

The two case studies presented are intentionally ambiguous in terms of client demographics and ask the reader to consider their own biases in making assumptions when beginning to work with a family. These case studies encourage the reader to think through the role that trauma may play throughout the generational development process and the long-term impact it may have as a family grows and develops while also taking into consideration how the positionality of the social worker may influence the assessment process. With this hopefully expanded perspective on generational development, the next chapter moves into exploring infancy and early childhood.

KEY TERMS

- Social groups: This is a term from social sciences in which two or more people who collectively have a sense of unity, interact with each other and may have similar characteristics

- Cultural groups: This is a group of people who are identified by ways of thinking, and behavior through a shared set of beliefs, values, and patterns of behavior. All cultural groups have intragroup variance.

- Disparate social groups: These are groups seen as 'different' or 'other' than the dominant social group. These groups have been historically and socially marginalized.

- Dominant social groups: This sociological term refers to a social group that controls the value system and rewards in a particular society.

- Subordinated social groups: Any group that has less power than the dominant group in a society.

- Cultural trauma: This phenomenon occurs when members of a collective group feel as if they have been subjected to a horrific event(s) that leaves permanent marks on group consciousness and impacts the future in irrevocable ways. This happens to both individual and a collectivity to which individuals belong.

- Historical trauma: This is a type of multigenerational, cumulative trauma experienced by a specific cultural, racial or ethnic group. It can be related to major events that oppressed a particular group of people because of their status as oppressed, such as slavery, the Holocaust, forced migration, and the violent colonization of Indigenous people. Its' origins are with the social construction of subordinate group statuses through migration, annexation of land, and colonialism

- Generational development: This term describes how people become a family and how people engage in the parenting system. This term that includes one or more people that are considering or finding themselves contributing to the next generation, which includes intentional or unintentional pregnancy, fostering to adopt, formal or informal adoption, kinship care, and traumatic or forced pregnancy and includes the influences of involuntary infertility, miscarriage, stillbirth, donor parents, and those who identify as childless by choice.

- Standard North American family (SNAF): This is a dominant (and mythical) schema of how family is defined in North America. This vision includes a heterosexual, legally married dyad, and any children who co-reside in the same household. The male partner is designated as the breadwinner, and the female partner may engage in paid work, but is mainly responsible for childcare and household labor.

- Placement cessation: This can also be known as an unplanned placement change, placement disruption or the early, premature or unintentional ending of a foster care placement by any party involved in the placement (the child welfare agency, the foster caregiver or the youth-in-care) and can be related to many different factors.

- Prenatal Care (PNC): Also known as antenatal care, it is a form of health care that a pregnant woman receives from an obstetrician or a midwife. This care can include dietary and lifestyle advice, weighing to ensure proper weight gain, checks on fetal development and examination for problems of pregnancy such as edema and preeclampsia.

- Womxn: This is an alternative and inclusive spelling of the word 'woman' and is meant to include anyone who has ever identified as a woman—all those that identify as women at any time in their life, including trans and nonbinary people. The term comes from intersectional feminism.

- Participatory action research: This approach to research highlights action and participation by community members through the principles of equality and justice. Power is situated in the community in which the research is taking place and often focuses on performance quality and knowledge production through social change.

DISCUSSION QUESTIONS

1. What is your relationship to the word "family"? What did this word mean to you growing up? What does this word mean to you now? How has this understanding been influenced by outside forces such as your culture, spiritual tradition, family of origin, and the context of important historical events that have occurred during your lifespan?

2. As a social work student, what have you learned and absorbed about how a family is created in your studies so far?

3. What are some traditions, rituals, and myths that you can identify related to generational development? How did you learn about these traditions, rituals, and myths? How might these be different or similar to those of your client(s)?

4. Grief and loss often simultaneously occur during the generational development experience. How might you hold the space of simultaneous joy and navigating the journey of loss when working with a client?

5. In your own words, define cultural trauma and historical trauma. How do you see these concepts impacting assessment and engagement with clients who are building a family?

6. In 2022, Serena Williams, an international tennis superstar and womxn of extraordinary financial means, wrote a personal essay for *Elle* magazine about her near-death experience during the birthing process as her concerns were ignored by medical professionals. If you do not yet have clients who have gone through the childbirth process, take a moment to read this article and reflect on the following question: How can you be an agent of change with the Western medical system around childbirth experiences?

REFERENCES

Alexander, J. (2004). Toward a theory of cultural trauma. In J. Alexander, R. Eyerman, B. Giesen, N. Smelser, & P. Zatompka (Eds.), *Cultural trauma and collective identity* (pp. 1–30). University of California Press.

Almeida, J., Bécares, L., Erbetta, K., Bettegowda, V., & Ahluwalia, I. (2018). Racial/ethnic inequities in low birth weight and preterm birth: The role of multiple forms of stress. *Maternal Child Health Journal*, *22*, 1154–1163. https://doi.org/10.1007/s10995-018-2500-7

Ayón C., Messing J. T., Gurrola, M., & Valencia-Garcia, D. (2018). The oppression of Latina mothers: Experiences of exploitation, violence, marginalization, cultural imperialism, and powerlessness in their everyday lives. *Violence Against Women*, *24*(8), 879–900. https://doi.org/10.1177/1077801217724451

Barton, A. & Bishop. (2014). Paradigms, Processes, and Values in Family Research. *Journal of Family Theory and Review*, *6*, 241–256. https://.doi.org/10.1111/jftr.12043

Barlow, A., Varipatis-Baker, E., Speakman, K., Ginsburg, G., Friberg, I., Goklish, N., Cowboy, B., Fields, P. Hastings, R., Pan, W., Reid, R., Santosham, M., & Walkup, J. (2006). Home-visiting intervention to improve child care among American Indian adolescent mothers: A randomized trial. *Archives of Pediatrics & Adolescent Medicine*, *160*(11), 1101–1107.

Barthloet, E., & Smolin, D. (2012). The debate. In J. Gibbons & K. Smith Rotabi (Eds.), *Intercountry adoption policies, practices, and outcomes* (pp. 233–251). Ashgate.

Bermudez, J. M., Bertranna A. M., & Jordan, L. S. (2017). Decolonizing research methods for family science: Creating space at the center. *Journal of Family Theory and Review*, *8*(2), 192–206.

Berthelot, N., Lemieux, R., Garon-Bissonnette, J., Drouin-Maziade, C., Martel, E., & Maziade, M. (2020). Uptrend in distress and psychiatric symptomatology in pregnant women during the coronavirus disease 2019 pandemic. *Acta Obstretics Gynecologica Scandanavica*, *99*, 848–855.

Bick & Dozier, (2013). The effectiveness of an attachment-based intervention in promoting foster mothers' sensitivity toward foster infants. *Infant Mental Health Journal*, *34*, 95–103. https://doi.org/10.1002/IMHJ.21373.

Blackmore, J., & Burns, G. (2020). "The very first thing that connected us to him": Adopters' experiences of sharing photographs, "talking" albums and other materials with their children prior to meeting. *Adoption & Fostering*, *44*(3), 225–241.

Braithwaite, V. (2010). *Compliance with migration law*. Department of Immigration and Citizenship. https://static1.squarespace.com/static/5c05f8595cfd7901fc57139d/t/5c07303a88251b7b4194f5eb/1543974976097/2010.compliance+with+migration+law.pdf

Brave Heart, M. Y. H., & DeBruyn, L. M. (1998). The American Indian holocaust: Healing historical unresolved grief. *American Indian and Alaska Native Mental Health Research*, *8*(2), 60–82.

Brown, R. (2020). The intergenerational impact of terror: Did the 9/11 tragedy impact the initial human capital of the next generation? *Demography*, *57*(4), 1459–1481. https://doi.org/10.1007/s13524-020-00876-6

Browning, A. S. (2015). Undertaking planned transitions for children in out-of-home care. *Adoption & Fostering*, *39*(1), 51–61.

Butts, J. B., & Rich, K. L. (2013). *Nursing ethics: Across the curriculum and into practice* (3rd ed.). Jones & Bartlett.

Carter, E., Elevate Women's Collective, & Mazzoni, S. (2021). A paradigm shift to address racial inequities in perinatal healthcare. *American Journal of Obstetrics and Gynecology*, *224*(4), 359–361.

Chamberlain, C., Gee, G., Brown, S., Atkinson, J., Herman, H., Gartland, D., Glover, K., Clark, Y., Campbell, S., Mensah, F. K., Atkinson, C., Brennan, S. E., McLachlan, H., Hirvonen, T., Dyall, D., Ralph, N., Hokke, S., & Nicolson, J. (2019). Healing the past by nurturing the future—co-designing perinatal strategies for Aboriginal and Torress Strait Islander parents experience complex trauma: Framework and protocol for a community-based participatory action research study. *BMJ Open*, *9*(6), Article e028397. https://doi.org/10.1136/bmjopen-2018-028397

Child Welfare Information Gateway. (2022). *Planning for adoption: Knowing the costs and resources.* https://www.childwelfare.gov/pubs/s-cost/

Collins English Dictionary. (n.d.) Global North. In *CollinsDictionary.com dictionary*. Retrieved November 30, 2021, from https://www.collinsdictionary.com/us/dictionary/english/global-north

Conching, A. K., & Thayer, Z. (2019). Biological pathways for historical trauma to affect health: A conceptual model focusing on epigenetic modifications. *Social Science & Medicine*, *230*, 74–82.

Coontz, S. (2000). Historical Perspectives on Family Studies. *Journal of Marriage and Family Therapy*, 62, 283–297. https://doi.org/10.1111/j.1741-3737.2000.00283.x

Crawford, S., Boulet, S. L., Mneimneh, A. S., Perkins, K. M., Jamieson, D. J., Zhang, Y., & Kissin, D. M. (2016). Costs of achieving live birth from assisted reproductive technology: A comparison of sequential single and double embryo transfer approaches. *Fertility and Sterility*, *105*(2), 444–450. https://doi.org/10.1016/j.fertnstert.2015.10.032

Creanga, A., Syverson, C. Seed, K., & Callaghan, W. (2017). Pregnancy-related mortality in the United States, 2011–2013. *Obstetrics and Gynecology*, *130*, 366–373.

Crear-Perry, J., Maybank, A. Keeys, M., Mitchell, N., & Godbolt, D. (2020). Moving towards anti-racist praxis in medicine. *The Lancet*, *396*(10249), 451–453. https://doi.org/10.1016/S0140-6736(20)31543-9

Czarnocka, J., & Slade, P. (2000). Prevalence and predictors of posttraumatic stress symptoms following childbirth. *British Journal of Clinical Psychology*, *39*(1), 35–51. https://doi.org/10.1348/014466500163095

Darling, E. K., Kjell, C., Tubman-Broeren, M., & Marquez, O. (2021). The effect of prenatal care delivery models targeting populations with low rates of PNC Attendance: A systematic review. *Journal of Health Care for the Poor and Underserved*, *32*(1), 119–136. https://doi.org/10.1353/hpu.2021.0012

Davis, L. M., Williams, M. V., Derose, K. P., Steinberg, P., Nicosia, N., Overton, A., Miyashiro, L., Turner, S., Fain, T., & Williams, E. (2011). The Impact of Incarceration on Families: Key Findings. In Understanding the Public Health Implications of Prisoner Reentry in California: State-of-the-State Report (pp. 117–142). RAND Corporation. http://www.jstor.org/stable/10.7249/mg1165tce.13

de Graaff L. F., Honig, A., van Pampus, M. G., & Stramrood, C. A. I. (2018). Preventing posttraumatic stress disorder following childbirth and traumatic birth experiences: A systematic review. *Acta Obstetricia et Gynecologica Scandinavica*, *97*(6), 648–656.

Domar, A., Gordon, K., Garcia-Velasco, J., La Marca, A. Barriere, P., & Fabiola Beligotti, B. (2012). Understanding the perceptions of and emotional barriers to infertility treatment: A survey in four European countries. *Human Reproduction*, *27*(4), 1073–1079. https://doi.org/10.1093/humrep/des016

Dozier, M., Grasso,. D, Lindheim, O. and Lewis., E. (2007). The role of caregiver commitment in foster care. In: Oppenheim, D. and Goldsmith, D. (Eds.) *Attachment Theory in Clinical Work with Children: Bridging the gap between research and practice*. New York: Guilford Press, Chapter 4.

Dunbar-Ortiz, R. (2014). *An Indigenous people's history of the United States*. Beacon Press.

Eriksson, P. (2016). Fear of loss of a wanted child: emotional accounts of Finnish prospective adoptive parents in pre-adoption services. *Adoption & Fostering, 40*(3), 209–218. https://doi.org/10.1177/0308575916661270

Ertel, K. A., James-Todd, T., Kleinman, K., Krieger, N., Gillman, M., Wright, R., & Rich-Edwards, J. (2012). Racial discrimination, response to unfair treatment, and depressive symptoms among pregnant Black and African American women in the United States. *Annals of Epidemiology, 22*(12), 840–846. https://doi.org/10.1016/j.annepidem.2012.10.001

Farmer, E. (2009). Making kinship care work. *Adoption & Fostering, 33*(3), 15–27. https://doi.org/10.1177/030857590903300303

Gadson A., Akpovi, E., & Mehta P. K. (2017). Exploring the social determinants of racial/ethnic disparities in prenatal care utilization and maternal outcome. *Seminal Perinatology, 41*(5), 308–317. https://doi.org/10.1053/j.semperi.2017.04.008

Gay and Lesbian Alliance Against Defamation. (2017). Accelerating Acceptance 2017: A Harris Poll survey of Americans' acceptance of LGBTQ people. https://www.glaad.org/files/aa/2017_GLAAD_Accelerating_Acceptance.pdf

Georgas, J., Berry, J., Van de Vijver, F., Kagitçibasi, Ç, & Poortinga, Y. (Eds.). (2006). *Families Across Cultures: A 30-Nation Psychological Study*. Cambridge: Cambridge University Press. doi:10.1017/CBO9780511489822

Goldberg, A. E., Moyer, A. M., Kinkler, L. A., & Richardson, H. B. (2012). "When you're sitting on the fence, hope's the hardest part": Experiences and challenges of lesbian, gay, and heterosexual couples adopting through the child welfare system. *Adoption Quarterly, 15*, 1–28.

Graml, G., Meyer-Lee, E., & Peifer, J. S. (2021). Decolonizing global learning and internationalization: A human-scale case study of innovation. In G. Malfatti (Ed.), *People-centered approaches toward the internationalization of higher education* (pp. 133–148). IGI Global. https://doi.org/10.4018/978-1-7998-3796-1.ch007

Green, T. L. (2018). Unpacking racial/ethnic disparities in prenatal care use: the role of individual-, household-, and area-level characteristics. *Journal of Women's Health, 27*(9), 1124–1134. https://doi.org/10.1089/jwh.2017.6807

Hardeman, R. R., Burgess, D., Murphy, K., Satin, D. J., Nielsen, J., Potter, T. M., Karbeah, J., Zulu-Gillespie, M., Apolinario-Wilcoxon, A., Reif, C., & Cunningham, B. A. (2018). Developing a medical school curriculum on racism: Multidisciplinary, multiracial conversations informed by public health critical race praxis (PHCRP). *Ethnicity & Disease, 28*(Suppl. 1), 271–278. https://doi.org/10.18865/ed.28.S1.271

Hariharan, B., Quarshie, L, Amdahl, C., Winterburn, S., & Offiah, G. (2020). Experiencing racism within medical school curriculum: 2020 ICCH student symposium. *Patient Education and Counseling, 105*(7), 2599–2602. https://doi.org/10.1016/j.pec.2021.12.018

Healthy City. (2011). *A short guide to community based participatory action research*. https://hc-v6-static.s3.amazonaws.com/media/resources/tmp/cbpar.pdf

Hoke, M. K., & McDade, T. (2015). Biosocial inheritance: A framework for the study of the intergenerational transmission of health disparities. *Annals of Anthropological Practice, 38*, 187–213.

Hull, K. E., & Ortyl, T. A. (2019). Conventional and cutting-edge: Definitions of family in LGBT communities. *Sexuality Research & Social Policy, 16*(1), 31–43. https://doi.org/10.1007/s13178-018-0324-2

Ickovics, J., Kershaw, T., Westdahl, C., Magriples, U., Massey, Z., Reynolds, H., & Rising, S. (2007). Group prenatal care and perinatal outcomes: a randomized controlled trial. *Obstetrics and Gynecology, 110*, 330–339.

Johnson, M. B. (2020). Prenatal care for American Indian women. *The American Journal of Maternal/Child Nursing, 45*(4), 221–227. https://doi.org/10.1097/NMC.0000000000000633

Juffer, F., & Tieman, W. (2012). Families with intercountry adopted children: Talking about adoption and birth culture. In I. J. Gibbons & K. Smith Rotabi (Eds.), *Intercountry adoption, policies, practices and outcomes* (pp. 211–229). Ashgate.

Justia. (2022). *Transgender parents and their rights*. https://www.justia.com/lgbtq/family-law-divorce/transgender-parents/

Kim, H. G., Harrison, P. A., Godecker, A. L., & Muyzka, C. (2014). Posttraumatic stress disorder among women receiving prenatal care at three federally qualified health care centers. *Maternal and Child Health Journal, 18*, 1056–1065. https://doi.org/10.1007/s10995-013-1333-7

Klitzman, R. (2017). How much is a child worth? Providers' and patients' views and responses concerning ethical and policy challenges in paying for ART. *PLoS ONE, 12*(2), Article e0171939. https://doi.org/10.1371/journal.pone.0171939

Kozhimannil K. B., Interrante J. D., Tofte A. N., & Admon L. K. (2020). Severe maternal morbidity and mortality among indigenous women in the United States. *Obstetrics & Gynecology, 135*(2), 294–300. https://doi.org/10.1097/AOG.0000000000003647

Lefkovics, E., Baji, I., & Rigo, J. (2014). Impact of maternal depression on pregnancies and on early attachment. *Infant Mental Health Journal, 35*(4), 354–365.

Lewis, L. (2018) Meeting my child for the first time: Adoptive parents' experiences of the period of adoption transition. *Adoption & Fostering, 42*(1), 38–48.

Light A., Wang L. F., Zeymo A., & Gomez-Lobo, V. (2018). Family planning and contraception use in transgender men. *Contraception, 98*, 266–269.

Loewen, G.V. (2005). A socio-ethnographic study of the academic professionalization of anthropologists. Lewiston, NY: Edwin Mellen Press.

Lynes, D., & Sitoe, A. (2019). Disenfranchised grief: the emotional impact experienced by foster carers on the cessation of a placement. *Adoption & Fostering, 43*(1), 22–34. https://doi.org/10.1177/0308575918823433

Mage, D. T., Donner, E., & Holmes, L. (2019). Risk differences in disease-specific infant mortality between Black and White U.S. children, 1968–2015: An epidemiologic investigation. *Journal of Racial & Ethnic Health Disparities, 6*, 86–93.

Malmquist, A., Martin, J., & Thiel, A. (2021). Childless bisexual and gay men's expectations of future parenthood. *Journal of GLBT Family Studies, 17*(4), 323–338. https://doi.org/10.1080/1550428X.202

Markin, R. D., & Coleman, M. N. (2023). Intersections of gendered racial trauma and childbirth trauma: Clinical interventions for Black women. *Psychotherapy, 60* (1), 27–38. https://doi.org/10.1037/pst0000403

Martin, J. A., Hamilton, B. E., Osterman, M. J. K., & Driscoll, A. K. (2019). Births: Final data for 2018. *National Vital Statistics Reports, 68*(13), 1–46.

McCubbin, L. & Moniz, J. (2015). Ethical Principles in Resilience Research: Respect, Relevance, Reciprocity and Responsibility. In: Theron, L., Liebenberg, L., Ungar, M. (eds) *Youth Resilience and Culture. Cross-Cultural Advancements in Positive Psychology*, vol 11. Springer. https://doi.org/10.1007/978-94-017-9415-2_16

McGregor, D., Morelli, P., Matsuoka, J., & Minerbi, L. (2003). An ecological model of well-being. In H. Becker & F. Vanclay (Eds*.), The international handbook of social impact assessment: Conceptual and methodological advances (pp. 109–126).* Northampton, MA: Edward Elgar.

McLemore, M. R., Altman, M. R., Cooper, N., Williams, S., Rand, L., & Franck, L. (2018). Health care experiences of pregnant, birthing and postnatal women of color at risk for preterm birth. *Social Science & Medicine, 201*, 127–135. https://doi.org/10.1016/j.socscimed.2018.02.013

Mohamed, S. A., Thota, C., Browne, P., Diamond, M., & Al-Hendy, A. (2014). Why is preterm birth stubbornly higher in African-Americans? *Obstetrics and Gynecology International Journal, 1*, Article 00019.

Moseson, H., Zazanis, N., Goldberg, E., Fix, L., Durden, M., Stoeffler, A., & Obedin-Maliver, J. (2020). The imperative for transgender and gender nonbinary inclusion. *Obstetrics & Gynecology, 135*(5), 1059–1068. https://doi.org/10.1097/AOG.0000000000003816

Movement Advancement Project. (n.d.). *Foster and adoption laws*. Retrieved April 13, 2023, from https://www.lgbtmap.org/equality-maps/foster_and_adoption_laws

Moyer, A., & Goldberg, A. (2017). "We were not planning on this, but …": Adoptive parents' reactions and adaptations to unmet expectations. *Child and Family Social Work, 22*, 12–21. https://doi.org/10.1111/cfs.12219

Mughal, S., Azhar, Y., & Siddiqui, W. (2022). *Postpartum Depression*. StatPearls Publishing.

Neil E., Beek, M., & Schofield, G. (2018). *Moving to adoption: A practice development project: Research Briefings*. Centre for Research on Children and Families, University of East Anglia.

Neil, E., Young, J., & Hartley, L. (2018). *The joys and challenges of adoptive family life: A survey of adoptive parents in the Yorkshire and Humberside region*. Centre for Research on Children and Families, University of East Anglia.

Petersen, E., Davis, N., Goodman, D., Cox, S., Syverson, C., Seed, K., Shapiro-Mendoza, C., Callaghan, W. M., & Barfield, W. (2019). Racial/ethnic disparities in pregnancy-related deaths—United States, 2007–2016. *The Morbidity and Mortality Weekly Report, 68*(35), 762–765. https://doi.org/10.15585/mmwr.mm6835a3

Ponting, C., Mahrer, N., Zelcer, H., Schetter, C., Chavira, D. (2020). Psychological Interventions for Depression and Anxiety in Pregnant Latina and Black Women in the United States: A Systematic Review. *Clinical Psychology & Psychotherapy 27*, 249–265. http://doi.org/10.1002/cpp.2424.

Redmond, M., & Martin, B. (2021). All in the (definition of) family: Transnational parent–child relationships, rights to family life, and Canadian immigration law. *Journal of Family Issues, 44*(3), 1–19. https://doi.org/10.1177/0192513X211054461

Rich, C., & Domar, A. (2016). Addressing the emotional barriers to access to reproductive care. *Fertility and Sterility, 105*(5), 1124–1127, https://doi.org/10.1016/j.fertnstert.2016.02.017

Richards, S. (2018). "I'm more than just adopted": Stories of genealogy in intercountry adoptive families. *Genealogy, 2*(25), 1–18. https://doi.org/10.3390/genealogy2030025.

Ross LE, Siegel A, Dobinson C, Epstein R, & Steele LS (2012). "I don't want to turn totally invisible": Mental health, stressors, and supports among bisexual women during the perinatal period. *Journal of GLBT Family Studies, 8*(2), 137–154.

Rotabi, K., & Bunkers, K. (2011). In an era of reform: A review of social work literature on intercountry adoption. *SAGE Open, 1*(3), 1–16. https://doi.org/10.1177/2158244011428160

Shah, J. S., Leem, F., & Toy, E. C. (2018). Improving rates of early entry prenatal care in an underserved population. *Maternal and Child Health Journal, 22*(12), 1738–1742. https://doi.org/10.1007/s10995-018-2569-z

Sidanius, J. (1993). The psychology of group conflict and the dynamics of oppression: A social dominance perspective. In S. Iyengar & W. J. McGuire (Eds.), *Explorations in political psychology (pp. 183–219)*. Duke University Press.

Smith, D. (1993). The Standard North American Family: SNAF as an ideological code. *Journal of Family Issues, 14*, 50–65.

Stangor, C. (2015). *Social Groups in Action and Interaction: 2nd Edition*. Routledge. https://doi.org/10.4324/9781315677163.

Soet, J. E., Brack, G. A., & DiIorio, C. (2003). Prevalence and predictors of women's experience of psychological trauma during childbirth. *Birth*, *30*(1), 36–46. https://doi.org/10.1046/j.1523-536X.2003.00215.x

Tam, B., Findlay, L., & Kohen, D. (2017). Indigenous families: who do you call family? *Journal of Family Studies*, *23*, 243–259.

Uttal, L. (2009). (Re)visioning family ties to communities and contexts. In S. A. Lloyd, & A. L. Few (Eds.), *Handbook of feminist family studies* (pp. 134–146). SAGE Publications. https://doi.org/10.4135/9781412982801.n11

Valencia-Garcia, D., Simoni, J. M., Alegría, M., & Takeuchi, D. T. (2012). Social capital, acculturation, mental health, and perceived access to services among Mexican American women. *Journal of Consulting and Clinical Psychology*, *80*, 177–185. https://doi.org/10.1037/a0027207

Vasileva, M., & Petermann, F. (2018). Attachment, development, and mental health in abused and neglected preschool children in foster care: A meta-analysis. *Trauma, Violence, & Abuse*, *19*(4), 443–458. https://doi.org/10.1177/1524838016669503

Vedam, S., Stoll, K., Taiwo, T. K., Rubashkin, N., Cheyney, M., Strauss, N., McLemore, M., Cadena, M., Nethery, E., Rushton, E., Schummers, L., Declercq, E., & the GVtM-US Steering Council. (2019). The giving voice to mothers study: Inequity and mistreatment during pregnancy and childbirth in the United States. *Reproductive Health*, *16*(1), Article 77. https://doi.org/10.1186/s12978-019-0729-2

Viguera, A., Whitfield, T., Baldessarini, R., Newport, D., Stowe, Z., Reminick, A., Zurick, A., & Cohen, L. (2007) Risk of recurrence in women with bipolar disorder during pregnancy: Prospective study of mood stabilizer discontinuation. *American Journal of Psychiatry*, *164*(12), 1817–1824.

Walker, A.J. (2009). A feminist critique of family studies. In S. A. Lloyd, A. L. Few, & K. R. Allen (Eds.), *Handbook of feminist family studies (pp. 19–27)*. Thousand Oaks, CA: Sage

Winokur, M., Holtan, A., Batchelder, K. B., Maynard, B., Littell, J., & Shlonsky, A. (2018). Systematic review of kinship care effects on safety, permanency, and well-being outcomes. *Research on Social Work Practice*, *28*(1), 19–32. https://doi.org/10.1177/1049731515620843

Wu, Y., Lu, Y.-C., Jacobs, M., Pradhan, S., Kapse, K., Zhao, L., Niforatos-Andescavage, N., Vezina, G., du Plessis, A. J., & Limperopoulos, C. (2020). Association of prenatal maternal psychological distress with fetal brain growth, metabolism, and cortical maturation. *JAMA Open*, *3*(1), Article e1919940. https://doi.org/10.1001/jamanetworkopen.2019.19940

Yehuda, R., Daskalakis, N., Lehrner, A., Desarnaud, F., Bader, H., Makotkine, I., & Meaney, J. (2014). Influences of maternal and paternal PTSD on epigenetic regulation of the glucocorticoid receptor gene in Holocaust survivor offspring. *The American Journal of Psychiatry*, *171*, 872–880.

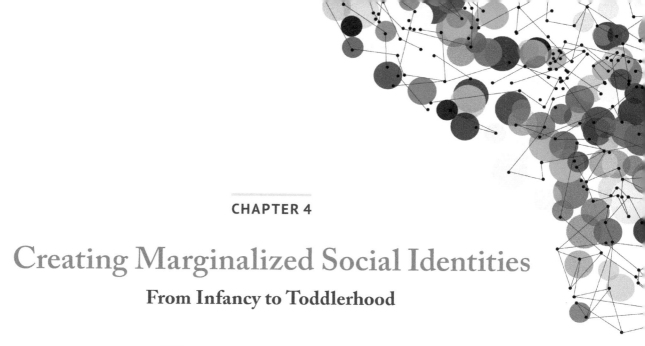

CHAPTER 4

Creating Marginalized Social Identities
From Infancy to Toddlerhood

TANIKA EAVES AND MELISSA MENDEZ

Competency 1: Demonstrate Ethical and Professional Behavior

Competency 2: Engage Difference and Diversity

1. Understand traditional theories of human lifespan development and consider and explore how those theories have excluded marginalized populations. (Competency 2)

2. Recognize the influence of identity and social location on early human development. (Competency 2)

3. Apply self-awareness and self-regulation to manage the influence of personal biases and values in working with diverse clients and constituencies. (Competencies 1 & 2)

Competency 7: Assess Individuals, Families, Organizations and Communities

1. Identify key concepts of the neurodevelopmental framework and the impact on lifespan development (Competency 7)

2. Connect key neurodevelopmental considerations with attachment and its classifications to better understand the impact of first relationships and experiences. (Competency 7)

Competency 8: Intervene with Individuals, Families, Groups, Organizations, and Communities

1. Identify links between intergenerational trauma and parenting practices perceived as "problematic." (Competency 8)

2. Recognize the impact of intergenerational trauma on the formation of attachment relationships as it relates to health and well-being throughout the lifespan. (Competency 8)

Introduction

In order to understand the intricate dynamics of the human ecosystem (i.e., individuals, families, groups, organizations, and communities), we need to start at the beginning. Early human experiences, including relationships and development, lay the foundation for the growth and evolution of individuals, families, communities, and society. Traditional theories of human development, like Bowlby's attachment theory, Erickson's stages of development, and Piaget's theory on cognitive development, have been the dominant narratives in shaping our understanding of early human development as social workers. Uri Bronfenbrenner's ecological model offers us a multilevel contextual framework in which to understand the phenomena of human development and how environmental contexts influence individual differences in life course development.

Social work's commitment to equity, diversity, and social justice, coupled with the national racial reckoning in recent years, has called for reexamination of theories and models explaining human development and early relationships. Our understanding of early development has been largely shaped by White, Western male traditions. The voices of those traditionally relegated to the margins of Western and U.S. society have been excluded from the discourse about early human development and experience. This exclusion has resulted in the pathologizing of relational patterns, parenting practices, family composition, and developmental trajectories within groups who do not follow White, Western ideals and norms.

Until recently, the field of social work has been complicit in characterizing largely immigrant, LGBTQIA+, and families of color as "deviant" from societal norms for not complying with the nuclear family structure, for having multiple primary caregivers and attachment figures, and for violating assumed gender roles and norms. Rigid norms involving raising children in a heteronormative, nuclear family (two parents, two children, and one pet) ideal where the mother is the primary caregiver diminishes the value of extended family and kinship networks and essentially blames the mother as the primary caregiver for developmental deviance or pathology.

In fact, traditional theories of attachment have only just begun to explore the implications of a societal context dominated by racism, discrimination, heteronormativity, and White supremacy on attachment relationships in race- and gender-minoritized children and adults (J. Stern et al., 2022). According to J. Stern and colleagues (2022), attachment theory can be enriched as a vehicle for antiracism by (a) considering relations between caregivers' racial-ethnic socialization and secure base provision, (b) diversifying researchers and research participants, and (c) using tenets of attachment theory to advocate for family support policies that reduce systemic inequities.

In other words, theoretical constructs explaining early development and relationships are being called to account to consider matters of identity (i.e., cultural, ethnic, gender, racial, religious), social and racial caste, and privilege and oppression that are inherently embedded in U.S. society and its institutions.

For example, as practitioners, how do we consider the contextual influences impacting the development of a secure attachment in an African American infant living in an impoverished, racially segregated community under the constant threat of violence and government-sanctioned separation from her parents? We know that traditionally, U.S. social policies have often intentionally harmed racially minoritized children and families, punishing them for not adhering to White norms of parenthood and family life. This sociopolitical context has implications for the developmental trajectory of marginalized children, who have not been studied or considered in most theories of early development. This chapter will seek to redress this marginalization.

REFLECT A MOMENT

How do you define a baby? Based on your upbringing, family traditions, and beliefs, how long does babyhood (i.e., a state of dependency for feeding, dressing, toileting, mobility, etc.) last?

What might autonomy mean for children reared in cultures where collectivism, not individualism, is the prevailing social value?

CASE INTRODUCTION

Later in the chapter, we will explore an in-depth case study of Shelby, a 19-year-old, single Black mother and her toddler, Devon, an 18-month-old male. Mother and toddler have a number of environmental and relational challenges that are very present in their life and put Devon's development at risk. They also have a historical trauma and racial trauma context that is ever-present in their experiences. As you read about the neurodevelopmental, ecological, and historical elements that impact child growth and development, think about how a young, Black single mother with a male toddler may experience services and systems and what types of barriers might be present for the family to fully engage and draw benefit from those services and systems.

Early Neurodevelopmental Considerations

Before we start to consider attachment and the role attachment plays in healthy development, we need to have a solid foundational understanding of how neurons, neural pathways, the brain, and the central nervous system build the template for development, specifically attachment and all social emotional and behavioral growth. From there, we can move on to consider how caregivers, who carry in their brains and bodies the templates from previous generations, influence and shape the trajectory of growth for very young children.

Over the past 30 years, research on early childhood brain development has immensely expanded our understanding of the growing brain and opened so many possibilities for intervention. We now know that 80% of brain growth occurs in the first 3 years of life, which means that during that time there is an exceptional amount of opportunity to influence an individual's growth trajectory (Shonkoff, 2003). We have learned that the brain is a **social organ** and that healthy human brain growth and development is critically dependent on human interactions and caregiving (Cozolino, 2014).

The infant brain contains approximately 100 billion neurons. This is the period during which the brain has the most neurons it will ever have. In the earliest months and years of life, these neurons will find each other and create **synaptogenesis**, the creation of connections, or neural pathways, between two neurons (Institute of Medicine and National Research Council 2000). When a baby is born, each neuron has a predetermined association with specific information and skills related to human species development. These come about from evolutionary processes. When the infant is provided an environment where these neurons can find each other, then connect, this neural connection becomes the new skill or information that the baby has learned. During the first few years of life, babies experience up to 1 million neural connections per second (Center on the Developing Child, 2007).

EXAMPLE

Babies are born with the evolutionary urge to stand up and walk. There are neurons that exist in the brain that are associated with that urge. Some would call it an "intuitive" process, but it is also a cognitive process. Babies are also born with neurons that can operationalize and send messages to the central nervous system to move those muscles and body parts that allow them to walk, a motor process. When the baby is given opportunities to pull up and practice walking, those cognitive neurons and motor neurons find each other and create the connection: The baby wants to pull up and walk, and the baby's body can pull up and walk. The baby learns the new skill and has activated that neural pathway between the cognitive and motor neurons that motivate and enable standing and walking. The more the baby gets opportunities to strengthen that neural pathway, the more efficient and stronger that connection becomes, and the baby is ultimately more successful at this important developmental task.

When babies are not given opportunities for these neurons to be "introduced" to one another and do not experience those neural pathway connections, we may see interruptions in healthy development and growth. We know that the brain is an organ of efficiency in that it will keep those pathways that are more frequently traveled and use a process called **pruning** to remove any pathways that are not used (Huttenlocher & Dabholkar, 1997). The rapid and extensive growth in the first few years causes an overproduction of neural pathways, and the brain must eliminate those less traveled pathways in order to strengthen the more frequently traveled ones. In essence, then, the brain has a "use it or lose it" quality that is especially potent in the first years of life. This has significant meaning for the neurons and neural pathways associated with personal and social development. We know that when we examine neural connections in the brains of children who have had histories of neglect, we can see decreased density in neural dendritic branches in parts of the brain that are associated with personal and social development, which means the neural pathways are less "firmly wired" within the brain's developing structure (Applegate & Shapiro, 1995). This results in disrupted personal and social growth trajectories for young children that can have lifelong negative impacts. For this reason, early intervention and support for children who are at risk of neglect is an important and urgent issue for us all.

To better understand this process as it relates to the development of personal and social development, we can use the **transactional model of development**, a theory of development that is focused on the infant's relationship to their environment, which is very closely connected to attachment theory. The transactional model suggests that the infant is a "product of continuous dynamic interactions between the child and environment" and that these transactions are "bidirectional" (Sameroff & Fiese, 2000, p. 138. The transactional model suggests that the infant is not just a passive recipient of their experiences but rather an active participant. The concept of "serve and return" is a closely related process that is more directly focused on the responsive care that infants and young children experience with caregivers. Serve and return behaviors between caregivers and infants—babblings sounds, gestures, facial expressions, and vocal tones—support the "architecture" of the infant's brain (Center on the Developing Child, 2007).

Consider the next two series of interactions between a new mother and her 2-month-old baby from the transactional model and the serve and return concept (see Figures 4.1 and 4.2). As you follow the interactions, think about what factors might be present in the environment to create the background for these two very different interaction series.

Interactions like these, happening hundreds of times a day, are the foundations for the infant's ability to organize and understand the world around them and their relationships to

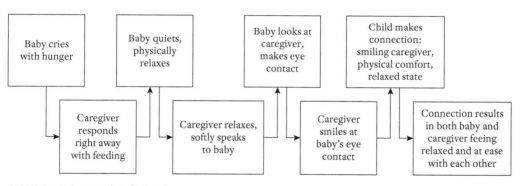

FIGURE 4.1 Interaction Series 1

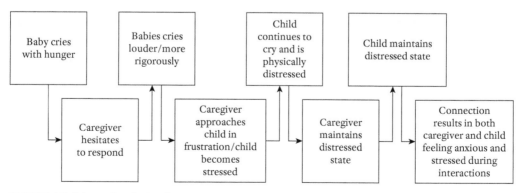

FIGURE 4.2 Interaction Series 2

other humans. These interactions are also the foundations of attachment. What might have been happening in the first series to allow the mother and infant to experience the positive set of transactions that ultimately result in an optimal neural pathway that solidifies trust and assurance for the infant? In the second series of interactions, what types of challenges may have been present in the environment to disrupt the development of the optimal pathway?

Attachment is the cornerstone of human social experience and relationships and provides us with a context in which to consider development. John Bowlby's work on **attachment theory** and Mary Ainsworth's expansion of attachment theory that establishes attachment patterns have been pivotal in the development of our understanding of young children's social and emotional needs and experiences. From attachment theory we know that children need consistent and nurturing primary caregivers, or a set of primary caregivers, in order to thrive and experience social and emotional health (Kobak et al., 2016). We also know from attachment theory that babies and young children will use their primary caregivers as a secure base from which they explore the world around them (D. Stern, 1977). We consider both attachment and secure base behavior as key ingredients to understanding how children bond and learn to trust, and we use both to assess the quality and predictability of child development and potential.

TABLE 4.1 How Young Children Experience Attachment Patterns

Secure	"I need you, and you are here for me. I feel good."
Insecure/Avoidant	"I need you, but you are not available, so I am OK on my own most of the time. I feel alone."
Insecure/Ambivalent	"I need you, and you are here sometimes, but I don't feel safe or secure when you are here. I feel scared and confused. I am not OK on my own."
Insecure/ Disorganized	"I need you, but you are scary. I can't trust you or anyone else. I don't know what to feel except fear and, sometimes, anger."

(Attachment patterns expanded by Mary Ainsworth)

Attachment forms in the same way that our earlier example of standing and walking forms: through experiences that activate the appropriate neural pathways in the baby's brain that are associated with personal and social connections. Infants and young children will have a spectrum of attachment preferences, depending on their family and environment, that may mean they have deep attachment to one caregiver, or they may form deep attachments to more than one caregiver (Davies et al., 2021). Attachment provides four main functions to support child growth and development:

- Attachment provides a sense of security for the baby.
- Attachment helps regulate affect and arousal.
- Attachment supports communication.
- Attachment provides a secure base for child exploration.

When attachment is of high positive quality and is meeting all these functions for the baby, then the baby can focus on gaining new skills and learning new concepts in their environments. That is, when attachment is secure and positive, the baby's mental bandwidth is "freed up" to focus on other tasks. If the baby is experiencing less than secure and healthy attachment, their brain will be preoccupied with those core functions and limited in its ability to engage in new and more complex learning experiences.

REFLECTION QUESTIONS

1. Can you think of an example of a secure attachment relationship from your personal experiences?

2. How might an insecure/avoidant or insecure/disorganized attachment system impact a young child's developing social skills (e.g., with peers and teachers in preschool or a group care setting)?

Parents, Trauma, and Toxic Stress

The role caregivers play in facilitating this brain growth is crucial. All learning happens in the context of human relationships, and we know that it is by being in relationships that young children learn how to be in relationships. Three key questions are implicit in a child's relationship with their caregiver(s): Am I safe? Can I trust? Am I loved and cared for? It is these questions that young children seek to reconcile in the first years of life. When these questions are answered in the affirmative ("Yes, I am safe. Yes, I can trust. Yes, I am loved/cared for"), young children can move to higher tasks like problem solving, self-control, and learning new skills. But when the brain is preoccupied with safety, trust, and connection and those things have not been firmly established, it is difficult for the brain to utilize those higher order functions, also called "executive functions." To this end, parents and caregivers—and all grownups who contribute to the world that children live in—have their own higher order task of creating experiences and environments where all children feel safe, trusting, and loved and cared for.

What happens then when parents/caregivers have high levels of toxic stress and trauma to manage in their own brains and bodies and are expected to also be present and nurturing to support the development of children's brains and bodies? This is the ultimate challenge of intervention work with very young children and their parents/caregivers: How do you hold the needs of the baby and the parent/caregiver simultaneously?

Toxic stress, the prolonged presence of stress in the absence of nurturing and caring support, is now known to have significant negative impact not only on young children during their first years of life but also their parents and caregivers (Shonkoff et al., 2012). Young children's attachment needs require parents/caregivers to be the "buffer" for young children who may be experiencing toxic stress, but systems often fall short of supporting the parents/caregivers themselves.

Toxic stress comes in many forms: family and community violence, work-related stress, and financial stress. One of the most prominent areas of toxic stress for families that have experienced historical and racial marginalization is in the area of financial stress. In the United States, 40.3% of babies, 11.4 million babies and toddlers, ages 0–3, live in poverty (Zero to Three, 2022). Very young children are by far the largest group of children experiencing poverty in the United States. While there are multiple factors that intersect with poverty that increase risks for young children and families, the impact of the lack of financial resources alone plays a significant role in parental experience of toxic stress. The cognitive burden of poverty—the experience of consistently lacking the financial resources to ensure basic care for one's family with food, shelter, clothing and to pay bills for basic needs, like heat, electricity, transportation—has significant impact on individual brain capacities. Poverty's impact on cognition has been shown to limit an individual's ability to focus on other important tasks, such as being successful at work, in training or education programs, and also in parenting (Mani et al., 2013). Historically, economic and social conditions that have held up institutions that create barriers for individuals to achieve financial security have simultaneously created a more difficult path for young children as well.

It is in this area of intervention work that we consider the intersection of attachment theory and **family systems theory.** Both focus heavily on parental influences by way of transactional relationships, and both make space to address historical personal and collective trauma experiences. Selma Fraiberg's pivotal 1975 article "Ghosts in the Nursery: A Psychoanalytic Approach to the Problems of Impaired Mother–Infant Relationships" shaped the way we consider parent/caregiver trauma and how it impacts the capacity for parents/caregivers to provide consistent, nurturing, and responsive care for young children. **Ghosts in the nursery** are described as "visitors of unremembered past of the parents" and refers to how parents will unconsciously experience their children, especially in infancy, through the lens of those "ghosts" (Fraiberg, 1975). This can result in the intergenerational transmission of abuse, neglect, or insecure attachment patterns that can disrupt healthy development. Fraiberg (1975) gives us a better understanding of how transgenerational patterns of negative parenting influences on child development thrive and survive, sometimes despite the parents' best efforts to resolve and expel their ghosts. Family systems theory, as a framework for understanding how family interactions largely determine individual family member's behaviors, similarly seeks to identify and extract hurtful patterns of family interactions that are generational and embedded (Johnson & Ray, 2016).

> **REFLECTION QUESTION**
>
> 1. How might you use traditional models of child development, like Erickson's stages of psychosocial development, to understand the impact of contextual influences like land displacement, migration, or community violence on the earliest stages of developmental crises where young children are learning a sense of trust in their world and beginning to develop a sense of autonomy?
>
> 2. Consider what autonomy might mean for children reared in cultures where collectivism, not individualism, is the prevailing social value.

The Overrepresentation of Children of Color in the Child Welfare System: Roots in Collective Historical Trauma

As social workers, we must always assess human experience within contexts. The previous section offered empirical and theoretical frameworks for considering early development of individuals within families. Now we need to reflect on meso- and macro-level forces that influence the capacity of families and care givers to provide a secure base for infants, toddlers, and young children. If we make an honest assessment of U.S. history, we have clear examples of social policies that have sabotaged parental autonomy and authority in racially minoritized populations right into the 21st century. Consider the irony and absurdity of social institutions that pathologize and punish families for "poor parenting" when those very institutions have systematically hindered the ability of parents to rear their own children.

In 2018, Black children accounted for about 14% of the U.S. population of children, yet they represented approximately 23% of children in the foster care system (Annie E. Casey Foundation, 2020). This overrepresentation of Black children in the foster care system has historical roots embedded in a legacy of slavery and Jim Crow segregation. Black parents have only held any legal sense of parental authority over their children in all 50 U.S. states for about 60 years (Ingram, 2022; Patton, 2017). This historical context of living in a society where for the first 246 years a mother's nursing infant could be ripped from her breast and sold on the auction block, then for an additional 100 years living under the constant threat of domestic terrorism and federally sanctioned segregation and economic inequity has had deep intergenerational impacts on attachment and early relationship development within this population.

Additionally, the horrors of separation and removal of Indigenous children from their families during the 19th and 20th centuries in the United States and Canada for the purpose of "civilizing" those children, when in fact they were being abused and sometimes starved to death at boarding schools, have only begun to be revealed in the 21st century. These are but a few examples of how U.S. and Western culture and policy have been designed to rupture family ties in racially minoritized families in the name of "helping" or making marginalized families more civilized or "normal." The standard for normalcy has always been embedded in White supremacy and places White, nuclear, heteronormative families at the top of the social hierarchy.

Traditional theoretical frameworks of early human development have often failed to take into account the impacts of collective and intergenerational historical trauma on parenting, attachment, and early relationships in infant and early childhood development.

Genocide and Colonization of Indigenous Populations—Displaced Children

"Kill the Indian, save the man." This was the mission of White America during the late 19th and early 20th centuries. By this time, the racial hierarchy was well underway, and Indigenous populations, though considered inferior, were initially encouraged to emulate White, Christian, capitalist ideals and norms, including holding enslaved Africans. However, during the 18th and 19th centuries, as White settlers craved more territory, assimilation became more elusive for Indigenous nations (Miles, 2021). The Indian Removal Act of 1830 resulted in the displacement of thousands of native people from a host of tribal nations. Indigenous people, much like their African and African-descendant counterparts, were quickly learning the brutal lesson that their autonomy would not be acknowledged or protected in this new America. They wouldn't even be entitled to protect their own children.

White settlers imposed a sort of cultural "tabula rasa" on Indigenous people in which if they shed their "savage" customs and ways, perhaps they might be "saved" as Christians with the potential to be civilized despite being denied full citizenship as Americans. This imposition of values started with the youngest and most vulnerable group: the children. **Indian boarding schools** were designed to assimilate and convert young Indigenous children to White, Christian American culture and society. Boarding schools operated and were funded by the U.S. government between 1860 and 1978. The advent of boarding schools followed nearly 2 centuries of dispossession of land and displacement of Indigenous peoples.

This collective, intergenerational trauma has been metabolized into the brains and bodies of Indigenous children and families. Children as young as 4-years-old were removed from their homes without parental consent and subjected to military-style methods of altering their identity. Their hair was cut, any tribal clothing artifacts or toys were taken from them, and they were forbidden from speaking their native language. The authoritarian doctrine of civilizing Indigenous children included conversion to Christianity and corporal punishment rooted in puritanical beliefs that children had to be broken of the stain of their "original sin" (Patton, 2017).

This approach to child-rearing and education was counterintuitive to Indigenous beliefs that children were gifts from the Creator and should be raised to be proud and independent. Gentle reprimand and guidance were the primary disciplinary practices for Native parents, and hitting children was rare and considered an act of violence (Brave Heart et al., 2011). The efforts of modern neuroscience to understand the impact of adverse early experiences on brain development and behavior offer compelling evidence suggesting that early separation and disruption of attachment relationships, abuse (physical, emotional, psychological, and sexual), and neglect (nutrition, hygiene, relational) disrupt neural wiring in the brain responsible for higher executive functioning (i.e., impulse control, planning, decision making; Shonkoff et al., 2012). This neural disruption can result in cognitive and behavioral difficulties throughout childhood and adolescence that interfere with socialization and school performance (Scott & Steinberg, 2008).

> Repeated exposure to toxic stress during the first 3 years of life in the absence of supportive, nurturing relationships can impair the areas of the brain designed to develop trust as well as disrupt the development of neural pathways responsible for higher level cognitive processes like memory and decision making.

Today, we see evidence of the impacts of collective historical trauma of Indigenous peoples and its transmission across generations in rates of infant and maternal mortality: Indigenous birthing parents' and babies' mortality rates are twice the rate of White birthing parents and babies. In addition, Indigenous youth are almost twice as likely to experience more than two adverse childhood experiences and are twice as likely to drop out of high school when they reach adolescence (Mejia, 2021).

Native mothers and babies have the lowest exclusive breastfeeding rates at 6 months. Breastfeeding is a major determinant of maternal–child health in the Native American community. Proper breastfeeding support and promotion must take into account potential intergenerational trauma due to the historical impact of dispossession, violence, and forced removal of children from their families.

The Legacy of Slavery and Corporal Punishment

African Americans are the descendants of the enslaved African people who were, second to Native Americans, among the earliest "forced Americans" (Miles, 2021). One of the most controversial issues related to child development and parenting in the African American community is the use of corporal punishment. A largely held belief among many African Americans is that physical discipline is a necessary, loving way to prepare their children for life in a society that will often regard them with suspicion at best and contempt at worst (Patton, 2017). In fact, it is considered to be almost never too early to start disciplining children, beginning as early as late infancy with a "pop" on the hand for touching something dangerous or forbidden. Physical discipline is also highly correlated with authoritarian and "harsh" styles of parenting, which empirical evidence suggests is more commonly practiced in African American families (Parker, 2021). Interestingly, the United States is the only Western, industrialized nation where corporal punishment in school is still legal—mostly in southern U.S. states (Ward et al., 2021).

This "tough love" approach to parenting, however, has not protected Black children from the violence of a racist society. In fact, African-descendant children in the United States are more likely to face more severe punishment at school, especially in states where school corporal punishment is still legal (Patton, 2017; Ward et al., 2021). Additionally, their rates of school suspension and expulsion are about twice as high as their White peers, starting as early as preschool (Gilliam et al., 2016). Findings from Gilliam et al. (2016) suggested that preschool teachers were most likely to attribute problem behaviors to a Black male child when observing four preschool-aged children, ages 3–4 (two White children, one male and one female, and two Black children, one male and one female) playing, even when none of the children were exhibiting problem behaviors. Despite at least 2 decades of empirical evidence countering the effectiveness of corporal punishment as a disciplinary or behavioral management strategy, reverence for its practice still looms large in the African American community.

As reported by Strauss (2020), Black preschool-aged children are disproportionately suspended from school. While Black male children make up 18% of national preschool program enrollment among males, Black male children make up 41% of male suspensions from preschool. Black girls account for 18% of female preschool attendants nationally but make up 53% of preschool suspensions among female students.

Physical discipline of children is often viewed as "cultural" and frequently linked to religion. Yet with regard to the African American community, there is no evidence that methods of physical punishment as part of parenting practices can be linked to West African parenting practices, which is where the majority of enslaved people were transported from (Patton, 2017).

Thus, a question arises: Is spanking, beating, and "whupping" a parenting practice inherent to the culture of African-descendant people or is it a trauma response to 12 generations of forced servitude and government-sanctioned dehumanization and brutality? When we think of the patterns of conditioning enslavers used to "break in" new enslaved people, there are parallels in the motivation for power and control that we see in modern parenting practices of many African-descendant families (Patton, 2017). As mentioned above, there is also a premise that if a child is not under control at home, they will be handled more brutally away from home by forces outside of the family (Patton, 2017). This prospect of threat and the intensity with which Black parents/caregivers respond to it may be rooted in an evolutionary context of survival.

Family Separations at the U.S.–Mexico Border

Since its inception, the United States has had a lengthy history of using family separation as a means to oppress and control marginalized populations. The separation of African families during the Transatlantic Slave Trade and of their descendants once enslaved people reached plantations in the New World; the forced enrollment of Indigenous children in boarding schools; and most recently, the separation of migrant families from Mexico and Central America at the U.S.–Mexico border all exemplify the disregard of Western society for the family life of "othered" peoples (Norona et al., 2018). Over the last 5 years, punitive prohibitive enforcement of immigration policies has increased, resulting in an unprecedented number of young children being impacted. Historically, the effects of immigration policy on very young children have been ignored (Finno-Velazquez et al., 2018). However, by 2017, 25% of children under the age of 6 in the United States were living with one or more parents who were born outside of the United States. The needs of young migrant children and young children of migrants can no longer go unmet.

Like a growing number of scholars, Norona et al. (2018) call on practitioners and policymakers alike to consider immigration as a psychosocial event that has broad implications across the lifespan in terms of "loss, family fragmentation and psycho-structural change which impacts the identity, health and mental health of migrants" (p. 10). This challenge to traditional theories of development is a prime example of how social workers must begin to integrate social contextual factors that have not typically been considered with any depth in human behavior in a social environment (HBSE) texts into their understanding of the human condition. If we do not take into account a young child's abrupt separation from a primary caregiver at the border due to prohibitive policies meant to discourage immigration and the values and biases driving such policies, we are failing to acknowledge the human ecosystem in which the child must grow and develop. How, then, can we properly assess the normativity of the child's development, behavior, and relational capacities if we are making comparisons to children whose experiences are completely different?

Finno-Velasquez et al. (2018) advocate for systems most likely to encounter undocumented families with young children, like early care and education, to establish safe and welcoming practices that are trauma sensitive. Early childhood programs, community health centers, churches, and public libraries—to name a few—are often considered ICE- (Immigration and Customs Enforcement) sensitive locations where immigration enforcement is limited (Finno-Velazsquez et al., 2018). These agencies can provide a host of support and concrete resources for newly settling migrant families with young children, reducing traumatic exposure and potential negative impact on child development. Programs and practitioners must also stay current and in compliance with federal immigration policies and consider how they are keeping the information of all families confidential to avoid inappropriate reporting about immigration status.

Attachment, Threat, and Social Contextual Factors

Human beings are designed to respond sharply and promptly to threat. Hartman and Belsky (2016) view Bowlby's attachment theory through the lens of evolution and survival. They suggest that the attachment system is activated in response to threat and further that a secure attachment relationship serves as a secure base for exploration and developing a sense of autonomy and competence when threat is absent. Thanks to recent discoveries in developmental neuroscience, traditional lifespan development theories are being challenged to consider the role of historical trauma and/or sociopolitical threat as social contextual factors in the human ecosystem that have significant implications for attachment and early relationship development (Opendak et al., 2017).

Within an attachment framework, the parent/caregiver is primarily responsible for regulating the brain and behavior of the infant. The role of regulating infant responses to the environment and making meaning of experience becomes particularly salient in times of distress or when there is a traumatic event (Norona et al., 2018). However, when the parent/caregiver themselves is navigating traumatic experience that may be either immediate and ongoing, coded into their DNA, or both, practitioners need to understand how this complicates the parent/caregiver–infant attachment system. Parents with a history of acute or chronic threat demonstrated by abrupt separations and disrupted attachments may adopt styles of caregiving that are perceived as problematic according to Western models of parenting and family dynamics. However, it is critical for practitioners to understand that what may be perceived as diagnostic in marginalized families, from a traditional lifespan development theoretical framework may actually be an adaptation to intergenerational and/or historical trauma.

Clinically, parent–infant dyads who have been classified as having insecure and especially disorganized attachment systems are considered at greater risk for development of behavioral pathology and relational difficulties throughout life (Main & Solomon, 1986; Lyons-Ruth et al., 2004). As social workers, it is essential to ask ourselves what may be the story or history behind an attachment system that presents as insecure. A child who is classified with an avoidant attachment system may have a parent/caregiver who thinks that by not responding immediately to the child's needs, they are preparing that child for survival and managing threat in a hostile world where basic needs will often go unmet. An anxious/ambivalent attachment classification may be the result of a parent who feels threat in their fear of losing their child and is therefore inconsistently available or emotionally unavailable. Living in constant fear and being on high-alert in threatening environmental contexts are adaptive from an evolutionary and neurocognitive perspective. However, the brain is unable to detect the difference between physical and emotional threats. This disconnect or misinterpreted communication between the brain and the body may compromise a parent's ability to self-regulate and regulate their child's distress, resulting in a disorganized attachment system where the source of the child's comfort is also the source of their fear.

These problematic attachment systems, while often viewed as pathological, may be adaptations to the social contextual forces influencing early parent/caregiver–child relationships. Considering collective historical narratives of marginalized groups is an integral component of comprehensive biopsychosocial-spiritual assessment. Although we must take caution not to treat every subgroup of a marginalized population as a monolith, we must also recognize how history and current sociopolitical context impact individuals, families, and communities in the most intimate ways. An expectant migrant mother may be afraid to seek prenatal care due to the violent handlings of other migrants she witnessed at the border. An Indigenous new mother may have difficulty feeling connected to her baby because she has been influenced by the public health narrative that she and her child are 2–3 times more likely to die during pregnancy and in the year following birth. An African American grandfather raising his toddler grandson may be perceived as harsh or authoritarian in his no-nonsense approach to child-rearing when he is in fact deeply fearful of how society will misperceive his grandson's mischief and curiosity. These scenarios all require an interrogation of the traditional models of attachment and lifespan development that we rely on to assess family functioning.

When we are unable to engage families in care, there is a tendency to label them as "hard to reach" or "resistant." We may label mothers struggling to attach to their babies as "disconnected" and similarly call families of color struggling to raise children in a world that doesn't value their lives or recognize their humanity "harsh." This deficits-framed approach to talking about children and families—families whom we have noted were never considered in the origins of attachment, lifespan, and other traditional developmental theories—further perpetuates oppression, exclusion, and biased practices while at the same time pathologizing their suffering (Shorters, 2022). A strengths-based approach that integrates a critical analysis of traditional theory through an antiracist, social justice, trauma-informed lens is essential to social work practice in the 21st century.

REFLECTION QUESTIONS

1. Should we, as practitioners, impose developmental expectations rooted in individualistic principles and ideals designed to prepare children to live in a Western, capitalist society on children and families who have historically been excluded from this cultural paradigm?

2. How might we consider empowering and supporting families in cultural adaptation while still preserving their identity and traditions?

Case Study

Background and Presenting Issues

Shelby is a 19-year-old single Black mother of 18-month-old Devon, referred for early intervention services by Devon's pediatrician. The pediatrician's primary concerns are Devon's social emotional and behavioral development, but there are also some concerns about speech and language delays. Devon has not yet started to develop receptive language skills, the ability to understand basic requests and directions (e.g., "Go get your shoes") and has not yet begun to say words. Shelby believes that Devon "doesn't want to listen" and that he "ignores" the grownups. Shelby had not followed through with previous referrals for services because she and Devon live with her mother, Lorraine, age 44, and her mother had indicated that she would not approve of services in her home. Lorraine's concerns are about her own privacy and her general skepticism about the effectiveness and helpfulness of services for children this young. Lorraine's belief is that most children "grow out of" any developmental or behavioral concerns and that intervention is not something that is usually necessary unless a child has significant medical conditions or delays.

> Consider the ecological system context for Devon and what systems are present and connected to create his experiences. How many different systems is the family involved with? How might the family's history of involvement with these systems impact Devon's involvement with these systems?

The family dynamic includes Lorraine, 44, as head of household who works full time as a cook in the schools. Lorraine's 21-year-old son, Aaron, lives in the home also and works part time for a temp agency. Shelby and Devon live in the home. Shelby works part-time hours at a call center, and when she is working either Aaron or Lorraine care for Devon. Shelby is also enrolled in adult learning to try to complete her GED. She left school at age 17 in her senior year because she was pregnant. That pregnancy ended in a miscarriage, and she did not return to school. She became pregnant again with Devon soon after the miscarriage. Shelby's older sister, Karina, lives close by with her two daughters, Kimmie, age 4, and Kiara, age 2. The family is prepared and excited to welcome home the youngest brother, Jaylen, age 17, who has been living in juvenile detention facilities for the past 9 months due to drug-related activities. Jaylen will be enrolled at the district's technical high school for his junior year when he returns home. The family is close and somewhat enmeshed. Everyone is deeply involved and concerned with each other's lives, children, and experiences. Extended family relationships are also very important in this family, and there are dozens of extended family members in the area that are part of Devon's daily life in any given week. Especially present in his life is his great grandmother Jo, age 62, who provides care for him often when others cannot.

What racial and historical influences have shaped our beliefs about Black fathers? In what ways does the family reflect those beliefs? Consider how powerful stereotypes can become internal working models for the way individuals and the collective perceive ourselves and each other's our worth and our value in society. What does this mean for Devon?

Devon's father, Derek, age 20, does have a presence in Devon's life, but it is limited to once or twice a week visits. He and Shelby had difficulties with their relationship and decided to not pursue a permanent relationship after Devon was born. There is constant struggle and conflict in the greater family dynamic about Derek's ability and willingness to provide financial help with raising Devon. Lorraine is very vocal about her disappointment in Derek's engagement and ability to "step up and take care of" his son. Shelby is also frustrated with Derek's limited support, but she also has empathy for him because his own family life, having grown up bouncing around in foster care, limits his ability to be fully available for his son. Derek reports that he experiences a "hot and cold" relationship with the family; some weeks he is welcomed and invited to visit and eat meals, and some weeks he is treated with disdain and disregard. This has left him feeling unsure, and so he tends to only now visit Devon at parks and fast-food restaurants instead of at the home. Derek lives with his paternal grandmother and extended family on his own side and does not feel like his home environment is an appropriate setting to visit with Devon. There are concerns about active drug use and drug dealing in the home, and Derek has concerns about safety. The result of all of this is that Derek's time with Devon is short and the visits do not always give them a chance to fully connect and be present with each other.

Developmental Evaluation and First Visits

Devon's early intervention (EI) developmental evaluation showed moderate delays in social-emotional development and more significant delays in speech and language. Almost immediately, the speech and language evaluator detected a concern about his hearing. It was revealed that he had failed an audiological screening at his 18-month well-child visit, but that information was not provided to the EI team conducting the evaluation. During the evaluation it was revealed that Devon had two ear infections in the past year but never received treatment with tubes. Shelby reported that the pediatrician did not see need for tubes and that she felt that the medication provided helped Devon stop "pulling his ears" and helped him "sleep through the night better."

Throughout the evaluation, many family members participated in different capacities. Despite the effort for the EI team to focus questions with Shelby, many other family members wanted to respond and encourage Devon to perform the tasks put forth by the EI team. Many responses were "I've seen him do that." It was clear to the EI team that this family was very invested with care and concern about Devon's growth and development. Devon's grandmother, Lorraine, was equally participatory as mom even though she kept encouraging Shelby to answer the questions and reminding her that she was his mother. The dynamic was somewhat challenging for the EI team but overall helpful to get so much information and perspective on Devon's skills and development. Derek was encouraged to attend the EI evaluation, but work demands made him unable to attend. Devon seems to enjoy having all the focus on him and enjoyed exploring the materials provided by the EI team to conduct the evaluation. Upon completing the scoring, the team let the family know that Devon was eligible for services by both a speech and language therapist, twice a month, and a developmental specialist, every week. The family agreed to the plan, and it was noted that at the end of the evaluation session, Lorraine, who was most adamantly against "people coming into (her) home" commented that this "was not that bad."

How do we generally feel about families that are highly interconnected and dependent? Do we see them as intrusive or overburdening? In this case, how much do you value Shelby's independence? Why might families function this way as a strategy for survival and success when they have had to struggle so much with institutions and systems?

The first few weeks of visits for the developmental specialist were focused on building relationship with Devon, Shelby, and the family. It was clear to the team that it would not be the case that Devon's services would be provided in isolation from the family. The team recognized that his daily life was embedded in this rather large and enmeshed family system and that the interventions would need to be developed with the family in this context. This was not without challenges though. From the very beginning several issues were presented that caused challenges for the working relationship:

- Family members frequently referring to Devon as "bad" or a "bad boy." Even Shelby at times used this term to reprimand him: "Devon, stop being so bad."

- Very loud and chaotic context for the visits resulted in distractions for Devon during the sessions. He was especially excited and interested in his uncles, and anything they were doing would pull him away from his EI session. Family members enjoyed fishing, so anytime that subject came up he would become very focused on going along or became upset if he could not go fishing with his grandmother and/or uncles.

- Concerns about drug use in the home were ongoing. While Shelby reported that she did not use marijuana, because it "made (her) feel sick," all other family members were forthcoming about their recreational use and joked about it frequently. The team concerns were less about supervision of Devon but more about safety issues related to strangers coming into the home at times to, the team presumed, either buy or sell drugs.

- While one EI team member, the developmental specialist who is of Mexican American ethnicity and is bilingual, enjoyed a trusted and positive working relationship with the family from the beginning, the speech and language therapist, who is Caucasian and monolingual, struggled with it. The family never missed a visit with the specialist and showed a very high level of interest all things of Mexican culture, especially food and language. It came up in almost every visit. Lorraine pushed for the developmental specialist to "teach Devon some Spanish" because she felt it was a skill that all kids should have for the future. Meanwhile, the speech and language therapist often experienced a "no-show" from the family, and this left her feeling disconnected and less valued in her role with the family.

Despite the challenges, the EI team experienced an effective working relationship with the family in the first 6 weeks of services that resulted in the family having some concrete tools to support Devon's language skills. Much of the work focused on helping reframe his behavior struggles as related to his inability to communicate his wants and needs. The family felt that withholding things and experiences from him would teach him to communicate better, but the team helped them understand that first he needs practice with the communication skills. The team also worked hard to help Shelby follow up quickly with audiology because there were concerns that Devon's pediatrician had missed his need for tubes due to chronic ear infections. The result was that he did indeed need tubes in his ears, which allowed for more potential for his speech and language progress.

Ongoing Services

Devon continued to receive early intervention services until his 3rd birthday. During that time period, the speech and language visits decreased to once a month due to progress in his communication skills, but his developmental specialist visits continued weekly. An infant mental health specialist (IMH) social worker joined the team at a point when Shelby expressed interest in having Derek be more present in the EI sessions. The IMH social worker focused with Shelby on how to nurture her son's relationship with his father while managing her own relationship with family, who continued to have a negative view of Derek and treated him with disdain and disregard. Shelby and Lorraine came to a high point in this conflict at Devon's 2nd birthday party when Shelby told her mother that she would need to "stop talking bad about Devon's dad" in front of him. This resulted in a higher level conflict that positioned Shelby and Lorraine in conflict over the living situation. Lorraine felt disrespected by her daughter and would not tolerate being "disrespected in (her) own house."

The 3 months that followed were difficult in the work because Shelby, determined to move out, realized her desperate financial situation and that she would likely not be able to move out anytime soon. She began to set some goals but vacillated between feelings of excitement and motivation to feelings of hopeless and being overwhelmed. It was at this time that she became pregnant again by Derek and decided not to tell her family right away.

CONCLUSION

To circle back to the top of the chapter, we have discussed the ways in which White, Western ideals and norms have shaped traditional standards for early childhood development. The voices of marginalized people have been excluded from the discourse about early human development and experience, and social policies have tended to reify this exclusion. Social work, with its dedication to diversity and social justice, must seek to redress this exclusion. As practitioners, then, understanding the contexts and challenges of marginalized populations is fundamentally important from infancy to toddlerhood. The next chapter will look at childhood through early adolescence.

KEY TERMS

- Social organ: the brain is described as a social organ because human beings are fundamentally shaped and co-created by relationships.

- Synaptogenesis: the formation of synapses which are the point of contact where information is transmitted between neurons. This process is essential to overall brain architecture.

- Pruning: the process during brain development in which the brain eliminates extra synapses. This process "cleans up" old and unimportant neural connections in favor of high quality and frequently used neural connections.

- Transactional model of development: continuous bi-directional and reciprocal influences between the developing child and contextual factors impacting the child.

- Attachment theory: developmental psychology theory postulating that human infants need to develop a close emotional bond with at least one primary caregiver for healthy social emotional development. Attachment is also considered an evolutionary relationship dynamic that ensures safety and survival.

- Toxic stress: response to strong, frequent and/or prolonged adversity. Toxic stress in early childhood has been linked to high blood pressure, inflammation and heart disease.

- Family systems theory: a theory of human behavior that defines the family unit as a complex system in which members interact to influence each other's behavior.

- Ghosts in the nursery: according to Selma Fraiberg and colleagues (1975), the relationship between a parent's early, often harsh or traumatic experiences of the way they were raised (parented) and their own parenting style.

- Indian boarding schools: residential schools founded in the mid-19th century by the government or Christian missionaries in the US and Canada to eliminate Indigenous culture (language, dress and customs) in children as young as 4, and replace them with mainstream (White) American culture. These children were typically forcibly removed from their families and placed in schools without parental consent.

DISCUSSION QUESTIONS

- Consider the family dynamics in the case study presented and what are some protective factors that may be considered and amplified to support the child's experience and growth of healthy development?

- If you are a social worker, working with this family, what areas of intervention might you want to begin with given what you know now about the importance of children's early experiences?

- How might you work with this family to integrate dad more into the child's experiences and what factors need to be considered in the context of the whole family?

REFERENCES

Annie E. Casey Foundation. (2020). Black children continue to be disproportionality represented in foster care. https://www.aecf.org/blog/us-foster-care-population-by-race-and-ethnicity

Applegate, J. S., & Shapiro, J. R. (2005). *Neurobiology for clinical social work: Theory and practice.* Norton.

Brave Heart, M.Y., Chase, J., Elkins, J., & Altschul, D. B. (2011). Historical trauma among Indigenous peoples of the Americas: Concepts, research, and clinical considerations. *Journal of Psychoactive Drugs, 43*(4), 282–290.

Center on the Developing Child. (2007). *A science-based framework for early childhood policy.* Harvard University. https://developingchild.harvard.edu/resources/a-science-based-framework-for-early-childhood-policy/

Cozolino, L. (2014). *The neuroscience of human relationships: attachment and the developing social brain* (2nd ed.). W. W. Norton & Company.

Davies, S. M., Silverio, S., Christiansen, P., & Fallon, V. (2021). Maternal–infant bonding and perceptions of infant temperament: The mediating role of maternal mental health. *Journal of Affective Disorders, 282*(1), 1323–1329. https://doi.org/10.1016/j.jad.2021.01.023

Finno-Velazquez, M., Cahill, B., Ulrich, R., & Matthews, H. (2018). Heightened immigration enforcement and the well-being of young children in immigrant families: Early childhood program responses. *Zero to Three, 39*(1), 27–32.

Fraiberg, S., Adelson, E., & Shapiro V. (1975). Ghosts in the nursery: A psychoanalytic approach to the problems of the impaired mother-infant relationships. *Journal of the American Academy of Child Psychiatry, 14*, 387–421.

Gilliam, W. S., Maupin, A.N., Reyes, C. R., Accaviti, M., & Shic, F. (2016). *Do early educators' implicit biases regarding sex and race relate to behavior expectations and recommendations of preschool expulsions and suspensions?* Yale Child Study Center.

Hartman, S., & Belsky, J. (2016). An evolutionary perspective on family studies: Differential susceptibility to environmental influences. *Family Process, 55*(4), 700–712. https://escholarship.org/uc/item/5qb3658v

Huttenlocher, P. R., & Dabholkar, A. S. (1997). Regional difference in synaptogenesis in the human cerebral cortex. *Journal of Comparative Neurology, 387*, 167–178.

Ingram, A. (2022). *This woman's work: A conversation about racial inequities in maternal child health and inclusive reproductive justice.* Fairfield University Black Lives Matter Course.

Institute of Medicine and National Research Council (2000). From neurons to neighborhoods: The science of early childhood development. Washington, DC: The National Academies Press.

Johnson, B., & Ray, W. (2016). Family systems theory. In *Encyclopedia of Family Studies.* https://doi.org/10.1002/9781119085621.wbefs130

Kobak, R., Zajac, K., & Madsen, S. (2016). Attachment disruptions, reparative processes, and psychopathology: Theoretical and clinical implications. In J. Cassidy & P.R. Shaver (Eds.), *Handbook of attachment: Theory, research, and clinical applications* (3rd ed., pp. 25–39). Guildford Press.

Lyons-Ruth, K., Melnick, S., Bronfman, E., Sherry, S., & Llanas, L. (2004). Hostile-helpless relational models and disorganized attachment patterns between parents and their young children: Review of research and implications for clinical work. In L. Atkinson & S. Goldberg (Eds.), *Attachment issues in psychopathology and intervention* (pp. 65–94). Lawrence Erlbaum Associates Publishers.

Main, M., & Solomon, J. (1986). Discovery of an insecure-disorganized/disoriented attachment pattern. In T. B. Brazelton & M. W. Yogman (Eds.), *Affective development in infancy* (pp. 95–124). Ablex Publishing.

Mani, A., Mullainathan, S., Shafir, E., & Zhao, J. (2013). Poverty impedes cognitive function. *Science*, *341*(6149), 976–980. https://doi.org/10.1126/science.1238041

Mejia, M. (2021, May 30). *The U.S. history of Native American boarding schools*. The Indigenous Foundation. https://www.theindigenousfoundation.org/articles/us-residential-schools

Miles, T. (2021). Dispossession. In N. H. Jones, C. Roper, I. Silverman, & J. Silverstein (Eds.), *The 1619 Project: A new origin story* (pp. 135–164). One World.

National Scientific Council on the Developing Child. (2010). Early experiences can alter gene expression and affect long-term development: Working Paper No. 10. Harvard University. https://developingchild. harvard.edu/resources/early-experiences-can-alter-gene-expression-and-affect-long-term-development/

Norona, C. R., Flores, L. E., Velasco-Hodgson, M. C., & Eiduson, R. (2018). Historical, sociopolitical, and mental health implications of forcible separations young migrant Latin American children and families. *Zero to Three, 39*(1), 8–20.

Opendak, M., Gould, E. & Sullivan, R. (2017). Early life adversity during the infant sensitive period for attachment: Programming of behavioral neurobiology of threat processing and social behavior. *Developmental Cognitive Neuroscience, 25*, 145–159. https://doi.org/10.1016/j.dcn.2017.02.002

Parker, A. (2021). Reframing the narrative: Black maternal health and culturally meaningful support for wellness. *Infant Mental Health Journal, 42*, 502–516. https://doi.org/10.1002/imhj.21910

Patton, S. (2017). *Spare the kids: Why whupping children won't save Black America*. Beacon Press.

Sameroff, A. J., & Fiese, B. H. (2000). Transactional regulation: The developmental ecology of early intervention. In J. P. Shonkoff & S. J. Meisels (Eds.), *Handbook of early childhood intervention* (2nd ed., pp. 135–159). Cambridge University Press.

Scott, E. S., & Steinberg, L. (2008). *Rethinking juvenile justice*. Harvard University Press.

Shonkoff, J. P. (2003). From neurons to neighborhoods: Old and new challenges for developmental and behavioral pediatrics. *Journal of Developmental and Behavioral Pediatrics, 24*(1), 70–76.

Shonkoff, J. P., Boyce, W., & McEwen, B. (2009). Neuroscience, molecular biology, and the childhood roots of health disparities: Building a new framework for health promotion and disease prevention. *Journal of the American Medical Association, 301*(21), 2252–2259.

Shonkoff, J. P., Garner, A. S., Siegel, B. S., Dobbins, M. I., Earls, M. F., McGuinn, L., & Wood, D. L. (2012). The lifelong effects of early childhood adversity and toxic stress. *Pediatrics, 129*(1), e232–e246.

Stern, D. N. (1977). *The first relationship: Mother and infant*. Harvard University Press.

Stern, J. A., Barbarin, O., & Cassidy, J. (Eds.). (2022). Attachment perspectives on race, prejudice, and anti-racism. *Attachment & Human Development, 24*(3), 253–259. https://doi.org/10.1080/14616734.2021.1976920

Strauss, V. (2020, November 26). New federal data shows Black preschoolers still disciplined at far higher rates than Whites. *The Washington Post*. https://www.washingtonpost.com/education/2020/11/26/new-federal-data-shows-black-preschoolers-still-disciplined-far-higher-rates-than-whites/

Tippet, K. (Host). (2022, February 3). Trabian Shorters—A cognitive skill to magnify humanity [Audio podcast episode]. In *On Being with Krista Tippett*. National Public Radio. https://onbeing.org/programs/trabian-shorters-a-cognitive-skill-to-magnify-humanity/

Ward, G., Petersen, N., Kupchik, A., & Pratt, J. (2021). Historic lynching and corporal punishment in contemporary southern schools. *Social Problems*, *68*(1), 41–62 https://doi.org/10.1093/socpro/spz044

Zero to Three. (2022). *State of babies yearbook: 2022*. https://stateofbabies.org

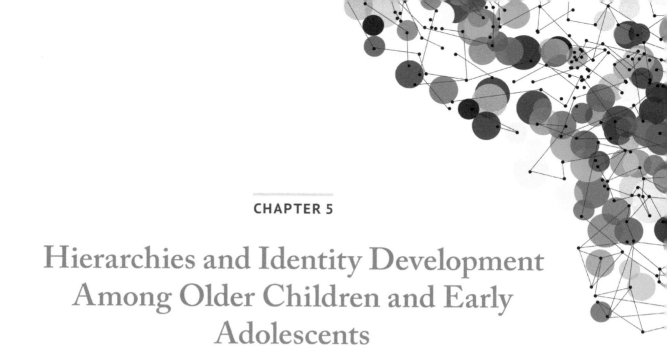

CHAPTER 5

Hierarchies and Identity Development Among Older Children and Early Adolescents

LAURA QUIROS AND ELISABETH COUNSELMAN-CARPENTER

Optimal learning depends on this process—a cycle of curiosity, exploration, discovery, practice, and mastery—which leads to pleasure, satisfaction, and the confidence to once again set out and explore.

—Bruce Perry, *New Direction for Adult and Continuing Education*

We would like to note that this chapter was cocreated by both authors but that the story told in the "use of self" narrative woven throughout the chapter is the singular story of author Laura Quiros.

LEARNING OBJECTIVES

1. Adopt an anti-oppressive and trauma-informed approach to practice that is client-focused, strengths-based, self-reflective, and creates egalitarian and accountable relationships of partnership with clients in recognition of clients' expertise regarding their own environments, concerns, needs, priorities, capacities, and resources (Corresponds Competencies 2–9).

2. Demonstrate a working knowledge of the National Association of Social Workers Code of Ethics, International Federation of Social Workers Global Social Work Statement of Ethical Principles, and National Association of Black Social Workers Code of Ethics, to acquire a clear understanding of how to apply social work values to practice. (Competency 1)

3. Be aware of and learn to manage personal feelings, attitudes, and values in the professional helping process and within the context of social work values. (Competencies 1, 3 and 6)

4. Identify, compare, and deconstruct classical developmental theories of adolescence through a decolonizing lens. (Competencies 1, 3, and 7)

1. When you think about your adolescence, what comes to mind?

2. Upon reflection, did you identify as an adolescent with a marginalized identity? If so, what parts of your social identity did you feel were marginalized? If not, when did you identify an aspect of your identity that was marginalized?

3. In what ways did you experience social domination and subordination? In what ways did social domination and subordination change and shift throughout your adolescence?

4. What helped you cope with the negative effects of social domination and subordination?

5. Experimenting with use of self: Do you imagine sharing any of these experiences with clients? What does that space of sharing look and feel like?

6. In what ways would sharing experiences facilitate or inhibit client–social worker interactions?

Introduction

This chapter began as a solitary reflection on my own adolescent identity development in hierarchical environments as a way to intentionally locate myself. The case study below rests on the roots of autoethnography and phenomenology. I begin with my lived experience and reflection to center my purpose and message. I invite the reader to join me in this space of vulnerability, nuance, complexity, and nonbinaries as I reveal aspects of myself in this case study. I model "use of self" for you as a practice and pedagogical tool by first locating myself and my story as an adolescent with marginalized social identities. The Licensed Independent Clinical Social Workers (LICSW) define **use of self** as the process of "sharing myself with my clients through skillful self-disclosure and empathy and authentically bringing all I'm made of into the therapeutic relationship for use as a therapeutic tool" (Daley, 2013, p. 3). Use of self as a pedagogical tool offers ways to relate to and make meaning of expressions of identities, care, structure, imagination, and nonbinary sensibilities.

The case study below explicitly highlights the social hierarchies of race, class, gender, culture, and religion in addition to interpersonal, sociopolitical, and intergenerational trauma that shaped my identity development during my early, middle, and late adolescence.

Please read and answer the questions below prior to reading the case study.

OPENING NARRATIVE: CASE STUDY

I was born in the Bronx, New York, but grew up in a perceived wealthy and White suburb in Westchester, New York. I was born into a two-parent family, with what felt like resources at the time, but quickly learned that those resources were fleeting. During my childhood, we moved several times in the same town because of financial constraints. At the age of 6, I lost my brother to sudden infant death syndrome, the rented home we were living at the time flooded, and we became homeless. We moved in with a family friend for a few years, and once back in our own home, my parents' marriage began to visibly disintegrate. At the end of my early adolescence, at the age of 13, my father was asked to leave our home; my parents separated and finally divorced. Having witnessed intimate partner violence, infidelity, and substance abuse, coupled with the experiences of growing up amidst mental illness and the sociopolitical and intergenerational traumas of racism, sexism, and antisemitism, my early and middle adolescence can be categorized as one of both survival and numbing—what I know now are manifestations of trauma. I needed an outlet for all the emotions and manifestations of trauma that arose from my home and social environments. The feelings and posttrauma reactions to those feelings felt confusing, unmanageable, and terrifying. As illustrated, my childhood and adolescence were full of **adverse childhood experiences (ACEs)**, which are defined as traumatic events that are experienced in childhood and adolescence. Such events include but are not limited to abuse, neglect, loss, divorce, mental illness, and domestic violence. Such traumas are experienced over a sustained period of time and have long-term biological, physical, emotional, and mental health effects (Finkelhor et al., 2015).

My mother and father were survivors of intergenerational trauma. **Intergenerational trauma** is defined as trauma that is passed down through generations (Dias & Ressler, 2013). More specifically intergenerational trauma is the "intergenerational transmission of risk for neuropsychiatric disorders, such as phobias, anxiety and posttraumatic stress disorder" (Dias & Resssler, 2013, p. 95). This research teaches us that children are shaped by their parents' experiences long before they were born. Yet traditional adolescent development theory does not account for the experiences of intergenerational trauma and the impact that trauma has on brain development and social and emotional development, in terms of both risk and resilience. As a result, transgenerational trauma and its impact often go unrecognized by practitioners (Hendrix et al., 2021).

As an adolescent with a marginalized identity, the manifestations of the traumas were not named as posttrauma responses by my parents, educators, or mental health providers. A systems perspective was not applied to my story. Instead, labels were assigned to me: unstable, broken, wild, out of control, too much, stupid, and emotional. My environment as well as my relationship to my environment was absent from everyone's assessment of me. Furthermore, these personality labels fit neatly into the U.S. social construction of an adolescent with a marginalized identity, particularly, in my case, a Latina. I was assessed from a nonsystems perspective, and that assessment was validated by the social constructions of race and gender. In this example, we see how systems of oppression impact the individual on a micro level. It was not uncommon to assign labels such as "emotional," "unstable," and "out of control" to a Latina adolescent who came from a "broken" home. More explicitly, we see here the coupling of bias and individual racism with systems of oppression.

Returning to case study, I internalized these labels, and they became a part of my identity and my essence. I want to emphasize that it was not necessarily the actual traumas that caused the disconnection to myself but how those traumas manifested, and then those manifestations were unrecognized as posttrauma reactions and then became part of my personality. The research tells us that adolescents can experience a wide range of reactions to trauma and loss. Yet the theories, thinking, and perspectives that were used to engage, assess, intervene, and evaluate me further constricted and pathologized my development and emerging sense of self. Social work students often worry that they are responsible for the livelihood of the client, and I share with students that while you are not responsible for the client's recovery or relapse—in the most broadest of sense—you are responsible for making sure to engage with systems theories, systems thinking, and systems perspectives throughout the life of a case.

Defining Adolescence

Often thought to encompass tweens and teenage years, the phase of **adolescence** has traditionally been defined, particularly by stage theorists, as starting in what has been considered late childhood: from around the age of 10 to one's early 20s. It is a time in which one establishes a true sense of identity as we seek our place in the world. We begin to move away from our family and community of origin into a larger world arena. However, it can also be a time in which structural oppression, historical racism, sexism, cisheteronormativity, and othering can do tremendous damage to one's development (National Scientific Council on Adolescence, 2021). Multifaceted personal identity development, working toward our adult sense of self, and social group definition are at the forefront during this particular time in one's life.

Stage Theories

Traditional human behavior texts often favor stage theories when conceptualizing adolescent development. **Stage theory**, as defined by the American Psychological Association (n.d.), is "any hypothetical construct used to describe phases or steps in a process that occurs over time, such as a theory that development involves discontinuous phases marked by changes in functioning." Perhaps two of the most well-known and oft-discussed theories of adolescent development is Piaget's (1972) theory of cognitive development, which defined adolescence as the "formal operational stage," and Erikson's (1963) psychosocial theory of development, which defined adolescence as the stage of "identity versus confusion."

Piaget (1972) believed the formal operational stage was the fourth and "final" stage of development that begins around the age of 12, with later theorists believing that it lasts into adulthood. Piaget posited that this was when abstract thoughts and deductive reasoning develops. He believed that around age 11, children develop abstract and hypothetical reasoning and are now more likely to consider moral and ethical questions in their decision-making process and weigh whether or not something may actually happen. Piaget believed this stage ended around the chronological age of 15.

Erikson (1968) initially conceptualized adolescence as ages 12–18, which he referred to as the stage of "identity versus confusion," followed by "intimacy versus isolation," which encompasses a broad range from 18–40 years old. Unlike Piaget, Erikson (1968) was more focused on how relationships impact growth and development and the role that social interaction plays in human development. Erikson (1962) believed that adolescents struggle with a sense of confusion and insecurity during this time as they seek to integrate a sense of self. He posited that this is time in which people seek an overall identity to carry through their life and thus experiment with different behaviors and roles as they "try on" new identities to see which fit (Erikson, 1962). For those who are unable to find a good fit with the identity that they have tried on, there can be role confusion and continued insecurity.

Kohlberg's (1985) theory of moral development, a third stage theory, was built off of Piaget's work and stated that "conventional morality" begins in early adolescence and continues through adulthood. This phase comprises Stages 3 and 4, in which interpersonal relationships are developed and social order is maintained. Kohlberg believed that this is when individuals begin to accept social rules of what is good and moral and that moral standards are internalized. He also believed this was a time of conforming to the norms of the larger social group and an acceptance of authority. Critiques of Kohlberg show that his work is (a) grounded in gender bias (Gilligan, 2016) since he based his theory primarily off the experiences of cisgender men and (b) purely Western in focus with an emphasis on upper- and middle-class values (Govrin, 2014).

Stage theories have significant limitations that have become more frequently acknowledged in scholarly work, particularly in the latter half of the 20th century. Among many other critiques, further research has shown that children develop the abilities described by Piaget much earlier than he mentioned and that he also overestimated the formal operational abilities. Like other Western-based theories, Piaget remained deficit-based and focused too much on what children could not do, versus what they could accomplish. Quite simply, Piaget did not discuss the influence of social systems or how a child processes and understand social situations. Erikson did not take into account the roles that race, culture, and gender play during this period and, like Piaget, has a deficit-based focus. In addition, his stages are not always linear, which makes the applicability of this theory quite limiting in practice. None of these theorists took into account ACEs, sociopolitical trauma, or intergenerational trauma in conceptualizing adolescent experience. In returning to the case study, for example, how can this be thought to be the final stage of development, when one has not yet had the opportunity to acknowledge, address, and begin to heal from both the traumas that were survived and the subsequent labels applied to trauma-related externalizing behaviors?

Piaget would acknowledge during his career that development is not linear in nature or even predictable. One positive is that what he did offer was the concept that children and adolescents think differently than adults. It should also be recognized that Piaget (2013) believed a supportive environment helps students learn better, that social interactions are important, and that peer teaching can be an important aspect to adolescent learning. While Piaget and Erikson have made some important contributions to understanding some of the tasks and experiences that influence adolescent development, their work is bound by the time in which it was conducted and lens of their own dominant positionality.

Another classic theory is Bronfenbrenner's (1977) ecological systems theory, which created a nested composite of interrelated structures, named the "microsystem," "mesosystem," "exosystem," "macrosystem," and "chronosystem." These systems were organized from most to least significant in terms of the impact they have on a child, and the influence of one system's development was dependent on its relationship with the other systems. Bronfenbrenner would revise his own theory in 1994, referring to it as the "bioecological model," as he became more interested in proximal processes of development—or how there were persistent forms of interaction with the immediate environment—and that these proximal processes affect people differently due to context (Bronfenbrenner & Ceci, 1994). Continued research has supported Bronfenbrenner's work, particularly around the influence of the school system on childhood and adolescent development (Kelly & Coughlan, 2019; Lippard et al., 2018). However, some of the limitations of this theory include very little work on understanding the impact of the mesosystem and the fact that it too is a deficit-based model, in which assumptions may be made that if one does not have a positive environment, one may develop "negatively." It is critically important to consider these historically significant theories with an understanding that variations in power, social support, access to resources, and the presence of community and historical risk factors play a significant role in development (National Scientific Council on Adolescence, 2021). It is also critically important to note the diversity of experience in adolescents who are grouped under one identity label (e.g., Latino youth, queer youth, or Black youth) and to honor the diversity of individual experiences due to these variations in structural factors. Perhaps the most significant limitations of the classically studied theories is that they were based on the adult perspective of other adults or youth with dominant identities.

By adolescence, individuals are well aware of racial discrimination in both their community and within school settings (Adam et al., 2020). English et al. (2020) found that Black youth experience an average of five instances of racial discrimination per day in both direct and online interactions. The impact of racial discrimination on adolescence for all youth of color must be highlighted when understanding the tasks and challenges that accompany adolescence. Benner et al. (2018) found that racial and ethnic discrimination has 11 different types of negative effects on well-being during adolescence, which include greater psychological distress; lower self-esteem; increased substance use; lower academic engagement, motivation, and achievement; and more internalizing and externalizing symptoms.

From a neurobiological perspective, adolescence is a vulnerable time in which social experience can have a significant impact. Regions of the brain that are maturing at this time relate to emotional regulation and social cognition (Blakemore & Mills, 2014). There are powerful physical changes that occur during adolescence along with cognitive, emotional, and social shifts (Blakemore & Mills, 2014; McCormick et al., 2010, Steinberg & Morris, 2001), and experiences during this key time in individual development may have a long-term impact on emotional, cognitive, behavioral, and overall health functioning in adulthood (Blakemore & Mills, 2014).

In addition to tremendous neurobiological and emotional change, there is profound social change as well. Peer and romantic relationships become a more primary focus (Adam et al., 2020) while ethic and racial identity (ERI) begins to solidify (Jugert et al., 2020; Umaña-Taylor et al., 2014). The social influence of peers at this time cannot be underscored, particularly as they serve as a reference point for ERI development (Umaña-Taylor et al., 2014, Veenstra et al., 2018). There are mixed results in which has more impact—friends of a same ethnic-racial identity versus cross-racial-ethnic identity—but most ERI studies find that same ethnic and cross-ethic friends can serve very different functions for teens with marginalized identities and that same ethnic friends may have more relevance in ethnic and racial identity development in adolescence (Chen & Graham, 2017; Jugert et al., 2020).

More specifically Jugert et al. (2020) found that teens do not necessarily purposefully select friends with similar ERI but that they adjust their ERI levels to those of their friends, which demonstrates the strength of peer influence at this age. It is also incredibly important to know that much of the ERI work has been done in the United States rather than in Europe and in developing countries and is not necessarily generalizable to adolescent ethnic-racial identity development in other countries.

In reflecting upon the earlier case study, we see the power of peer influence at this age. Although I identified as Latina and Jewish, my friends at the time were predominantly White identified; our commonality was that each of us had experienced some form of childhood and adolescent trauma. We found refuge in each other, the creative arts, or, in my case, on the soccer field, thereby shifting my social identity away from my racial and cultural affiliations and leaning into my identities of being from a lower socioeconomic class and a survivor of adolescent trauma. That is not to say race and culture were not present, nor is it to say that I did not experience racial discrimination. I did, yet the manifestations of trauma associated with the traumas I experienced were salient. It is important for students to consider the complexity of intersectionality when working with marginalized adolescents. Having a White-identified mother was also a factor in my racial and ethnic identity and perhaps played a role in why my female peers were mostly White identified. Again, we see the complexity in marginalized adolescents who occupy a biracial identity. Identity theory has taught us that identification takes place in the context of society through interpersonal relationships while constantly undergoing reconstruction and redefinition (Quiros, 2009).

Identity and Sexuality

Adolescence is a time in which sexual development flourishes. For some teens, it is a time in which self-identification about their sexual identity may shift, while others have been clear on their orientation from childhood (Rosario et al., 2008). Similar to other adolescent identity formation models, sexual identity formation was initially characterized by stage theories, primarily those by Cass (1979) and Troiden (1989), but these are both considered extremely dated. They were developed at a time in which there was not a lot of access to information about sexual orientation, resources for the studies were limited, and there were more significant levels of stigma toward queerness (Cass, 1979; Troiden, 1989), Boxer & Cohler, 1989). It is also important to note that these two models were developed based on a sample of White adults reflecting retrospectively on their experiences (Cass, 1979; Troiden, 1989, not from adolescents themselves (Institute of Medicine, 2011). Boxer et al. (1993), who were the first to study queer adolescents (whom they identified as LGB, and more than half of whom also identified as youth of color), found that sexual identity development is not a series of phases or stages but something ongoing through the lifespan. This work was later supported by Diamond's (2015) research on sexual fluidity.

Research remains extremely limited on the experienced of queer youth with other historically and socially marginalized identities. Queer youth of color are at an even greater risk for behavioral health problems (Di Giacomo et al., 2018; Ross et al., 2018). There continue to be significant gaps in research on queer youth of color and how they can be supported during such a vulnerable developmental time. It is important to note that limited research (e.g., Rosario et al., 2008) has shown that developmental experiences can be different for adolescents who are navigating both ethnic and racial identity and sexual orientation identity. And within the diverse identities under the umbrella of "youth with marginalized sexual identities," even less is known about asexual and aromantic youth and the unique and nuanced aspects of their identity development.

Adolescence—as well as emerging adulthood, as discussed in the next chapter—is often a time in which youth "come out" in terms of their sexual orientation identity. Early queer developmental theorists have found that for gay and lesbian youth, a developmental task that occurs in adolescence is the process of deconstructing internalized heterosexual expectations and constructing a new set of future expectations in a "queer life course" (Boxer et al., 1993). For all adolescents, there are milestones around sexual and romantic awareness and first sexual experiences, but for queer youth, this includes additional pieces, including the experience of self-labeling as queer and disclosing same-sex orientation. Although there have been myths around first awareness of sexual attraction, much work with queer youth found similarities of first awareness of sexual attraction for heteronormative youth and queer youth to be around the age of 10 (D'Augelli et al., 2007; D'Augelli & Hershberger, 1993; Boxer et al., 1993, Rosario et al., 1996).

Transgender and Gender Expansive Youth

It is important to note that identity development for transgender and gender expansive (TGE) adolescents has its own unique aspects to the developmental trajectory. Most of the work on TGE youth is conducted on and with White, Western-identified, and North American samples, which we name at the forefront of this discussion. TGE adolescents (please see the *SAGE Encyclopedia of Psychology and Gender* [Nadal, 2017] for a more thorough discussion) have gender identities and/or gender expressions that "do not conform to society's conventional binary sex/gender system. They may combine [biological] sex and gender in unconventional ways in their own identities ... or they may appear entirely conventional while having unconventional identities or sex/gender histories that belie their normative appearances" (Pardo & Devor, 2017, p. 1690). All adolescents, regardless of gender identity, engage in age-appropriate identity self-exploration and social exploration during this time, but puberty and the social pressures that accompany adolescence can be powerfully triggering and lead to crises for TGE adolescents: Bodies mature in ways that may feel powerfully dysphoric, and social and familiar support may not be there (Pardo & Devor, 2017). There are high rates of mental health challenges and startlingly high rates of suicidal ideation and death by suicide in TGE adolescents. It is also important to know that gender identity is not just developing or fluid in adolescence, but for all individuals, and particularly TGE folx, gender identity continues to evolve and develop through the lifespan.

It is of critical importance for social workers and behavioral health providers to under-stand the extreme vulnerabilities and sociopolitical traumas that TGE adolescents experience and to actively work as advocates to educate themselves about the additional developmental challenges for TGE teens and to increase protective factors. This includes creating space and connection for all youth with multiple marginalized identities to connect in affinity spaces to support positive identity-building; conduct discussions around what is being seen, heard, and consumed from in-person and online messaging about their identities; provide resources for support within the community at large; and continue to decrease barriers and stigma toward mental health resource provision.

THEORY ↔ PRACTICE

Assessments gather data from several domains of a client system, including employment history, living situation, medical status and history, family history and dynamics, and developmental history. Be careful to be aware of potential biases as you move through the assessment process. One way to mitigate this is to name the potential biases in the beginning of the case. This data is then used in a case formulation that links theories of human behavior with a client system's experiences, practice wisdom, and sense of itself. Using a social justice lens, apply the theoretical information in this chapter to the case study using the following questions:

- Create a genogram and ecomap for the case study. The idea here is to gather the facts of the case through the use of a genogram and ecomap. This visual representation of the facts of the case allows for both the social worker and the client to see one's lineage, rela-tionships, and patterns of behaviors across generations. Include in the genogram the ways in which the trauma is evident across generations—interpersonally and socioculturally.

- Using the ecomap, depict how larger systems in communities and societies aid in facil-itating or inhibiting the intergenerational transmission of trauma.

- Create a treatment goal and three objectives that focus on applying theories of behav-ior change to intergenerational transmission of trauma. Hint: Focus the objectives on both the family member and caregiving system (see Chapter 3).

As discussed, one of the most significant strengths of understanding and naming the impact of intergenerational trauma is that it removes, or at least limits, the binary conflation of labels and stereotypes. The adolescent is assessed within a larger context of family history, ancestry, and as a person in a hierarchical environment, an environment that has history attached to it. A critical reminder: Context shapes the human development of populations marginalized because of their social identity or location. In the words of Schwartz (2021), "When you tell a person they are sick and ignore the larger context in which their symptoms make sense, not only do you miss leverage points that could lead to transformation, but you also produce a passive patient who feels defective" (p. 60).

The limitation of incorporating an intergenerational trauma framework is that a deficit lens may surface and then ultimately prevail in the assessment and treatment of the adolescent, particularly for adolescents with marginalized identities.—meaning, the adolescent is seen as only the trauma, diagnosed and treated as unstable, broken, wild, out of control, too much, stupid, emotional. This becomes their "filter" through which they will later interpret experiences.

Returning to the case study we are using to illustrate identity development among adolescents with marginalized social identities and locations in a hierarchical environment, my mother who was White and Jewish and my father who is Black and Latino parented from their personal histories, the only way they knew how. And so I navigated my middle adolescence on my own without much, if any, supervision, protection, or guidance. Traditional theories on parenting might label my parents as permissive and neglectful (Baumrind, 1991), without any understanding of their own intergenerational trauma, historical context, and/or the lived experience they are carrying as parents, who are also people. Again, if we lean on traditional parenting theories and sideline history, we have the potential to negate the power of institutional and social hierarchies and forget that social domination and subordination create structures, systems, and interpersonal interactions that negatively and positively influence the development of all populations, but particularly people with multiple marginalized identities.

THEORY ↔ PRACTICE

Behavior change theories typically focus on the individual, yet people are encouraged and discouraged by systems in the social environment, such as peers and school. Considering the information provided in the case study, apply the theoretical information in this chapter to the case study using the following questions:

- Create a new ecomap based on the additional information provided in the case study. Remember to stick with the facts. Compare the initial case study and the revised one to identify additional systems that facilitate or inhibit family and individual behavior change.

- Create two additional treatment objectives that target client systems facilitating or inhibiting family or individual behavior change. In these treatment objectives, identify tasks for the family and individual systems to complete as part of the treatment goal. Hint: Consider the level of perceived power that the client systems describe when discussing their problems and potential solutions.

When working with youth with marginalized identities, we must identify protective and promotive factors. The research tell us that protective and promotive factors can reduce the adverse impact of trauma: "*Protective* factors buffer the adverse effects of trauma and its stressful aftermath, whereas *promotive* factors generally enhance children's positive adjustment regardless of whether risk factors are present" (NCTSN Core Curriculum on Childhood Trauma Task Force, 2012, p. 6). Often times, students begin with the deficits of a case; they focus is on "what is wrong" rather than noticing and naming what is working to help this adolescent survive. Returning to the case study for an illustration of a protective factor, a protective factor for me during my early adolescence was the soccer field. My talent as an athlete and specifically a goalkeeper kept me sane, grounded, and disciplined. It was an outlet for my manifestations of trauma: The movement, leadership, and diversity were healing. It served as a form of positive stress versus the toxic stress of the micro, meso, and macro spaces of my home, school, and community (Shonkoff et al., 2009). I strongly identified as an athlete, and during the season, this positive social identity stayed with me on and off the soccer field.

We see the shifting of social identity formation in late adolescence. This is yet another illustration that identity development is not a stagnant and linear process. Late adolescence brought with it a new college terrain to navigate. I went to a predominately White liberal arts college in Upstate New York to play soccer, but after the first year I quit because of repeated injuries and a desire to socialize with a new group of friends who physically, racially, and ethnically looked like me. Here we see the strong pull of peer influence and specifically my need to connect more deeply to my racial and ethnic identities. Although they were not yet integrated, I started to find a sense of belonging in my Latina and Jewish identities. Compartmentalization of different components of the self is not uncommon for individuals from marginalized identities, where we alternate between aspects of our heritage, giving attention to different parts of the self during different times. Moving even further away from nonlinear theories of identity development, we learn that identity and identification are social and interactional processes. At different times and in different context, certain aspects of identity are more relevant than others (Dewane, 2006). These new friend groups provided me with the opportunity to embrace and reclaim my racial and cultural social identities that had been absent during my middle adolescence in high school. The pull of belonging and acceptance from my peers drew me away from the soccer field and my studies. Particularly in this predominantly White college, the soccer field was dominated by White females with long brown ponytails, and the coaching staff was all White males. Because of this context, I no longer felt that strong sense of belonging I did in high school. Although I majored in psychology and graduated within 4 years, at the end of college I did not have a stable and integrated sense of identity and still found myself in trauma-laden reactionary spaces, unable to navigate intimate relationships, not sure where I belonged, and holding onto a deep fear of abandonment. For students who desire to work in high education settings, how are you holding space for college students with marginalized identities?

THEORY ↔ PRACTICE

Risk, vulnerability, and protective factors facilitate or inhibit lasting behavior changes and the generalization of treatment insights to other situations. Using the ecomap and genogram, color the risk, vulnerability, and protective factors red, yellow, and green, respectively. Next, apply the theoretical information in this chapter to the case study using the following questions:

- Examine the treatment objectives created and identify how risk, vulnerability, and protective factors are included. If these factors are not included, then rewrite the treatment objective and compare the two.

- Using purple, color the negative effects of social domination and subordination that are presented in the genogram and ecomap. Hint: Consider earlier developmental stages and the influence of other systems.

- Using orange, color the coping mechanisms used to respond to the negative effects of social domination and subordination.

- Compare these changes to the genogram and ecomap to the treatment plan, and if necessary, edit the treatment plan to include the factors, social domination, subordination, and coping mechanisms.

The Impact of Mainstream Social Work Theory on Marginalized Adolescents

Fast-forward, during my young adulthood, I found social work to be my "calling" and applied to Hunter College School of Social Work. I vividly remember sitting in my master's in social work program's human behavior course in the late 1990s. The professor was a South Asian tenured female, and every human behavior theory she taught was created by a White and cisgender man. I remember sitting there questioning the monolithic and linear Eriksonian-representation of human behavior that seemed unrelatable and unattainable. I now think about the professor's own indoctrination into a White world where development was experienced only through the dominant gaze. The lectures in the classroom as well as the readings and case studies were void of adolescents with marginalized identities and the impact of hierarchical environments and intergenerational or sociopolitical trauma on adolescent identity development.

At the same time, as a student with a marginalized identity who had also internalized the previous negative experiences with teachers in high school, I recall feeling nervous to raise my hand and question the professor's teachings. The human behavior textbooks were written with the understanding that I would be White. Within each chapter there were inserted paragraphs on "how to work with" African Americans, Hispanics, and Asians—our identities conflated and reduced to a few paragraphs, full of stereotypes. Even though critical and creative thinking were explicit learning objectives of the course, I stayed silent due to a fear of questioning and disrupting the theoretical frameworks of White men. I would have been questioning the frameworks not only of these White males but, by extension, that of a non-White male who was seemingly cosigning the validity of these theories. Instead, what surfaced were familiar feelings of exclusion, inferiority, and self-doubt. My trajectory, grounded in traumatic experiences and a biracial, multiethnic, and Jewish identity, was not aligned with Erik Erikson's static states of human development. As mentioned, my adolescence was about surviving, coping, and navigating hierarchical environments and primarily White spaces, not identity and role confusion. Questions surfaced for me that I can now name an internalization of racial and cultural inferiority: If this social work classroom—essentially a hierarchical environment—was the normative way of being, then how could I have the audacity to disrupt that space? My internal dialogue went like this: "After all, I was permitted entrance into this intellectual community; Don't I have to follow the normative ways of being?" Furthermore, it soon became clear that student engagement did not and does not necessarily mean curiosity is welcomed, nor was there a modeling of permission to disrupt the established status quo. In fact, in that class, the advancement of the status quo through new inquiries was what was always expected—and discussed with most excitement (Quiros, 2021).

I have noticed in my teaching that students are most drawn to theories that align with their epistemologies. Those more rigid and concrete lean toward linear models, while those who embrace complexity and nuance and are themselves marginalized lean toward humanistic, narrative, and social constructionist frameworks. I encourage students to make these connections and use critical-thinking tools to interrogate theoretical frame while also interrogating themselves.

Can we reorient ourselves toward thinking about adolescent identity development in a new and inclusive way? As detailed in the above case study, it was only through the reflective practices of my lived experiences that I came up against the ways that my identity was being pathologized, my cultures conflated, my intergenerational and personal traumas ignored, my experiences seen and dealt with by others, including mental health professionals, as only obstacles, not as opportunities. Adolescents with dominant identities do not experience resistance to these traditional theories; they swollen them, flowing through the texts, lectures, and subsequent institutions without much if any internal or external barriers. Ahmed (2012) shares, "When a category allows us to pass into the world, we may not notice that we inhabit that category" (p. 178).

What if we looked at diversity as a strength? Social work, by its very nature, is supposed to be a strength-based profession, yet often we live in the world of micro diagnosis and pathology. We live in fear and despair rather than hope, love, and possibility. This is most glaring in the language that we use to identify and describe populations who are challenged by fitting into status quo spaces. Terms such as "as risk," "addict," and "victim" not only conflate identity but inherently ignore the person-in-environment framework that grounds the profession. When my students describe their internships, they use phrases such as, "I am working with at-risk adolescents." My first question back to them is "At risk of what?" followed by "Are you considering the White spaces these adolescents enter into every day? Are the environments that they live and learn in trauma informed?" This chapter is a resistance to traditional models of identity development peppered with the love and compassion needed to look deeply at new ways of learning and teaching human behavior in the social environment. Let's positively disrupt (Quiros, 2021) that traditional space with social work practice that is grounded in love, compassion, inclusion, and equity. Practice that starts with yourself and a willingness to expand one's constricted eyes. Next, let's consider some mechanisms for change.

Mitigating the Negative Effects of Social Domination and Subordination

This section of the chapter discusses mechanisms designed to limit the negative effects of social domination and subordination, as well as the biological, social, emotional, and cognitive processes that affect social interactions and identities. We begin by defining and offering a trauma-informed social justice lens as a mechanism designed to limit the negative effects of social domination and subordination.

Trauma-Informed Social Justice Lens

The definition of **trauma** is an experience or set of experiences that overwhelms one's ability to cope. The COVID-19 pandemic presented the world with an opportunity to not only normalize trauma but also engage with trauma from a sociopolitical lens—meaning, the traumas of systemic oppression that impact well-being and mental health. Furthermore, the spring and early summer of 2022 brought with it a wave of hate crimes, fueled by racism, anti-Semitism, and mental illness. The world is an increasingly unsafe place, particularly for individuals and, in this case, adolescents with marginalized social identities. Trauma-informed spaces in the classroom and in the practice are necessary now more than ever. Essentially, **trauma-informed spaces** are spaces that recognize the impact of past and present trauma on well-being and on the ability to learn (Imad, 2022).

To first understand and practice in a trauma-informed space, it is necessary to deconstruct the word "trauma." When you hear the word "trauma" used in any space, are you using the skills of curiosity and asking what it means, how it is related to the topic at hand, or are you assuming that you know and then concluding and making a judgment or diagnosis based on your way of knowing? Begin with this exercise of defining trauma because we generally see and respond to the world through our individual lens that is grounded in our personal histories and ways of knowing. Any interruption of this way of knowing may feel uncomfortable. That means when we hear the word "trauma," we may have an emotional reaction that impacts how we define the word, regardless of how it is being used. Remember, when we hold onto our ways of knowing and constructions of our identities so tightly, we constrict ourselves and limit our learning, literally and figuratively. As a result, we may miss opportunities to expand our lens, thus blocking or obstructing our ability to engage with different ways of being and knowing.

What Does It Mean to Be Trauma Informed from a Social Justice Lens?

As Quiros (2021) explains, "Becoming trauma-informed is an ongoing process, an ongoing lesson, and a journey. Rather than claiming expertise, we develop it by sharing what we have learned from our individual and collective experiences and by inviting others to join us in developing a community that embodies equity-based, trauma-informed leadership and practice."

The below principles are operationalized from a trauma-informed social justice lens (Harris & Fallot, 2001; Layne et al., 2011; Quiros, 2021; Thompson & Carello, 2022). As you read these, take notes and think about the many ways you can incorporate each of these principles into your classroom and into practice, remembering that each of these principles build off of one another:

- safety: Ensure physical, emotional, spiritual safety; "do no harm." This means not "claiming" a space to be safe but actively working in collaboration to make it safe, slowly and consistently. Building safety requires the naming of the connection between intergenerational and systemic trauma and individual well-being. Distinguish between safety and comfortability. Oftentimes, students and clients name feeling "unsafe" when the feeling is discomfort that arises when talking about topics such as oppression. One way to begin working on safety is to define it. What does safety mean? What does safety look like and feel like? Pay close attention to the language that is used on intake forms, policies, and course outlines. Using preferred names and honoring the use of pronouns are examples of ways to create safety for students and clients to learn and ask questions.

- trust/trustworthiness: Maximize trustworthiness and transparency by making tasks clear, maintaining boundaries that maintain relationships, and modeling positive disruption and accountability. Understand that building trust takes time and is very much based on power, identity, and positionality in context. Building trust requires us to be vulnerable. We model that vulnerability by admitting when we have made a mistake and sharing parts of ourselves so that we can be in relation to and with one another.

- choice: This involves prioritizing choice and providing decision-making means that support participants' control over their own (healing) journey. It also means honoring the diversity of healing practices and offering and inviting choice. For example, in the classroom I often revisit assignments with students as opposed to assigning them without any choice.

- collaboration: Maximize collaboration and share power by honoring and practicing equity and inclusion-based approaches and interventions. For example, inclusion is practiced and honored in decision making, inviting cocreation of policies, and creating consistent opportunities for feedback. It also means helping students and clients understand that there is power in collaboration; we do not need to do things alone.

- empowerment and voice: Identify strengths and prioritize building skills and a community that promotes student/survivor/organizational healing and growth. In other words, everyone has a value to add, and every voice should have the opportunity to be heard. Finally, uplift voice by challenging the silence, inviting conversation, and modeling vulnerability.

REFLECTIVE QUESTIONS

1. Where do you see each of these principles showing up in your work with individuals, families, and communities?

Liberated Classrooms, Curricula, Pedagogy, and Practice

Let's talk about what a liberated classroom, curricula, pedagogy, and practice looks and feels like. Before we begin, close your eyes, and write down or share out loud what you see, feel, and hear in a liberated space. What are the adjectives that come to mind? What are the smells in this space? What is in the room? What kind of language is used? Perhaps in this vision you are folding in the trauma-informed practice principles, so words like "safety," "choice," "collaboration," "empowerment," and "trust" show up in this space. Spend some time sharing your liberated space with the class.

REFLECTIVE QUESTIONS

1. How might an adolescent with a marginalized identity benefit from this activity?

2. What are the benefits of a liberated space?

Classrooms, Curricula, Pedagogy, and Practice

Ideally, the classroom space, in both pedagogy and curriculum, is a mechanism designed to limit the negative effects of social domination and subordination. At the same time, "classrooms cannot change if professors are unwilling to admit that to teach without biases requires that most of us learn anew, that we become students again" (hooks, 2010, p. 31). Instructors can lean on and integrate the trauma-informed principles to create classrooms that are liberated, do not perpetuate the status quo, and limit the negative effects of social domination and subordination. In order to do this, we must not think about the classroom or the practice arena as neutral spaces. Our bodies, our positionalities, our social locations occupy that space, and without understanding that and naming that, we may unintentionally create spaces of domination and subordination.

This position echoes hooks's (1994) description of classrooms and the bodies in them:

> The erasure of the body encourages us to think that we are listening to neutral, objective facts, facts that are not particular to who is sharing the information. We are invited to teach information as though it does not emerge from bodies. ... We must return ourselves to a state of embodiment in order to deconstruct the way power has been traditionally orchestrated in the classroom. ... If professors take seriously, respectfully, the student body, we are compelled to acknowledge that we are addressing folks who are a part of history. (p. 139)

Curricula do not show us how or provide a way to teach. If we are meant to center relationships in an antiracist social work practice, the practice of teaching and learning can involve our felt and historicized experiences of being in relationship. I encourage you to try to make those moments visible and explicit in your teaching. Lean into use of self as a mechanism for change (Dewane, 2006).

Using the practice principles of trauma-informed care, how are we collaborating and soliciting feedback from our students and clients when it comes to the curricula and healing practices? For example, I discuss with students when assignments are due, as opposed to assigning a date. We begin every class with a check-in and end every class with a check-out. I communicate with students in between classes so our work in the classroom becomes embodied and they lean into the learning rather than just focusing on what is on the test. How are we making spaces for readings that are both financially accessible and diverse? Are we working in collaboration to interrogate and unpack the language we use in our intake forms, process recordings, and syllabi? In our pedagogy and practice, are we actively working to transcend social constructions that limit our heart and mind from expanding beyond our socialization (Love, 2013)?

The theories of identity that were presented to me along the way did not help me make sense of my world or my adolescent development. The theories did not provide comfort; rather, they confused me, othered me, and further contributed to the stereotypes that made up my single story (Adichie, 2009). While social work felt like a fit for my career choice, I also realized, early on in my studies, that it was encapsulated by a White savior mentality: a mentality and way of being that assumed "we" were all the same and did not make room for the teachings of how social hierarchies shape identity development processes among adolescents with marginalized social identities and locations in a hierarchical environment.

As an adolescent, I needed help moving through obstacles; I needed help healing and finding beauty and joy in my complexity and multiculturalism. I needed help making person-in-environment connections and a better understanding of how systems of oppression impact individual mental health. I needed to learn about mechanisms designed to limit the negative effects of social domination and subordination, as well as the biological, social, emotional, and cognitive processes that affect social interactions and identities. I did not need to be saved.

The work of decolonizing and liberation involves awareness, intentionality, and imagination. It requires us pay attention to ourselves, spaces, other people, and interactions that intentionally, or not, are complicit in upholding the status quo. It also requires us to imagine spaces that are grounded in love and hope and empathic accountability (Quiros, 2021).

Below is a case study of a soccer field: a relatively "neutral" space that is loaded with biological, social, emotional, and cognitive processes that affect social interactions and identities. As a mother of an adolescent, cisgender female, I am hyperaware of the ways in which her identities and those of her peers show up. Raising a child from a racially and culturally mixed background, I am forever striving to parent from a social justice lens. I often wonder how visible the lack of diversity and attention to diversity on the athletic fields for adolescent youth is. What is needed in these spaces to limit the negative effects of social domination and subordination? I chose this case study because the sports field is a place that impacts biological, social, emotional, and cognitive processes that affect social interactions and identities.

Ponytails that Swing Side to Side

Standing on the sideline of my 14-year-old's soccer games, I see the confidence in many of these White-identified middle adolescent girls. Soccer is a predominantly White sport, and the highly competitive leagues often reside in affluent suburbs, many of which are also politically conservative. Regardless of the political affiliation, I see and feel the confidence of these adolescent girls on the field. My hypothesis, based on my research and lived experience, is that growing up with financial resources and social capital, in addition to being White identified, gives adolescents a psychological advantage over adolescents with marginalized identities. Even those who do not have innate soccer talent step onto the field with a way of being that demands respect. It's "their" world. The research tells us that self-confidence—in this case, trusting their abilities on the field—is a benefit of traditional theories of identity formation during adolescent stage of development for adolescents with *dominant* social identities, and what about those with marginalized identities who enter this very White space? Where is the social lens of person-in-environment and the impact of that environment on well-being? Is there an awareness or investment in the psychology of stigma consciousness on the playing field? While playing a sport is a protective factor, there is a responsibility to nurture identity development on the field with an awareness of how the field may unintentionally be a hierarchical space of domination and subordination.

CONCLUSION

This chapter opened with a personal case study from the primary author, Laura Quiros, about her adolescence and ways in which she struggled to process the trauma she had experienced, ways in which she tried to numb the pain of interpersonal and intergenerational trauma, and her quest for safety and belonging within the multitude of her identities. Through her story, we reflect on the impact adverse childhood experiences have on adolescent development and the manifestations that intergenerational trauma can have during the teen years. A discussion followed about the traditional stage theories that have been historically taught, including those by Piaget, Erickson, Bronfenbrenner, and Kohlberg, with a particular focus on critiquing these theories for their dominant lens, the White-centric perspective, and the absence of any trauma-informed perspective. We argue for a systems perspective that includes how adolescents negotiate race, ethnicity, sexual orientation, and gender identity while also contending with the rapid neurobiological shifts that puberty brings. In bridging theory to practice, we explored how to engage in trauma-informed assessments that are grounded in a social justice framework when working with adolescents and asked the reader to reflect upon ways in which their own positionality impacts their assessment skills. Finally, we advocated for an intersectional lens through which adolescent assessment can be conducted rather than using a linear or stage model. The chapter concluded with a return to Laura's story and how social work school has typically leaned heavily on linear theories of development and amplified dominant voices in what is taught and experienced, and she challenges the reader to step back from internalizing the White savior lens and instead embrace the work through a decolonizing, intersectional, and liberatory lens. The next chapter looks at emerging adulthood.

KEY TERMS

- Use of self: This term, in social work, is the process and experience of combining one's personal self, including personal experiences, heritage, belief systems and personality traits with professional knowledge, skills and values to enhance our work with clients through authenticity and genuine-ness.

- Adverse childhood experiences (ACEs): These are traumatic events experienced in childhood (before the age of 18) that often include verbal, physical and/or sexual abuse and challenging situations within a household and community. These experiences have a long-term impact on individual development and overall health and wellbeing through the lifespan. There are ten categories of ACEs.

- Intergenerational trauma: Transmission of oppressive, traumatic, historic events that get passed down through generations.

- Adolescence: A period of time in one's life often chronologically marked between the ages of 10–19 years old, and can extend to age 26 in which a person experiences the completion of physical puberty. Different cultures recognize different periods in which adolescence is recognized, and in which physical and emotional development occurs through the teenage years.

- Stage theory: These theories typically divide human development into 'stages', or linear periods of time in which a human completes certain tasks, exhibits certain behaviors that are deemed 'typical' of the stage or participates in certain life activities during this time period. These theories do not typically take into consideration the impact of trauma and structural factors or influences.

- Trauma-informed spaces: Spaces that hold and acknowledge the normalization of trauma at its center and using the principles of choice, safety, collaboration empowerment and trustworthiness to create belonging.

- Trauma: Authors note: We encourage students and instructors to explore the Substance Abuse and Mental Health Administration's website to explore a current definition of trauma. https://www.samhsa.gov/trauma-violence

DISCUSSION QUESTIONS

1. Explain the connection between intergenerational trauma and trauma informed spaces for marginalized adolescents.

2. What did you learn from the case study that affects your understanding of the impact of race/ethnicity/class on marginalized adolescents and the intervention?

3. When you reflect on your own adolescence, what are the markers within your family, your neighborhood and your community that indicated you had 'entered' adolescence or 'concluded' adolescence? What was the expectations of this period of time?

4. Review the parameters of Adverse Childhood Experiences (ACEs). How do you see the impact of ACEs manifesting in adolescence? What are important aspects of a holistic treatment plan that can begin to address the impact of ACEs in adolescence?

5. Review the five foundations of trauma-informed practice through a social justice lens. How do you ensure these foundations are in place in your own individual practice? How does your agency implement (or not) these foundations? Identify any gaps in which these foundations could be strengthened in your internship or workplace. What plan could you come up with to address these gaps and which stakeholders should be involved to secure the plan's implementation?

REFERENCES

Adam, E., Hittner, E., Thomas, S., Villaume, S., & Nwafor, E. (2020). Racial discrimination and ethnic racial identity in adolescence as modulators of HPA axis activity. *Development and Psychopathology*, *32*(5), 1669–1684. https://doi.org/10.1017/S095457942000111X

Adichie, C. N. (2009, July). *The danger of a single story* [Video]. TED Conferences. https://www.ted.com/talks/chimamanda_ngozi_adichie_the_danger_of_a_single_story

Ahmed, S. (2012). On being included: Racism and diversity in institutional life. Duke University Pres.

American Psychological Association. (n.d.). Stage theory. In the *APA Dictionary of Psychology*. Retrieved April 17, 2023, from https://dictionary.apa.org/stage-theory

Baumrind, D. (1991). The influence of parenting style on adolescent competence and substance use. *The Journal of Early Adolescence*, *11*(1), 56–95. https://doi.org/10.1177/0272431691111004

Benner, A. D., Wang, Y., Shen, Y., Boyle, A. E., Polk, R., & Cheng, Y. P. (2018). Racial/ethnic discrimination and well-being during adolescence: A meta-analytic review. *American Psychologist*, *73*, 855.

Blakemore, S.-J., & Mills, K. L. (2014). Is adolescence a sensitive period for sociocultural processing? *Annual Review of Psychology*, *65*, 187–207. https://doi.org/10.1146/annurev-psych-010213-115202

Boxer, A. M., & Cohler, B. J. (1989). The life course of gay and lesbian youth: An immodest proposal for the study of lives. *Journal of Homosexuality*, *17*(3–4), 315–355. https://doi.org/10.1300/J082v17n03_07

Boxer, A. M., Cohler, B. J., Herdt, G., & Irvin, F. (1993). Gay and lesbian youth. In P. H. Tolan & B. J. Cohler (Eds.), *Handbook of clinical research and practice with adolescents* (pp. 249–280). John Wiley & Sons.

Bronfenbrenner, U. (1977). Toward an experimental ecology of human development. *American Psychologist*, *32*(7), 513.

Bronfenbrenner, U., & Ceci, S. J. (1994). Nature-nurture re-conceptualised: A bio-ecological model. *Psychological Review*, *10*(4), 568–586.

Burstow, B. (2003). Toward a radical understanding of trauma and trauma work. *Violence Against Women*, *9*(11), 1293–1317. https://doi.org/10.1177/1077801203255555

Cass, V. (1979). Homosexual identity formation: A theoretical model. *Journal of Homosexuality*, *4*(3), 219–235.

Chen, X., & Graham, S. (2015). Cross-ethnic friendships and intergroup attitudes among Asian American adolescents. *Child Development*, *86*, 749–764. https://doi.org/10.1111/ cdev.12339

Daley, J. C.W. (2013). *Clinical social workers' use of self and the impact of personal therapy on practitioner development* [Unpublished master's thesis]. St. Catherine University. https://sophia.stkate.edu/msw_papers/166

D'Augelli, A., Rendina, J., Sinclair K., & Grossman A. (2007). Lesbian and gay youth's aspirations for marriage and raising children. *Journal of LGBT Issues in Counseling, 1*(4), 77–98.

D'Augelli A., & Hershberger, S. (1993). Lesbian, gay, and bisexual youth in community settings: Personal challenges and mental health problems. *American Journal of Community Psychology, 21*(4), 421–448.

Dewane, C. J. (2006). Use of self: A primer revisited. *Clinical Social Work Journal, 34*(4), 543–558. https://doi.org/10.1007/s10615-005-0021-5

Diamond, L. (2015). *Sexual fluidity.* In *The international encyclopedia of human sexuality.* Wiley. https://doi.org/10.1002/9781118896877.wbiehs452

Di Giacomo, E., Krausz, M., Colmegna, F., Aspesi, F., & Clerici, M. (2018). Estimating the risk of attempted suicide among sexual minority youths. *JAMA Pediatrics, 172*(12), 1145–1152. https://doi.org/10.1001/jamapediatrics.2018.2731

English, D., Lambert, S. F., Tynes, B. M., Bowleg, L., Zea, M. C., & Howard, L. C. (2020). Daily multidimensional racial discrimination among Black U.S. American adolescents. *Journal of Applied Developmental Psychology, 66*, Article 101068. https://doi.org/10.1016/j.appdev.2019.101068

Erikson E. (1963). *Childhood and society* (2nd ed.). Norton.

Erikson, E. (1968). *Identity: Youth and crisis.* Norton.

Fallot, R.D., (2011). *Creating cultures of trauma-informed care.* Substance Abuse and Mental Health Services Administration (SAMHSA). Treatment for Homeless Program Workshop.

Finkelhor, D., Shattuck, A., Turner, H., & Hamby, S. (2015). A revised inventory of adverse childhood experiences. , 48, 13–21. https://doi.org/10.1016/j.chiabu.2015.07.011

Gilligan, C. (2016). In a different voice. Harvard University Press.

Govrin, A. (2014). From ethics of care to psychology of care: Reconnecting ethics of care to contemporary moral psychology. *Frontiers of Psychology, 5*, 1135. https://doi.org/10.3389/fpsyg.2014.01135

Harris, M., & Fallot, R. D. (Eds.). (2001). *Using trauma theory to design service systems.* Jossey-Bass.

Hendrix, C. L., Dilks, D. D., McKenna, B. G., Dunlop, A. L., Corwin, E. J., & Patricia A. Brennan, P. A. (2021). Maternal childhood adversity associates with frontoamygdala connectivity in neonates. *Biological Psychiatry: Cognitive Neuroscience and Neuroimaging, 6*(4), 470–478. https://doi.org/10.1016/j.bpsc.2020.11.003

hooks, b. (1994). *Teaching to transgress.* Routledge.

hooks, b. (2010). *Teaching critical thinking.* Routledge.

Imad, M. (2022). Trauma-informed education for wholeness: Strategies for faculty & advisors. *New Directions for Student Services, 2022*(177), 39–47. https://doi.org/10.1002/ss.20413

Institute of Medicine (US) Committee on Lesbian, Gay, Bisexual, and Transgender Health Issues and Research Gaps and Opportunities. (2011). *The health of lesbian, gay, bisexual, and transgender people: Building a foundation for better understanding.* National Academies Press. https://www.ncbi.nlm.nih.gov/books/NBK64808/

Jugert, P., Leszczensky, L., & Pink, S. (2020). Differential influence of same- and cross-ethnic friends on ethnic-racial identity development in early adolescence. *Child Development, 91*(3), 949–963, https://doi.org/10.1111/cdev.13240

Kelly, M., & Coughlan, B. (2019). A theory of youth mental health recovery from a parental perspective. *Child and Adolescent Mental Health, 24*(2), 161–169.

Kohlberg, L. (1985). *Essays on moral development.* Harper & Row.

Layne, C. M., Ippen, C. G., Strand, V., Stuber, M., Abramovitz, R., Reyes, G., Jackson, L. A., Ross, L., Curtis, A., Lipscomb, L., & Pynoos, R. (2011). The core curriculum on childhood trauma: A tool for training a trauma-informed workforce. *Psychological Trauma: Theory, Research, Practice, and Policy*, *3*(3), 243–252. https://doi.org/10.1037/a0025039

Lippard, C. N., La Paro, K. M., Rouse, H. L., & Crosby, D. A. (2018). A closer look at teacher–child relationships and classroom emotional context in preschool. *Child & Youth Care Forum*, *47*(1), 1–21.

Love, B. (2013). Developing a liberatory consciousness. In W. B. M. Adams (Ed.), *Readings for diversity and social justice* (pp. 601–605). Routledge.

McCormick, C. M., Mathews, I. Z., Thomas, C., & Waters, P. (2010). Investigations of HPA function and the enduring consequences of stressors in adolescence in animal models. *Brain and Cognition*, *72*, 73–85.

Nadal, K. (2017). *SAGE encyclopedia of psychology and gender*. SAGE Publications.

National Scientific Council on Adolescence. (2021). *The intersection of adolescent development and anti-Black racism*. UCLA Center for the Developing Adolescent. https://developingadolescent.semel.ucla.edu/adolescence-and-anti-black-racism

NCTSN Core Curriculum on Childhood Trauma Task Force. (2012). *The 12 core concepts: Core curriculum on childhood trauma*. UCLA-Duke University National Center for Child Traumatic Stress.

Olmstead, S. (2020). A decade review of sex and partnering in adolescence and young adulthood. *Journal of Marriage and Family*, *82*, 769–795. https://doi.org/10.1111/jomf.12670

Pardo, S. & Devor, A. (2017). Transgender and gender nonconforming identity development. In K. Nadal (Ed.), SAGE encyclopedia of psychology and gender (pp. 1689–1692). SAGE Publications.

Piaget, J. (1972). Intellectual evolution from adolescence to adulthood. *Human Development*, *15*(1), 1–12.

Piaget, J. (2013). *The moral judgment of the child*. Routledge.

Quiros, L, (2009). *The social construction of racial and ethnic identity among women of color from mixed ancestry: Psychological freedoms and sociological constraints* [Unpublished doctoral dissertation]. City University of New York. https://academicworks.cuny.edu/gc_etds/1960

Quiros, L. (2021). *Incorporating diversity and inclusion into trauma-informed social work*. Routledge.

Rosario, M. Meyer-Bahlburg, H., Hunter, J., Exner, T., Gwadz, M., & Keller, A. (1996). The psychosexual development of urban lesbian, gay, and bisexual youths. *Journal of Sex Research*, *33*(2), 113–126.

Rosario, M., Schrimshaw, E. W., & Hunter, J. (2008). Predicting different patterns of sexual identity development over time among lesbian, gay, and bisexual youths: A cluster analytic approach. *American Journal of Community Psychology*, *42*(3–4), 266–282. https://doi.org/10.1007/s10464-008-9207-7

Ross, L. E., Salway, T., Tarasoff, L. A., MacKay, J. M., Hawkins, B. W., & Fehr, C. P. (2018). Prevalence of depression and anxiety among bisexual people compared to gay, lesbian, and heterosexual individuals: A systematic review and meta-analysis. *Journal of Sex Research*, *55* (4–5), 435–456. https://doi.org/10.1080/00224499.2017.1387755

Schwartz, R. (2021). *No bad parts: Healing trauma and restoring wholeness with the internal family systems mode*. Sounds True.

Shonkoff, J. P., Boyce, W., & McEwen, B. (2009). Neuroscience, molecular biology, and the childhood roots of health disparities: Building a new framework for health promotion and disease prevention. *Journal of the American Medical Association*, *301*(21), 2252–2259.

Steinberg, L., & Morris, A. S. (2001). Adolescent development. *Annual Review of Psychology*, *52*, 83–110.

Thompson, P., & Carello, J. (2022). Trauma-informed pedagogies: a guide for responding to crisis and inequality in higher education. Palgrave Macmillan.

Troiden R. (1989). The formation of homosexual identities. *Journal of Homosexuality*, 17(1–2):43–73.

The National Scientific Council on Adolescence (2021). *The intersection of adolescent development and anti-Black racism* (Council Report No. 1). Retrieved from https://developingadolescent.org.

Umaña-Taylor, A. J., Quintana, S. M., Lee, R. M., Cross, W. E., Rivas-Drake, D., Schwartz, S. J., … Seaton, E. (2014). Ethnic and racial identity during adolescence and into young adulthood: An integrated conceptualization. *Child Development, 85*, 21–39.

Veenstra, R., Dijkstra, J. K., & Kreager, D. A. (2018). Pathways, networks, and norms: A sociological perspective on peer research. In W. M. Bukowski, B. Laursen, & K. H. Rubin (Eds.), *Handbook of peer interactions, relationships, and groups (2nd ed., pp. 45–63)*. New York, NY: Guildford

CHAPTER 6

Hierarchies and Identity Development from Adolescence to Young Adulthood

AMELIA ORTEGA AND JAMALI MOSES

Introduction

This chapter explores the implications of the transition from adolescence into young adulthood and its implications for families of origin and choice as well as socioeconomic status, educational processes and outcomes, risk and protective behaviors, and social identity. We will heavily emphasize the school setting, where much of the socialization within this age cohort occurs.

This chapter employs self-reflexive praxis, a practice of critically understanding the self within the environment and within dynamic processes that unfold between human beings in social work. The vignette and case study illustrate the dynamic nature of self-development and healing for young people moving into early adulthood. This chapter includes a clinical vignette that has been co written with a young adult who engages multiple emerging identities as a source of his strength and healing generational trauma. This chapter also focuses on why and how schools can utilize restorative justice as a healing practice.

LEARNING OBJECTIVES

1. Develop knowledge about healing-centered, community-based practices for engaging emerging adults in trauma-informed, liberation-focused wellness support. (Competency 6)

2. Identify culturally attuned, anti-oppressive approaches to addressing the impacts of racial trauma with young adults. (Competency 3)

3. Identify ways educational settings can facilitate personal and systemic racial trauma healing for young adults. (Competency 4)

4. Develop and challenge the current description of social work in educational settings. (Competency 2)

Before continuing with this chapter, let's take a moment for some reflective engagement. Reflective engagement supports critical reading and self-reflection about your internal responses: How does your body feel? What thoughts are coming into your mind? What are you sensing emotionally within yourself? Prior to reading this chapter, you are encouraged to write down your responses to the following questions and to share with either a peer who is also reading this chapter or a small group that you are working with. Exchanging reflections and personal insights with peers aligns with the following National Association of Social Work (NASW, 2017) ethical principle: "Social workers recognize the central importance of human relationships" (Ethical Principles section). We learn and grow in social settings, connected to other humans and through collaborative, shared meaning making. Together, consider the following:

1. When you hear the term "legacy healing," what comes to mind?

2. What significant experiences first come to mind when you consider your transition from adolescence to young adulthood? Was this a time in your life that was marked by any cultural celebration/expectation/new role within the family?

3. When you think through your own multiple social locations, what assumptions do you think are made most often about young adults of your generation? Do you respond to these assumptions? If so, how?

4. How has your transition from adolescence to emerging adulthood reflected parts of your family's generational story? How has it been a departure from prior generations?

Transitional Aged Youth

Transitional aged youth (TAY) are generally between the ages of 16 and 25 years old. Within this diverse age cohort are individuals transitioning from child- and youth-serving institutional supports to adult services. While there is socialized pressure to transition to adulthood, it is important to remember that "the age may not match the stage." In other words, the chronological age of the individual may not synch up with the client's emotional needs. Many TAY need additional socioemotional care and community-based assistance to navigate toward emerging adulthood and the tasks required for the transition to more independence. Critically understanding that TAY may need additional support for school, housing, and mental health care navigation is key to collaboration within a liberation health model framework—a concept we will delve into later in the chapter.

Healing in Schools

We open our discussion of TAY by starting in the setting and institution in which youth may spend a lot (or a little) amount of time and may serve as not only a place in which trauma may be experienced but also a place, we argue, in which healing can occur. Educational institutions have incredible power over the well-being of individuals in any society. On the surface, most will associate educational institutions with academic learning or skills training. Less discussed is the long withstanding impact of educational systems on young people, especially those who do not identify as heterosexual, Anglo-Saxon, neurotypical, and male. The disparity of positive educational experiences and impact is evident in the United States. From *Brown v. Board of Education* in the Supreme Court of the 1950s to contemporary issues of Black and Latinx students in New York City having the highest suspension, drop out, and incarceration rates, holistic, equitable, and healing (or at least trauma-informed) educational experiences are not as prevalent as they should be. School violence such as Parkland and Columbine showed the world that young people with severe mental health issues may also suffer at the hands of ill-equipped school systems. It can be easy for social work professionals who are not formally trained educators, but are employed in schools, to provide services that are only targeted toward academic enhancement and improvement while neglecting holistic and emotional well-being. In being unilaterally focused on academics, school social workers can miss opportunities to facilitate healing spaces, activities, and therapy while challenging and changing harmful subsystems in educational settings. In this chapter, we will discuss healing and effective restorative justice practices in schools that disrupt the school-to-prison pipeline (a collaborative paradigm between schools with zero-tolerance policies and the justice system) and how to be a practitioner who goes beyond managing symptomatology.

 THEORY ↔ PRACTICE

Moving Beyond Managing Symptoms

Many of the tools developed to address a young adult's mental health in an educational setting tend to lean toward symptom management exclusively. Such helpful tools include social emotional learning curriculums, anger management programs, and mindfulness programs. Symptom management is necessary in helping young adults self-regulate. The skill of self-regulation is needed to exhibit skills and behaviors that lead to academic success (Leenarts, 2013). However, focusing on symptom management without assessing or treating the possible core beliefs or trauma at the root of the young person's dysregulation may only be a short-term solution. School clinicians should also keep in mind that the emotional dysregulation that many young people exhibit is a human response (hyper or hypo arousal) to high stress or traumatic experiences (Schupp, 2015). If symptomology and behaviors are left unassessed for trauma, it can be under- or overdiagnosed and treated exclusively as other disorders, such as attention-deficit/hyperactivity disorder, conduct disorder, generalized anxiety disorder, and other *DSM* personality disorders (Kaminer et al., 2005). These disorders may be applicable as a secondary diagnosis but are often designated and treated as the primary diagnosis. School clinicians who are interested in moving beyond symptom management and treating stress and trauma should consider the following:

- *time and resources*: School social workers tend to have many roles in schools with a huge caseload and limited time. Clinically addressing trauma and stress can be time and energy consuming as a clinician. If a school social worker is interested in moving past symptom management into helping students process their trauma, they may need to get creative. Some possible ideas include using groups, asking school leadership to use classes like homeroom/advisory and health classes for socioemotional learning, and teaching techniques around healthy coping and self-regulation strategies (instead of the clinical space). School social workers should also consider monetary resources for training and supplies (if applicable) and having a consistent physical space for healing to take place.

- *support from educator colleagues and school leadership*: School social workers should not work apart or siloed from their educator colleagues. Educators are often the first people in the school setting to encounter students emotionally and mentally. Creating trusting allyship with educators is a necessity for successful therapeutic intervention. The same is true with regard to school leadership, as they are the gatekeepers of the school resources and culture. Ideally, school social workers should assess if their school communities have or are interested in being trauma informed before implementing this practice.

- *support from the parent/caregiver body*: If possible, a school social worker who is interested in healing should also consider how to do so from a systems perspective. Though there may not be enough time and resources to address healing the family working in a school setting, having the support from primary caregivers to work with their children in a healing way while at school is necessary.

- *ongoing education and training in therapeutic modalities*: Many therapeutic modalities are oriented in managing symptoms or lack supportive quantitative data on their effectiveness. School social workers should stay abreast and/or get training on evidence-based interventions. Offering the best of what our field has to offer to students who historically have been neglected and oppressed is revolutionary. Currently, trauma-focused cognitive behavior therapy (TFCBT) and eye movement desensitization and reprocessing (EMDR) are two evidence-based interventions for trauma.

- *non-Westernized healing (decolonizing therapy)*: Traditional social work education and training is rooted in White centrality and Westernized ideology. However, healing emotionally and mentally is not a White or Westernized concept exclusively. School clinicians should consider incorporating forms of healing that have origins in cultures and histories from different parts of the world. Decolonizing healing and therapy by using ideologies that are founded by various cultures of the **global majority** has the potential to centralize a healing process that may feel more genuine to the student client. Healing circles and mindfulness/meditation are two well-known therapeutic modalities that are being used increasingly and have origins that are not White and Westernized.

It is imperative that a school social worker assess if they can hold healing time and spaces in the school setting for students struggling with stress and trauma. Starting this work without carefully assessing if the support and resources are available can cause disruption of services, which can do more harm to student clients.

Demolishing the School-to-Prison Pipeline with Restorative Justice

According to data for 2021 on the NYC Department of Education (NYC DOE, n.d.) the NYC DOE is the largest school district in the United States, with 1,058,888 students. Amongst this student population of over a million children, adolescents, and young adults, 82% of them identify as the world majority (predominantly Latinx, Black, and Asian). These statistics potentially point to the NYC DOE as one of the largest educational agencies serving youth of the world majority. Keeping in mind that structural, institutional, and individual racism are woven into the fabric of U.S. systems and culture (DeGruy, 2017), it is imperative that clinicians who work in schools and are interested in healing should consider ways of dismantling parts of education culture that sustain harm and racism. There are many subsystems that need healing and dismantling in education. Shifting traditional curriculum and pedagogy from a Eurocentric to a critical race lens with inclusion of real-life skills and concepts (e.g., understanding credit cards and paying taxes) are ways schools can begin to heal and dismantle racist ideologies in education. While social workers can have an influence in curriculum and pedagogy creation, they can have the most influence of change within systems involving student mental health and behavior. One system influenced by these factors is what has become known as the school-to-prison pipeline.

The School-to-Prison Pipeline

According to Bacher-Hicks et al. (2019), youth who attend school regularly are less likely to be involved in criminal activity. Conversely, there is a positive correlation between missing school and criminal justice involvement amongst youth. The disciplinary practice in schools of punishing youth by forcing absenteeism (suspension and expulsion) can increase the likelihood of criminal activity, arrest, and eventual incarceration, a process known as the **school-to-prison pipeline**. According to the NYC DOE's (2020) *Annual Report on Student Discipline 2019–2020*, Black and Latinx students have the highest suspension rates. One can argue that this is because the majority of the youth in the NYC DOE educational system racially identify as a member of the global majority. However, this staggering statistic is true nationwide. According to Kamenetz (2018), Black high school–aged youth are twice as likely to be suspended from school than their White counterparts and students with disabilities are twice as likely to be suspended than their counterparts without a disability. Comparatively, according to Nellis's (2021) *The Color of Justice*, for every 100,000 residents in the United States there are 1,240 Black people imprisoned, 349 Latinx people imprisoned, and 261 White people imprisoned.

Juxtaposing suspension rates and incarceration rates in the United States, it becomes obvious that people who are descendants of the African diaspora are the most vulnerable to the school-to-prison pipeline.

Restorative Justice: Choosing a Healing Approach Instead of Punishment

Most unsafe and undesirable behaviors begin with emotional distress or dysregulation (Selby et al., 2008). People of the world majority are more at risk to have experiences that can trigger emotional distress due to (but not exclusively) all forms of racism and discrimination (Saleem et al., 2019). This should be the groundwork for **restorative justice (RJ)** practices in schools and programs that serve transitional aged youth of the global majority. Additionally, RJ should be a practice exclusively of healing and restoration from harm and not punishment (Davis, 2019). RJ practices in schools can dismantle the school-to-prison pipeline by offering healing spaces for students' behavior instead of punishment.

The practice that many RJ practitioners utilize are circles. Mostly called **healing circles, talking circles, or fairness circles**, the practice of community members coming together to address important issues can be found in many Indigenous cultures around the world (Davis, 2019). In schools, the circles can be used to address interests, needs, and concerns about the school and larger community while allowing youth to build trust and rapport with one another (Boyes-Watson & Pranis, 2015). Circles can also be used to address when a member of the school community harms themselves or the community with their behavior. An example of harm can be a student who is late to school every day or verbal altercations between two school community members. Harm in this context does not mean suicidal or homicidal ideation or actions; instead, it means some sort of disruption to the harmony of the school community, the individual learning process, and community learning process.

RESTORATIVE CIRCLES: GUIDELINES

Have participants seated in a circle. Sitting in a circle means no one is the head or gatekeeper of the process. A person can facilitate the process but should not monopolize the process.

All participants should engage in active listening. Facilitating circle trainings where active listening skills are taught can help. Also, having a talking piece (an object that is passed around to participants when they want to speak) can help participants with this process.

Use a problem-solving lens and not a judicial lens. The circle process should not be about innocence or guilt, but healing, accountability, and problem solving.

Review the process with participants before you start. Letting participants know the steps in the process beforehand can alleviate any stress and anxiety.

Everyone in the circle should agree to be there, including the person who is responsible for the harm to the community.

The process used in facilitating circles to address harm should be tailored to fit the school's identity and needs. However, here are some important elements that should be prioritized for successful implementation of RJ practices that addresses harm:

- true equity: Harm can be done by anyone in the school community. Keeping this in mind, all members in the school community can participate in or be referred for an RJ circle (staff and students alike).

- community buy-in: The circle process is one that involves the whole community. Therefore, it is important for RJ practitioners to be mindful of building trust and relationships with school community members before implementing RJ.

- formal referral system: Creating a formal referral system for the school community is helpful with management and formalizing the beginning of the entire circle process.

- RJ point person(s): There should be a person (or people) who is the RJ entity in the school. This person trains, facilitates, and holds circles and other RJ practices. This should also be the person who receives all RJ referrals.

- balanced circle: After a referral is made, the RJ point person should find participants within the school community of various roles and titles to participate in the circle. All participants, including the school member who caused harm, should agree to participate in the process.

- the circle process: The circle process should start with an explanation of the process. There are many ways circles can be facilitated, but there are some universal components, such as active listening, "I" statements, giving the person who caused harm a chance to tell their perspective of what happened, and everyone in the circle committing to an action to help the person who caused harm to grow and heal so that the harm does not happen again.

- following up: The RJ point person or another community member who participated in the circle should follow up with everyone else about the process and if any everyone is meeting their commitment made in the circle. There should also be follow up with the community member whom the circle was held for and, if necessary, clinical services offered or referred.

RESTORATIVE JUSTICE TRAINING CENTERS AND FACILITIES
The Restorative Center
New York Peace Institute
Suffolk University (Boston)
Restorative Justice Ed

Limitations to Restorative Justice

School social workers who want to use RJ in their practice can get training or certifications at a variety of institutions. Aspiring RJ practitioners should be aware that some youth with severe neurodivergence or cognitive disabilities may need other forms of RJ in addition to or instead of a circle. Daily counseling, reaching out to parents, and giving access to safe quiet spaces are ways to enhance the circle experience.

There are many ways healing can happen in schools. As a social work student (many, many years ago), the mantra at the time was to "start where the client is." This still rings true for social workers in schools. However, a wider lens is required: Taking an inventory of the school culture, systems, and student needs will point the school social worker toward what needs to be enhanced, challenged, or facilitated. Being an agent of change will come with challenges, resistance, and gatekeeping that may cause the school social worker to want to submit to the systems and policies that sustain oppression. Going against the grain will always take immense amounts of courage, energy, and constant healing of self for the school social worker.

Liberation-Centered Social Work Practice

Another model that can be powerful in terms of healing when working with youth and can be used in outside-of-school settings is the liberation-centeremmodel. Historically, social work education has used a Westernized approach to understanding human development (Clarke, 2022; Chapman & Withers, 2019), which is an approach that has been centered in a deficit analysis particular to the chronological aging process. While traditional human development perspectives used words such as "stages" and "phases" to organize the process of aging, more current thinking offers a "person-in-environment" approach (Hutchinson, 2005). The **developmental life course perspective (DCLP)** offers an intersectional lens through which to view the key turning points and transitions of our lives in an environmental context (Hutchinson, 2005). There is much to explore in terms of the transitions that occur between adolescence and young adulthood. We can understand that there is great diversity in the outcomes of our transitions between adolescence and young adulthood due to the complexities of family structure, community surrounding us, and our own sense of selfhood. The DLCP is a framework that supports building a critical perspective *with* those that we are working alongside and can help to illuminate the root causes of present-day inequities, challenges, and points of access to healing and health. Working alongside or using a collaborative practice with a client supports reduction in the power differential traditionally experienced between a provider and client. Drawn from a principle of feminist psychology, "working with" promotes egalitarian relationships (Maass, 2021, p. 105) and a deeper understanding that the client is an expert of their own experience. Applying a theory as detailed as the DLCP requires building trust and rapport. Traditionally, the DLCP has been taught as a framework from which we can build a detailed life course narrative. Social workers do not often have the opportunity to explore an individual's full life story due to structural constraints, which can include short sessions regulated by third-party insurance, agency limitations, and a grounding of services in community-based short-term engagement.

The **liberation health model** (Belkin-Martinez & Fleck-Henderson, 2014) similarly offers a framework that can be more easily engaged in a variety of health and healthcare settings. The Liberation Health Model asserts that direct practice must be informed by structural analysis (Belkin-Martinez & Fleck-Henderson, 2014). This analysis can be collaborative and supports new meaning making for young adult clients who are considered transitional aged youth.

The following narrative illustrates the use of a liberation health model in framing growth, healing, and making meaning of complex family context. This narrative was fully coauthored in a partnership with Ethan, a young adult who received counseling services through my practice for many years. Using a queer feminist psychotherapy lens in our work supported an egalitarian relationship over the years. Ethan remains the expert of his own experience and developed his voice throughout our work together to share his narrative and insights both within and outside of the counseling relationship. The author, remains a compassionate witness and partner in the work that is liberation health centered here. The coauthoring process was trauma informed and structured through transparent conversations about the intended use of this text, Ethan's reflections on his transition from adolescence to young adulthood, and Ethan and I building the text together with a focus on him telling his own story.

DEVELOPMENTAL LIFE COURSE PERSPECTIVE

An organizing framework that we can use to understand human development across the life course (from birth to death). This framework supports us to examine the impact of time and social context (Hutchinson, 2005) and utilizes an intersectional perspective based on six core principles:

- lives in historical time and place
- timing in lives
- diversity of the life course
- linked lives
- human agency in constrained environments
- development risk and protection

LIBERATION HEALTH FRAMEWORK (BELKIN-MARTINEZ & FLECK-HENDERSON, 2014)

A method of practice that helps individuals, families, and communities understand the personal, cultural, and institutional factors that contribute to their problem and act to change these conditions; to liberate themselves from both internal and external oppressions.

Case Study: Writing a New Way—Queerness, Latinidad, Young Adulthood

Ethan and I met when he was 16 years old, he having been referred to a community based mental health group practice by his mother. At the time, I was working as a trauma-focused therapist at a Latinx-owned and Latinx-serving group psychotherapy practice where Ethan and I met for weekly sessions together. Ethan is now 25 years old and he has continued to engage with behavioral health care through my individual psychotherapy practice for the last 7 years. When we first met, Ethan's mother shared that he was experiencing violent bullying at school, had stopped attending classes, and had been absent from school for most of the semester. Ethan lived a few blocks from my office, with his two brothers, mother, father, and his paternal grandmother. Ethan's intergenerational household was described to me as very busy and full of perpetual noise; space was limited, and there was frequent conflict about the scarcity of resources. When describing his home environment, Ethan states, "If you had money to spend, you were expected to spend it on everyone you lived with. If you could save money, spend it immediately." Ethan used his sessions with me to share his experiences with school bullying, his awareness of his own non heteronormativity within his Latino family, and his passion for writing and music. We often explored the gendered and socialized norms of his family, the direct messages he received about growing older, and how his identities pushed against these expectations. Ethan shares about these expectations, "You grow up with two values. The first was to stay in school, and the second was to make a lot of money. You're not sure how they correlate or how that works, but don't need to know. You are going to be the savior your parents need, and that's enlightening enough." Ethan was fearful of both sharing his political viewpoints and newly discovered insights about his sexuality with specific family members due to the outward homophobia and sexism he witnessed; and he worried that rejection would also mean rejecting his family's collective needs. Together, we worked using somatic approaches for anxiety self-management and to support Ethan to share his truth in the therapeutic space as a way of holding the complexity of all his identities—with no part left behind. Ethan states:

> When you're a teenager you decide you don't like school because you don't like feeling small or insignificant and you don't like that everyone talks to you like you know less than them. Sometimes you know more, sometimes people like that you know more, but who can you trust, anyway? It's hard to go outside. Your values are warped. Your parents don't make you feel like the savior you were supposed to be.

Sessions with Ethan were structured by lighting a candle when we began to talk, included breaks for brief meditations, games to build connection, and writing prompts for him to use and explore his inner wisdom outside of our weekly meetings. About his experience following these prompts, Ethan remembers:

> I took a whimsical approach to getting to know myself: writing about myself like a character in a movie. The rest of the cast was the city, my family, and the

feelings that surrounded me the more I neglected them. Through writing I got more practice with identifying and processing my feelings. This act directly contradicted my family, masculinity, and my role as an angsty, secretly angry teenager in New York City.

Ethan was often escorted to the office for our sessions by his aunt, his brother, and sometimes multiple family members. There was curiosity about what he was doing "in therapy." Occasionally, sessions also included a "chosen" family member, usually a friend, and we were able to discuss the importance and power of naming and choosing family as we age. Queer youth in transition may experience family-of-origin rejection and, like Ethan, find reflection in shared representation with peers. Kinship family structures are diverse in structure and complex in function as adolescents move through unique identity formation processes. When working with TAY it can be useful to evaluate and explore notions of family that are expansive and encompass individuals and communities unique to the social and emotional needs of the individual—and are not bound by birth or family of origin.

As a teenager, Ethan spent most days alone at his grandmother's house. His brothers were in school, and older adults were working or outside the home. We worked together to address his mother's concerns about a safety transfer to a new school, as he increasingly expressed interest in returning to school and it was clear that he felt ready to socialize again. I provided Ethan's mother with psychoeducation about sexuality, gender, and adolescent development. These collaborative sessions were important to building trust with Ethan's family, supporting Ethan's self-advocacy skills, and understanding the generational narrative of his family. The stories shared in these sessions illuminated grief for the loss of his mother's own adolescence and the disappointments and guilt that she has carried. The family's cultural perspectives about Ethan's role in the family and the constant labor of managing a large family with housing instability often left Ethan feeling invisible. Ethan's requests to bring in a friend or family member broadened my capacity to understand and connect with the larger context of this environment he was in while moving through adolescence. Ethan shared the following about this time in our work together:

> The truth is that I wasn't entirely aware of what I was doing. I didn't want to go to school, I didn't want to talk to people my age, I didn't want to participate in anything. Still, these were things that were expected of me, and I couldn't stand to disappoint anyone. Before I was an adult driven to do right by myself and my complex relationship with my inner child, I was a teenager driven toward my goals by a deep fear of disappointing people. A reflex rooted in Catholic guilt, or by how heartbroken I felt when I disappointed my mother as a kid. If I let someone down, they would hate me and I would be unlovable. I was an empathetic kid who often tried to guess what my parents were thinking and feeling. I would take on the task of fixing whatever was stressing them out because that's how I understood my role in the family. My mom confessed to me that when I was a kid, she would sometimes want to shake me by the shoulders and go, "Please

act like a kid!" I found that if I fixed my own behavior, my own personality and habits, I could make life for my parents just a little bit better. It was how I learned to approach every problem: How am I wrong, and what can I do differently?

Ethan's internalization of his family's conflicts and stress contributed to a sense of responsibility that collided with his developmental tasks to individuate, to come out and to express himself. We worked together, exploring his outlets for queerness in film, writing, and music while he simultaneously balanced a need for safety with his growing sense of self.

Within a year of collaborative sessions, Ethan felt ready to transition to a new school, and I supported a referral to an all-LGBTQ high school in New York City. Ethan's new school was made up of many transitional aged youth, small classes, and personalized support for life outside the classroom. The high school offered wrap-around case management services through a partner LGBTQ-youth-serving organization, a food pantry, community meals, afterschool programs, and college readiness support. When Ethan entered high school again, he took a risk by not only joining a new community but also breaking a legacy cycle. When we reflected on this school transfer experience, Ethan included this narrative:

> There was a time in my 11th year where I skipped a day of school and I panicked over the teachers I was letting down. To avoid those feelings, I skipped the next day and the day after that. My principal, a sharp and direct woman, had a meeting with my mom and I where I confessed I didn't show up because I couldn't face disappointing anyone. "I'm not going to lie, Ethan, I was incredibly disappointed," she said. She was calm, she sounded sad, and for the first time I wasn't heartbroken. I'd disappointed my community, but they weren't going to close any doors on me. I spent an afternoon at school one semester trying to explain my feelings for a chosen family member in my life. One of the many readily available guidance counselors at school explained: "I think it's safe to say you hold love for this person." That is what it was: a deep respect and love for the community that showed me unconditional support. It was a personal and fundamental component to who I am today and to what I needed to disassemble my family's legacy cycles. I've learned later as an adult that my mother used to sleep with the weight of the world every night, and in the moments where she was just as confused and scared as I was, she was her most human. But she was never disappointed in me.

Prior to the school transfer, Ethan spent his days writing chapters of a novel that he was dreaming up and organizing musical playlists for different emotions for each day of the week. We incorporated reading his novel chapters and engaging in creative writing together in our sessions. Ethan increasingly agreed to read his own work out loud and to practice hearing his own voice. These listening and reflection sessions became a strategy for building confidence to engage in school groups, writing projects, and eventually an LGBTQ youth public speaking board. As a member of the youth speak-out project, Ethan traveled city-wide to schools and organizations telling his coming out story and describes this experience:

> With a narrative focusing on defining queer identity, we shared our most vulnerable stories with audiences from middle school to college, answered their questions, connected with them. In the end we were trying to help young people recontextualize their vision of LGBTQ people from what they'd previously known to the human beings we are, to the kids we were.

At 18, Ethan's narrative about his struggle shifted from centering a personal pathology of depression and anxiety to a nuanced narrative that spoke to the socioeconomic conditions of his family's life at home, the complexity of his relationship to gender and sexuality in his Latinx family, and his analysis of the impact of his internalized oppression.

Ethan's ability to use writing for emotional catharsis and as a strategy to connect with others supported him to gain a summer internship at *The Huffington Post*. Ethan describes this time:

> I spent two summers with that internship. The second time was fueled by the success of finishing high school and fitting into stylish clothes for the first time, so I had both the confidence and shamelessness to harass my internship managers for an essay spot on their online arts and culture publication. I'd always been a writer, only now with the backing of published work.

Key adults who worked with TAY supported Ethan as he made the transition from high school. His guidance counselor, teachers, therapist, and friends created a network of resources as he left the school and planned what was next. Ethan's confidence to show up as himself with a multitude of identities, including his queerness and Latinidad, represented his process of self-actualization as his self story grew to encompass pride. In his senior year, Ethan applied for scholarships as he continued to focus on his writing while starting classes at a local undergraduate institution. Ethan's journey from adolescence to young adulthood was marked by risk-taking to try on new identities such as "intern," "graduate," and "writer." Ethan now produces *7 the Magazine*, an arts-focused magazine printed in New York City. Ethan says that he chose the name because the number 7 represents a complete cycle. Ethan continues to live with his family in lower Manhattan, where he continues to write and attend college.

You can access *7 the Magazine* by scanning the QR code below.

Visit: https://www.7thezine.com/

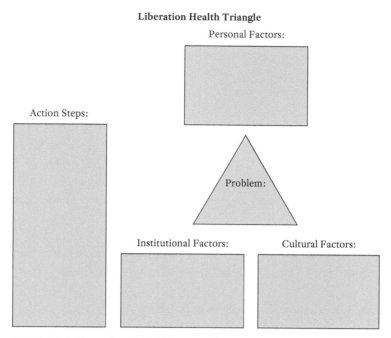

FIGURE 6.1 Liberation Health Framework

Figure 6.1 illustrates the **liberation health triangle**, a visual map of the three contextual areas of consideration when practicing from this perspective. In my work with Ethan, we collaborated to understand the personal, institutional, and cultural factors that were informing his experience of the "problem," which was originally believed to be Ethan's depression. Over time, we came to change this story to understand together what a complex web of problems were manifesting in all the members of his family, the neighborhood, and larger society. While Ethan's separation from school came to represent his pathology (depression and anxiety), it became clear that his queerness also allowed for the family system to culturally identify him as the problem. Ethan shares this insight: "To be queer meant to think differently than my family. To be the second generation of an immigrant family meant that my struggles were mental, and not anything that can be measured against what others in my family had been through." Entering therapy with a core belief that he must be measured against the suffering of others led us to explore community-based trauma, cultural transmissions of trauma responses, and the validity of healing. Ethan states, "I went from 'How am I the problem?' to 'How has everything both within and beyond our control moved together to lead us to where we are now?' I didn't know it then, but understanding the DNA of our community trauma was understanding how to heal."

THEORY ↔ PRACTICE

Tips and Tools for Using a Liberation Health Model in Practice

tool: Print out or screen share the liberation health model triangle. This visual tool can be used collaboratively to support egalitarian relationship building and can become a shared document to record changes in shared understanding of the problem being worked on.

tip: Take a personal inventory of your own experiences with transitioning to young adulthood. What parts of your narrative feel present today? What assumptions about adulthood or family inform your social work practice? How might these be showing up with clients as well?

tool: Mapping! Use Google Maps or another mapping service to create a unique map or list of services, organizations, and resources for TAY in the local area. Pick out different places and pin them virtually, or create a list in the notes section of their phone to access at any time outside of session. You can share this virtual map with TAY that you are supporting and collaboratively add resources that are being recommended or used frequently by local TAY.

tip: Engage with the liberation health model through additional reading, training, or peer-to-peer supervision. Articles and additional reading can be found on the Boston Liberation Health website (https://bostonliberationhealth.org/resources).

In practice, the liberation health framework supports:

- thinking broadly and through a queer lens regarding who constitutes family (also see Chapter 3) and including friends and chosen family in mental health sessions to reduce stigma

- critical analysis of how to navigate chronic family conflict and how to understand this as a manifestation of institutional and socioeconomic oppression

- strengths-based story sharing about family lineages of resiliency, resistance, and *ganas* (Spanish for "motivation")

- cultivating new meaning about the stories we have been told about ourselves and stories we want to rewrite

- critical analysis of the barriers to transitioning from high school and youth services to codevelop action plans for the transition process.

- individuals identifying personal actions to take as a part of social justice advocacy within systems designed with large gaps in care

Centering our humanity in the work of healing is a project that pushes directly against the systems of oppression that mold us all. Claiming our full humanity, our right to liberation from negative self-beliefs, and finding power in collective action are possible in mental health practice. As social workers, we carry a history of "benevolent violence" (Chapman & Withers, 2019). This can be seen in the history of our profession, which has embodied the colonial projects of erasure and minimization of the realities of oppression in the daily lives of Black, Indigenous, and communities of the global majority. Use of the liberation health model can support clients to move outside a traditional binary narrative of "sickness/wellness" and aid in building personal agency, unburdening legacy traumas, and making visible all that is active and present in the room. I have had the honor of collaborating on this narrative summary and analysis with Ethan throughout this chapter. This cowriting decision is a direct contradiction to the histories of our collective people being written *about* without consideration of impact and ownership. This process has provided both Ethan and I a space to reflect on the significance of this therapeutic relationship and to engage with larger stories of healing and growth together. Consent, agency, and voice are vital components in the work of healing our deepest wounds, and it is my hope that we continue to examine the constructed divide between lived experience and classroom education in social work schools. What follows are a few suggestions regarding where to start if you are interested in using this model with TAY and additional resources for your mental health liberation path.

CONCLUSION

This chapter discussed two contemporary approaches to healing from the impacts of structural oppression and experiences of trauma. This chapter encourages social workers to consider family and school environments as primary sites for healing and liberation practices. The liberation health model was explored as a client-centered framework that offers a culturally oriented relational model for working with clients toward healing and wholeness. Additionally, mental and emotional healing can happen in schools. School social workers can be social and culture agents of change by utilizing holistic and healing approaches with students and with school community. Restorative justice is an approach that school social workers can utilize to dismantle the extremely harmful school-to-prison pipeline. Having looked at the transition from adolescence to young adulthood, the next chapter examines young adulthood more closely.

KEY TERMS

- Transitional aged youth (TAY): a demographic of young people aged 15–26 who are engaged with any organized service (such as mental health, health care, school programming, housing support etc.). This diverse demographic spans adolescence through young adulthood, and experiences the challenges of aging out of pediatric or youth services however is culturally and socially too young for adult services.

- Global majority: sometimes used to describe the majority of people globally who are non-white. Statistically, BIPOC communities are the global majority. This term is used to illuminate the disparities which impact the majority of people across the world.

- School-to-prison pipeline:school-based disciplinary actions that forces students to be absent from school or class (i.e.- suspension) which increases the likelihood of student involvement in the justice system. This type of discipline is primarily targeted towards TAY of the world majority.

- Restorative justice (RJ): a set of Indigenous community-based practices that promote exploration and healing in lieu of punishment.

- Healing circles/talking circles/fairness circles: a specific RJ practice that uses groups within a community to address topics and issues that affect the community. The groups typically gather and sit in a circle which has significant symbolism of healing and equality.

- Developmental life course perspective (DCLP): a framework for understanding human development across the life course (birth to death) which centers an intersectional analysis through the use of six core principles.

- Liberation health model: a wellness model that supports an intersectional and collaborative approach to understanding and working with the context for healing and health goals.

- Liberation health triangle: a visual map of the three primary points of analysis within the Liberation Health Model (personal, institutional, and cultural). The triangle is a concrete and collaborative tool which can be used directly with clients.

DISCUSSION QUESTIONS

1. Consider the area of practice you are most interested in, how might the Liberation Health Model be integrated into this area of work? What do you imagine may facilitate this integration? What barriers might exist?

2. Consider a current dilemma in your own community, family or a peer group that you belong to. How might you understand this dilemma or struggle through a critical application of the liberation health model? What personal, institutional and cultural factors are influencing this dilemma or struggle?

3. What feelings or emotions emerged for you while reading through Ethan's personal narrative? What might these emotions help you to understand about your own journey through young adulthood? What social norms or expectations did you experience during young adulthood or your transition aged years? How are these social norms or expectations informing your experience of reading this narrative?

4. Take a moment and reflect on your educational experiences when you were a TAY. What emotional support systems (non-academic) did you have at your school setting at this time in your life? If you had a lot of support, why do you think that is? Conversely, if you did not have much support, why do you think that is?

5. Are there other institutions and systems that you think can have a direct effect on demolishing the school to prison pipeline?

6. Restorative justice is a practice that is contrary to traditional educational culture. What are some barriers you can foresee trying to implement this practice in schools? Develop some ideas about how you would address these barriers.

REFERENCES

Bacher-Hicks, A., Billings, S., & Deming, D. (2019). *The school-to-prison pipeline: Long-run impacts of school suspensions on adult crime.* National Bureau of Economic Research. https://doi.org/10.3386/w26257

Boyes-Watson, C., & Pranis, K. (2015). *Circle forward.* Living Justice Press.

Chapman, Chris, and A.J. Withers. A Violent History of Benevolence: Interlocking Oppression in the Moral Economies of Social Working. University of Toronto Press, 2019. https://doi.org/10.3138/9781442625082.

Clarke, K. (2022). Reimagining social work ancestry: Toward epistemic decolonization. *Affilia*, *37*(2), 266–278. https://doi.org/10.1177/08861099211051326

Davis, F. (2019). *Race and restorative justice.* Skyhorse Publications.

DeGruy, J. (2017). *Post traumatic slave syndrome: America's legacy of enduring injury and healing.* Joy DeGruy Publications.

Diaz, J. (2022, May 25). *27 school shootings have taken place so far this year.* NPR. https://www.npr.org/2022/05/24/1101050970/2022-school-shootings-so-far

Duran, E., Firehammer, J., & Gonzalez, J. (2008), Liberation psychology as the path toward healing cultural soul wounds. *Journal of Counseling & Development*, *86*(3), 288–295. https://doi.org/10.1002/j.1556-6678.2008.tb00511.x

Elder, G. H., & Shanahan, M. J. (2006). The life course and human development. In R. M. Lerner & W. Damon (Eds.), *Handbook of child psychology: Vol. 1. Theoretical models of human development* (6th ed., pp. 665–715). John Wiley & Sons.

Hutchison, E. D. (2005). The life course perspective: A promising approach for bridging the micro and macro worlds for social workers. *Families in Society*, *86*(1), 143–152. https://doi.org/10.1606/1044-3894.1886

Kamenetz, A. (2018, December 17). *Suspensions are down in the U.S. schools but large racial gaps remain.* NPR. https://www.npr.org/2018/12/17/677508707/suspensions-are-down-in-u-s-schools-but-large-racial-gaps-remain

Kaminer, D., Seedat, S., & Stein, D. (2005). Post-traumatic stress disorder in children. *World Psychiatry*, *4*(2), 121–125.

Leenarts, L. E., Diehle, J., Doreleijers, T. A., Jansma, E. P., & Lindauer, R. J. (2012). Evidence-based treatments for children with trauma-related psychopathology as a result of childhood maltreatment: A systematic review. *European Child & Adolescent Psychiatry*, 22(5), 269–283. https://doi.org/10.1007/s00787-012-0367-5

Maass, V. S. (2021). *Feminist psychology: History, practice, research, and the future.* ABC-CLIO.

Martinez, D. B., & Fleck-Henderson, A. (Eds.). (2014). *Social justice in clinical practice: A liberation health framework for social work.* Routledge

National Association of Social Workers. (2017). *Code of ethics of the National Association of Social Workers.* https://www.socialworkers.org/about/ethics/code-of-ethics/code-of-ethics-english

Nellis, A. (2021). *The color of justice.* The Sentencing Project.

New York City Department of Education. (n.d.). *DOE data at a glance*. https://www.schools.nyc.gov/about-us/reports/doe-data-at-a-glance

New York City Department of Education. (2020). *Annual report on student discipline 2019–2020.* https://infohub.nyced.org/reports/government-reports/suspension-reports

Saleem, F., Anderson, R., & Williams, A. (2019). Addressing the "myth" of racial trauma: Developmental and ecological considerations for youth of color. *Clinical Child and Family Psychology Review, 23*(1), 1–14. https://doi.org/10.1007/s10567-019-00304-1

Schupp, L. (2014). *Assessing and treating trauma and PTSD*. PESI Publishing & Media.

Selby, E., Anestis, M., & Joiner, T. (2008). Understand the relationship between emotional and behavioral dysregulation: Emotional cascade. *Behaviour Research and Therapy, 46*(5), 593–611. https://doi.org/10.1016/j.brat.2008.02.002

Sokol, B., Grouzet, F., Muller, U. (2013). *Self-regulation and autonomy: Social and developmental dimensions of human conduct.* Cambridge University Press.

Wald, J., & Losen, D. (2003). Defining and redirecting school-to-prison pipeline. *New Directions for Youth Development, 2003*(99), 9–15. https://doi.org/10.1002/yd.51

CREDIT

Fig. 6.1: Source: https://bostonliberationhealth.org/.

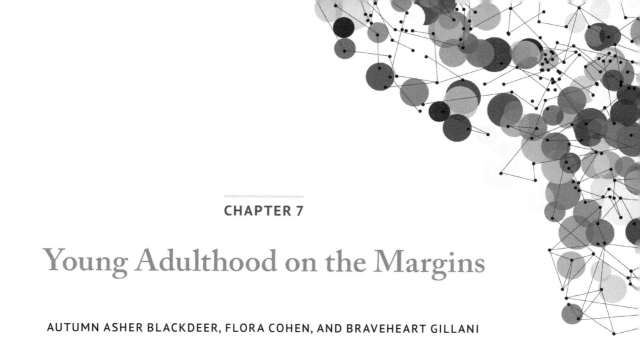

CHAPTER 7

Young Adulthood on the Margins

AUTUMN ASHER BLACKDEER, FLORA COHEN, AND BRAVEHEART GILLANI

LEARNING OBJECTIVES

1. Understand and be able to delineate specific developmental markers of young adulthood and emerging adulthood (Competencies 3, 4 & 7)

2. Use knowledge of human behavior and the social environment to understand the process of transitioning into emerging and young adulthood (Competencies 3 & 7).

3. Understand the reciprocal interactions between emerging and young adults and their environments (Competency (3, 4, & 5).

4. Recognize how the dominant culture's structure and values may oppress, marginalize, alienate, or enhance privilege or power (Competency 3, 4, 5, & 7).

Introduction

The aim of this chapter is to explore the transition into emerging and young adulthood. We will introduce relevant theoretical frameworks for understanding emerging and young adulthood. Through centering multiple marginalized identities, we will understand the processes of ethnic and racial identity formation and sexual and gender identity formation. These processes are further explored through several intersecting axes, including socioeconomic status, immigration and acculturation, religion and spirituality, caregiving, and communal responsibilities. Finally, we will consider the practical implications for social workers.

To begin, consider this brief vignette:

VIGNETTE

A novice child welfare social worker walked up to the house and knocked on the door. She could hear muffled music inside. When the door swung open, she was immediately assaulted by the smell of marijuana and feces. Her new client Taylor answered and demanded to know who she was and why she was at the door. She explained, "I'm here with the family treatment program. I'll be your new case manager. I'm just here to help." Taylor responded, "Are you trying to take my kids away?!" She answered, "No, I am just here to talk and to see how I can help you keep your kids here with you."

Upon an initial assessment, the social worker found that the client lived in a two-bedroom house with their partner Peyton, their 2-year-old child, and the client's elderly and infirm grandmother. The house was full of scattered clothes and dirty dishes, but there appeared to be no food in the refrigerator. The 22-year-old client and their partner both had left school during their 10th-grade year and neither had a stable income at the time. The social worker asked, "How can I help?"

Reflection Questions

1. What is your first impression about this situation?

2. How does your individual positionality impact your view of the situation?

3. What unconscious biases might you have toward the client?

4. What is the first action you would take in this situation?

5. What is your most pressing concern upon entering this scenario?

Young Adulthood

As originally conceived, **young adulthood** ranged from late teens to early 40s. This timeframe was more applicable when "average" American individuals were married and had stable jobs by their early 20s. It is important to acknowledge that this timeframe (1890s to early 2000s) is based on cisgendered, heterosexual, upper-income, White, male-identified individuals. Traditional conceptualizations of adulthood are often characterized by specific life events, such as completing school, obtaining permanent employment positions, achieving financial independence, leaving the parental home, and ultimately settling down by getting married and starting a family (Mary, 2014), as outlined in the family life cycle theory that was developed by Carter and McGoldrick (1998). This theory assumes that all families go through predictable changes based upon life events (both predictable and unpredictable). Historically, individuals within the stage of young adulthood ideally have greater emotional maturity, associated with a change in personality traits (Bleidorn & Schwaba, 2017). Indicators of emotional maturity include showing empathy, setting healthy boundaries, and owning up to mistakes.

Normative markers of adulthood traditionally center cisgendered, heterosexual, middle-class, White people. These markers include independence, interdependence, role transitions, norm compliance, biological transitions, chronological transitions, and family capacities (Tagliabue et al., 2016). Here, the cultural value distinctions between independence and interdependence must be recognized. Western culture prioritizes independence over interdependence, whereas Eastern and Indigenous societies are opposite. Independence can be psychological, emotional, physical, or geographic. *Independence* usually includes accepting responsibility for the consequences of one's actions and no longer residing in the parental home (Tagliabue et al., 2016). *Interdependence* in adulthood is defined as being less self-oriented and missing a demarcation between the self and the community (Tagliabue et al., 2016). It must be noted that the traditional definition of adulthood is from a cisgendered, heteronormative, Western focus. Other communities that fall outside of the heteronormative and Western world have different understandings of where they fall on the spectrum between independence and interdependence, as well as what that means for them.

The role transitions we mentioned above—completing an education, getting married, having children and having a career—vary wildly based upon an individual's identity. For example, obtaining a college education is not a marker of success or growth in all families and cultures. Similarly, forming intimate relationships and marriage practices vary deeply across cultures, wherein some cultures have extended periods of dating before marriage and other cultures have marriages that may occur before dating at all. Additionally, a cisgendered heterosexual woman bearing a child has a very different experience as compared to a transgendered individual or a couple in a same-sex relationship. In the United States, drinking alcohol or smoking marijuana, becoming biologically capable of bearing children, going to college, obtaining a job, and reaching the chronological transitions age of 18 are all considered normative markers of reaching adulthood (Tagliabue et al., 2016). The final traditional marker of adulthood can be seen as running a household (Tagliabue et al., 2016). Running a household includes managing the finances, cooking, cleaning, and ensuring the safety and well-being of the house. However, these roles in household management may differ by gender and culture.

SEVEN TRADITIONAL CRITERIA FOR DEFINING ADULTHOOD

1. Independence
2. Interdependence
3. Role transitions
4. Norm compliance
5. Biological transitions
6. Chronological transitions
7. Family capacities

THEORY ↔ PRACTICE

Understanding and conceptualizing developmental trajectories can inform interventions with client systems. Time lines are a graphical tool that depicts significant events in a client's life across their developmental stages. Apply theories about roles and developmental periods in the following activities:

1. Select a client system and create a time line that starts at birth and ends at the current age or phase of the client system's development.

2. Ask the client system to indicate any significant events in their life, like individual or family role transitions, work or family achievements, and community-level changes.

3. As the client system is building the time line along with the helping professional, identify the client system's views on the events as negative (-), positive (+), or positive <u>and</u> negative (+-).

4. Overlay the finished time line with an indication of developmental stages, and ask the client system about the insights they have gained from this assessment process.

There is a burgeoning uncertainty surrounding the criteria used to define adulthood (Tagliabue et al., 2016). Traditional transitional markers of adulthood are increasingly delayed in present-day society (Tagliabue et al., 2016), and it is suspected that the COVID-19 pandemic and subsequent lockdown may have an even greater impact on "launching" into adulthood (Sarkar et al., 2022). People with multiple marginalized identities will experience differences in role transitions compared to their peers who follow more "traditional" models of identity development. It remains debatable if factors such as financial independence, employment, home ownership, marriage, and parenthood are still the important and relevant markers to define adulthood (Tagliabue et al., 2016).

Current views of development can be described as ahistorical or outdated. The typical transition to adulthood has shifted in the past 50 years for people from a range of backgrounds. While some people have profited from the changing economic landscape, many have encountered a formidable, inflated cost of living, with salaries lagging behind. While previously most families could move away from home and begin investing in developing financial assets within their 20s, this is not feasible for most families today. Low-wage workers are increasingly challenged to support their families, save, and invest in long-term financial stability (Abel et al., 2018). Many young adults live at home with their families for extended periods of time and are forced to find their independence amidst financial constraints.

Role transitions such as becoming a parent can be a drastically different experience for people of different identities. For example, a heterosexual, White, adolescent, cisgendered girl compared to an older, homosexual, transgender man will have different experiences becoming a parent. Assumed within the experience of becoming a parent is the experience of childbearing, which is not possible for all families. Additionally, a two-parent family is often treated as the standard for nuclear families, while many families with young children are either headed by single parents, extended families, or chosen families (see Chapter 3 for a more in-depth discussion on generational development). Therefore, the transitional markers listed above may be insufficient to describe the wider experience of development across populations with different backgrounds, identities, and experiences. It is no longer feasible to continue to understand the experience of becoming a parent as something heterosexual people do through a monogamous, financially stable marriage, while many families experience vastly different trajectories to child-rearing.

Emerging Adulthood

Emerging adulthood was coined by Arnett (2000, 2007) as the period between adolescence and full-fledged adulthood occurring between the late teens and the mid- to late-20s. This in-betweenness is described as not feeling much of either an adolescent or adult (Bleidorn & Schwaba, 2017; Tagliabue et al., 2016). Emerging adults themselves report perception of this developmental phase as largely ambivalent (Tagliabue et al., 2016). Typical individuals in this stage are young adults with no children, who do not yet live in their own home, and who do not have sufficient income to be considered fully financially independent (Arnett, 2000, 2007).

Internationally, perspectives on emerging adulthood are remarkably different. In some contexts, adolescents (especially boys) are expected to work in order to support their families. In many contexts throughout the world, young girls may begin to be engaged in marriage and child-bearing from the age they begin their menstrual period. These differences in culture and context can have profound impacts on individuals who move between countries, especially within the refugee experience. As adolescents and young adults travel to new contexts as immigrants, refugees, or asylum seekers, they may experience processes of acculturation that challenge their perception of normative development. For example, kissing in the hallways of a high school may be normative within some cultures while it is extremely taboo in others (Cohen et al., 2022). These different markers of normative adolescent development can be jarring and place emerging adults in the difficult position of managing perspectives from their home and host cultures.

Emerging adulthood is defined by individuals exploring their identities more than any other period in their lives (Bleidorn & Schwaba, 2017). Most research at the emerging adulthood life stage explores identity exploration in terms of ethnicity, gender, class, or sexual orientation. However, this definition of identity exploration is limited because people may experience those roles intersectionally, and they may be defined at different points in their lives. For example, there is emerging literature on gender identity and how it impacts mental health and suicidality within older adulthood (Gaveras et al., 2023).

5 FEATURES OF EMERGING ADULTHOOD ACROSS CULTURES

1. identity exploration: possibilities in love, work, and worldview

2. feeling in-between: adolescence and adulthood

3. self-focus: free from obligations and restrictions in adulthood

4. instability: too many possibilities can lead to distress and confusion

5. possibilities: generally optimistic about opportunities and time

While previous developmental periods have defined the transition to adulthood by achieving specific roles, Arnett (2000) has described this phase of emerging adulthood as the "roleless role" (p. 471). Emerging adults are not yet firmly committed to a certain role or identity and report an increase in openness to new experiences (Bleidorn & Schwaba, 2017). However, this concept of "choosing an identity" is not always available to people of identities that are treated as monolithic. For example, the Black identity in the United States could refer to Afro-Hispanic, African, African American, Caribbean, or others, but many people with a Black identity are treated as if they fall into one monolithic category. While emerging adulthood is a period of exploration, these explorative experiences are bounded by social realities.

Emerging adulthood is generally seen as a time of greater self-focus rather than other-focus (Tagliabue et al., 2016). However, this concept is different across individualist or more collectivist societies. The core aspect of individualist cultures is that individuals are independent from one another, while in collectivist cultures individuals are mutually obligated to one another. The individualist worldview prioritizes personal goals, unique attributes, and individual control (Hofstede, 2001). The collectivist worldview prioritizes community, common goals, and values. Although individual perspectives on individualism versus collectivism may vary along a spectrum, larger contextual influences affect individual identity formation. In more collective cultures, emerging adulthood may be a period when the individual bears additional responsibility for their community. Meanwhile, in more individualistic cultures, emerging adulthood is typically a time when people begin to separate themselves from their families and communities.

 THEORY ↔ PRACTICE
Apply theories about roles and developmental periods in the following activity:

1. Draw a large circle on a piece of paper.

2. Using a pencil, have the client system indicate what portions of the "pie" should encompass identity exploration, feeling in-between, self-focus, instability, and possibilities.

3. On a separate piece of paper, draw another circle, and using the same process, have the client system indicate the portions of the pie that significant others believe should encompass identity exploration, feeling in-between, self-focus, instability, and possibilities.

4. Compare the differences in the pies and explore areas of potential agreement and conflict.

Individualist and Collectivist Cultures

Individualist cultures stress the needs of the individual over the needs of the group and are defined by independence and autonomy. People in individualistic cultures tend to behave according to self-interest and personal preferences. **Collectivist cultures**, conversely, emphasize the needs and goals of the whole group over the needs and desires of each individual member.

There is an emphasis on relationships between members of the group and a strong sense of community identity.

Identity exploration during emerging adulthood is not only about racial, gender, cultural, or class awareness but also about one's worldview, work or career aspirations, and ultimately their love interests or lack thereof (asexual or aromantic people may have different experiences regarding interpersonal relationship development). As emerging adults today experience less pressure to get married or start a family, they can explore additional possibilities for their own development and life goals (Bleidorn & Schwaba, 2017).

Life transitions influence personality development. Personality changes within emerging adulthood are said to be a result of responding to life transitions and developmental tasks, even if these transitions and tasks do not directly lead to committed adult roles (Bleidorn & Schwaba, 2017). Examples of these transitions and developmental tasks that can influence personality changes within emerging adulthood include graduating from school, traveling, dating, moving out of the parental home, and making new friends (Bleidorn & Schwaba, 2017). Examples of related shifts include a widened perspective on cultures and communities, focusing on alternative habits or priorities, and engaging in more social or less social behaviors. The defining features of this phase are exploration, flexibility, and noncommitment; as such, emerging adulthood is the most heterogeneous and least structured period within the life course (Bleidorn & Schwaba, 2017). However, for more interconnected families, the influencing transitions may be less likely. In many cultures, it is unacceptable for people to date before marriage. In some parts of the world, girls are not enrolled in school and do not often experience moving outside of their homes. Limiting the social network of emerging adults can also limit opportunities to engage with explorative experiences that influence personality development. Being from a marginalized identity may also make it unsafe to be extremely explorative.

TABLE 7.1 Hallmarks of Young Adulthood Versus Emerging Adulthood

Young adulthood	Emerging adulthood
Firm foundation	Feeling in-between
Role-oriented	Self-focus
Dedication	Instability
Commitment	Possibility

While some state that emerging adulthood is a new stage in development, others have criticized the concept by stating that individuals are neither extending their youth nor experiencing a new life phase (Mary, 2014). Indeed, it is plausible that emerging adulthood is less of a reflection of a new developmental stage and more of an indication of socioeconomic restructuring. Thus, emerging adulthood is simply the next generation developing new coping strategies in response to this socioeconomic restructuring (Mary, 2014). However, it is altogether plausible that young adults are simply following alternate patterns of transition based on the available socioeconomic opportunities and social possibilities.

VIGNETTE (CONTINUED)

Taylor and Peyton talk after the child protection worker leaves. They sit at the foot of the stairs while Grandma sits across the room on her pull-out couch.

[television is on in the background]

Taylor: I don't want to go out there, there are protests going on. Let's stay in and smoke.

Peyton: C'mon, it'll be fun. And it's important. You remember what happened to your brother.

Taylor: That's exactly why I don't want to out there—cops will be there.

Grandma: Y'all need to calm down. I am trying to get some rest.

[toddler picks up a pen from the floor and starts chewing on it]

Taylor: I am trying to get a job so we can get out of here.

Peyton: What kind of job are you fittin' to get? You know you aren't smart. You won't be able to get nothin'.

Taylor: We can't stay here forever.

Peyton: Yes, we can. Your grandma will write us into her will; she is going soon anyway.

Taylor: We can't even pay the electric bill as it is. How do you think that's going to change?

[They all sit on the sofa bed. It creaks, and the springs poke out from under the mattress.]

Reflection Questions

1. What are some assumptions you make about the intersecting identities that are presented?

2. What are your hypotheses about resources and needs?

3. With this additional information, how would your plan to support the family change?

4. How does your positionality affect your assumptions and hypotheses?

5. What is the most pressing need for the family right now?

Theoretical Frameworks

We have discussed some of the key theoretical frameworks in previous chapters, but let's review them with a special eye to their applicability to young adulthood. Please keep in mind that theoretical frameworks help us ground our understanding, observations and data. The following section reviews the ecological, the psychological, and critical theoretical frameworks.

The Ecological Perspective

Bronfenbrenner's (1979) social ecological theory is a traditional theoretical model used to understand human behavior and the social environment. The key tenet of the social ecological model is that individuals are embedded within many social contexts, both **proximal** (family, peer, community) and **distal** (local, national, global). Problems, then, are seen as located within the stresses created by the interactions between individuals, families, groups, organizations, and institutions within the environment at the micro, meso, and macro levels. For example, a queer, disabled young adult may be contending with navigating their family's response to their sexuality within the micro level while also contending with the larger cultural issues of residing within a homophobic society and seeking queer disability justice within the overall macrosystem. Special attention is paid to the **goodness of fit** between an individual or group and the places they live their lives (Sands, 2001).

One significant criticism of this model is that culturally specific concepts of the social environment are typically unseen; for example, it does not include the lasting effects of colonization, structural violence, or acculturation stress. Without accounting for these unseen forces from an ecological perspective, attempting to understand how a young or emerging adult comes to understand their identity will be ultimately incomplete.

ECOLOGICAL ASSESSMENT FRAMEWORK

Consider the person-in-environment and goodness of fit.

1. Is there adaptation or maladaptation?
2. What external or internal stressors exist?
3. What are the developmental factors at play (age-related tasks)?
4. What are the risk factors present?
5. What are the challenges for this individual?
6. What environmental factors are present?

Systems theory is an interdisciplinary study of systems and how they impact each other. General systems theory (GST) was initially conceptualized by Ludwig von Bertalanffy, a biologist seeking to theorize the study of living systems (Keidrwoski, 2010). By the early 1950s GST began to spread transdisciplinary. "Systems theory" is an umbrella term with a series of distinct theories, such as chaos theory, living systems theory, control theory, complex systems theory, and many more. The ecological model is a part of systems theory (Ceci, 2006). Within social work, systems theory is a lens through which social workers can look holistically at a client's condition and environmental factors and develop more comprehensive interventions. Bronfenbrenner's ecological model proposes that an individual's environment is a nested arrangement of structures, each contained within the next (Ceci, 2006). He named these structures the "microsystem," "mesosystem," "exosystem," "macrosystem," and "chronosystem." It should be noted that even though Bronfenbrenner's structure was primarily focused on child development, it is applicable to all stages of life.

Bronfenbrenner's ecological model's adaptation to emerging adulthood is demonstrated in Figure 7.1, where each arrow indicates impacts and correlations between variables and the hash line between variables indicates significant time intervals. Figure 7.1 indicates that

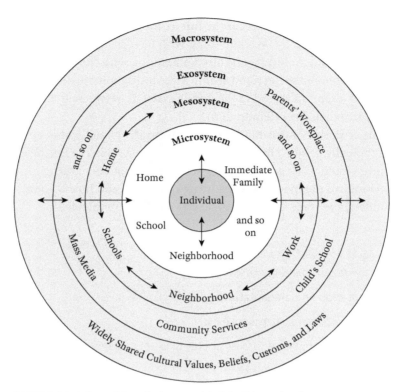

FIGURE 7.1 Adapted Bronfenbrenner Model of Emerging Adulthood

emerging adults are deeply influenced by their peers, family, and neighborhood at the micro level. However, there is a feedback mechanism associated with each of those factors, demonstrating how an emerging adult is influenced by their family, but the emerging adult also impacts the family. Similarly, the emerging adult is affected by their peers, but the emerging adult also impacts their peers. Examples of the meso system–level influencers include job contexts, educational institutions, and religious or spiritual communities. The position of the influencing variable is dependent upon the family and social context, as they all impact emerging adults engaged in identity and self-formation. The impact of the emerging adult on the meso-level factors may be affected by the factor's size and the emerging adult's intensity of engagement with it.

Visualizations of concentric circles are often utilized to model relevant factors at each environment level, and application typically stops there. Appropriate utilization of the ecological perspective would account for the feedback loops that occur when individuals interact with their environment rather than a simple unidirectional relationship. All the variables mentioned above constantly impact the emerging adult, and the emerging adult is impacting them. All of this happens within the particular socioeconomic and temporal contexts covered by the macro- and chronosystems. These interactions across multiple levels of systems create a complex dynamic system that is difficult to predict or manage.

This system is more complicated for emerging adults of multiple minoritized identities. With elements such as racism, sexism, **xenophobia** engaging at all levels (micro, meso, exo, macro) of the society, emerging adults of multiple minoritized identities experience additional challenges. There are no detailed mechanisms for how an individual's environment impacts their development. Further, there is no delineation of the strength or overall measure of impact each space may have upon the individual. A flat concentric circle representation presents all levels as equal; however, we know that overarching experiences of oppression weigh more heavily in certain spheres of development than others. Finally, the framework is difficult to implement into practice, as all factors are meant to be mutually and systematically influential, but how can one consider all of these at once?

The Psychosocial Development Theory

Erikson (1968) posits that identities emerge and develop because of dynamic interactions between individuals and their social contexts. There are a total of eight stages of psychosocial development in Erikson's model. Three stages most relevant to emerging and young adulthood are Stages 5, 6, and 7 of identity versus identity confusion, intimacy versus isolation, and generativity versus stagnation, respectively. Prior to emerging and young adulthood, the Stage 5 of identity versus identity confusion is where the teenager must achieve a sense of identity in their occupation, sex roles, politics, and religion. Stage 6 is the best fit for emerging and young adulthood, as the conflict of intimacy versus isolation models the challenges young adults face in developing intimate relationships or suffering isolation. Finally, Stage 7, where young and emerging adults are headed, is the conflict of generativity versus stagnation, which is defined by adults finding some way to satisfy and support the next generation.

TABLE 7.2 Erikson's Psychosocial Stages of Development

Stages	Crisis	Goal
Birth–1 year	Basic trust versus mistrust	Build faith in environment and future
2 years	Autonomy versus shame and doubt	Develop self-control and adequacy
3–5 years	Initiative versus guilt	Able to initiate own activities
6 years–puberty	Industry versus inferiority	Learn and understand how things work
Adolescence	Identity versus Identity confusion	See oneself as a unique individual
Early adulthood	Intimacy versus isolation	Make meaningful commitments to others
Middle age	Generativity versus stagnation	Display concern for family and general society
Aging years	Integrity versus despair	Develop sense of integrity and fulfillment

These stages are limited in their applicability to young and emerging adults with multiple marginalized identities, particularly in the consideration of interdependent and collectivist communities. For example, the developmental event of leaving the home typically happens later in life, especially for young adults from marginalized backgrounds. As such, their struggle for identity versus role confusion may not emerge until later in life rather than adolescence as the original framework suggests. Further, individuals grounded in community may have the generativity concern for their collective community well-being and survivance well before later adulthood as the original framework suggests.

The typical example considered is a young adult, recently graduating from high school, moving out of the parental home, and focusing on building intimacy with romantic partners and others outside of the family unit. However, for individuals with multiple marginalized identities, this milestone of intimacy versus isolation may not occur until later in life. For example, many Indigenous emerging adults do not leave their familial homes or communities until later in life and, as such, may not face the challenge of isolation until they are closer to middle age rather than adolescence as proposed in Erikson's framework. Further, the middle age conflict of generativity versus stagnation is likely experienced earlier, particularly for those from collectivist communities, like Indigenous and immigrant communities. The entire worldview is focused on interdependence rather than independence, like with the dominant U.S. culture; as such, these individuals are raised within communities that learn and value concern for one another and society well before they are considered middle aged. Ultimately, Erikson's psychosocial stages fail to account for various worldviews and processes of development from those with multiple marginalized identities.

Critical Theory

Critical theory is a Marxist-inspired philosophical and sociological movement distinguished from traditional theories according to its specific purpose: "A theory is critical to the extent that it seeks human emancipation, acts as a liberating influence, and works to create a world that satisfies the needs and powers of human beings" (Horkheimer, 1972, p. 246). According to Horkheimer's (1972) definition, critical theory must explain what is wrong with a "current social reality, identify the actors to change it, and provide both clear norms for criticism and achievable practical goals for social transformation" (p. 244). In this sense, critical theory should be utilized as a liberatory praxis that acknowledges history while simultaneously encouraging action (hooks, 1990; Mignolo & Walsh, 2018).

CRITICAL THEORY SUMMARY

- Critical theories challenge the status quo by explicitly naming the underlying assumptions.
- It was initially developed with the goal to examine, understand, and potentially deconstruct ideologies such as fascism.
- Critical theories are a praxis; they utilize both theory and practice to challenge social ills that are caused by power differences.
- Critical theory has expanded in the latter 20th century to include other praxis, such as critical race theory, critical feminist theory, and queer theory.

Through witnessing current social, political, and environmental movements, many emerging and young adults are emboldened to become activists. This is especially true for youth with marginalized identities, who have been given voice and language with the development of various critical theories. Emerging and young adults have enhanced executive functioning coupled with a wider range of experiences that bring to light social ills such as racism, capitalism, and climate change. At the same time, as they enter higher education or employment, they have more opportunities to be taken seriously. These experiences can lead to critical consciousness and a new generation of activists. However, severely curtailed education about racism, LGBTQIA+ issues, and other key social concerns can be detrimental to the social and political involvement of young adults, along with building up frustration and resentments against the "established" educational, political, and social institutions within them.

Within views of young adulthood, critical theory probes us to interrogate the historical and current dimensions of power that impact individuals and community. Specifically, critical race theory (CRT) invites individuals of all backgrounds, races, and ethnicities to investigate histories of racism and how they have impacted social demographics and accumulated advantages for certain races. Similarly, critical gender theory investigates the notion of a binary gender system itself and its impacts upon modern society. By uplifting basic assumptions, critical theory galvanizes emerging adults to make radical choices for themselves.

TABLE 7.3 Major Theories for Emerging Adulthood

Theory	Summary	Critique
Ecological perspective	Individuals are embedded within social contexts.	It lacks culturally specific concepts.
Systems theory	Use a holistic lens to view a client's condition and environmental factors.	Models can be unwieldy and difficult to target intervention.
Psychosocial development	Identities emerge from dynamic interactions between individuals and their social contexts.	It is not representative of those with multiple marginalized identities.
Critical theory	Explore and challenge underlying assumptions within society.	There is no clear structure. It is more confrontational than community building.

VIGNETTE (CONTINUED)

The social worker meets Taylor at a homeless shelter where they have been living for a few months with their son. Taylor just obtained a holiday job delivering mail during the busy Christmas season and they are excited to be able to afford gifts for their son. They state that the shelter managers have been giving them a hard time because they think their clothes are too revealing. They won't help out, and there are problems in the shelter with leaking pipes and cockroaches. They cuddle up with their son at night because they don't want bugs crawling all over them. They report that they often cry themselves to sleep, missing their grandmother and feeling incredibly alone in the shelter with their toddler.

Reflection Questions

1. What is your first impression about this situation?

2. How does your individual positionality impact your view of the situation?

3. What unconscious biases might you have toward the client and the shelter?

4. What is your most pressing concern upon entering this scenario?

5. What is your plan to support the family?

Weaving Multiple Identities Together: A Tapestry of Being

Young adulthood is not unidimensional. Individuals bring various aspects of their identity together, combining it all together in a unique tapestry of racial identity, ethnicity, socio-economic status, family and belonging, (different) abilities, sexual and gender identity etc. In the pages below, you will learn how various dimensions of identity reveal themselves individually and combine to form lasting impacts on the young adults.

Ethnic and Racial Identity Formation

Ethnic and racial identity (ERI) is a multidimensional construct of beliefs and attitudes that individuals have about their ethnic-racial group membership in combination with the processes by which these beliefs and attitudes are attained over time (Umaña-Taylor et al., 2014). ERI is not merely an exclusive self-categorization or an ethnic/racial identification label that an individual chooses; however, the process of ERI can lead to different choices in self-categorization (Umaña-Taylor et al., 2014). Ethnic and racial identity is not an endpoint for how one chooses to self-identify, define what one believes, or delineate how one feels about one's group (Umaña-Taylor et al., 2014). ERI is the interaction between maturation and context and, as such, takes different forms and meanings across the lifespan (Umaña-Taylor et al., 2014). It must be understood that identity may be chosen but can at the same time be influenced by genetic or nurtured factors. Therefore, the development of multiple identities within individuals is a nuanced and dynamic process, with the emerging adult often examining and reexamining pieces of their identity and how they mesh with other parts of their preexisting and currently forming identities. This is true for one's ethnic and racial identity, ancestry connection, and community belonging along with their sexual and gender identity. With the development of each piece of identity, an emerging adult might reexamine all other parts of their self. Research within identity formation and development of emerging adults should therefore not be considered from a siloed and generic perspective and rather seen as a holistic, iterative, and healthy process.

From a life course perspective, ethnic and racial identity changes and develops over time. In early-middle childhood, ERI is defined through processes of ethnic-racial labeling, knowledge and behaviors, and constancy; these processes prepare children for ERI formation and meaning-making in adolescence (Umaña-Taylor et al., 2014). These experiences during early-middle childhood happen simultaneously among peers, which can be dangerous for marginalized children (Umana-Taylor et al., 2014)). For biracial children, it is common to feel ostracized from both parts of their racial identities. ERI also leads to broad assumptions among peers that inadvertently stereotype people of different racial identities. ERI in adolescence fits with Erikson's psychosocial development theory as a time when personal identity emerges (Umaña-Taylor et al., 2014). ERI in young adulthood is defined by complexity as an expansion of life domains where ERI may be potentially relevant in realms of relationships, education, and career choices (Umaña-Taylor et al., 2014). Further within young adulthood, ERI becomes increasingly integrated with other aspects of the self in order to create a cohesive overall identity (Umaña-Taylor et al., 2014). Moving on into adulthood, ERI becomes part of an individual's psychological platform for negotiating employment, community and political participation, and partner intimacy related to family formulation (Umaña-Taylor et al., 2014). Previous work has failed to accurately and appropriately account for these multiple identities, often limiting representations to group descriptions and stereotypes.

Many adult members of ethnic-racial minority groups enter adulthood with an identity that is psychologically functional and positive yet culturally limited or even corrupted by miseducation, such as believing negative stereotypes about one's racial or ethnic group (Umaña-Taylor et al., 2014). For example, prior research has reported that Black American emerging adults face challenges in sorting out their own assessments of who and what they want to become while also rejecting and overcoming negative stereotypes society holds about them (Arnett & Brody, 2008). For LGBTQIA+ Latinx young adults, scholars have begun to intersectionally examine the unique cultural stressors and attitudes that may stigmatize nonnormative sexualities, particularly within the context of religious ideologies (Schmitz et al., 2019). For American Indian youth, previous research has conceptualized that a belief in negative stereotypes can lead to a self-fulfilling prophecy about fulfilling a negative Native stereotype (Gonzalez & Skewes, 2016). This may look like Indigenous young men drinking alcohol irresponsibly due to belief in the "drunken Indian" stereotype.

It is critical to understand the social environmental context within which individuals are embedded in order to understand how one's ERI develops and the consequences of ERI for an individual's adjustment (Umaña-Taylor et al., 2014). Family is one of if not the most important proximal social context that guides ERI formation (Umaña-Taylor et al., 2014); however, other important influences outside of the family (e.g., peers, mentors, and neighbors) have been less studied. For example, Indigenous youth who are raised within a tight-knit community close to elders and traditional medicine and ceremonies may have stronger identities as being Indigenous when compared to urban Native youth who were raised in urban contexts. However, urban Native youth could have a mentor or neighbor deeply immersed in their traditional culture who could also help them develop a strong racial and ethnic identity.

Sexual and Gender Identity Formation

An understanding about sexual and gender identity formation must be grounded in queer theory. **Queer theory** is a strengths-based framework for understanding sexual and gender identities that are outside of current social norms (Bragg et al., 2018). The term "queer theory" began with Gloria Anzaldua and other scholars in the 1990s and was influenced by critical theory and Foucault, who viewed sexuality as socially constructed and rejected identity politics. Queer theory rejects heteronormativity and posits that queerness is a "collective contestation" (Butler, 1993) of gender- and sex-based binaries. The goal of queer theory is to undo hierarchies and fight against social inequalities. Queer theory positions young adults to critically interrogate gender and sexual binaries, power inequalities, and the heteronormatively that prescribes sexual identity development.

Sexual and gender identities develop in queer time, in opposition to the institutions of family, heterosexuality, and reproduction (Halberstam, 2005). In queer identity development, and individual moves through the stages of building an awareness, exploring their gender and sexual identities, potentially committing to an identity that fits them, and integrating that identity into themselves and the way they navigate their communities (Hall et al., 2021). For some people, this process can happen in their childhood or teenage years, and for others, the added independence of entering young adulthood provides an opportunity to explore queer identity formation in new ways. Young adulthood is often the period of time when individuals leave their childhood homes and seek community in new settings. Still, some people do not have the opportunity to explore and discover their own queerness until later adulthood, when they have completed heteronormative milestones like heterosexual marriage and childrearing.

Queer identity formation is complex: It involves not only individual processes but dynamic processes with families, communities, and the larger political context. Individuals who remain at home or remain enmeshed with home cultures that are restrictive in terms of sexual and gender identity formation can have an even more challenging time navigating their queer identities. Some families may not be accepting of queer identities, especially within certain religious sects. Furthermore, some communities may endorse quite queer-phobic attitudes through explicit practices like bathroom policing or implicit assumptions of heteronormative sexual identities. Frankly, even the grouping of trans identities within sexual identities (the "T" in LGBT) represents a lack of understanding about the differences between sexual and gender identities.

Individuals with multiple marginalized identities may have an even more difficult time "coming out" because of the intersectional identities they already carry. Holding a racial, gender, or socioeconomic identity that is already marginalized may cause an individual to think that holding onto a queer identity may make their life even more challenging. In young adulthood, it can help for individuals to find communities of like-minded people who can support the navigation of queerness alongside other intersecting identities.

Ageism is another factor queer emerging adults often experience, which adds to their overall marginalization. For instance, queer community is often developed within queer clubs and bars, spaces that are often not appropriate or inviting for younger emerging adults. Hence, it is important to create support groups, meeting spaces, and resources that are age and identity specific.

A critical piece for queer emerging adults is around the notion of coming out, which is a Western cultural phenomenon despite often being universalized. It implies clearly expressing our sexual and gender identity, if it is deviant from the normative heterosexual, cisgendered standard to those within our smaller and larger circles of influence and contact. Coming out is seen as a "coming of age" ritual for many emerging adults. However, the concept itself must be handled with care. Within many cultures, such as in India or Pakistan, sexuality is considered to be a private matter and does not need to be shared. Additionally, the notion of sexuality being a static term and gender existing within binary notions is a colonial idea and is not existent across cultures or traditions.

Socioeconomic Status Identity Formation

A salient part of identity development within young adults is to learn about, engage with, and make progress in career or professional arenas. This shift in roles—from being cared for and focused upon to becoming more responsible and engaging in complex systems, engaging in nuanced decision making, and providing financial capital—may be particularly stark for young adults with marginalized backgrounds. Intergenerational poverty, lack of financial education, and exposure to violence can build coping mechanisms and behaviors detrimental to a youth's long-term financial well-being (Moore, 2005). Additionally, accumulation of financial resources may not be the primary focus of many developing adults from nondominant cultures, as they may have collectivistic and community-based values.

Young adults from marginalized communities are not monolithic; They have different identities, potentials, capacities, supports and goals. Therefore, the above-mentioned barriers may show up in a variety of ways for them. In the United States, many young adults of color experience challenges to saving and accumulation of financial assets. A recent study showed that Black young adults aged 17–23 years saved about 3% the amount saved by their White counterparts, suggesting that young adults' savings may be patterned after disparities in the distribution of assets and families may transfer a financial advantage to young, White adults. Secondly, young adults of marginalized identities may not inherit the same generational wealth as young adults who are White, leading to worse socioeconomic status over a lifetime.

Even with similar income, young adults and professionals of color experience a different set of demands. Due to historical and institutional racism, young adults of color often come from families and communities that are not abundant in capital. The influx of money in the young adult's life may create a multitude of complications very difficult to navigate. Notions of familial respect, expectations, and hierarchy may be challenged due to inordinate amounts of resources in either direction. Additionally, young adults of color who are successful in navigating the systems of capitalistic wealth accumulation may be seen as examples within the community. They may experience exclusion and tokenism from the larger White society while at the same time experiencing estrangement, separation, or being put on the pedestal within their own community. They may also experience pressure to share their financial and social resources with their community and invest time and energy in guidance and mentorship for community members.

Immigration and Acculturation Identity Formation

Young adults experience a strong need for community and belonging within their social worlds. While acculturating to life in a new environment, they may feel a need to assimilate to find community. However, many young adults with immigrant backgrounds may feel torn between maintaining the cultural practices they were raised in and adapting those of the dominant culture. They may spend additional time and resources communicating with family in their home countries and finding their own cultural enclaves within their new communities.

Many emerging adults who are immigrants support immediate and extended families by sending them remittances. This money is critical for their families, especially in countries with lower socioeconomic status. This increase in responsibility puts undue burden and pressure on the young adults. However, the process of sending remittances also increases a sense of belonging and community. With values on interdependence, family support, and belonging, adults who are immigrants may often define their success as attached to the overall success and well-being of their families.

Young adults with immigrant identities may experience a myriad of challenges. The challenges that people with immigrant identities contend with vary based on intersecting identities, such as country of origin, gender, age, socioeconomic status, and academic achievement. For example, the 2017 ban on immigration from specific countries, colloquially entitled the "Muslim Ban" was fueled by xenophobic beliefs following the September 11, 2001, terrorist attacks. While many immigrants from the Middle East and North Africa (MENA) region contend with challenges associated with being labeled as terrorists, others from regions that are more phenotypically White, such as from Ukraine, may experience less discrimination upon entering new host country contexts like the United States.

Young immigrant adults of marginalized identities may experience discriminatory behaviors and xenophobia from their peers and new communities. Questions such as "Where are you from?" may be well-intentioned but do a lot of damage to a young person's sense of belonging to a space. Immigrant young adults grappling with their sense of identity and belonging often express a feeling of unbelonging in both the countries of their birth along with the country where they are living. Additionally, those who might not be legalized citizens are subjected to a constant threat of removal, which perpetuates a constant sense of hypervigilance and sense of unbelonging within themselves. Furthermore, it perpetuates a sense of instability and may cultivate notions of self-hate and distrust for themselves along with the authorities.

Spirituality and Religious Identity Formation

Emerging adulthood is a prime time for individuals to question their religions of origin and explore their spirituality. This is in line with the belief that young adults are curious and eager to develop a deeper understanding of themselves (Braskamp & Ward, 2008). The formation of the prefrontal cortex, which supports executive tasks such as metacognition, planning and future thinking, supports the capacity for abstract topics like a higher power and the reckoning between good and evil in the world. Additionally, young adults are going through a series of changes in their bodies and the sociocultural environment. Physically, they experience hormonal shifts through puberty and changes in neurotransmitters in the process. Socially, they begin to experience increased social capital and responsibilities. With all these changes, religion and spirituality may act as a supportive coping mechanism or it may add to the young adult's difficulties.

Intersectional factors such as race, ethnicity, immigration status, and sexual orientation may all impact an emerging adult's relationship with religion and spirituality. Research has proven that similarities may exist more between parents and their children in religious beliefs over practice (Francis, 1993). Parents are the primary factors in initiating children into a set of religious practices. However, comparatively less research has been done on this topic regarding emerging adults.

Three important factors that contribute to the variability in emerging adults' religiosity and spirituality are culture, community, and gender. These factors may lead to differences to the level of development and importance of these beliefs. Additionally, culture, community, and gender impact the way these beliefs are socialized. Finally, they may impact the practices and outcomes of individuals. All these factors may support or dissuade young adults from engaging in religion and/or spirituality.

Young adults with identities that do not align with heteronormative ideals, gender binary norms, or homonormative sexual and gender expressions may experience ostracization from majority religions. It is critical for social workers to be impartial, inclusive, and supportive toward their clients, irrespective of their personal or religious beliefs. Social workers must work hard not to project their own stereotypes on their clients. They must educate themselves regarding this population, the kinds of discrimination experienced by queer individuals, and safe resources for the queer community.

Caregiving and Communal Responsibilities

In young adulthood, individuals begin to understand their role as independent adults, but they are also met with additional responsibilities. In the past, many people moved out of their parents' homes in young adulthood, but due to inflation and high rates of unemployment, more and more young adults are remaining at home. In 2015, a third of people aged 18 to 34 lived under their parents' roofs (Hong & Kui, 2020). During the COVID-19 pandemic, with school and work moving online, growing numbers of people moved back to their parents' homes.

For many young adults of marginalized identities, their independence is uniquely tied to their communities. Many young adults are tasked with caregiving for older people in their families. In families of marginalized identities, it is often fiscally irresponsible and culturally inappropriate to send aging adults to nursing homes. Caring for the matriarchs and patriarchs of families is seen as an ethical responsibility.

Many young adults of marginalized identities care for young children. Although teen pregnancy rates have declined, Black and Latina girls are more than twice as likely as White girls to become pregnant before they leave adolescence (Hong & Kui, 2020). With higher rates of teen pregnancy, women of marginalized identities who are entering young adulthood may face additional challenges. They may be stigmatized by their communities, ostracized by their families, or experience extended financial strain both due to child-rearing and difficulty finding a job while also performing caregiving duties.

Practice Implications

Now that you have read about the theoretical frameworks, it is important to consider how they can be applied to Social work practice. In the pages below, we will review how to engage with the young adults from various levels of practice.

Mental Health

Most mental health conditions are diagnosed in young adulthood. Roughly half of lifetime mental disorders have their onset by the mid-teens, and 75% by the mid-20s (Kessler et al., 2007). For families of marginalized identities, mental illness may have a high stigma and treatment seeking may be discouraged. In many cultures, depression or anxiety are seen as weaknesses, and more severe mental illnesses like schizophrenia or bipolar disorder may cause incredible shame for families (Office of the Surgeon General, 2001). Furthermore, discussing family challenges with outside actors, such as therapists, may be seen as highly inappropriate (Ahmedani, 2011).

Mental health services may be ill-equipped to support people with marginalized identities. Histories of institutionalizing people with severe mental illnesses causes distrust in the mental health care system. Currently, there is an insufficient number of mental health providers (social workers, psychologists, and psychiatrists) who hold marginalized identities (Ahmedani, 2011). Mental health curricula seldom support an understanding of intersectionality and impacts on well-being. Furthermore, current diagnostic criteria and "evidence-based practices" were developed by and for a majority White population. This disconnect between available services and the identities of individuals being served is an extreme barrier to appropriate care for people with mental illnesses.

Curiosity

A social worker should always enter a client interaction from a place of not knowing. Even with all of the research and perspective that the social work field offers, there is no way to truly know what is happening for a client. Even though evidence may lead the social worker to believe that the main concern for a client is their queer identity or racialized experiences, they may be contending with other consuming challenges. Always enter an interaction with a client from a place of humble questioning and exploring how they view their own challenges. At the same time, a social worker must be aware of their own blind spots and not use their clients to "educate" them on specific issues and topic. Unnecessary, irrelevant, and inappropriate questions regarding a client's identity and experience may create more harm for the client and come across as voyeuristic behavior. Ultimately, social workers need to honor their client's dignity and probe in areas that are beneficial for the client's growth and development.

Involving Communities

Communities, especially marginalized communities, are interconnected. Too often, the social work field focuses on individual well-being while ignoring the interconnected relationships and concerns within community. Many marginalized people take on caregiving roles within their families, are connected to churches, and are expected to meet certain expectations due to their ethnic group or culture. When working with individuals, it is important to remember to support community cohesion and well-being simultaneously.

CONCLUSION

This chapter on young adulthood delineated developmental markers between young and emerging adulthood while drawing attention to their expanding social environments. While young adulthood has historically been cast as a wide range of years, emerging adulthood pinpoints the in-between time to merge the gap between adolescence and full-fledged adulthood. This chapter discussed several reciprocal interactions that occur between emerging and young adults and their environments, particularly along the axes of individual and collectivist cultures, theoretical frameworks, and multiple marginalized identities. Several theoretical perspectives were presented to understand the social environment of young and emerging adults, such as the ecological perspective, psychosocial development, and critical theories. Multiple historically marginalized perspectives were presented and placed in conversation with how the dominant culture can exacerbate these disparities for young and emerging adults. This chapter concluded with practice implications ranging from micro to macro practice. From here, the next chapter dives deeper into adult development with multiple marginalized identities.

KEY TERMS

- Young adulthood: traditional developmental stage ranging from late teens to early 40s characterized by a dedication to social role commitment.

- Emerging adulthood: in-between developmental phase between adolescence and full-fledged adulthood characterized as a time of self-focus, ambivalence, and curiosity.

- Individualistic cultures: stress the needs of the individual over the needs of the group and are defined by independence and autonomy.

- Collectivist cultures: emphasize the needs and goals of the whole group over the needs and desires of each individual member.

- Proximal: situated nearby social contexts, such as one's family, peers, and community.

- Distal: situated further away from an individual, such as one's local, national, or global social contexts.

- Goodness of fit: refers to how well an individual fits within or matches with their social contexts.

- Systems theory: the interdisciplinary study of systems and how they impact each other.

- Queer theory: a subfield of critical theory characterized by the rejection of heteronormativity in order to critically interrogate gender and sexual binaries and power inequalities.

- Xenophobia: prejudicial beliefs and discrimination against individuals from other countries.

- Critical theory: Critical theory aims to critique and challenge power structures and societal norms, with the goal of promoting social justice and equity. It emphasizes the examination of power relations and the ways in which dominant ideologies maintain and reproduce social inequality.

- Ethnic and racial identity (ERI): a multidimensional construct of beliefs and attitudes that individuals have about their ethnic-racial group membership in combination with the processes by which these beliefs and attitudes are attained over time (Umaña-Taylor et al., 2014).

DISCUSSION QUESTIONS

1. How can social workers fully support young adults on the margins in stepping into healthy and mature adulthood?

2. How can social workers be aware of their personal bias while engaging with young adults on the margins?

3. How can different theories help social workers in supporting young adults on the margins?

4. Describe some nuances social workers must consider while helping young adults on the margins navigate social barriers into becoming their whole selves.

REFERENCES

Abel, J. R., Florida, R., & Gabe, T. M. (2018). *Can low-wage workers find better jobs?* (Report No. 846). Federal Reserve Bank of New York Staff Reports. http://doi.org/10.2139/ssrn.3164963

Ahmedani, B. (2011). Mental health stigma: Society, individuals, and the profession. *Journal of Social Work Values and Ethics*, *8*(2), 41–416.

Arnett, J. J. (2000). Emerging adulthood: A theory of development from the late teens through the twenties. *American Psychologist*, *55*(5), 469–480. https://doi.org/10.1037//0003-066X.55.5.469

Arnett, J. J. (2007). Emerging adulthood: What is it, and what is it good for? *Child Development Perspectives*, *1*(2), 68–73. https://doi.org/10.1111/j.1750-8606.2007.00016.x

Arnett, J. J., & Brody, G. H. (2008). A fraught passage: The identity challenges of African American emerging adults. *Human Development*, *51*(5–6), 291–293. https://www.jstor.org/stable/26764871

Bleidorn, W., & Schwaba, T. (2017). Personality development in emerging adulthood. In J. Specht (Ed.), *Personality development across the lifespan* (pp. 39–51). Academic Press.

Bragg, J., Havig, K., & Muñoz, R. (2018). Absent in theory, invisible in practice: Queering HBSE for a more inclusive social work profession. *Journal of Human Behavior in the Social Environment*, *28*(1), 44–57.

Braskamp, L. A., & Ward, K. A. (2008). Reducing stress for new faculty at church-related colleges and universities. *Journal of Human Behavior in the Social Environment*, *17*(1–2), 129–156. https://doi.org/10.1080/10911350802168928

Bronfenbrenner, U. (1979). *The ecology of human development*. Harvard University Press.

Butler, J. (1993). Poststructuralism and postmarxism. *Diacritics*, *23*(4), 3.

Carter, B., McGoldrick, M., & Whitbourne, S. (1999). The expanded family life cycle: Individual. *Family. and Social Perspectives* (3rd ed. I. Boston: Allyn and Bacon.

Ceci, S. J. (2006). Urie Bronfenbrenner (1917–2005). *American Psychologist*, *61*(2), 173–174. https://doi.org/10.1037/0003-066X.61.2.173

Cohen, F., Meyere, S. R., Seff, I., Bennouna, C., Allaf, C., & Stark, L. (2022) Intersectionality: Experiences of gender socialization and racialization for Iraqi students resettled in the United States. *Journal on Education in Emergencies*, *8*(2), 111–138.

Erikson, E. H. (1959). Identity and the life cycle: Selected papers. *Psychological Issues*, *1*, 1–171.

Erikson, E. H. (1968). *Identity: Youth and crisis*. Norton.

Francis, L. J. (1993). Parental influence and adolescent religiosity: A study of church attendance and attitude toward Christianity among adolescents 11 to 12 and 15 to 16 years old. *International Journal for the Psychology of Religion*, *3*(4), 241–253. https://doi.org/10.1207/s15327582ijpr0304_4

Gaveras, E. M., Fabbre, V. D., Gillani, B., & Sloan, S. (2023). Understanding past experiences of suicidal ideation and behavior in the life narratives of transgender older adults. *Qualitative Social Work*, *22*(1), 159–175. https://doi.org/10.1177/14733250211051783

Gonzalez, V. M., & Skewes, M. C. (2016). Association of the firewater myth with drinking behavior among American Indian and Alaska Native college students. *Psychology of Addictive Behaviors: Journal of The Society of Psychologists In Addictive Behaviors*, *30*(8), 838–849. https://doi.org/10.1037/adb0000226

Halberstam, J. J., & Halberstam, J. (2005). *In a queer time and place: Transgender bodies, subcultural lives* (Vol. 3). NYU press.

Hall, S. (2021). *The hard road to renewal: Thatcherism and the crisis of the left*. Verso Books.

Hofstede, G. (2001). *Culture's consequences: Comparing values, behaviors, institutions, and organizations across nations* (2nd ed.). SAGE.

Hong, P., & Cui, M. (2020). Helicopter parenting and college students' psychological maladjustment: The role of self-control and living arrangement. *Journal of Child and Family Studies*, *29*, 338–347.

hooks, B. (1990). Postmodern blackness. *Postmodern Culture, 1*(1).

Horkheimer, M., & Adorno, T. W. (1972). *Dialectic of Enlightenment: Max Horkheimer and Theodor W. Adorono.* New York: Seabury Press.

Kessler, R., Amminger, G. P., Aguilar-Gaxiola, S., Alonso, J., Lee, S., & Üstün, T. B. (2007). Age of onset of mental disorders: A review of recent literature. *Current Opinion in Psychiatry, 20*(4), 359–364. https://doi.org/10.1097/YCO.0b013e32816ebc8c

Mary, A. A. (2014). Re-evaluating the concept of adulthood and the framework of transition. *Journal of Youth Studies, 17*(3), 415–429.

Mignolo, W. D., & Walsh, C. E. (2018). *On decoloniality: Concepts, analytics, praxis.* Duke University Press.

Moore, K. (2005). Thinking about youth poverty through the lenses of chronic poverty, life-course poverty and intergenerational poverty. *SSRN Electronic Journal.* https://doi.org/10.2139/ssrn.1753655

Office of the Surgeon General, Center for Mental Health Services, & National Institute of Mental Health. (2001). *Mental health: Culture, race, and ethnicity: A supplement to* Mental Health: A Report of the Surgeon General. Substance Abuse and Mental Health Services Administration. https://www.ncbi.nlm.nih.gov/books/NBK44249/

Sands, R. G. (2001). *Clinical social work practice in behavioral mental health: a postmodern approach to practice with adults.* Pearson.

Sarkar, U., Sahatgija, H., & Kyo, M. (2022). *The impact of COVID-19 on young people.* Generation Unlimited. https://www.generationunlimited.org/stories/impact-covid-19-young-people

Schmitz, R. M., Sanchez, J., & Lopez, B. (2019). LGBTQ+ Latinx young adults' health autonomy in resisting cultural stigma. *Culture, Health & Sexuality, 21*(1), 16–30. https://doi.org/10.1080/13691058.2018.1441443

Tagliabue, S., Crocetti, E., & Lanz, M. (2016). Emerging adulthood features and criteria for adulthood: Variable-and person-centered approaches. *Journal of Youth Studies, 19*(3), 374–388.

Umaña-Taylor, A. J., Quintana, S. M., Lee, R. M., Cross, W. E., Jr., Rivas-Drake, D., Schwartz, S. J., Syed, M., Yip, T., Seaton, E., & Ethnic and Racial Identity in the 21st Century Study Group. (2014). Ethnic and racial identity during adolescence and into young adulthood: An integrated conceptualization. *Child Development, 85*(1), 21–39. https://doi.org/10.1111/cdev.12196

von Kiedrowski, G., Otto, S., & Herdewijn, P. (2010). Welcome home, systems chemists! *Journal of Systems Chemistry, 1,* Article 1. https://doi.org/10.1186/1759-2208-1-1

CREDIT

Fig. 7.1: Source: Adapted from https://cormac404.wordpress.com/2017/05/18/some-thoughts-on-an-ecological-perspective-of-social-media-research/.

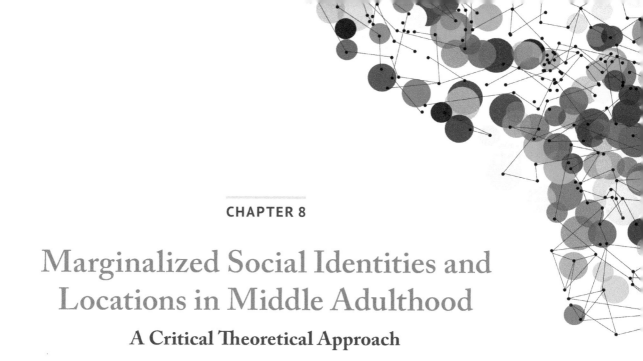

CHAPTER 8

Marginalized Social Identities and Locations in Middle Adulthood

A Critical Theoretical Approach

GIO IACONO AND LISA WERKMEISTER ROZAS

There is no "the truth," "a truth"—truth is not one thing, or even a system. It is an increasing complexity.

—Adrienne Rich

LEARNING OBJECTIVES

1. Develop an understanding of the intergenerational aspects of biological, social, emotional, and cognitive processes that become pivotal points of intervention during adulthood.

(Competencies 2, 3 and 7)

2. Explore how daily stressors and life-changing events challenge development processes and lead to subsequent processes in family, community, and social environments.

(Competencies 2, 3, and 7)

3. Recognize how a critical theoretical framework, informed by queer theory, matrix of coloniality, critical race theory, and critical realism, can deepen social workers' understanding of human behavior in the social environment.

(Competencies 2, 3, and 7)

4. Apply the aforementioned critical theoretical framework to three predominant traditional HBSE theories in social work: (a) Erickson's stages of psychosocial development as it relates to middle adulthood; (b) adult attachment theory; and (c) Bronfenbrenner's ecological systems theory. (Competencies 2, 3, and 7)

Introduction

The process of "growing up" is unique to every individual, yet finding meaning to where one is in life is something most people have in common. By the time people enter into adulthood, most have been socialized by caregivers, family and community members, friends, or others central in their development. The messages we receive around what to value, believe, and accomplish, either intentionally or unintentionally relayed, are most likely in concert with the norms and expectations of the people with whom we are surrounded as well as the larger dominant culture. Through this process and the recognition of their own intersectional identities, typically, people develop their own set of beliefs, values, and "truths" and seek to share that with others. Whether or not a person's lived experience is recognized or validated often depends on the level of conformity (or nonconformity) their identities have to dominant cultural standards and/or if an identity is a target for discrimination or stigmatization. The truth that lies in one's identity is dynamic, unique, mutable, and complex. Many traditional HBSE theories lack a critical analysis that takes power and privilege into consideration, presenting a one-dimensional understanding of development. Social workers who work with individuals at all phases of development must seek to understand, hold on to, and rely on the complexity that is the human condition. Think about your upbringing: What messages do you remember receiving about your own and different social group identities? How similar or different were the people who lived in your neighborhood, went to your schools, and shopped in your community? What beliefs do you remember being taught when you were younger but no longer have? Consider these questions as you read the following vignettes.

VIGNETTES

Brian: You are a social work intern in a community mental health agency. You have been assigned Brian, who is a 38-year-old Black, bisexual, intersex, male-identified individual. He has a small frame and wears an oversized jacket. As he sits in the chair, he looks down, takes off his glasses, and starts talking about how much he wants to be in a long-term relationship but doesn't know how to do the "intimacy thing." He lists the various relationships he has had and explains that none of them have lasted more than a month or two. He explains that he wants a relationship that is about more than "just sex." As he pulls back and puts on his glasses, he looks at you and says, "So, do you think you can help me?"

Chantal: As a new social worker at a behavioral health clinic, Chantal was recently referred to you for individual therapy. Chantal is 45-years-old, Black, transgender, and is living with HIV. She has reported significant traumatic experiences related to racism, xenophobia, and abuse as a result of growing up as a gender-nonconforming child and adolescent. In your first session, she appears distraught and preoccupied, stating that she has come for therapy to "get rid of these nightmares" and to "feel better." She also states, "I really don't know if this therapy stuff is going to work."

Reflection Questions

1. What might be some of the first questions that come to mind?

2. Which ones would you actually ask the clients?

3. Which might you hold off on asking, and which might you decide not to ask at all?

4. What assumptions might you have about each client?

5. What aspects of their stories or identities might make you feel unprepared?

6. How might your identity influence the way you see and work with each client?

Road Map

This chapter will begin by identifying our social locations and **positionalities** (e.g., race, gender, class, **sexual identity**, etc.). We will follow by describing our theoretical framework that provides a critical lens to exploring human behavior in the social environment. These critical approaches are queer theory, matrix of coloniality, critical race theory, and critical realism. Following this, we will present three predominant traditional theories in social work that help us examine human behavior in the social environment. While helpful, these theories often overlook important factors that negatively impact a client or a community's well-being. Utilizing a critical theoretical framework, traditional mainstream theories we will examine are (a) Erickson's stages of psychosocial development as it relates to middle adulthood, (b) adult attachment theory, and (c) Bronfenbrenner's ecological systems theory. Finally, we will present two case studies where we will apply a critical theoretical framework to provide a deeper and more critical exploration of a person's social realities in adulthood.

Locating Ourselves

To begin, it is important to identify and determine how our social locations, positionalities, and places of privilege and disadvantage inform how we critically explore adulthood and human behavior in the social environment. Our frames of reference are situated within a particular local, political, and historical context (Probst & Berenson, 2014). I, Gio (coauthor), am a queer, White, male-identified, Canadian-born social work educator, researcher, and practitioner. My clinical and community social work practice has largely focused on populations who hold multiple and intersecting forms of oppression. My identification of privilege (e.g., White and male identities) leads me to critically reflect on how I conduct social work assessment and intervention within a racist, White supremacist, patriarchal, **cis/heteronormative** context and how client–practitioner relations and power dynamics are upheld by these systems of oppression.

I, Lisa (second coauthor), identify as a first-generation Peruvian American, light-skin Latina, queer cisgender female research-activist, educator, and clinician. My identity as a bilingual, bicultural, first-generation Peruvian American informs my research and practice. My light-skin privilege shields me from many overt forms of racism and at the same time often requires me to divulge my racial/ethnic identity after being misidentified. This experience is an example of the complexity that exists within a person's identity, particularly when one's own truth does not match society's expectations.

Theoretical Framework

For this chapter, we have decided to focus on four main critical theories/frameworks that challenge dominant and traditional ways of understanding human behavior in the social environment during middle adulthood. The following approaches have been invaluable in helping us disrupt White, ableist, classist, cis/heterosexist, and sexist clinical assumptions and approaches when working with adult clients and service users living with marginalized social identities and locations. While there are a multitude of critical theories and frameworks social workers can draw upon to support their practice, these four theories/frameworks—queer theory, matrix of coloniality, critical race theory, and critical realism—have especially helped us as practitioners consider how stigma, discrimination, and cultural and intergenerational trauma shape and unfairly impose upon the lives of individuals and communities.

Within the context of these important theories/frameworks, it is important to recognize the dramatic effect traumatic events can have on overall development, beginning in childhood and extending into adulthood. Events such as physical or psychological abuse, neglect, and household dysfunction experienced in early development are associated with physical, mental, and behavioral health consequences later in life. These signifying events have become known as **adverse childhood experiences (ACEs)**, and a measure has been developed to identify the prevalence of trauma in a child's life. Although these biopsychosocial impediments affect and cut across sociopolitical and socioeconomic status, the prevalence of ACEs is greater among disadvantaged populations (Merrick et al., 2018). Research that has focused on understanding the connections between traumatic experiences and well-being has found that for most people, greater exposure to trauma results in poorer physical/mental health, emotional, and educational outcomes (Hughes et al., 2017). The premise being that toxic stress actually changes people's genetic and molecular structure as well as neurological and immune functioning (Boullier & Blair, 2018).

Queer Theory

Queer theory is a critical perspective that emerged in the early 1990s in order to challenge and deconstruct sexuality and gender. While there is no singular agreed-upon definition of queer theory, it is grounded in questioning, or rather *queering*, deeply held societal beliefs and assumptions related to sexuality and **gender identity** to better understand the ways in which social systems and institutions impose and oppress marginalized sexual and gender identities and expressions (Filax, 2006). Generally speaking, queer theorists see sexuality and gender as a fluid **social construction** rather than a fixed identity (Meyer et al., 2021). This theoretical position provides a critical lens to social workers that questions dichotomous and categorical thinking related to sexual and gender binaries (e.g., straight/gay; transgender/cisgender). This theory challenges deeply held assumptions of what is natural (e.g., heterosexuality) and unnatural and deviant (e.g., same-sex relationships; Callis, 2009). Importantly, queer theory allows for social workers to consider the societal impact and imposition of rigid binaries related to sexual and gender identities and actively resist the reification of these harmful binaries in their practice.

Given the emphasis on engaging diversity, equity, and inclusion in social work education (Council on Social Work Education, 2022), utilizing queer theory in social work education and practice can be useful in providing social work students and practitioners with a critical lens to deepen their understanding in relation to sexual and gender diversity. However, this perspective, which disrupts binary categories of sexual and gender identity, remains largely absent and rarely discussed in social work education and research (Bragg et al., 2018; Gringeri & Roche, 2010; Iacono, 2017).

Bragg and colleagues (2018) argue for the queering of human behavior and the social environment (HBSE) courses as a way to enhance the implicit and explicit curriculum in social work education. They posit that "queer theory is uniquely positioned to change the view on those deemed different or queer as being deviant and reshape this from a truly strengths-based perspective" (Bragg et al., 2018, p. 48). The Council on Social Work Education's (CSWE, 2022) Educational Policy and Accreditation Standards (EPAS) explicitly centers the importance of the explicit (e.g., learning plans, course material) and implicit (e.g., student supports, inclusive policies, school environment, institutional climate) curriculum. Queer theory aligns with the EPAS by enhancing the social work curriculum to better prepare students in engaging diversity within social work practice, policy, and research. For instance, queer theory may support students in deepening **critical reflexivity** in relation to the multiplicity and diversity of sexual and gender identities; this process could allow for the provision of more culturally responsive and affirming supports to clients holding these diverse identities. Queer theory also lends itself to strengthening lesbian, gay, bisexual, transgender, queer, questioning, **intersex**, asexual (LGBTQIA+) affirmative social work practice (Gates & Kelly, 2017) by challenging normative and binary structures related to sexuality and gender and honoring our client's lived experiences and ways of identifying and expressing themselves.

The Matrix of Coloniality

The **matrix of coloniality** is a framework developed by Anibal Quijano (2007). The matrix examines the structures of White supremacy, capitalism, patriarchy, and Christianity and the power that they hold individually and as a matrix in keeping the hegemonic social order. Although much of the power exists on unseen causal levels, the mechanisms that are created by the matrix affect myriad forces and events that are identified on other levels of reality (Werkmeister Rozas, 2022).

The history and effects of colonialism on a global scale are profound. Although most nations reject this form of political oppression, it is far from being eradicated. Just as important to recognize is the remnants of colonialism that continue to be a disruptive and pernicious force that upholds inequity and oppression. In his conceptualization of the coloniality of power, Quijano (2000) contends that the present-day political-economic-social order exists within the context of enduring "colonial situations" (p. 218). The colonial situation uses race as a unit of value, placing Black, Indigenous, and non-White individuals at the bottom of the sociopolitical hierarchy. The power of White supremacy is used to distribute and assign value to the various types of labor based on racial identity. Patriarchy functions in a similar fashion, undervaluing the feminine and overvaluing the masculine, denying the undervalued gender of power. Capitalism then uses these valuations to assign a particular monetary merit based on who inhabits and has access to the most prized occupations and social status. By restricting the more respected, lucrative, and credible forms of labor to White men, people of color are exploited and devalued and their labor rendered dispensable. The result was to consider people of color, particularly Black and Indigenous people, less than human, assigning them the status of slave or subordinate to White people. Christianity was used to support this ideology because most White people were Christian and most Black and Indigenous people were not. Christianity became a proxy for race.

What this means is that Black, Indigenous, and people of color (BIPOC) today live not only with the ongoing effects of colonialism but also with the current and very tangible elements of coloniality. The oppressive forces that formed the coloniality of power continue their pernicious effects on individuals who exist outside of the overvalued identities constructed by society. Many of the socio-economic-political issues that immiserate the nondominant populations of the United States today are the result of the power of coloniality. Recognizing these forces that are omnipresent in the lives of our clients is crucial to facilitating social work interventions that work toward their liberation and well-being.

Critical Race Theory

What is important about acknowledging the role that **White supremacy** has had on the social construction of race is the ramifications it has had, particularly in the United States. What is most important is to consider **critical race theory (CRT)** not as an "add-on" approach but rather a central aspect to the way social relations have developed in structural relationship to access to power and privilege within a racially diverse society. The task is not merely expanding more access to resources and opportunities but disrupting the dominant narrative of who is overvalued and who is undervalued in today's society. CRT examines the social construction of race as central to the way that people of color are ordered and constrained in society (Limbert & Bullock, 2005; Treviño et al., 2008). "Race is a powerful social construct that is created and recreated over time to regulate 'racial progress' and to preserve white privilege" (Limbert & Bullock, 2005, p. 254). The legacy of the construction of Whiteness as synonymous with humanity rather than simply a racial characteristic is still present today (Sullivan, 2003). The queer of color critique, which highlights the important intersections of queerness and race, implies the necessity of examining the unique experiences of queer and trans people of color (Ferguson, 2004; Karpman et al., 2018).

The politics of respectability are a performative praxis of minorities hoping to gain status in the minds of dominant groups through assimilation (Moore, 2011), especially as it relates to performing White middle- and upper-class heteronormative identities. The aim in respectability politics is to display behaviors worthy of respect to not only gain social status but also confirm the marginalized subject's humanity. Multiple and intersecting realities are related to social identities, such as gender, sexual orientation, socioeconomic background, and cultural/racial group, and the level of power and privilege related to those intersecting identities (Crenshaw, 1989). Within the social realities that exist, social problems exist due to oppressive human conditions and structural inequality. Experiences of exploitation and oppression related to living in a hierarchical system that affords privilege to more valued groups also function as a source of imbalance (Goodrich & Silverstein, 2005).

Critical Realism

Critical realism is a concept that considers the structure of reality as multidimensional. Roy Bhaskar (2013) believed that true reality existed in three dimensions: the empirical, the actual, and the causal. The *empirical* exists of that which could be observed and authenticated. It is the realm of what each individual experiences. The *actual* is what occurs, whether you as an individual experiences what occurs or not. The individual may not have access to that experience and how it influences them in the moment, but they are still influenced by the occurrence. In the realm of the *causal*, it is the range of unseen experiences, such as forces of racism, poverty, patriarchy, and other forms of oppression, that influence the way one perceives the world and affects their life experiences. What is important to understand about this framework is that we are affected/influenced by a variety of events experienced on various levels, some of which remain subliminal and unseen.

Acknowledging that reality occurs on more than one level allows for all aspects of an individual's lived experience to be validated. The empirical experiences of individuals possessing targeted identities have long been discounted, questioned, or invalidated. The recognition that what occurs on an individual level is real should be respected. Such an experience is then supported by the notion of the actual level, which exists even though others may not see or experience what occurred. In this case, it matters not whether or not someone disbelieves that something occurred on the empirical level because they did not see it (Werkmeister Rozas & Henry (2022). The actual level gives credence to the lived experience of those individuals whose perspectives are generally diminished. It also indicates that these empirical experiences, not experienced by those with dominant identities, impacts them in the realm of the actual. The causal level is created by the oppressive forces that, although unseen, manifest themselves in very real circumstances that perpetuate and maintain social, economic, and political inequity. It also places responsibility on the larger society for the circumstances in which people with stigmatized identities find themselves. It establishes that issues such as poverty, violence, and criminality go beyond the responsibility of the individual and include the larger society. It takes issue with the idea that individuals are to blame for their poor mental/physical health, economic situation, or social position. In other words, through the oppressive systems, institutions, and structures it has created and maintained, society is not only complicit but has a direct role in the inequity and injustice that operates within the three levels of reality.

When individuals resist contact with oppressed populations claiming fear or lack of commonality, rewarding only those who "made it" because they conformed to the dominant culture's standards of success, they are effectively choosing not to understand the empirical experience of those who are oppressed. When working with oppressed populations, we must take into account the multiple levels, not only of lived experience but of the impact on those lived experiences. The following section will introduce three predominant traditional HBSE theories that social workers use to inform assessment and intervention with clients.

Traditional HBSE Theories

Traditional and mainstream theories of human behavior and the social environment largely fail to deeply explore harmful sociopolitical factors (e.g., colonialism, racism, homophobia, transphobia, etc.) that impact people across the lifespan. We have selected three predominant theories social work students are introduced to that would benefit from applying a critical lens. We will briefly introduce each traditional theory and apply the aforementioned critical theories/frameworks (queer theory, matrix of coloniality, critical race theory, and critical realism) in order to provide a deeper understanding of the interaction between one's social environment, human development, and behavior. We will explore Erickson's (1993) stages of psychosocial development as it relates to middle adulthood (e.g., generativity versus stagnation), Ainsworth (1978) and Bowlby's (1969) adult attachment theory, and Bronfenbrenner's (1979) ecological systems theory.

Stages of Identity Development (Erikson)

Erik Erikson's (1993) eight stages of psychosocial development offers a conceptual framework for how an individual's identity develops using the ego as the unit of growth. Beginning with infancy and ending in older adulthood, the theory illustrates the various tasks needing to be accomplished in order for a person to develop and mature. Although Erikson contends that stages may overlap, there are consequences for the next stage of development if a task is not mastered in the previous stage.

The two stages that correspond to adult development are young adulthood and middle age. In young adulthood the task that is to be mastered is intimacy. Between the ages of 19 and 40 years old, the ability to develop intimacy is considered to be key in the creation, maintenance, and sustainability of relationships. The concept of intimacy is broad and includes sexual as well as emotional closeness. In order for intimacy to occur, an individual must have the ability to be vulnerable (which requires trust developed in the first stage) as well as a strong sense of self (which requires personal identity developed in the fifth stage).

Applying a Critical Lens

According to Erikson (1993), in order for individuals to have healthy and successful relationships at some point, these two stages are critical to master. Difficulty arises, however, when individuals experience trauma that affects them both psychologically as well as physically. A strong sense of self is often challenged by self-blame and insecurity. In the United States, a strong sense of self is supported and recognized as possessing the individual traits necessary to become a successful, productive, and self-reliant member of society. In other cultures, a strong sense of self can be viewed as selfish, self-absorbed, and lacking care and connection to their community. Is the culture of a particular community to blame if an individual is not supported in the development of a strong sense of self?

If an individual develops a strong sense of self that falls outside of the dominant norms and values of a positive identity, the result may be that the person experiences a sense of shame about who they are. For example, an individual in the LGBTQIA+ community may experience a meaningful relationship with a same-sex partner only to be told that the relationship does not represent the values of the larger society. What perhaps could have been a positive experience on the level of developing intimate relationships instead relegates that experience to immoral and shameful when compared to the dominant values (e.g., heteronormativity) of society.

A similar question could be posed within the stage of generativity versus stagnation, which occurs in middle adulthood. The standards most often used for generativity are family building, career satisfaction, and success, which allows for an individual to feel useful and accomplished as a member of society. The individual feels a sense of having made a difference in the world as the result of one's contributions to the betterment of humanity through positive change and parenting that produces children who are responsible, accomplished, and functioning members of society.

Yet the measure of success is often tied to dominant societal values that may or may not be in line with every individual. For example, money, fame, social influence, and power are often noted as standard measures of career success. If a person's sphere of influence is small and perhaps not valued by the dominant society, their life work may not be considered sufficiently generative. Capitalism is a force that tends to be responsible for designating standards for career success. If your work and initiative are not considered to be contributing to the capitalist system, your efforts tend to be diminished.

For some, not having children is a responsible and important decision. Some may believe it to be the best action to take in a world that is overpopulated and has diminishing resources. For others, it is about knowing their limitations as a caregiver or the difficulties that could be imposed on the family if children were introduced. There are also the individuals who want to have children or build a family that is not centered on children but are unable due to various bio-psycho-socio-political-economic barriers. Without a critical understanding of how socialization works, the propagation of children assures the ongoing proliferation of dominant values, ideals, and practices—the continuation of the matrix of coloniality.

> **REFLECTION QUESTIONS**
>
> 1. How might you understand the role culture and historical context might play in the standards Erikson's theory explains to be important in adulthood?
>
> 2. What important aspects of adulthood might the theory exclude or minimize?

Adult Attachment Theory (Ainsworth & Bowlby)

Mary Ainsworth (1978) and John Bowlby (1969) have significantly contributed to our understanding of attachment, relationships, and human bonding as it relates to human development. Attachment theory, which we first encountered in Chapter 4, provides social workers an understanding of the ways in which an individual relates with others (i.e., attachment figures) in intimate relationships. Attachment theory posits that there are three main patterns of attachment: secure, indicating a healthy connection and bond with others; anxious, indicating an overdependence on others; and avoidant, indicating difficulties relying on others. Ainsworth later added a fourth attachment pattern: disorganized, indicating a fearful, disoriented and conflicted approach toward others (Levy et al., 2018). The crux of the theory is the idea that in order for children to go out and explore the world, they need a secure base (Feeney, 2004, 2007), which is mostly provided by a caregiver.

As an infant, receiving reliable and consistent care from a caregiver is what is believed to contribute to healthy development and a secure bond (or attachment) between the infant and caregiver. In adult relationships, attachment tends to be more reciprocal in nature compared to infant–caregiver bonds in that these relationships (e.g., romantic partnership) tend to provide mutual care to one another (Ainsworth, 1978). As for the influence early attachment styles have on adult attachment, researchers acknowledge the origin may in part be in early experiences but do not always determine insecure or secure attachment in adulthood (Fraley & Roisman, 2018). There is a growing body of research that is examining the effects having or not having a secure base has on adult functioning and the potential for further growth through attachment in adulthood (Feeney & Van Vleet, 2010).

Applying a Critical Lens

Although much of the early research focused on the role that caregivers had on maintaining stable attachment styles over time, more attention has been given to how changes in attachment styles may be based on various psychosocial factors, such as relationship changes and disruptions, experiences of trauma, and potentially participating in psychotherapy (Fraley, 2002; Grossman & Grossman, 2005; Levy et al., 2018). However, there is a lack of research exploring the impact of systemic and institutional oppression on adult attachment.

An important aspect of attachment theory is that it was created largely within a particular cultural context. The Eurocentric importance of individualism is an undisclosed value in this theory resulting in specific standards of interpersonal distance, proximity to caregiver, and caregivers' response to infant cues deemed more appropriate than others. Concomitantly, there is an assumption that children are raised with one primary caregiver, most often identified as the mother; in fact, many cultures rely on multiple caregivers, including other adults and older children (Quinn & Mageo, 2013). In short, caregivers of all cultures encourage select behaviors they and their society deem to be virtuous. These virtues are consistent with the values and norms of the larger culture and are seen to contribute to successful adulthood. Longitudinal research conducted in various cultures and societies with differing values and virtues suggest that infant development is constructed within particular cultural contexts and definitions of attachment (Keller, 2013). It does not necessarily follow the same Eurocentric markers outlined in attachment theory that focuses on individualism and independence and, importantly, does not result in difficulties in adult attachment.

What this means is that expanding attachment theory into culturally informed frameworks is important (Keller, 2013). Understanding adult attachment requires having a clear sense of the cultural virtues, values, and norms in which a person was raised. Attachment behavior that may be pathologized within a Eurocentric context may be normalized and highly prized within other cultural contexts. In every cultural setting there are incidences of attachment styles that fall outside of societal and cultural expectations and may be problematic to an individual's overall development. Differential lived experiences, such as trauma, physical/mental health, and oppression, for example, can have an effect on attachment to various extents. When observing adult attachment styles, it is imperative to acknowledge that they are based on the same Eurocentric, heteronormative assumptions that privilege adult pair bonding as the ultimate expression of adult attachment. In cultural settings that favor communalism over individualism, an adult's bond with a group may be favored over the bond with another individual (Quinn, 2013). Within every attachment system there exists a range and variability, and the importance of this lies with recognizing these variations and, together with the client, understanding the implications it has on relationships, identity, and overall well-being.

> **REFLECTION QUESTIONS**
>
> 1. How might you understand how being the target of racial oppression can impact an individual's adult attachment style?
>
> 2. How might you address attachment theory's inherent Western, Eurocentric, cis/heteronormative assumptions when applying it to social work practice with diverse clients?

Ecological Systems Theory (Bronfenbrenner)

Ecological systems theory provides social workers a framework for understanding the interconnectedness of humans and the various systems (e.g., micro, meso, macro) in their environment (Bronfenbrenner, 1979). This theory posits that humans develop in relation to various proximal and distal relationship systems, such as their immediate family and friends, and broader social systems, such as their work and community (Fearnley, 2022). A *system* can be seen as a set of elements that impact or influence one another. Bronfenbrenner identified various levels of nested and interconnected systems that interact between individuals and their social environments: microsystem, mesosystem, exosystem, and macrosystem. These systems are thought to contribute to an individual's development (Fearnley, 2022).

Bronfenbrenner (1979) regarded the *microsystem* as the most immediate environment around an individual, such as the interpersonal relations with one's parents, siblings, teachers, and peers. The *mesosystem* is seen as the interactions among two or more settings an individual participates in, such as one's school and neighborhood. The *exosystem* involves elements that an individual may not be an active participant in but impact the person's behavior and development. Examples of the exosystem include various institutions in society, such as the government, workplace, mass media, and the criminal justice system. Bronfenbrenner regarded the *macrosystem* as consisting of broader culture and society's dominant ideologies, overarching values, and beliefs.

Applying a Critical Lens

This theoretical approach can help social workers attend to the person-in-environment as it relates to their client and the various interactions within and between systems that clients are impacted by. However, while this theory may acknowledge the existence of systemic oppression, this approach largely remains silent on how human oppression operates within these various systems. Further, ecological systems theory does not acknowledge causal mechanisms of oppression, leaving a lack of critical analysis of harmful sociopolitical factors that impact clients' lives. This poses challenges in being able to support clients and service users. Centering CRT, for instance, would allow social workers to ask crucial questions about the systems that a client interacts with. Using a CRT lens, a social worker may ask, "How does racism impact a client's ability to access important services and resources within a particular institution or system?" Applying a queer theory lens, for example, may allow social workers to consider how matters of safety, or lack thereof, impact clients' level of outness or gender expression as they navigate and interact with various societal systems. Further, these critical perspectives could provide a more nuanced understanding of how systems of oppression impose on people's lives, influence intra/interpersonal relationships, and exacerbate daily stressors.

REFLECTION QUESTIONS

1. Why is it important to understand how various societal systems clients interact with have been oppressive?

2. How might exploring with a client the ways in which various systems have been oppressive be helpful or unhelpful?

Moreover, while Bronfenbrenner (1975) acknowledged and aimed to incorporate the impact of societal factors on human development, there has been greater emphasis placed on the impact of family as opposed to the impact of broader systems in their environment, such as systems that perpetuate oppression (e.g., racism, homophobia, sexism, etc.). Critical frameworks such as those presented in this chapter can disrupt the tendency to deemphasize the harmful impact of broader systems and structures on the lives of clients and challenge social workers to think more critically in how they conduct social work assessment and intervention.

The following case studies help elucidate how the aforementioned critical and traditional theories of human behavior and development can provide social work practitioners guidance in working with diverse populations in middle adulthood, who oftentimes hold a myriad of diverse and intersecting identities. We will be revisiting Chantal and Brian, whose vignettes appeared at the beginning of the chapter.

Case Studies

Chantal

Chantal is a 45-year-old Black, transgender, pansexual woman. She is a U.S. citizen and first-generation Jamaican American who immigrated to the United States with her parents when she was 5. She uses she/her/hers pronouns. She is currently not working and is seeking employment. Chantal was diagnosed with HIV in her 20s and has been accessing services at the behavioral health clinic where you work.

Growing up, Chantal experienced significant psychological and emotional abuse by her family, teachers, and peers due to presenting as gender nonconforming. Her father consistently put pressure on Chantal to "stop acting like a girl." Peers in school constantly bullied Chantal due to her race and being gender nonconforming. At age 16, she dropped out of school and shortly thereafter left her family home permanently. She has experienced intermittent homelessness since. She is currently stably housed, living with her good friend Michelle.

At age 22, she attempted suicide and was subsequently hospitalized. At present, Chantal is on HIV antiretroviral medications and has been able to maintain medication adherence with the support of her friend. Chantal has experienced significant trauma growing up (i.e., ACEs) and was diagnosed with PTSD, major depression, and generalized anxiety disorder in her early 20s. She is currently taking antidepressant medication. She also has a history of substance misuse and began using when she was 16 years old. Currently, Chantal uses alcohol to cope with daily stressors and drinks throughout the day. She is also deeply spiritual and finds a source of strength in a higher power. Chantal's friend Michelle works long hours and she is extremely isolated, often in her room, without much access to supports in the community. Recently, with Michelle's encouragement, Chantal has been willing to regularly attend therapy due to her struggles with depression, anxiety, and nightmares. You have just started working with Chantal. Before reading ahead, take a moment to reflect on and respond to the questions below.

CRITICAL REFLECTIVE QUESTIONS TO CONSIDER

1. Reflecting on your social location and positionality (e.g., intersectional identities related to race, sexual orientation, gender identity, class, etc.), what might you need to consider in working with Chantal? Think about issues related to power, privilege, and oppression.

2. Taking a critical perspective, what specific risk factors and challenges are present in Chantal's life? Think individually (e.g., biologically, psychologically, spiritually), interpersonally, institutionally, systemically, and culturally.

3. What questions might you ask Chantal in order to thoroughly assess and gain a deeper understanding of the challenges she faces?

4. In applying traditional (e.g., systems, attachment) and critical (e.g., CRT) perspectives, how might you intervene to support Chantal?

5. What strengths do you see in Chantal?

First, it is imperative that social work practitioners develop competency and cultural responsiveness when working with LGBTQIA+ populations (Gates & Kelly, 2017). In Chantal's case, having the knowledge and skills for **LGBTQIA+ affirmative practice** is essential; it will be important to be knowledgeable of transgender identity development and coming out processes in particular, as well as issues impacting trans people. Critical perspectives like queer theory and CRT can help us in exploring how Chantal interacted within her environment, specifically a hostile environment toward immigrants and Black and transgender people, and guide us in exploring the ways in which she was able to exercise power and resistance in the face of great adversity and oppression. Informed by critical and traditional HBSE theories outlined in this chapter, below are some main areas to consider within the context of supporting Chantal.

It is important to consider Chantal's history, from early life stages, adolescence, and young adulthood. As we explore Chantal's history, including the impact of ACEs, it is especially important to be cognizant of the potential impact of intergenerational trauma stemming from systemic and institutional oppression, such as racism, xenophobia, classism, and sexism, to name a few. While we may explore trauma with Chantal from a more individualistic lens, it is equally important to consider the impact of collective and cultural trauma imposed on Chantal, her family, and her community. Relatedly, it would be important to consider the impact of Chantal's family immigration experience in her development as a child, young adult, and adult and how this impacted attachment patterns with her parents and family.

We may also consider and explore the potential impact of Chantal's environment and particular systems she interacted with—namely, the family and school system, as well as the community in which she grew up in. It would be helpful to explore these systems and how they may have impacted her development and sense of self as a young Black trans woman. Critical social work practice takes into account the role of agency in a person's life and how they might be able to exercise power individually and collectively to bring about personal and collective change (Fook, 2016). This broader critical and systems perspective may help us in understanding Chantal's experiences better and help us better determine how to intervene as social workers, not only on an individual level but potentially on a community level.

Additionally, we would want to explore Chantal's family history of mental health and substance use, not only to gain a deeper understanding of family mental health and substance use patterns but also to explore intergenerational patterns of resilience and coping with these challenges. Chantal experienced significant abuse and bullying from her family, teachers, and peers; these early experiences may likely play a role in her attachment style as an adult and would be important to assess. Carefully exploring and understanding how this pervasive abuse contributes to her PTSD symptoms (e.g., nightmares, flashbacks) may help lay the groundwork for establishing grounding and coping skills, as well as facilitate deeper trauma therapy to process some of these ongoing traumatic experiences.

Even though it is clear that Chantal has empirical experience of the abuse of which she was the target, others interacting with her may or may not be aware of her history. Critical realism would suggest we recognize that whether or not others in Chantal's community are aware of abuse, it affects them. How she presents herself in relationship to others is in part influenced by the abuse she endured and continues to endure. On a causal level, the social forces of gender, oppression, transphobia, and racism continue to reinforce the messages Chantal received about her identities, even if none are specifically directed toward her as an individual. It is also worth exploring how her continuous experience of being homeless and unstably housed may contribute to ongoing lack of a secure base. Without experiencing security in the context of a meaningful relationship as an adult, she has little opportunity for growth in attachment. This is most likely adding to her anxiety and depression as an adult. Chantal also experienced a suicide attempt as a young adult, which may be something to attend to as a potential risk factor for subsequent suicide attempts. There may also be an opportunity to explore and process this potentially traumatic experience in your work with her.

In terms of substance use, it would be worth exploring Chantal's desires and goals. It may be reasonable to work toward abstinence or harm reduction, which seeks to mitigate the harms associated with substance use (Vakharia & Little, 2017). Focusing on Chantal's strengths, we may explore strategies beyond using alcohol to cope with daily stressors and possible supports (e.g., substance use treatment, peer support groups) in the community to help either abstain or reduce harm. We may also devise a safety plan with Chantal should she experience a crisis and/or suicidality. A safety plan may include specific strategies to support herself (e.g., coping skills) and how to obtain supports (e.g., trusted friends, crisis lines, community supports).

It will be important to ask about Chantal's physical health and communicate with her primary care provider if anything needs to be further assessed. While not always pertinent, discussing the physiological and psychological effects of living with HIV for over 20 years may be warranted, especially considering the historical legacy of the HIV/AIDS epidemic, as well as its disproportionate impact on people of color. It may also be worth exploring what it means to her living with these various diagnoses and "labels" (e.g., HIV, PTSD, major depression, etc.).

Informed by CRT, it is essential to attend to intersecting factors of Chantal's identity and how she constructs her identity. While various institutions and cultural norms in society impose and construct social identities, it will be crucial to explore and understand how Chantal sees herself, from earlier life stages to present day, and whether internalized oppression (e.g., internalized racism and transphobia, **cis/heterosexism**) has an impact on her life and well-being. This critical practice of exploring one's social identities and how one's "problems" are connected to and influenced by institutional, structural, and legal forces (e.g., employment discrimination, lack of legal protection for trans people) may be helpful in externalizing Chantal's problems (i.e., the person is not the problem) and deconstructing unhelpful dominant discourses (e.g., harmful narratives of Black and trans identities).

Further, this exploration may facilitate the construction of alternative ways of understanding her intersectional identities and the development of empowering narratives that create opportunities for cherished values to become more richly described (Healy, 2005). Through this deconstruction/construction process, we may facilitate critical consciousness-raising (Friere, 1970) with Chantal, which involves the reflexive process of increasing one's awareness of their experiences in the context of oppressive structures and social systems. Ultimately, these various reflexive processes may facilitate awareness and resistance to oppressive structural realities and center empowering stories and possibilities that can build resilience (Dominelli, 2002; Fook, 2016).

On a more practical level, a case management approach may support meeting some of Chantal's desires or needs. For instance, a collaborative plan to support medication adherence may be developed, and referrals may be made to other health services and community organizations that support Black trans women. As a social worker, it will be important to be aware of potential community groups and culturally responsive supports (virtually or in person) that may help with reducing her social isolation. Connecting to an LGBTQIA+ affirming spiritual community may also be helpful given Chantal's strong spirituality. Political engagement may also be an avenue to explore with Chantal; engaging in strategies to exercise power, such as self- and collective advocacy, may facilitate empowerment and support her well-being (Iacono et al., 2022). At the same time, it is important to recognize that aspects of the matrix of coloniality may have a presence in some of these groups. Similar to her father not wanting Chantal to throw away her male and heterosexual privilege, some community groups of color are less open to including LGBTQIA+ individuals because of the limited power they hold. Similarly, White supremacy often plays a role in predominantly White LGBTQIA+ community groups welcoming BIPOC individuals.

In the process of working with Chantal, it will be important to maintain your own critical consciousness as a social worker. As you deeply listen, ask important and critical questions, and try to deepen understanding, we must explore our own reactions and implicit and explicit biases. This will help us challenge inherent power imbalances and reduce oppressive beliefs and actions in the social work therapeutic relationship (Sakamoto & Pitner, 2005). Ultimately, this process of working with and supporting Chantal must be driven by her and not by our own preconceptions of what she needs. Alongside working with Chantal, engaging in social advocacy with community groups to address broader macro-level issues that affect Chantal can support dismantling broader systems of oppression.

Brian

Brian is a 38-year-old Black, bisexual, intersex, male-identified individual who received a high school associate's degree. He explains that he was "OK" at school but didn't really like it. He worked at a computer software company where his job was to input data into large data banks. He grew up with a single mother; his father left the family shortly after his birth. He explains being self-conscious about his genitalia, as he has a nonfunctioning penis as well as a urethra that comes out of a vaginal hole. Throughout much of his childhood, he had several invasive surgeries to facilitate urological control and genital construction. These surgeries were physically traumatic and painful, requiring months of rehabilitation and restricted movement. He currently lives alone in an apartment and reports feeling lonely.

He relayed multiple stories of his feeling out of place and isolated in high school. He said he almost never used the restroom at school because it made him feel so uncomfortable. As a male-presenting and -identified person, Brian would use the men's bathroom but would always have to go into the stall because the way his urinary function worked, he needed to sit down so could not use the urinal. He repeated how embarrassed he would feel if someone was in the bathroom using the urinal because they could hear that he was "peeing" in the stall. He also says that it doesn't help that he has a small physical stature, which sometimes makes people think he is trans. He and his mother did not discuss his difficulties. He said it seemed she always felt uncomfortable when anything about "how he was born" was brought up. He said she would say things like, "You are just like any other Black man on the outside, so just act like one on the inside." He said that often confused him because he wasn't sure what outside and inside she was talking about.

He describes the few relationships he has had as purely sexual with not a lot of emotion. His relationships were mostly with men and tended not to last very long. He believes he has difficulties with intimacy and wishes he could be attracted to a woman enough in a sexual way so that he could pursue a long-term relationship. He wonders if that might make a difference. His mother is not aware of his relationships with men, and he feels as though she would not be supportive. He wants to have a home with "a mate" so that he doesn't have to be alone and can share things with them but doesn't know how to be in a long-lasting relationship with his intimacy issues.

He came into treatment because he wanted to work on what he called "intimacy issues." All of Brian's sexual and romantic interests have been with cisgender men. Some identified as gay, some as bisexual, and others as straight. How would you begin to understand Brian's circumstance and begin your work?

CRITICAL REFLECTIVE QUESTIONS TO CONSIDER

1. Reflecting on your own positionality, how might your identities facilitate engaging Brian in your work together? Which may present as potential barriers?

2. How might you understand Brian's intersectional identities as a Black, bisexual, intersex man, within the context of the coloniality of power? Think about his sense of masculinity, sexuality, and gender.

3. Considering the developmental stage in which he finds himself, what questions might you ask Brian about the future he desires? What significance might his multiple surgeries at an early age have on his sense of self?

4. Recognizing what traditional theories might offer to facilitate an understanding of Brian's sense of self, how might your understanding of attachment theory, ecological theory, and psychosocial development be strengthened by a critical theoretical framework?

Whether we find ourselves working with a client who has similar or overlapping identities to ours or identities that are entirely different, it is always important to reflect on how the sociopolitical context plays a role in relational dynamics. Thinking about the power differentials that may exist as a result of education, race, gender, or level of conformity to dominant standards offers an opportunity to build a conscious level of empathy.

Considering what we know about Brian's developmental history, how might we understand the effects larger social forces, such as racism, sexism, cisgenderism, and homophobia, have had on Brian? How has being a Black man, small in stature, with female- and male-associated genitalia affected his sense of self growing up? His mother's messages to him about being a man on the inside and outside most likely put pressure on Brian to conform to traditional standards of masculinity and cisnormativity. They also reinforced the importance of holding on to the only power the matrix of coloniality bestowed on him by being male in a patriarchal, White supremist society. For Brian to align himself with any element of femininity would be to his disadvantage. Similarly, having been subjected to multiple surgeries at a young age to construct a penis, even though it would not be a functioning one, impressed on Brian the value of being a cisgender male in society.

A traditional theory such as Erikson's stages of psychosocial development would echo the potential impasse Brian might experience in not being able to biologically procreate. The expectation of generativity in adulthood, mostly accomplished by building a family, may seem out of reach because of the reproductive and relational challenges. It would be important here to understand what Brian's expectations are for himself as an adult and what larger systemic institutions and structures have influenced these expectations. Can he recognize his own values outside of dominant standards? How might you go about gaining an understanding of Brian's sense of purpose and the contributions he is making to various aspects of his life and larger society? It would be important to explore what things hold meaning for him and his future goals, hopes, and dreams. How might queer theory assist in understanding how Brian's goals may be similar to those recognized in a hetero/cisnormative population and may be realized differently?

When thinking about his identity, what levels of reality are at play? Empirically, for Brian, he is Black, intersex, bisexual, and male identified. On an actual level, he may be perceived as a Black (or mixed race), gay male or transgender man. On a causal level, a variety of systemic and structural forms of oppression affect the way he is perceived by others in society and restrict the way he is able to identify. The prescriptive socially constructed male/female gender binary requires a certain stereotype of masculinity for males and femininity for females. This narrow categorization leaves little room for individuals whose presentation or identification may not conform to these rigid standards, diminishing their ability to authentically express who they are. Imagine the consequences that this unseen oppressive force may have on Brian's ability to fully realize all aspects of himself. The people with whom he associates are likely to be unaware of the manifestations of gender, sexual, and racial oppression and how they impact Brian on a daily basis. Not being able to acknowledge, embrace, or define his intersectional identity because it does not conform to dominant societal standards or exist in a one-dimensional view of reality affords Brian little opportunity to grow or develop. It is crucial that any social worker working with him is critically conscious of the systemic oppressive forces that are working on all levels of reality.

Finally, it would be important to understand the kinds of social supports Brian has and what aspects of him feel welcomed and understood and which does he feels go unrecognized or devalued. Often for LGBTQIA+ people of color, there is a feeling that they may have to prioritize one identity over another in order to find a community. Many LGBTQIA+ communities are predominantly White, leaving issues of race and racism unaddressed. Similarly, due to the consequences of the matrix of coloniality and the privilege that Black men possess due to gender oppression, in many BIPOC communities issues of homophobia, transphobia, and cisgenderism are present. Finding a BIPOC LGBTQIA+ social support network would potentially assist Brian in feeling connected to a community where all of his identities are recognized and validated.

TABLE 8.1 Taking A Critical Approach When Utilizing Traditional Human Behavior and Development Theories In Middle Adulthood

Traditional middle adulthood HBSE theories	Applying a critical lens
Erickson's stages of psychosocial development	• As the stages of psychosocial development model rarely takes into account the impact of trauma and trauma history (e.g., ACEs), consider and explore with your client what their understanding of growth and development means to them and whether they even subscribe to these cultural values.
	• Consider your client's cultural and ethno-racial background when trying to apply the this model. Does the model fit with their worldview and cultural reality?
	• Challenge rigid ideals and hetero/cisnormative assumptions of where one should be in terms of relationships and a sense of generativity (e.g., raising a family, career, success) in middle adulthood, given that many LGBTQIA+ adults do not necessarily follow traditional trajectories related to relationships and what it means to be generative.
	• Consider how a client's intersectional identities (e.g., race, ethnicity gender identity, sexual identity) inform their middle adulthood developmental process.
	• Acknowledge and honor how clients identify in terms of their sexuality and gender.
	• In terms of human development, consider the multiplicity and fluidity of sexual and gender identities rather than seeing them as singular and fixed identities.
	• Question dichotomous and categorical thinking related to sexual and gender binaries (e.g., straight/gay; transgender/cisgender).
	• Challenge deeply held assumptions of what is natural (e.g., heterosexuality, cisgender) and unnatural and deviant (e.g., LGBTQIA+).
	• In assessing adult identity development, consider whether you validate and honor clients' multidimensional levels of reality, that which can be observed and authenticated, as well as experiences that may be subliminal, unseen, or inaccessible to our clients.
	• Aim to take into account the multiple levels—the empirical, the actual, and the causal—of a client's reality and how this impacts their understanding of their life stage of development.
Adult attachment theory (Ainsworth & Bowlby)	• Consider the impact of systemic and institutional oppression on adult attachment.
	• Consider whether you are resisting engagement and attachment with clients who experience multiple and interlocking forms of oppression due to a lack of commonality and whether you engage more with clients who "made it" because they conformed to the dominant culture's standards of success.

(Continued)

TABLE 8.1 Taking A Critical Approach When Utilizing Traditional Human Behavior and Development Theories In Middle Adulthood (*Continued*)

Traditional middle adulthood HBSE theories	Applying a critical lens
	• Question Eurocentric attachment assumptions:
	• Individualism, which results in specific standards of interpersonal distance, proximity to caregiver, and caregivers' response to infant cues that are deemed more appropriate than others.
	• Assumption that children are raised with one primary caregiver, most often identified as the mother when in fact, many cultures rely on multiple caregivers, including other adults and older children, which is perfectly healthy and common.
	• Hyperfocus and valuing of individualism and independence, which would deem certain communities as having difficulties in adult attachment if they do not possess them.
	• Pathologizing attachment behavior and patterns that deviate from Eurocentric ideals, such as those related to hetero/cisnormativity and the nuclear family, two-parent household model.
Ecological systems theory (Bronfenbrenner)	• Engage in critical analysis of harmful sociopolitical factors that impact your clients.
	• Consider how human oppression operates within these various systems and the causal mechanisms of oppression.
	• Centering CRT, ask critical questions about the systems that a client interacts with and how racism may impact BIPOC clients' ability to access important services and resources within a particular institution or system.
	• Apply the matrix of coloniality to explore how powerful structures of White supremacy, capitalism, patriarchy, and Christianity, individually and as a matrix, impose a hegemonic social order in your clients' lives. Colonialism lives on and has not been completely eradicated; aim to recognize the remnants of colonialism that continue to be disruptive and harmful in your client's life.
	• Applying a queer theoretical lens, consider how matters of safety, or lack thereof, impact your clients' levels of outness or gender expression as they navigate and interact with various societal systems.
	• Assess beyond the impact of the family system and consider the impact of broader systems (e.g., school, employment, culture) in your clients' environment that perpetuate oppression (e.g., racism, homophobia, sexism, etc.).
	• Critical frameworks, such as matrix of coloniality, CRT, and queer theory, can disrupt the tendency to deemphasize the impact of broader systems on the lives of clients and challenge social workers to think more critically about how they conduct social work assessment and intervention.
	• Critically reflect on how BIPOC clients specifically are negatively impacted by not only the ongoing effects of colonialism but the current and very tangible elements of coloniality; recognizing these forces that are omnipresent in the lives of our clients is crucial to collaboratively facilitating interventions that work toward their liberation and well-being.
	• Utilizing a critical realism lens, question whether you see your client's experiences related to poverty, mental health/health, violence, criminality, for example, as their sole responsibility or as a result of the impact of larger oppressive societal systems and structures.

CONCLUSION

This chapter on middle adulthood development sought to examine intergenerational aspects of biological, social, emotional, and cognitive processes that become pivotal points of intervention during adulthood. We demonstrated how daily stressors and life-changing events challenge development processes and lead to subsequent processes in family, community, and social environments. Through the critical theories/frameworks we presented in this chapter (i.e., matrix of coloniality, CRT, queer theory, critical realism), we sought to highlight the importance of complexity. Using these theories/frameworks, we critically examined and interrogated three predominant and traditional theories (i.e., Erickson's stages of psychosocial development related to middle adulthood, adult attachment theory, Bronfenbrenner's ecological systems theory) that social workers use to understand our clients' development and behavior in the social environment. We argued that these traditional theories can be helpful in social work assessment and intervention; however we contend that they often fail to consider complex, crucial factors that negatively impact our clients' day-to-day realities. The two case studies presented in this chapter, as well as their related critical reflection questions, provide some guidance to social workers when working with clients who experience multiple and interlocking forms of oppression and live with stigmatized identities.

This chapter focused on weaving traditional theories with critical theories/frameworks and frameworks utilized in social work: Complexity is ultimately the centerpiece of the approach we offer. We understand the complexity, and oftentimes chaos, that is the human condition. As a model for social work practice with adults, we did not attempt to step away from classical theorists and their ideas, which heavily inform practice, but instead we aimed to weave together these theories, like a tapestry or quilt, with critical theories/frameworks in order to unveil the complexity. In doing so, we highlighted the limitations of traditional theories and incorporated a critical lens that thoughtfully considers and more deeply integrates the impact of the larger sociopolitical context when working with clients. We hope that you have grappled with the ideas presented in this chapter and will weave these critical theoretical approaches into your practice as a way to uphold the standards of the profession and to promote a more social justice–oriented approach to social work practice (National Association of Social Workers, 2021). The next chapter looks at later adulthood.

KEY TERMS

- LGBTQIA+ affirmative practice: an overarching framework that informs social work and clinical practice with LGBTQIA+ individuals. Affirmative practice aims to affirm and celebrate LGBTQIA+ identity and expression, and explore and address anti-LGBTQIA+ minority stressors that negatively impact mental health and wellbeing.

- Cis/heteronormativity: an oftentimes unrecognized form of systemic prejudice towards sexual and gender minority individuals (i.e., LGBTQIA+ population) through commonplace assumptions that all people in society are cisgender and heterosexual, and this being seen as the "norm".

- Cis/heterosexism: the societal privileging (e.g., power, status, access, resources) of cisgender identity and heterosexuality.

- Critical race theory (CRT): examines the social construction of race as central to the way that people of color are ordered and constrained in society. CRT highlights how racism is not merely the product of individual bias or prejudice, but also something embedded in all societal systems (legal, education, etc.) and policies.

- Critical realism: a theory used to explain perceptions of reality. It states that reality is experienced on three levels: the empirical which are events that are experienced first-hand, the actual which are all events, whether experienced by the self or not, and the causal which accounts for the mechanisms that generate events.

- Matrix of coloniality: a framework comprised of four invisible forces—White supremacy, patriarchy, Christianity, and capitalism which function together to form a political, social relational, economic and epistemological structure of subjugation, exploitation, and domination that determine social roles and status.

- Positionalities: a recognition of the various social group identities a person holds (both dominant and targeted identities) within a particular socio-political setting and how it influences the way a person understands and experiences the world.

- Queer theory: examines the ways in which power operates to institutionalize and legitimate certain sexual and gender expressions and identities while stigmatizing others (i.e., those that exist outside of heterosexuality and cisgender identity).

- Adverse childhood experiences (ACEs): traumatic experiences that occur before a child turns 18. Experiences such as physical and emotional abuse, neglect, domestic violence, parental substance abuse, mental illness, and incarceration can negatively affect a person's health, mental health, and overall life trajectory.

- Social construction: a term used to explain a concept or meaning that has been created by society within that particular social context. Although the concept is the result of subjective reality, because the concept has been adopted by society it is perceived as an objective truth.

- Sexual identity: one's perceptions of how they think of themselves in terms of who they are romantically and/or sexually attracted to. This term can also refer to sexual orientation.

- Gender identity: one's innermost concept of self as man/male, woman/female, a blend of both or neither. One's gender identity may be the same or different from their sex assigned at birth (i.e., female/male).

- Critical reflexivity: involves an examination of one's own perspective, assumptions, beliefs and values that are the result of our social relations and our relationship to power within the larger social order.

- Intersex: referring to a person who is born with sex characteristics (e.g., chromosomes, sex hormones, genitals) that do not fit traditional medical definitions of male or female bodies. Intersex may also be an identity one adopts.

- White supremacy: an ideology used to support a racial hierarchy where White people are superior to all other racial groups and should therefore dominate all others.

DISCUSSION QUESTIONS

1. What do I take away after reviewing this chapter?

2. How are the major ideas and concepts presented in this chapter support my work with the communities I work with?

3. How might I apply the major ideas and concepts in this chapter to my social work practice?

4. How do the chapter's major ideas and concepts align with anti-racist and anti-oppressive practice?

REFERENCES

Ainsworth, M. D. S. (Ed.). (1978). *Patterns of attachment: A psychological study of the strange situation.* Lawrence Erlbaum.

Bhaskar, R. (2013). *A realist theory of science.* Routledge.

Boullier, M., & Blair, M. (2018). Adverse childhood experiences. *Paediatrics and Child Health, 28*(3), 132–137. https://doi.org/10.1016/J.PAED.2017.12.008

Bowlby, J. (1969). *Attachment and loss: Vol. 1: Attachment.* The Hogarth Press and the Institute of Psycho-Analysis.

Bragg, J., Havig, K., & Muñoz, R. (2018). Absent in theory, invisible in practice: Queering HBSE for a more inclusive social work profession. *Journal of Human Behavior in the Social Environment, 28*(1), 44–57. https://doi.org/10.1080/10911359.2017.1383959

Bronfenbrenner, U. (1975). The origins of alienation. In U. Bronfenbrenner & M. Mahoney (Eds.), *Influences on human development* (2nd ed., pp. 485–501). The Dryden Press.

Bronfenbrenner, U. (1979). The ecology of human development: Experiments by nature and design. Harvard University Press.

Callis, A. S. (2009). Playing with Butler and Foucault: Bisexuality and queer theory. *Journal of Bisexuality, 9*(3–4), 213–233. https://doi.org/10.1080/15299710903316513

Council on Social Work Education. (2022). *2022 educational policy and accreditation standards for baccalaureate and master's social work programs.* https://www.cswe.org/accreditation/standards/2022-epas/

Crenshaw, K. (1989) Demarginalizing the intersection of race and sex: A black feminist critique of antidiscrimination doctrine, feminist theory, and antiracist politics. *University of Chicago Legal Forum*, 139–167.

Dominelli, L. (2002). Anti-oppressive practice in context. In R. Adams, L. Dominelli & M. Payne (Eds.), *Social work: Themes, issues, and critical debates*. Basingstoke: Palgrave.

Erikson, E. H. (1993). *Childhood and society*. W.W. Norton & Company.

Fearnley, B. (2022). Becoming a reflexive and reflective practice educator: Considering theoretical constructs of Bronfenbrenner and Bourdieu for social work student field placements. *Social Work Education*, *41*(1), 50–62. https://doi.org/10.1080/02615479.2020.1796954

Feeney, B. C. (2004). A secure base: Responsive support of goal strivings and exploration in adult intimate relationships. *Journal of Personality and Social Psychology*, *87*(5), 631–648. https://doi.org/10.1037/0022-3514.87.5.631

Feeney, B. C. (2007). The dependency paradox in close relationships: Accepting dependence promotes independence. *Journal of Personality and Social Psychology*, *92*(2), 268–285. https://doi.org/10.1037/0022-3514.92.2.268

Feeney, B. C., & Van Vleet, M. (2010). Growing through attachment: The interplay of attachment and exploration in adulthood. *Journal of Social and Personal Relationships*, *27*(2), 226–234. https://doi.org/10.1177/0265407509360903

Ferguson, R. A. (2004). *Aberrations in Black: Toward a queer of color critique*. University of Minnesota Press.

Filax, G. (2006). Politicising action research through queer theory. *Educational Action Research*, *14*(1), 139–145. https://doi.org/10.1080/09650790600585632

Fook, J. (2016). *Social work: A critical approach to practice*. SAGE.

Fraley, R. C. (2002). Attachment stability from infancy to adulthood: Meta-analysis and dynamic modeling of developmental mechanisms. *Personality and Social Psychology Review*, *6*(2), 123–151. https://doi.org/10.1207/S15327957PSPR0602_03

Fraley, R. C. (2019). Attachment in adulthood: Recent developments, emerging debates, and future directions. *Annual Review of Psychology*, *70*(1), 401–422. https://doi.org/10.1146/annurev-psych-010418-102813

Freire, P. (1970). *Pedagogy of the oppressed*. Continuum.

Gates, T. G., & Kelly, B. (2017). Affirming strengths-based models of practice. In M. P. Dentato (Ed.), *Social work practice with the LGBTQ community: The intersection of health, mental health, and policy factors* (pp. 235–248). Oxford Universtiy Press.

Goodrich, T. J., & Silverstein, L. B. (2005). Now you see it, now you don't: Feminist training in family therapy. *Family Process*, *44*(3), 267–281.

Gringeri, C. E., & Roche, S. E. (2010). Beyond the binary: Critical feminisms in social work. *Affilia*, *25*(4), 337–340. https://doi.org/10.1177/0886109910384194

Grossman, K. E., & Grossman, K. (2005). Universality of human social attachment as an adaptive process. In C. S. Carter, L. Ahnert, K. E. Grossmann, S. B. Hrdy, M. E. Lamb, S. W. Porges, & N. Sachser (Eds.), *Attachment and bonding: A new synthesis* (pp. 199–228). Boston Review.

Healy, K. (2005). *Social work theories in context: Creating frameworks for practice*. Palgrave Macmillian.

Hughes, K., Bellis, M. A., Hardcastle, K. A., Sethi, D., Butchart, A., Mikton, C., Jones, L., & Dunne, M. P. (2017). The effect of multiple adverse childhood experiences on health: A systematic review and meta-analysis. *The Lancet Public Health*, *2*(8), e356–e366. https://doi.org/10.1016/S2468-2667(17)30118-4

Iacono, G. (2017). Epistemic injustice: Towards uncovering knowledge of bisexual realities in social work research. *Advances in Social Work*, *18*(2), 563–582. https://doi.org/10.18060/21427

Iacono, G., Craig, S. L., Crowder, R., Brennan, D. J., & Loveland, E. K. (2022). A qualitative study of the LGBTQ+ youth affirmative mindfulness program for sexual and gender minority youth. *Mindfulness*, 1–16.

Karpman, H.E., Ruppel, E.H., & Torres, M. (2018). "It wasn't feasible for us": Queer women of Color navigating family formation. *Family Relations*, *67*(1), 118–131.

Keller, H. (2013). Attachment and culture. *Journal of Cross-Cultural Psychology*, *44*(2), 175–194. https://doi.org/10.1177/0022022112472253

Levy, K. N., Kivity, Y., Johnson, B. N., & Gooch, C. V. (2018). Adult attachment as a predictor and moderator of psychotherapy outcome: A meta-analysis. *Journal of Clinical Psychology*, *74*(11), 1996–2013. https://doi.org/10.1002/jclp.22685

Limbert, W. M., & Bullock, H. E. (2005). 'Playing the fool': US welfare policy from a critical race perspective. *Feminism & Psychology*, *15*(3), 253–274.

Merrick, M. T., Ford, D. C., Ports, K. A., & Guinn, A. S. (2018). Prevalence of adverse childhood experiences from the 2011–2014 Behavioral Risk Factor Surveillance System in 23 states. *JAMA Pediatrics*, *172*(11), 1038–1044. https://doi.org/10.1001/jamapediatrics.2018.2537

Meyer, S. J., Dale, E. J., & Willis, K. K. (2021). "Where my gays at?" the status of LGBTQ people and queer theory in nonprofit research. *Nonprofit and Voluntary Sector Quarterly*, *51*(3). https://doi.org/10.1177/08997640211021497

Moore, M. R. (2011). *Invisible families: Gay identities, relationships, and motherhood among Black women*.

National Association of Social Workers. (2021). *Code of ethics*. https://www.socialworkers.org/About/Ethics/Code-of-Ethics/Code-of-Ethics-English

Quijano, A. (2000). Coloniality of power and Eurocentrism in Latin America. *International Sociology*, *15*(2), 215–232. https://doi.org/10.1177/0268580900015002005

Quijano, A. (2007). Coloniality and modernity/rationality. *Cultural Studies*, *21*(2–3), 168–178.

Quinn, N. (2013). Adult attachment cross-culturally: A reanalysis of the Ifaluk emotion fago. In N. Quinn & J. Mageo (Eds.), *Attachment reconsidered: Cultural perspectives on a Western theory* (pp. 215–240). Springer.

Quinn, N., & Mageo, J. (Eds.). (2013). *Attachment reconsidered: Cultural perspectives on a Western theory*. Springer.

Sakamoto, I., & Pitner, R. O. (2005). Use of critical consciousness in anti-oppressive social work practice: Disentangling power dynamics at personal and structural levels. *British Journal of Social Work*, *35*(4), 435–452. https://doi.org/10.1093/bjsw/bch190

Sullivan, N. (2003). *A critical introduction to queer theory*. New York University Press.

Treviño, A. J., Harris, M. A., & Wallace, D. (2008). What's so critical about critical race theory?. *Contemporary Justice Review*, *11*(1), 7–10.

Vakharia, S. P., & Little, J. (2017). Starting where the client is: Harm reduction guidelines for clinical social work practice. *Clinical Social Work Journal*, *45*(1), 65–76. https://doi.org/10.1007/s10615-016-0584-3

Werkmeister Rozas, L. (2022). Coloniality of power, critical realism and critical consciousness: The three "C" framework. *Journal of Ethnic & Cultural Diversity in Social Work*, *31*(3–5), 162–172.

Werkmeister Rozas, L., & Henry, A. (2022). The use of critical theory in social work international study program: Instilling racial and epistemic justice. *Social Work Education*, 1–17.

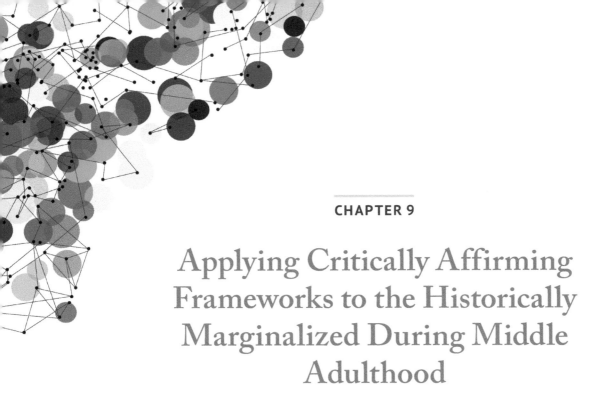

CHAPTER 9

Applying Critically Affirming Frameworks to the Historically Marginalized During Middle Adulthood

MAYRA LOPEZ-HUMPHREYS, ROSE M. PEREZ, AND BEVERLY ARAÚJO DAWSON

Introduction

"Midlife" as a construct in human behavior has moved from an unstudied terrain to an interesting, important, uncharted developmental stage that is now acknowledged to be experienced differently across diverse identities. According to the 2010 U.S. Census, as cited in Lachman (2015), 28% of the U.S. population falls into this category. This period in one's life extends over a large part of the lifespan and plays an important role in the lives of both younger and older generations. Researchers have paid less attention to this life stage in the past, a situation that has recently begun to change (Infurna et al., 2020). A recent study showed that people perceive midlife to range from 44 to 64 (Lachman, 2015), but this can vary over time and across surveys.

LEARNING OBJECTIVES

1. Provide an overview of middle adulthood and the rationale for including critical frameworks that expand dominant developmental theories and assumptions. (Competency 6)

2. Examine critically affirming frameworks (liberation psychology, relational cultural theory, intersectionality, and strengths-based perspectives) that reject deficit-oriented, individualistic perspectives and center the narratives of individuals with historically marginalized identities. (Competency 2 & 6)

3. Presenting a biological, psychological, social, natural environment, and spiritual framework within the context of a case study. (Competency 6)

4. Apply critically affirming frameworks that include the multiple ways members of historically marginalized groups experience oppression and marginalization. (Competency 2 & 4)

Common developmental tasks of middle adulthood have traditionally included establishing a family, focusing on one's career, raising children while attending to aging parents and the social community, and witnessing noticeable biological changes due to the normative aging processes (Hutchinson, 2015). Alternately, some theorists argue that middle adulthood should be assessed based on developmental milestones rather than chronologic age and is historically characterized as a time of reflection on the milestones achieved in career, family, and social development (Hutchison, 2015).

As with any life stage, this new developmental phase is associated with new challenges and constraints, which may be associated with internal confusion and chaos (Hutchinson, 2015). Carl Jung is described to have been the first thinker to focus on the psychological work of what he called the "second half of life," inclusive of a "mid-life crisis" (Jung et al., 2014). According to Jung et al. (2014), middle adulthood focuses on family relations, spirituality, and humanistic values.

The study of middle adulthood has typically consisted of a developmental approach, analyzing the effect of early life experiences and its impact on middle adulthood and the balance of growth and decline in middle adulthood.

Given the increase in life expectancy, scholars have started to examine the period between ages 30 and 45, coining it "established adulthood" and describing it as a time of focus on career trajectories, relationships, and family (Mehta et al., 2020). The recent increase in life expectancy across racial and ethnic groups has also contributed to the interest in middle adulthood. While the age-adjusted death rate for the total population increased by 16.8% from 715.2 per 100,000 standard population in 2019 to 835.4 in 2020, between 2000 and 2019, the overall life expectancy in the United States increased among Latinx (2.7 years), Black (3.9 years), and White (1.7 years) individuals (Dwyer-Lindgren et al., 2022). When studying middle adulthood, most scholars have highlighted the increased life expectancy and a post–World War II baby boom in the United States as contributing to what is referred to as "mass longevity" and a large cohort of adults in midlife (Hutchison, 2015).

It is also important to note that while life expectancy has increased for most groups, the top leading causes of death for individuals include heart disease, cancer, COVID-19, unintentional injuries, stroke, chronic lower respiratory diseases, Alzheimer's disease, diabetes, influenza, pneumonia, and kidney disease (National Center for Health Statistics, 2016b). Unfortunately, the top leading causes of death are most prevalent among historically marginalized populations.

A current analysis of middle adulthood development must consider the complex nature of a person's multiple identities (e.g., race/ethnicity, gender, class, sexual orientation, [dis]ability). This analysis must consider how intersecting forms (individual, institutional, and structural) of power, control, and oppression impact the well-being and dynamic life processes (Crenshaw, 1991; Willis & Martin, 2005). Additionally, Western perspectives of middle adulthood development among historically marginalized populations place a disproportionate focus on individual harm and give minimal attention to the complex, multifaceted ways that historically minoritized people are traumatized through interactions with systems and structures (Metzl & Hansen, 2014; Singh et al., 2020). Examining the impact of attitudes and bias on the individual does not account for the intersecting forms of stigmatization in the processes, policies, and norms of social/healthcare delivery systems, markets, institutions, and structures (Hatzenbuehler et al., 2013; Jacobs et al., 2003). Researchers are also highlighting the unique strengths of historically marginalized, middle-aged individuals and the capacity of many to manage stressors despite the accumulation of stressors throughout the life course (Baltes, 1987). We argue that cumulative assets, strengths, healthy mutual relationships, multisystem (micro, meso, and macro) trauma, and marginalization accrue across the lifespan into middle adulthood. Therefore, we offer critically affirming frameworks as a means for centering humanization, addressing systemic injustices, cultivating one's own power and agency, and fighting the collective struggle for freedom from oppressive systemic forces (Deepak, 2011; Freire, 1970; Martín-Baró, 1994).

This chapter acknowledges the connections between assets, strengths, thriving relationships, multifaceted contexts, intersecting identities, the cumulative effects of ongoing systemic barriers to economic stability as well as the historical and current trauma of colonialism and oppression throughout middle adulthood. Throughout this chapter, we will use the term historically marginalized individuals (HMIs) to refer to members of groups (i.e., women; certain racial/ethnic groups; people who identify as lesbian, gay, bisexual, transgender, queer/questioning, intersex, and asexual [**LGBTQIA+**]; immigrants; individuals with mental or physical disabilities; older individuals; and those of lower socioeconomic status) who were and continue to be denied full participation in dominant structures (political, social, cultural, economic) and who have been intentionally reduced via violence, exploitation, and stigmatization to the peripheral edges of society (Tate et al., 2014).

We begin by affirmatively examining the strengths of **historically marginalized individuals (HMIs)**. Additionally, rather than **homogenizing** HMIs as one group, we will reflectively explore the wide-ranging lived experiences that constitute middle adulthood development. Lastly, this chapter will explore ways to apply **critical affirming frameworks** to assist social workers in understanding how to address systemic injustices and leverage the agency, assets, and strengths of HMIs during mid- development. Let's begin with a case study vignette, which we will refer to throughout the chapter.

CASE VIGNETTE: ASSETS, STRENGTHS, AND THEN ADVERSITIES

Tanya is a 42-year-old, **cisgender**, straight, single, Afro-Latinx, middle-class ad executive living in a metropolis city on the East Coast who postponed starting a family to focus on her career goals. Tanya has a long-held aspiration to become a lead executive in promotions at work, and she has close friends with whom she connects consistently. Her parents, who immigrated from the Dominican Republic when she was 7, instilled in her a love and passion for learning and success, which fueled her to pursue a graduate degree in business administration.

Growing up in an Afro-Latinx household, Tanya had valuable early experiences where she received messages about the importance of a positive racial identity and the realities of discrimination in society. Tanya's parents, lawyers in their home country, immigrated to the United States due to a lack of career opportunities and started a family quickly after. Tanya is one of three daughters and the darker-skinned of the three siblings. The experiences of growing up in a family that openly discussed racism and witnessing the skin color privilege her siblings experienced provided Tanya with inner resources to confront racial oppression and adversities throughout her life.

As a Black Latinx woman, Tanya faces **microaggressions** moved and commercial buildings.

After a year of living in a new apartment complex, she has yet to make genuine connections with neighbors or find local eateries where she can decompress and feel "at home." Despite these negative experiences, Tanya remains motivated to have a successful career and relies on her family and close friends to reinforce her identity and strengths. As Tanya entered middle adulthood, she reconsidered her choice to delay having children. As a Black Latinx woman, Tanya's personal decision about procreation challenges the structural and systemic assumptions that have historically scrutinized and attempted to control the reproductive patterns of Black women (Neubeck & Casenave, 2001). These combined stressors and isolating experiences have impacted her ability to get pregnant successfully. She is currently looking into in vitro fertilization (IVF) to start a family but is concerned about the social stigmas attached to being a single black mother and is unsure about the possibility of identifying a safe, affirming, and inclusive community to raise her child.

Theoretical Frameworks

Theorists such as Erickson, Bronfenbrenner, and Elder have historically framed the "normative" understanding of human behavior development. For example, stage theorist Erik Erikson (1950) posited that the goal in middle adulthood is generativity. Attaining generativity, as we learned in Chapter 8, means transcending above and beyond one's self-interests to care for others. *Generativity* is characterized by achieving productivity, finding creativity, and offering guidance, inspiration, instruction, and leadership to others, including future generations (Syed & McLean, 2017). Examples of activities propagating generativity might include teaching, mentoring, volunteer work, telling stories, and caring for others. Without this other-centeredness, Erikson (1950) described middle-aged adults as running the risk of stagnating, which may include self-absorption and self-indulgence. They may feel as though they have little responsibility to the next generation. However, Erikson's staging is limited in examining the role of race and ethnicity regarding generativity and social involvement (Hart et al., 2001). For

REFLECTION QUESTIONS

Consider the sources of these messages when reflecting on your own experiences with affirmation and person-centered support.

1. Who and where have these messages come from?

2. How did these messages shape your identity?

example, U.S. policy has often been used to deny full participation of HMIs in the U.S. social system (e.g., exclusion of agricultural and domestic workers from the Social Security Act of 1935; Carlton-LaNey, 1999), resulting in the overwhelming need to practice generativity and develop larger networks of social supports.

Urie Bronfenbrenner's (1977) ecological perspective, introduced in the previous chapter, is a widely used framework that examines structural, institutional, and dynamic interactions within the lives of HMIs. This perspective offers a macro-level lens that focuses on broader environments and provides an approach to critically understand the larger systems, such as the global economic environment and educational and political systems (Bronfenbrenner, 2005). The physical ecology a person engages in can also provide an understanding of how one's material environment shapes one's cultural values and practices. For example, collectivistic values expressed within Chinese culture have been significantly shaped by the physical landscape of ancient China. The geographic landscape of China's maneuverable rivers and abundant fertile land fostered communal practices among neighbors that were also vital to sustaining one's survival (Nisbett, 2003). Within the United States, the ecological perspective has been utilized extensively to understand the experiences of first-generation immigrants and the complexities and opportunities of navigating settlement in the host society (Bronfenbrenner, 2005; Negi et al., 2018).

In response to the limited scope of existing theories, critical, person-centered, liberatory, and feminist scholarship have a long history of transforming Western frameworks and theories in ways that center the voices, bodies, and experiences of HMIs (Kagan et al., 2004). The following frameworks will be applied to HMIs' biological/physical, psychological, social, natural environment, and spiritual dimensions. Tonya's case study will also be integrated within the dimensions to demonstrate how frameworks could be applied.

Liberation Psychology

Heavily influenced by liberation theology (Gutierréz, 1988) and Freire's (1970) critical inquiry process, the founder of liberation psychology Ignacio Martín-Baró and scholar who challenged psychologists to include social transformation within their practice with HMIIs:

> This is not a question of whether to abandon psychology; it is a question of whether psychological knowledge will be placed in the service of constructing a society where the welfare of the few is not built on the wretchedness of the many, where the fulfillment of some does not require that others be deprived, where the interests of the minority do not demand the dehumanization of all(Martín-Baró, 1994, p. 46).

Martín-Baró (1994) argued that psychologists should be attuned to the following tenets:

- critical realism: identifying the sociopolitical context and the sources of inequities on disenfranchised within society.

- recovering historical memory: supporting just actions that acknowledge the historical context of HMIs.

- *concientización* (Spanish for "consciousness-raising"): engaging with HMIs in developing an awareness of the forms of oppression (e.g., racism) and the impact of structural violence on the life experiences of HMIs (e.g., internalized oppression).

- de-ideologized reality: collaboratively work to transform the structural causes of oppression.

These tenants have been applied to understand human development in several ways. For example, to understand immigrant women's experiences of homelessness, critical realism can be a resource in leveraging their strengths and resiliencies (Hordyk et al., 2014). In regard to the recovery of historical memory, Singh (2016) explored how transgender and nonbinary clients could be supported in reclaiming the historical memory of gender fluidity within historically marginalized communities before colonization. Liberation becomes a fully emancipatory process when HMIs develop the capacity to resist and attain social, political, and psychological well-being (Burton & Kagan, 2009).

Strengths-Based and Asset-Based Approaches

The question of how to decenter powerful false stigmatizing narratives that serve to control and rescue HMIs is an ongoing discourse within helping professions (psychology, counseling, and social work). There is growing evidence to support the use of strengths-based and asset-based approaches that can counter false narratives that give way to negative social and economic determinants of health (Craig et al., 2018; Scerra, 2012). At the same time, the dominance of deficit-based approaches in helping professions has contributed to a deficit discourse that often assesses HMIs primarily focusing on their experiences with marginalization (Fogarty et al., 2018). For example, Halpern (2015) notes how the routine practice of reporting prevalence rates and negative labeling (e.g., resistant or disengaged) of HMIs in professional documentation (case notes) can perpetuate unhealthy behaviors. Strengths-based approaches are not defined by a prescriptive set of practices but are best viewed as conceptual frameworks for well-being and development. Fundamental principles of strengths-based approaches integrate an individual's capacity for continual growth and the community's capacity to provide health-promoting resources (Saleebey, 1992, 2012). The term "assets" is often used synonymously in the literature with "strengths." Equally important, asset-based approaches shift the framing of how we approach the multifaceted narratives of HMIs. The starting point for asset-based approaches is the strengths (knowledge, aspirations, skills, social capital, historical, familial, and cultural connections; Brough et al., 2004; Glasgow Centre for Population Health, 2017). The framework underscores the importance of avoiding discussions of problems (e.g., obesity) experienced by HMIs without attributing responsibility to the source of the problem (e.g., inadequate access to affordable healthy food). It is easy to see how relying heavily on this framework tends to blame the victim and fails to account for the intersecting forms of oppression that create, sustain, and perpetuate social problems.

Intersectionality

Crenshaw's (1989, 1991) work joins work by Black feminist theorists who also asserted that when Black women and other minoritized communities are conceptualized along a single-axis framework, there is further marginalization and disempowerment because of their multiple and intersecting identities, such as gender, sexual orientation, racial, class, ethnic, linguistic, (dis)ability, and social class (Collins, 1998; hooks, 1984). Most individuals occupy both privileged and oppressed social locations. The conceptualization of intersectionality is now applied broadly across diverse populations. The theory serves to understand not only intersect, but each force is also a significant shift in how social problems can be analyzed; the theory views all systems of oppression as part of a continuous, all-encompassing construct of domination (Neubeck & Casanave, 2001). Defining "domination" as an overarching structure allows the analysis of social problems to be broad enough that its interconnecting exchanges and connected oppressive forces can be holistically assessed, evaluated, and addressed. For example, the interaction of race, gender, and class regularly determined private and public spheres of Black mothers. The economic, social, and cultural assaults experienced by thesocial support networks of Black mothers (e.g., for trade and childcare). The development of a communal private sphere (e.g., other mothering), which was fostered as a means to survive structural barriers (e.g., low-wage employment, unaffordable childcare, and segregated housing markets), made it impossible to sustain White middle-class nuclear family norms. The theory's structural implications of an interlocking system of oppressive forces can serve to address the intellectual, social, and political construction of social problems experienced by HMIs.

Relational Cultural Theory

Interdependence, human connections, and growth through relationships are critical to helping people develop and navigate challenges (Comstock, 2005; Jordan, 2017). Every society adheres to a *relational orientation*, which refers to a person's relationship with others (Anderson & Carter, 2003). *Lineal orientations* view the goal of continuity of the group as most important; *collateral orientations* strive to attend to the welfare of the extended group (Anderson & Carter, 2003). Within Western values, an individualistic relational orientation dominates; it emphasizes individual goals over collateral or lineal goals. In addition, dominant development theories often address developmental processes through step-like developments, "fixed" states, or one-dimensional goals of development.

In contrast, *relational cultural theory (RCT)* views development as "a dynamic process that encompasses increasing levels of complexity, structure, and formation within the context of human bonds and attachments" (Jordan, 1991, p. 36). Much of the RCT model was conceptualized during the second wave of U.S. feminism in the publication of *Towards a New Psychology of Women* (Miller, 1976). The model offers a distinctive view of strengths in the context of relationships, not strengths in isolation. Experiencing isolation causes suffering; in contrast, relationships with mutual empathy and mutual support are understood as the path out of isolation (Jordan & Hartling, 2002). For genuine mutual empathic encounters to occur, the process must encompass the growing, healing, and deepening of both individuals in the relationship. RCT considers that relational goals will have different expectations depending on the relational orientation system from which one operates (Jordan, 2017). For social workers, RCT broadens the individualistic assumptions and intrapsychic dynamics to assist the practitioner in viewing the client within the context of the worldview that has shaped and defined the client's values on what constitutes growth-fostering relationships. RCT scholars have noted the theory's valuable implications for understanding HMIs and forms of structural oppression (racism, sexism, and hetero/cisgenderism; Jordan, 2002; Singh & Moss, 2016).

Integral Human Development

Integral human development (IHD) provides a helpful conceptual framework for understanding why adding additional models to human development is necessary (see Figure 9.1). IHD models acknowledge the access and influence of systems and structures. They holistically value an individual's cultural, economic, political, social, and spiritual wholeness: "a wholeness that all humans want to experience and that, in concern for the common good, we want others to experience as well" (Heinrich et al., 2008, p. 3). The human development of an individual cannot be reduced or bifurcated into siloed components. Therefore, communal and personal

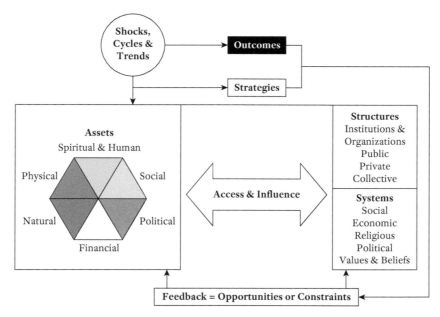

FIGURE 9.1 Integral Human Development (Heinrich et al., 2008)

well-being can only be cultivated in a holistic context of just and peaceful relationships that foster equilibrium (Heinrich et al., 2008).

Defining Historically Marginalized Individuals

It is important to note the within-group differences that exist with HMIs. For example, Latinx individuals are often studied as a homogenous group; however, as a result of mass European enslavement and colonization of the Antilles, Caribbean Latinx individuals have a higher percentage of Afro-Latinx individuals due to the mixture of African, Spaniard, and Taino background compared to other Latinx populations (Araujo Dawson, 2015). Previous studies have examined the experiences of Latinx people through a cultural lens, overlooking the significance and impact of race and ignoring the unique racialized experiences of Latinx individuals (Mazzula & Sanchez, 2021). Such within-group **heterogeneity** and the impact of intersectional identities renders a complex understanding of middle adulthood for Latinx individuals.

Let's consider the case study vignette from earlier in the chapter. When considering Tanya's family, social workers must consider how skin color shapes Tanya's lived experiences. As commonly found among racially and ethnically diverse families, various skin colors ranging variety of skin colors. Tanya is the darkest of her siblings. In the United States, individuals are racialized and categorized based on skin color and physical features (Telles, 2018). Therefore, darker-skinned individuals are more likely to be identified as Black, regardless of how a person personally identifies. Not only are these labels dichotomous in nature (meaning the choice of racial identity is either Black or White) but the labels are also loaded with stereotypes and power differentials that inform disparate experiences with access and opportunity (Golash-Boza & Bonilla-Silva, 2013). Therefore, it is probable that Tanya experiences higher levels of discrimination than her siblings and lighter-skinned family members.

THEORY ↔ PRACTICE: LET'S APPLY CRITICAL AFFIRMING FRAMEWORKS
Developing one' critical awareness of how race and which race and White supremacy were used to legitimate and expand colonization of the African Caribbean diaspora; reclaiming historical memory of African identities before colonialism.

    RCT: Fostering mutually empathic relationships with Afro-Latinx women who have cultivated healthy narratives about their identity can be an effective means for minimizing isolation.

Historically Marginalized Individuals and Physical/Biological Factors in Middle Adulthood

As we age, biological change becomes physically noticeable in most people. In middle adulthood, these changes include, among others, changes in appearance, mobility, the activity of the reproductive system, and susceptibility to chronic disease. Middle-aged adults are more likely to develop what is referred to as *multimorbidity*, which refers to experiencing two or more chronic diseases (Goodman et al., 2016). The *cumulative disadvantage or cumulative inequality hypothesis*, which posits that disadvantages in factors such as healthcare access and low socioeconomic status accumulate over time, resulting in more significant adverse effects for HMIs, has been utilized to explain the decline in health outcomes in middle adulthood (Yearby, 2018).

Higher rates of chronic health issues and mortality have been found among racially/ethnically diverse HMIs, particularly African Americans in middle and older life stages (National Center for Health Statistics, 2016a; Davis et al., 2017; Masters et al., 2014). In fact, several scholars have reported that Black individuals, compared to White individuals, have higher rates of multiple conditions diagnosed in middle adulthood and continue into future life stages (Quiñones et al., 2019). For example, among Latinx individuals, cancer and heart disease are the leading cause of death (Centers for Disease Control and Prevention, 2013). Disparities in dementia risk are likely due in part to a cumulative effect of social, demographic, and health factors over the life course, including underresourced neighborhoods and limited health care options (Sisco et al., 2015), poor childhood living conditions (Zhang et al., 2016), and high prevalence of chronic health conditions (Noble et al., 2012). Notably, African Americans have been identified as having a greater risk of developing dementia (Barnes & Bennett, 2014). It is important to note that the expansion of Medicaid has been found to reduce racial disparities in health coverage and outcomes, which is essential to addressing key disparities in middle adulthood for HMIs (Cross-Call, 2020).

THEORY ↔ PRACTICE: LET'S APPLY CRITICAL AFFIRMING FRAMEWORKS
Strengths-based (asset framing): During engagement, therapeutic support, and professional note-taking, social workers can hold off on naming disparities without identifying the larger structural forces responsible for the inequities.

Liberation psychology: Social workers must be aware of the detrimental effects of health inequities, support empowerment, and advocate with clients for change in systems and policies that perpetuate health disparities.

Physical Activity

A significant predictor of health is physical activity. The negative association between low socioeconomic status and female gender identity on health has been established. As such, these trends in physical activity carry out into midlife and beyond. Chalabaev et al. (2022) examined the effect of socioeconomic status on physical activity on adults older than age 50 using data from an extensive 13-year longitudinal study in Europe and found that for women, not men, the early-life disadvantage was negatively related to physical activity. The physical environment features of divested HMI neighborhoods, many in urban cities, provide indicators for lower rates of physical activity, including crowded streets, limited walkable green spaces, and residential apartment living that limits forms of exercise at home (Meijer et al., 2012; Zhang et al., 2020). It is important to address the physical environment when seeking to support changes in physical activity: "Rather than addressing obesity as an individual health problem, this new, transdisciplinary field of active living is focusing on how the built environment—including neighborhoods, transportation systems, buildings, parks, and open space—can promote more active lives" (Active Living Research, 4).

THEORY ↔ PRACTICE: LET'S APPLY CRITICAL AFFIRMING FRAMEWORKS
RCT: Explore mutual relationships that could participate in supporting the client's commitment to physical activity.
 Strengths-based (asset framing): Consider mapping with client spaces that support physical activity within their local community.

Fertility

Fertility in women begins to decline between the ages of 25 and 30, yet many are delaying childbirth for personal reasons, including pursuing careers (Vander Borght, & Wyns, 2018). It has been reported that the median age at last birth for females is 40–41 years without technical, medical assistance, such as in vitro fertilization (IVF; Eijkemans et al., 2014). Additionally, studies confirm that fertility in middle adulthood declines; however, with medical advances, we have witnessed an increase in births to women aged 40 and older and a decline in births during young adulthood (Hamilton et al., 2019; Smock & Schwartz, 2020). Risk factors associated with IVF include age, ovarian reserve, body mass index, endometrial receptivity, and male factors (Practice Committee of the American Society for Reproductive Medicine, 2015).

Researchers have reported racial disparities in IVF outcomes, citing that HMIs are more likely to experience spontaneous miscarriages (McQueen et al., 2015). These disparities have been explained by economic and racial/ethnic inequities impacting the quality of care (Practice Committee of the American Society for Reproductive Medicine, 2015). When considering Tanya's engagement with women's health care, the intersectionality of gender and race and its impact on the health of Black women is important to examine. Black women's access to gynecological health care within the U.S. medical care system is deeply intertwined with the historical enslavement of Black bodies. Racist biological assumptions of Black women as innate "breeders," whose fertility must be socially regulated to coincide with the needs of an ever-changing economy, informed an emergence of gynecology for Black women that was rooted in exploitation and unethical experimentations that continued into present-day gynecology (e.g., sterilization and family caps for women receiving public assistance; Carvalho et al., 2021; Neubeck & Casenave, 2001). Racist biological assumptions have also served to control the bodies of Latinx and Indigenous/Native American women. For example, between the 1930s and the 1970s, a program endorsed by the U.S. government led to approximately one-third of the female population being coercively sterilized in Puerto Rico (an unincorporated U.S. territory). Despite the highest sterilization rate in the world, this historic exploitation has been largely overlooked and understudied (Briggs, 1998). The impact of the harm caused by the U.S. medical establishment, particularly in gynecology, contributes to the present-day health disadvantages among Black, Latinx, and Indigenous/Native American women. For example, research shows that Black women receive a lower quality of care than White women (Khan et al., 2022). Often, women living in intentionally divested communities report experiencing discrimination and unequal access to culturally responsive women's health care (Khan et al., 2022).

When assessing Tanya's case, social workers should consider how the prevalence of the onset of chronic diseases in middle adulthood, particularly for HMIs, may impact her success with IVF. While Tanya may have health risks due to race and age, it is important to consider medical professionals who value relational support and empathy with historically marginalized women seeking IVF and actively engage in improving Black maternal health outcomes.

REFLECTION QUESTION

Intersectionality: As an Afro-Latinx woman living in a predominantly White neighborhood, what are some questions Tanya could consider when seeking out culturally responsive maternal health care?

Menopause

Menopause is defined as the cessation of menses in women. Although menopause is typically included as a biological marker by virtue of an estrogen deficiency, a competing debate shows variation across cultures in how menopause is socially constructed and experienced. Consider that in Japan there was no word for menopause (Charlap, 2015) until one was created by the popular media (Chandler & Tang, 2021). In India this concept is seen as a natural part of life. In China, menopause is seen as a rebirth (Chandler & Tang, 2021). Using narrative inquiry, Erol (2009) found that Turkish women thought of the concept as a "second spring."

Diet and Healthy Nourishment

Research continues to explore the effects of diet, especially its effect on estrogen in midlife women. For HMIs who live in economically divested communities, information and support to address the risks involved in aging are lacking, and subsequently, many women may not consume the proper quantities of foods rich in calcium that would mitigate the risk of osteoporosis in adulthood (Wilson-Barnes et al., 2022). The diet differences in intentionally divested communities may include minimal or limited access to healthy, affordable food (i.e., food deserts) and budgetary and time constraints (Bower, 2014).

Given Tonya's Afro-Latinx identity, the existing literature has also confirmed that inequities in systems of health are connected to diversity factors such as race, ethnicity, and immigration. Subsequently, HMIs, like Tonya, have a high risk of experiencing poor health outcomes in middle adulthood.

THEORY ↔ PRACTICE: LET'S APPLY CRITICALLY AFFIRMING FRAMEWORKS
Liberation psychology: Explore ancestral practices and embodied rituals that historically marginalized women engaged in to ritualize the changes in the body before colonization.

RCT: Consider asking trusted friends and family members who have experienced menopause to share medical care and emotional supports that were helpful.

Historically Marginalzied Individuals and Psychological Development in Middle Adulthood

Cognitive Performance

Many researchers have documented age-related decline related to cognitive domains, including memory, executive functioning, and processing speed (Erickson & Kramer, 2009; Morris et al., 2016). *Cognitive functioning* is an essential aspect of functioning and consists of how individuals obtain and process information (Richards & Deary, 2014). *Executive functioning* is defined as a goal-focused behavior that includes abilities such as planning, problem-solving, and decision-making, which are higher-order skills (Miller & Cohen, 2001; Zelazo et al., 1997). Additionally, *social cognition*, an approach to examining behavior, is defined as "how ordinary people think about people and how they think they think about people" (Fiske & Taylor, 1991, p. 1). For many HMIs, psychological well-being has necessitated developing psychological mechanisms, including social cognition, to successfully navigate experiences with racism and discrimination (Sue & Constantine, 2003). Key cognitive abilities might include keen perceptual insights, a capacity to interpret nonverbal and contextual meanings, and bicultural flexibility—skills that allow one to engage, negotiate, communicate, and facilitate with people from diverse social identities (Sue, 2003). Given Tanya's experience with living and working in predominantly White spaces, identifying ways to affirm and leverage her bicultural flexibility and social cognition to help her astutely negotiate and communicate within her relationships could be a valuable resource.

Existing research has documented a decline in cognitive functioning throughout the lifespan, particularly starting in middle adulthood (Erickson & Kramer, 2009; Liverman et al., 2015). It is also important to highlight the experiences of HMIs and its impact on cognitive functioning. Several scholars highlighted the cumulative effects of discrimination during the life course and its negative impact on cognitive functioning (Geronimus, 1992; Lupien et al., 2009; Muñoz et al., 2022). One study found that ethnic discrimination was related to cognitive decline among middle-adult Mexican immigrants after controlling for variables such as education (Muñoz et al., 2022). Another study reported that hypertension and diabetes were associated with greater rates of cognitive decline among middle-aged adults, including African Americans (Knopman et al., 2001). Marquez et al. (2017) found that structured Latin dancing contributed to less cognitive decline than regular exercise among Latino middle adults. Therefore, while HMIs may be at risk from cognitive decline more than White individuals, there are important cultural protective factors that can minimize the decline.

THEORY ↔ PRACTICE: LET'S APPLY CRITICALLY AFFIRMING FRAMEWORKS
Strengths-based (asset framing): Explore possible assets in social cognition as well a protective factors that can minimize cognitive decline.

RCT: Identify bicultural relationships that are mutually supportive and provide an opportunity for positive and empathic connection.

Environmental/Physical Environment

Concerns about access to the natural and accessible built environment have increased, particularly among the aging population. The **natural environment** refers to undisturbed natural spaces such as parks and gardens, while the *physical or built environment* includes the infrastructure developed within living spaces to meet the needs of inhabitants (Prescott & Logan, 2016; Ravi et al., 2021). The Council on Social Work Education (CSWE, 2022) has even incorporated environmental justice into the 2022 competencies. This move demonstrates that the social work profession recognizes the detrimental impact of climate change and environmental injustice and how HMIs are disproportionately impacted (CSWE, 2022). Nevertheless, within the United States, the conservation and environmental justice movement has largely been dominated by White leadership and Western perspectives (Purdy, 2015).

The U.S. policy of genocide and the forced removal of Indigenous/Native Americans from their lands has threatened Indigenous forms of ancestral knowledge, ritual, and practices that hold a strong relationship to land and nature. For Black and Afro-Latinx Americans, the ancestral inheritance of agrarian knowledge and skills was historically exploited through mass enslavement and wage corruption to build the immense wealth of the initial farming economy in the Americas (grain, cotton, and sugar). Despite a long history and symbiotic relationship shared by many HMIs with nature, the U.S. government has utilized policy and violence to systematically segregate, forcibly remove, and exclude HMIs from public lands and natural resources (Rowland-Shea et al., 2020). More recently, in a report examining the ethnic, racial, and socioeconomic disparities in the current distribution of natural areas in the United States, results showed that HMIs, including LGBTQIA+ individuals and people with disabilities, are almost 3 times more likely than White.

Additionally, the built dimensions of nature-deprived urban spaces have fostered living environments with the social stress of crowding, few public green spaces, and poor air quality (Peen et al., 2010). Evidence is also mounting that living in nature-deprived, urban communities is positively associated with depression and a higher prevalence of mental disorders (Peen et al., 2010; Rowland-Shea et al., 2020; van den Bosch et al., 2015). Tanya, in our case study vignette, currently lives in an apartment complex located in an area predominantly zoned for offices and commercial space. Exploring the impact of living in a nature-deprived environment on her emotional and mental well-being is an area of critical importance.

STRENGTHS-BASED (ASSET FRAMING): THEORY ↔ PRACTICE: LET'S APPLY CRITICAL AFFIRMING FRAMEWORKS

Consider mapping with clients green spaces and natural spaces that they can frequent in their local community when they are feeling stressed.

Liberation psychology: Within our advocacy efforts, social workers must take into account ancestral connection with the land and the impact of nature-deprived spaces on the physical, emotional, and mental well-being of HMIs. Consider cultivating and integrating natural resources (e.g., facilitating a gardening group) within your support services.

Assets, Resiliencies, and Coping Mechanisms

It is important to recognize the strengths and assets that contribute to HMIs' success through the middle adulthood trajectory. *Resiliency* has been defined as a positive reaction to stressors and adversity and has been linked to positive mental health and health outcomes among HMIs in middle adulthood (Masten, 2014). How one copes with stress, for example, is an important consideration when working with middle-aged adults, who often face adversities related to aging, careers, relationships, and loss of family or friends in this life stage (McGinnis, 2018). Relatedly, HMIs may face an accumulation of stressors from multiple systemic levels based on a history of oppression that may impact them in middle adulthood (Wilson-Barnes et al., 2022). Although traditional human behavior theorists did not initiate their research with HMIs, it is important to attend to the existing theories while also critically assessing them.

Spirituality and Religion

Spirituality and/or religion can often provide both a source of coping from stressors and a resource for cultivating hope. Lopez et al. (2003) describe emotion-based models of hope "as being a reinforcing affective state that is used to propel individuals towards goals but can also be used as a coping mechanism in dire situations' (as cited in Martin & Stermac, 2010, p. 694). In addition, cognitive-based models of hope assert that thoughts and beliefs provide agency for the hope that supports achieving one's goals (Martin & Stermac, 2010). Numerous studies highlight the protective function spirituality plays against stressors and adverse events among HMIs, particularly among African Americans (Ellison et al., 2010; Taylor et al., 2004). Equally important, research continues to affirm that when faith-based organizations are at their best, their partnerships with local communities are significant resources in contextually addressing the community needs and concerns of immigrant groups and African Americans (Maduka-Ezeh et al., 2022; Sutton & Parks, 2013). Historically, Catholicism has dominated the religious practices within the Dominican Republic; given Tanya's identity as a second-generation Dominican American, she may practice Catholicism. However, given her consciousness regarding her Black racial identity, she may be drawn to African American Christian churches that hold a more Black-centered identity and are civically engaged in social issues impacting the well-being of Black individuals.

THEORY ↔ PRACTICE: LET'S APPLY CRITICALLY AFFIRMING FRAMEWORKS
Strengths-based (asset framing): Finding ways to collaborate and partner with faith-based initiatives while also maintaining one's social work values and ethics is a vital skill for practitioners. Social workers in faith-based settings have the obligation to inform the standards and procedures of service by ensuring the rights of recipients to refuse to participate in any religious activity while also facilitating an open space for recipients of faith to integrate their values and beliefs as a resource.

Humor

Researchers have also documented humor as an effective coping strategy (Marziali et al., 2008). Coping through mature humor occurs when an emotion or thought is expressed through comedy, allowing a painful situation to be faced without individual pain or social discomfort (Martin, 2003; Karou-ei et al., 2009). The use of humor has been classified into adaptive and non-adaptive (Martin, 2003). *Adaptive humor* consists of self-enhancing humor, while *nonadaptive humor* often consists of self-defeating humor. Regarding middle adulthood, existing research highlights the increased use of adaptive humor and stabilizing during progression through the life stages and how it contributes to happiness and resiliency (Damianakis & Marziali, 2011).

When considering Tanya, social workers should explore how among Latinx individuals, a sense of family and respect for others can be positive aspects of their experience amidst adverse **migration** experiences and other adversity. While there is a paucity of research exploring the life satisfaction of HMIs, this chapter has highlighted a fair number of protective factors that help fight against the systemic risks faced by these groups.

Historically Marginalized Individuals and Social Development in Middle Adulthood

Education and Career Trajectories

Educational attainment (the number of years of formal education an individual completes) is a well-established determinant of one's overall health (Phelan et al., 2010). Unfortunately, as noted by Pickard (2020), "Deficit stories about race, gender, class, and literacy (dis)ability saturate policy and practice, often with negative consequences for the large numbers of low-income adults and adults of color who populate the classrooms" (p. 1). These deficit stories can often overlook the assets that Yosso (2005) defines as the "community cultural wealth" that historically marginalized adult learners hold. The community cultural wealth that learners of color contribute to educational settings can include many forms of capital, including:

- *linguistic capital*: the skill of navigating interpersonal relationships in multiple languages and forms of communication.

- *social capital*: social networks rooted in trust, cooperation, and reciprocity that help to facilitate social and economic support.

- *aspirational capital*: the capacity to access hope when faced with forms of oppression.

- *familial capital*: a commitment to the betterment and mutual support among an extended network of relatives.

- *navigational capital*: an aptitude for successfully navigating microaggressive and oppressive spaces designed to deter and invisibly minimize HMIs (Yosso, 2005).

For example, the cultivation and preservation of cultural orientation and values that exist outside of dominant Western norms can provide essential assets (e.g., communal support) and an affirming ethnic-racial identity that supports engagement in formal education (Knight et al., 2016; Neblett & Carter, 2012; Shen et al., 2016). In addition, a communal orientation toward one's community, ethnic/racial group, or family can reduce psychological distress and unhealthy behaviors and support educational goals and aspirations (Rivas-Drake & Marchand, 2016; Shen et al., 2016; Sellers et al., 1998). As a result, many middle adult HMIs pursue educational opportunities as a pathway to health, economic, and social prosperity, notwithstanding the impact of economic and social barriers. Facets of Tanya's community cultural wealth are likely to have played a considerable role in her successful attainment of higher education.

Educational and racial disparities across HMI groups also profoundly impact economic well-being (Adeyemo, 2021) and present a cumulative lifelong disadvantage. The persistence of lower earnings in Black and Latinx adults continues compared to Asian and White adults (Bowdler & Harris, 2022). Using data from the National Longitudinal Survey of Youth, Killewald and Bryan (2018) showed that the already wide wealth gap that starts in early adulthood between White individuals and Latinx and Black individuals widens even more through middle adulthood as the accumulation of wealth continues at a slower rate for Black and Latinx people.

THEORY ↔ PRACTICE: LET'S APPLY CRITICALLY AFFIRMING FRAMEWORKS
Liberation psychology: Engaging in concientización with HMIs by developing an awareness of the implicit and explicit false narratives/deficit stories within educational policies and practices that have been used to uphold White supremacy and deter HMIs from furthering their education.

Strengths-based (asset framing): As a means for priming possible assets with HMI adults returning to an educational setting, how could Yosso's (2005) "community cultural wealth" typology be used to assess resources that can be strategically leveraged in preparation of educational goals?

Marketplace Challenges for the Midlife Sandwich Generation

At a time when many midlife adults, especially those in lower skilled jobs, need work retraining to keep up with changing labor demands, they are also caring for—"sandwiched" between—young adults and aging parents. Changing marketplace demands in the United States have evolved toward a more service-oriented economy, and technological shifts have been at the forefront of this change; as such, the U.S. job market is continuing to face labor, productivity, and capital challenges (Qureshi, 2020). These labor market shifts have resulted in a skill mismatch between what employers now need and the available pool of applicants (Cappelli, 2015). Over time there has been a great deal of interest paid on skill shortages, and some argue that the United States is overeducated (Cappelli, 2015).

Indeed, many job shifts have benefitted high-skilled labor and created a greater number of lower skilled jobs in the service sector. The income gap has widened between the rich and the poor. Those in low-skilled sectors have been particularly hard hit as manufacturing or middle-sector jobs have gone offshore. The economic and labor market fluctuations are important to keep up with, and they vary constantly. Consider that much attention has been paid to education, and yet according to recent research, workers without a bachelor's degree are seeing workforce advantages, as employers prefer those with skills to those with a college education (Lanahan, 2022). This is particularly advantageous for HMIs. Consider that 62% of Americans lack a bachelor's degree, and of these, 72% of Black adults and 79% of Latinx adults lack a bachelor's degree (Lanahan, 2022).

Perhaps because of the COVID-19 pandemic and other factors, the percentage of young adults living with their parents is higher now than in any prior historical period (Fry et al., 2020). The children of midlife adults may be in school over more years, obtaining advanced degrees, which means delaying their work careers later in life and needing to be cared for by parents in midlife who are themselves in need of staying abreast of marketplace demands. As such, it is not unusual for adult college students, especially those from African American and Latinx families, to have dependent children while also attending college (Nelson et al., 2013).

Continuing technological shifts in the marketplace (Parker et al., 2016) mean that many middle-aged adults have had to return to school to remain employable. Since middle-aged adults often care for other family members while also holding full-time jobs (Gordon et al., 2012), their time back in school often occurs after completing their full-time work day. Online and virtual jobs are helpful to homebound and/or mobile adults. These economic forces affect domestic life, and roles between family members adapt to the circumstances. In some families, night shift work and caregiving of children and parents can create role stress.

Relationships in Middle Adulthood

In middle adulthood, the network of social relationships is thought to be more expansive than in other age groups (Hutchison, 2018). This can help navigate the challenges of this period. Midlife adults make up the generation in the middle, and as such, they serve as kin keepers (Hutchison, 2018). Close kin is also more broadly defined than before. Unmarried adults can define their close friends to be kinship. Kin-like communities can also be virtual.

Multigenerational Families

Complexity in the family is a trend that more and more includes a wider circle that extends beyond the nuclear family and one that includes multigenerational and multiethnic diversity. In many Western societies, the parent–child relationship is the most important relationship. Yet in immigrant families and other minoritized groups, a multigenerational family has been a defining characteristic all along. According to Cohen and Casper (2002), middle-aged adults, primarily women, in the sandwich generation have a higher likelihood of living in multigenerational homes. In this same study, Latinx and Black adults were shown to have a higher rate of multigenerational living arrangements than White adults.

Triandis (2001) and others have explored differences between individualistic and collectivist societies. According to Markus and Kitayama (1991), in Asia, Africa, and Latin America, for example, the view that the self is part of a larger social network constitutes a level of interdependence that may be expressed differently in societies characterized by a more individualistic ethos. In a collectivist society, there is a wider definition of family, which can involve caregiving for elders and other kin. Thus, with increased migration and the growth of ethnic groups, the so-called **sandwich generation** more and more allow for a widened definition of family in American society.

Most middle-aged adults of any culture are involved with their parents. Caregivers typically include daughters and daughters-in-law. For many, caregiving is both a burden and offers its rewards. Certainly, for adults, caregiving can be a source of generativity. One's outlook can contribute to how caregiving is perceived—if burden or gain. Viewed systemically, many privileged families hire caregivers who, in turn, must have someone else care for their children and/or aging relatives. Thus, the macro world is intertwined—a theme of this period in life. It is difficult to disentangle the macro-level factors from the meso or micro.

Some families find it rewarding to care for elders. African Americans have been found to have a higher likelihood of caring for aging parents than their White counterparts (Dilworth-Anderson et al., 2005; Fingerman et al., 2011). Intergenerational relationships can include extended family and fictive kin (Stewart, 2008).

Elders have a prominent place in African American families; they help the young to weather challenges (McCoy, 2011). African American families' focus is often centered on children (Revell & McGhee, 2012), and messages to younger family members are often mediated through the elders. Raising children amidst adversity is associated with a position of honor for African American mothers (Shambley-Ebron & Boyle, 2006a).

While grandparenting can be the case for some adults in midlife, so can singlehood. Some single adults in midlife remain childless, while others avail themselves of assisted reproductive technologies and surrogates to have a child with no coparent present. The diversity of family in midlife is perhaps more expanded now than ever.

Kinship no longer needs to be bound by geography, and this meets the needs of the upwardly mobile who find themselves isolated from family by virtue of jobs away from their home, which in the global era can be anywhere. The concept of social tribes can serve important functions, especially for single adults who seek kinship communities (e.g., social groups). For those who may be isolated for health or scarce resources, the smartphone can now connect them through social media wherever they may be.

Life Satisfaction and Middle Adulthood Relationships

According to Lachman (2015), there is a vast literature showing a consistent finding: low levels of life satisfaction or happiness during the middle years, ages 30–50, in what has been described as a U-curve. A vast literature of cross-sectional studies has posited that the U-curve of happiness in marital satisfaction may be the effect of parenting adolescent children (Miller, 2000), a time when teens tend to outpace their parents and parents find it difficult to adapt to teens' newfound freedom and interest in peer relationships (Csikszentmihalyi, 2003). This is referred to as the

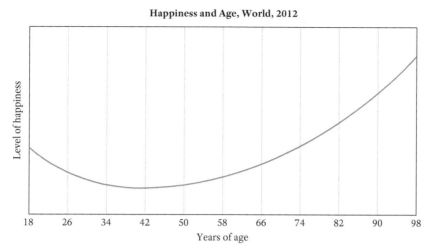

Happiness and Age, World, 2012

FIGURE 9.2

U-curve hypothesis. More recently, the effect of the U shape in happiness has been called into question. Galambos et al. (2020), like Miller (2000), draws attention to methodological issues in examining this hypothesis. According to Galambos et al. (2020), cross-sectional and longitudinal study designs and the variables chosen to designate well-being and the diversity of pathways in the course of an individual life challenge the steadfastness of this popular hypothesis. Consider that the diversity involved in the populations we study can also not be easily pegged or assessed. For example, one cannot compare a person who grew up marginalized all of their lives in the United States to an immigrant who recently arrived and whose life has significantly improved simply by virtue of moving to a location with higher economic well-being, but who has become a perpetual mourner of all that was lost.

CONCLUSION

Middle adulthood, despite being one of the longest stages in duration in a typical lifespan, has been historically underresearched. Moreover, it has typically been viewed through lenses that do not account for the experiences of the historically marginalized individual. We have tried here to examine some of the critically affirming frameworks, focusing on how they might be applied to contemporary social work practice. The next chapter will focus on later adulthood.

KEY TERMS

- **Cisgender:** denotes a person whose personal identity and gender are the same as the sex assigned to them at birth.

- **Critical affirming frameworks:** assist social workers in understanding how to address systemic injustices; leverage the agency, assets, and strengths of HMI; attend to the dynamics of intersecting identities and structures; and support mutual relationships in individuals and groups.

- **Heterogeneity:** refers to groups involving members who differ from one another on some aspects. An example is Latinx, which is a group involving members who are of different races yet share a similar ethnicity, traced back to Latin American origin or descent.

- **Historically marginalized individuals (HMIs):** have been relegated to lower societal status, including being barred from full political, cultural, and economic participation. Examples include enslaved people and their descendants, LGBTQIA+ individuals, senior citizens, racial/ethnic minorities, people with low intelligence, people who are disabled, people with serious mental illness, and people with cognitive impairment.

- **Homogenizing:** refers to a blending of potentially dissimilar characteristics. So, for example, when we assume that all of the members of a group act similarly, we are mis-attributing that each individual within the group would think or feel the same about a particular topic. Consider that not all Latinx people are Democrats, for example. Alternatively, consider that with technological advances and increased globalization, we are witnessing an increase in shared characteristics of people across different countries.

- **Latinx:** a relatively new gender-neutral term for people of Latin American origin or descent. Historically, and still commonplace, is the use of the term "Latino/a." The term "Latinx" is not entirely agreed upon, as shown in some polls.

- **LGBTQIA+:** an acronym that refers to "lesbian, gay, bisexual, transgender, queer/questioning (one's sexual or gender identification), intersex, and asexual/aromantic/agender" individuals (Merriam-Webster, n.d.). The "+" represents other sexual identities.

- **Microaggression:** refers to intentional or unintentional gestures or environmental or verbal slights directed at another person, which can come across or be perceived as offensive to the intended target. There are frequent complaints by marginalized groups who experience these from members of dominant groups.

- **Migration:** involves moving from one's place of birth to another. This typically refers to moving from one country to another but may also involve within-country migration. In the United States, currently, there are approximately 11 million undocumented migrants, many of whom crossed the border or overstayed their visas. Following emancipation, many freed enslaved people moved to the northern states, for example.

- **Natural environment:** refers to undisturbed natural spaces, such as parks and gardens, while the physical or built environment includes the infrastructure developed within living spaces to meet the needs of inhabitants

- **Othermothering:** involves caring for children who are not one's biological children.

- **The sandwich generation:** refers to the middle-aged adults caring for both their parents and their children.

- **The U-curve hypothesis:** refers to the relationship between adult happiness and age. It has been hypothesized and studied that parents' happiness dips during children's adolescent ages, perhaps because of parents being unable to adapt to their children's growing independence.

DISCUSSION QUESTIONS

1. Identify the social and structural forces that affect human behavior.

   a. *possible responses*: family, health care access, control of resources, language, culture, colonization, housing, forms of oppression (racism, sexism, ableism, cis/genderism, heterosexism)

2. What are the cultural forces that affect human behavior?

   b. *possible responses*: attitude, art/drama/music, beliefs, faith, rituals, costumes, attitudes, language, and food.

3. What are the cultural forces that affect human behavior?

4. What nonverbal messages might you be communicating unknowingly to your clients?

REFERENCES

Active Living Research. (2004). *What is active living?* Retrieved February 19, 2004, from http://www,activelivingresearch,org/index,php/What_is _Active_Living/i03

Adeyemo, W. (2021). *The American rescue plan: Centering racial equity in policy making.* U.S. Department of the Treasury. Retrieved September 22, 2022. from https://home.treasury.gov/system/files/136/American-Rescue-Plan-Centering-Equity-in-Policymaking.pdf

Anderson, J., & Carter, R. W. (2003). *Diversity perspectives for social work practice.* Pearson College Division.

Araujo-Dawson, B. (2015). Understanding the complexities of skin color, perceptions of race, and discrimination among Cubans, Dominicans, and Puerto Ricans. *Hispanic Journal of Behavioral Sciences, 37*(2), 243–256.

Baltes, P. B. (1987). Theoretical propositions of life-span developmental psychology: On the dynamics between growth and decline. *Developmental Psychology, 23*(5), 611–626. https://doi.org/10.1037/0012-1649.23.5.611

Barnes, L. L., & Bennett, D. A. (2014). Alzheimer's disease in African Americans: Risk factors and challenges for the future. *Health Affairs, 33*(4), 580–586.

Bower, K. M., Thorpe Jr, R. J., Rohde, C., & Gaskin, D. J. (2014). The intersection of neighborhood racial segregation, poverty, and urbanicity and its impact on food store availability in the United States. *Preventive medicine, 58*, 33–39.

Bowdler, J., & Harris, B. (2022). *Racial inequality in the United States*. U.S. Department of the Treasury. Retrieved September 22, 2022, from https://home.treasury.gov/news/featured-stories/racial-inequality-in-the-united-states#_ftn8

Briggs, L. (1998). Discourses of "forced sterilization" in Puerto Rico: The problem with the speaking subaltern. *Differences: A Journal of Feminist Cultural Studies, 10*(2), 30–33.

Bronfenbrenner, U. (1977). Toward an experimental ecology of human development. *American Psychologist, 32*(7), 513.

Bronfenbrenner U. (Ed.). (2005). *Making human beings human: Bioecological perspectives on human development*. SAGE Publications.

Brough, M., Bond, C., & Hunt, J. (2004). Strong in the city: Towards a strength-based approach in Indigenous health promotion. *Health Promotion Journal of Australia, 15*(3), 215–220.

Burton, M., & Kagan, C. (2009). Towards a really social psychology: Liberation psychology beyond Latin America. In C. C. Sonn & M. Montero (Eds.), *Psychology of liberation* (pp. 51–72). Springer. https://doi.org/10.1007/978-0-387-85784-8_3

Cappelli, P. H. (2015). Skill gaps, skill shortages, and skill mismatches: Evidence and arguments for the United States. *ILR review, 68*(2), 251–290.

Carlo, G., Raffaelli, M., Laible, D. J., & Meyer, K. A. (1999). Why are girls less physically aggressive than boys? Personality and parenting mediators of physical aggression. *Sex Roles, 40*(9), 711–729.

Carlton-LaNey, I. (1999). African American social work pioneers' response to need. *Social Work, 44*(4), 311–321.

Carvalho, K., Kheyfets, A., Maleki, P., Miller, B., Abouhala, S., Anwar, E., & Amutah-Onukagha, N. (2021). A systematic policy review of Black maternal health-related policies proposed federally and in Massachusetts: 2010–2020. *Frontiers in Public Health, 9*, Article 664659.

Centers for Disease Control and Prevention. (2013). CDC health disparities and inequalities report—United States, 2013. *Morbidity and Mortality Weekly Report, 62*(3). https://www.cdc.gov/minorityhealth/CHDIReport.html https://www.cdc.gov/mmwr/pdf/other/su6203.pdf

Chalabaev, A., Sieber, S., Sander, D., Cullati, S., Maltagliati, S., Sarrazin, P., Boisgontier, M. P., & Cheval, B. (2022). Early-life socioeconomic circumstances and physical activity in older age: Women pay the price. *Psychological Science, 33*(2), 212–223.

Chandler, J., & Tang, A. (2021). *Menopause around the world*. Mindset Health. https://www.mindsethealth.com/matter/menopause-around-the-world

Charlap, C. (2015). *La fabrique de la ménopause: genre, apprentissage et trajectoires* [Unpublished master's thesis]. Université de Strasbourg. https://theses.hal.science/tel-01316559

Cohen, P. N., & Casper, L. M. (2002). In whose home? Multigenerational families in the United States, 1998–2000. *Sociological Perspectives, 45*(1), 1–20. https://doi.org/10.1525/sop.2002.45.1.1

Collins, P. H. (1998). Fighting words: Black women and the search for justice (Vol. 7). U of Minnesota Press.

Comstock, D. (Ed.). (2005). *Diversity and development: Critical contexts that shape our lives and Relationships*. Brooks Cole Publishing.

Council on Social Work Education. (2022). *2022 educational policy and accreditation standards for baccalaureate and master's social work programs*. https://www.cswe.org/accreditation/standards/2022-epas/

Craig, P., Di Ruggiero, E., Frolich, K. L., Mykhalovskiy, E., White, M., Campbell, R., & Poland, B. (2018). *Taking account of context in population health intervention research: guidance for producers, users and funders of research*. National Institute for Health and Care Research. https://www.ncbi.nlm.nih.gov/books/NBK498645/

Crenshaw, K. (1989). Demarginalizing the intersection of race and sex: A Black feminist critique of antidiscrimination doctrine, feminist theory, and antiracist politics. *University of Chicago Legal Forum*, *14*(1), 538–554.

Crenshaw, K. (1991). Mapping the margins: Intersectionality, identity politics, and violence against women of color. *Stanford Law Review*, *43*(6), 1241–1299. https://doi.org/10.2307/1229039

Cross-Call, J. (2020). *Medicaid expansion has helped narrow racial disparities in health coverage and access to care.* Center on Budget and Policy Priorities.

Csikszetmihalyi, M. (2003). Personal communication. September 13, 2003. Claremont Graduate University, In Claremont, CA.

Damianakis, T., & Marziali, E. (2011). Community-dwelling older adults' contextual experiencing of humour. *Ageing and Society*, *31*(1), 110–124.

Davis, J., Penha, J., Mbowe, O., & Taira, D. A. (2017). Prevalence of single and multiple leading causes of death by race/ethnicity among U.S. adults aged 60 to 79 years. *Preventing Chronic Disease*, *14*, Article E101. https://doi.org/10.5888/pcd14.160241

Deepak, A. C., & Biggs, M. J. G. (2011). Intimate technology: A tool for teaching anti-racism in social work education. *Journal of Ethnic & Cultural Diversity in Social Work*, *20*(1), 39–56.

Dilworth-Anderson, P., Brummett, B. H., Goodwin, P., Williams, S. W., Williams, R. B., & Siegler, I. C. (2005). Effect of race on cultural justifications for caregiving. *The Journals of Gerontology Series B: Psychological Sciences and Social Sciences*, *60*(5), S257–S262.

Dwyer-Lindgren, L., Kendrick, P., Kelly, Y. O., Sylte, D. O., Schmidt, C., Blacker, B. F., Daoud, F., Abdi, A. A., Baumann, M., Mouhanna, F., Kahn, E., Hay, S. I., Mensah, G. A., Nápoles, A. M., Pérez-Stable, E. J., Shiels, M., Freedman, N., Arias, E., George, S. A., Murray, D. M., … Mokdad, A. H. (2022). Life expectancy by county, race, and ethnicity in the USA, 2000–19: A systematic analysis of health disparities. *The Lancet*, *400*(10345), 25–38.

Eijkemans, M. J., Van Poppel, F., Habbema, D. F., Smith, K. R., Leridon, H., & te Velde, E. R. (2014). Too old to have children? Lessons from natural fertility populations. *Human Reproduction*, *29*(6), 1304–1312.

Ellison, C. G., Burdette, A. M., & Bradford Wilcox, W. (2010). The couple that prays together: Race and ethnicity, religion, and relationship quality among working-age adults. *Journal of Marriage and Family*, *72*(4), 963–975.

Erickson, K. I., & Kramer, A. F. (2009). Aerobic exercise effects on cognitive and neural plasticity in older adults. *British Journal of Sports Medicine*, *43*(1), 22–24.

Erikson, E. H. (1950). *Childhood and society.* Norton.

Erol, M. (2009). Tales of the second spring: Menopause in Turkey through the narratives of menopausal women and gynecologists. *Medical Anthropology*, *28*(4), 368–396. https://doi.org/10.1080/01459740903303969

Fingerman, K. L., VanderDrift, L. E., Dotterer, A. M., Birditt, K. S., & Zarit, S. H. (2011). Support to aging parents and grown children in Black and White families. *The Gerontologist*, *51*(4), 441–452.

Fiske, S. T., & Taylor, S. E. (1991). *Social cognition.* Mcgraw-Hill.

Fogarty, W., Lovell, M., Langenberg, J., & Heron, M. J. (2018). *Deficit discourse and strengths-based approaches: Changing the narrative of Aboriginal and Torres Strait Islander health and wellbeing.* The Lowitja Institute.

Freire, P. (1970). *Pedagogy of the oppressed.* Continuum.

French, S. E., & Chavez, N. R. (2010). The relationship of ethnicity-related stressors and Latino ethnic identity to well-being. *Hispanic Journal of Behavioral Sciences*, *32*(3), 410–428.

Fry, F., Passel, J., & Cohn, D. (2020). *A majority of young adults in the U.S. live with their parents for the first time since the Great Depression.* Pew Research Center. https://www.pewresearch.org/

short-reads/2020/09/04/a-majority-of-young-adults-in-the-u-s-live-with-their-parents-for-the-first-time-since-the-great-depression/

Galambos, N. L., Krahn, H. J., Johnson, M. D., & Lachman, M. E. (2020). The U shape of happiness across the life course: Expanding the discussion. *Perspectives on Psychological Science*, 15(4), 898–912.

Geronimus, A. T. (1992). The weathering hypothesis and the health of African-American women and infants: Evidence and speculations. *Ethnicity & Disease*, 2(3), 207–221.

Glasgow Centre for Population Health. (2011). Asset-based approaches for health improvement: Redressing the balance. http://www.gcph.co.uk/publications/279_concepts_series_9asset_based_approaches_for_health_improvement.

Golash-Boza, T., & Bonilla-Silva, E. (2013). Rethinking race, racism, identity and ideology in Latin America. *Ethnic and Racial Studies*, 36(10), 1485–1489.

Goodman, R. A., Ling, S. M., Briss, P. A., Parrish, R. G., Salive, M. E., & Finke, B. S. (2016). Multimorbidity patterns in the United States: implications for research and clinical practice. In (Vol. 71, pp. 215–220): Oxford University Press US.Gordon, J. R., Pruchno, R. A., Wilson-Genderson, M., Murphy, W. M., & Rose, M. (2012). Balancing caregiving and work: Role conflict and role strain dynamics. *Journal of Family Issues*, 33(5), 662–689.

Gutierréz, G. (1988). *A theology of liberation*. Orbis Books.

Halpern, D. (2015). Inside the nudge unit: How small changes can make a big difference.

Hamilton, B. E., Martin, J. A., Osterman, M. J., & Rossen, L. M. (2019). *Births: Provisional data for 2018* (Vital Statistics Rapid Release Report 007). National Center for Health Statistics. https://www.cdc.gov/nchs/data/vsrr/vsrr-007-508.pdf.

Hart, H. M., McAdams, D. P., Hirsch, B. J., & Bauer, J. J. (2001). Generativity and social involvement among African Americans and White adults. *Journal of Research in Personality*, 35(2), 208–230. https://doi.org/10.1006/jrpe.2001.2318

Hartman, S. (1997). *Scenes of subjection*. Oxford University Press.

Hatzenbuehler, M. L., Bellatorre, A., Lee, Y., Finch, B. K., Muennig, P., & Fiscella, K. (2014). Retracted: Structural stigma and all-cause mortality in sexual minority populations. *Social Science & Medicine*, 103, 33–412. https://doi.org/10./1016/j.socscimed.2013.06.005

Hatzenbuehler, M. L., Phelan, J. C., & Link, B. G. (2013). Stigma as a fundamental cause of population health inequalities. *American Journal of Public Health*, 103, 813–821.

Heinrich, G., Leege, D., & Miller, C. (2008). *A user's guide to integral human development (IHD): Practical guidance for CRS staff and partners*. Catholic Relief Services. https://www.crs.org/our-work-overseas/research-publications/users-guide-integral-human-development-ihd

hooks, b. (1984). *Feminist theory: From margin to center*. South End Press.

Hordyk, S. R., Soltane, S. B., & Hanley, J. (2014). Sometimes you have to go under water to come up: A poetic, critical realist approach to documenting the voices of homeless immigrant women. *Qualitative Social Work*, 13(2), 203–220. https://doi.org//10.1177/1473325013491448

Hutchison, E. D. (2018). *Dimensions of human behavior: The changing life course*. SAGE publications.

Infurna, F. J., Gerstorf, D., & Lachman, M. E. (2020). Midlife in the 2020s: Opportunities and challenges. *American Psychology*, 75(4), 470–485. https://doi.org/10.1037/amp0000591

Jacobs, E. A., Kohrman, C., Lemon, M., & Vickers, D. L. (2003). Teaching physicians-in training to address racial disparities in health: A hospital-community partnership. *Public Health Reports*, 118, 349–356.

Jordan, J. V. (1991). The meaning of mutuality. In J. V. Jordan, A. G. Kaplan, J. B. Miller, I. P. Stiver, & J. L. Surrey (Eds.), *Women's growth in connection* (pp. 81–96). The Guilford Press.

Jordan, J. V. (2002). A relational-cultural perspective in therapy. In F. Kazlow (Ed.), *Comprehensive handbook of psychotherapy* (pp. 233–254). Wiley & Sons.

Jordan, J. V. (2017). Relational–cultural theory: The power of connection to transform our lives. *The Journal of Humanistic Counseling, 56*, 228–243. https://doi.org/10.1002/johc.12055

Jordan, J. V., & Hartling, L. M. (2002). New developments in relational-cultural theory. In M. Ballou & L. S. Brown (Eds.), *Rethinking mental health and disorders: Feminist Perspectives* (pp. 48–70). The Guilford Press.

Jung, C. G., Adler, G., Fordham, M., & Read, H. (2014). *The structure and dynamics of the psyche.* Routledge.

Kagan, C., Burns, D., Burton, M., Crespo, I., Evans, R., Knowles, K., & Sixsmith, J. (2004). Working with people who are marginalized by the social system: Challenges for community psychological work. In A. Sánchez Vidal, A. Zambrano Constanzo, & M. Palacín Lois (Eds.), *Psicología Comunitaria Europea: Comunidad, Poder, Ética y Valores/European Community Psychology: Community, Power, Ethics and Values* (pp. 400–412) Publicacions Universitat de Barcelona.

Karou-ei, R. A., Doosti, Y. A., Dehshiri, G. R., & Heidari, M. H. (2009). Humor styles, subjective well-being, and emotional intelligence in college students. *Journal of Iranian Psychologists, 5*(18), 159–169.

Khan, S. U., Yedlapati, S. H., Lone, A. N., Khan, M. S., Wenger, N. K., Watson, K. E., Gulati, M., Hays, A. G., & Michos, E. D. (2022). A comparative analysis of premature heart disease-and cancer-related mortality in women in the USA, 1999–2018. *European Heart Journal-Quality of Care and Clinical Outcomes, 8*(3), 315–323.

Killewald, A., & Bryan, B. (2018). Falling behind: The role of inter-and intragenerational processes in widening racial and ethnic wealth gaps through early and middle adulthood. *Social Forces, 97*(2), 705–740. https://doi.org/10.1093/sf/soy060

Knight, C. G., Mahrer, N. E., & Davis, A. N. (2016). The socialization of culturally related values and prosocial tendencies among Mexican-American adolescents. *Child Development, 87*(6), 1758–1771. https://doi.org/10.1111/cdev.12634

Knopman, D., Boland, L. L., Mosley, T., Howard, G., Liao, D., Szklo, M., McGovern, P., & Folsom, A. R., & Atheroscelerosis Risk in Communitites (ARIC) Study Investigators. (2001). Cardiovascular risk factors and cognitive decline in middle-aged adults. *Neurology, 56*(1), 42–48.

Lachman, M. E. (2015). Mind the gap in the middle: A call to study midlife. *Research in Human Development, 12*(3–4), 327–334. https://doi.org/10.1080/15427609.2015.1068048

Lachman, M. E., Teshale, S., & Agrigoroaei, S. (2015). Midlife as a pivotal period in the life course: Balancing growth and decline at the crossroads of youth and old age. *International Journal of Behavioral Development, 39*(1), 20–31. https://doi.org/10.1177/0165025414533223

Lanahan, Lawrence (2022) "More workers without degrees are landing jobs. Will it last?" Washington Post, https://www.washingtonpost.com/education/2022/07/08/ jobs-no-college-degrees/.

Levin, D. T. (2000). Race as a visual feature: Using visual search and perceptual discrimination tasks to understand face categories and the cross-race recognition deficit. *Journal of Experimental Psychology, 129*(4), 559–574. https://doi.org/10.1037/0096-3445.129.4.559

Liverman, C. T., Yaffe, K., & Blazer, D. G. (Eds.). (2015). *Cognitive aging: Progress in understanding and opportunities for action.* National Academies Press.

Lopez, S. J., Snyder, C. R., & Pedrotti, J. T. (2003). Hope: many definitions, many measures. In S. J. Lopez & C. R. Snyder (Eds.), *Positive psychological assessment: A handbook of models and measures* (pp. 91–106). American Psychological Association.

Lupien, S. J., McEwen, B. S., Gunnar, M. R., & Heim, C. (2009). Effects of stress throughout the lifespan on the brain, behaviour and cognition. *Nature Reviews Neuroscience, 10*(6), 434–445.

Maduka-Ezeh, A., Bagozzi, B. E., Gardesey, M., Ezeh, I. T., Nibbs, F., Nwegbu, S., & Trainor, J. (2022). "Inspired to action": Immigrants' faith-based organizations' responses across two pandemics. *Journal of Immigrant & Refugee Studies.* Advance online publication. https://doi.org/10.1080/15562948.2022.2035036

Markus, H. R., & Kitayama, S. (1991). Culture and the self: Implications for cognition, emotion, and motivation. *Psychological Review, 98*(2), 224–253.

Marquez, D. X., Wilson, R., Aguiñaga, S., Vásquez, P., Fogg, L., Yang, Z., Wilbur, J. Hughes, S., & Spanbauer, C. (2017). Regular Latin dancing and health education may improve cognition of late middle-aged and older Latinos. *Journal of aging and physical activity, 25*(3), 482–489.

Martin, K., & Stermac, L. (2010). Measuring hope. *International Journal of Offender Therapy and Comparative Criminology, 54*(5), 693–705.

Martín-Baró, I. (1994). *Writings for a liberation psychology.* Harvard University Press.

Marziali, E., McDonald, L., & Donahue, P. (2008). The role of coping humor in the physical and mental health of older adults. *Aging and Mental Health, 12,* 713–718. https://doi.org/10.1080/13607860802154374.

Masten, A. S. (2014). *Ordinary magic: Resilience in development.* Guilford Press.

Masters, R. K., Hummer, R. A., Powers, D. A., Beck, A., Lin, S. F., & Finch, B. K. (2014). Long-term trends in adult mortality for U.S. Blacks and Whites: An examination of period- and cohort-based changes. *Demography, 51*(6), 2047–2073. https://doi.org/10.1007/s13524-014-0343-4

Mazzula, S. L., & Sanchez, D. (2021). The state of Afrolatinxs in Latinx psychological research: Findings from a content analysis from 2009 to 2020. *Journal of Latinx Psychology, 9*(1), 8–25.

McCoy, R. (2011). African American elders, cultural traditions, and the family reunion. *Generations, 35*(3), 16–21.

McGinnis, D. (2018). Resilience, life events, and well-being during midlife: Examining resilience subgroups. *Journal of Adult Development, 25*(3), 198–221.

McQueen, D. B., Schufreider, A., Lee, S. M., Feinberg, E. C., & Uhler, M. L. (2015). Racial disparities in in vitro fertilization outcomes. *Fertility and Sterility, 104*(2), 398–402.

Mehta, C. M., Arnett, J. J., Palmer, C. G., & Nelson, L. J. (2020). Established adulthood: A new conception of ages 30 to 45. *American Psychologist, 75*(4), 431–444. https://doi.org/10.1037/amp0000600

Meijer, M., Rohl, J., Bloomfield, K., & Grittner, U. (2012). Do neighborhoods affect individual mortality? A systematic review and meta-analysis of multilevel studies. *Social Science Medical, 74,* 1204–1212. https://doi.org/10.1016/j.socscimed.2011.11.034.

Merriam-Webster. (n.d.). LGBTQIA. In *Meriam-Webster.com dictionary.* Retrieved April 23, 2023, from https://www.merriam-webster.com/dictionary/LGBTQIA

Metzl, J. M., & Hansen, H. (2014). Structural competency: Theorizing a new medical engagement with stigma and inequality. *Social Science & Medicine, 103,* 126–133.

Miller, J. B. (1976). *Toward a new psychology of women.* Beacon Press.

Miller, E. K., & Cohen, J. D. (2001). An integrative theory of prefrontal cortex function. *Annual Review of Neuroscience, 24*(1), 167–202.

Miller, R. B. (2000). Misconceptions about the U-shaped curve of marital satisfaction over the life course. *Family Science Review, 13*(1–2), 60–73.

Morris, R., Lord, S., Bunce, J., Burn, D., & Rochester, L. (2016). Gait and cognition: Mapping the global and discrete relationships in ageing and neurodegenerative disease. *Neuroscience & Biobehavioral Reviews, 64,* 326–345.

Muñoz, E., Robins, R. W., & Sutin, A. R. (2022). Perceived ethnic discrimination and cognitive function: A 12-year longitudinal study of Mexican-origin adults. *Social Science & Medicine, 311,* Article 115296.

National Center for Health Statistics. (2016a). *Health, United States, 2015: With special feature on racial and ethnic health disparities.* Centers for Disease Control and Prevention. https://stacks.cdc.gov/view/cdc/39108

National Center for Health Statistics. (2016b). *National Vital Statistics System, mortality.* Centers for Disease Control and Prevention. https://www.cdc.gov/nchs/nvss/deaths.htm

Neblett, E. W., & Carter, S. E. (2012). The protective role of racial identity and Africentric worldview in the association between racial discrimination and blood pressure. *Psychosomatic Medicine, 74*(5), 509–516. https://doi.org/10.1097/PSY.0b013e3182583a50

Negi, N. J., Maskell, E., Goodman, M., Hooper, J., & Roberts, J. (2018). Providing social services in a new immigrant settlement city: A qualitative inquiry. *American Journal of Orthopsychiatry, 88*(1), 16–25.

Nelson, B., Froehner, M., & Gault, B. (2013). *College students with children are common and face many challenges in completing higher education.* Institute for Women's Policy Research. https://iwpr.org/iwpr-issues/student-parent-success-initiative/college-students-with-children-are-common-and-face-many-challenges-in-completing-higher-education-summary/

Neubeck, K. J., & Cazenave, N. A. (2001). *Welfare racism: Playing the race card against America's poor.* Routledge.

Nisbett, R. E. (2003). *The geography of thought: How Asians and Westerners think differently ... and why.* Free Press.

Noble, J. M., Manly, J. J., Schupf, N., Tang, M. X., & Luchsinger, J. A. (2012). Type 2 diabetes and ethnic disparities in cognitive impairment. *Ethnicity & Disease, 22*(1), 38–44.

Parker, K., Rainie, L., Kochhar, R., & Rohal, M. (2016). *Changes in the American workplace.* Pew Research Center. https://www.pewresearch.org/social-trends/2016/10/06/1-changes-in-the-american-workplace/

Peen, J., Schoevers, R. A., Beekman, A. T., & Dekker, J. (2010). The current status of urban-rural differences in psychiatric disorders. *Acta Psychiatrica Scandinavica, 121*(2), 84–93.

Phelan, J. C., Link, B. G., & Tehranifar, P. (2010). Social conditions as fundamental causes of health inequalities: Theory, evidence, and policy implications. *Journal of Health and Social Behavior, 51,* S28–S40.

Pickard, A. (2022). Adult learners' community cultural wealth: Seeing ABE learners through a CRT lens. *Dialogues in Social Justice: An Adult Education Journal, 7*(1).

Practice Committee of the American Society for Reproductive Medicine. (2015). Testing and interpreting measures of ovarian reserve: a committee opinion. *Fertility and Sterility, 103*(3), e9–e17.Prescott, S. L., & Logan, A. C. (2016). Transforming life: a broad view of the developmental origins of health and disease concept from an ecological justice perspective. *International journal of environmental research and public health, 13*(11), 1075.

Purdy, J. (2015, August 13). Environmentalism's racist history. *The New Yorker.* https://www.newyorker.com/news/news-desk/environmentalisms-racist-history

Quiñones, A. R., Botoseneanu, A., Markwardt, S., Nagel, C. L., Newsom, J. T., Dorr, D. A., & Allore, H. G. (2019). Racial/ethnic differences in multimorbidity development and chronic disease accumulation for middle-aged adults. *PLoS One, 14*(6), Article e0218462. https://doi.org/10.1371/journal.pone.0218462

Qureshi, Z. (2020, February 25). *Technology and the future of growth: Challenges of change.* Brookings Institution. https://www.brookings.edu/blog/up-front/2020/02/25/technology-and-the-future-of-growth-challenges-of-change/

Ravi, K. E., Fields, N. L., & Dabelko-Schoeny, H. (2021). Outdoor spaces and buildings, transportation, and environmental justice: A qualitative interpretive meta-synthesis of two age-friendly domains. *Journal of Transport & Health, 20,* Article 100977.

Revell, M. A., & McGhee, M. N. (2012). Evolution of the African American family. *International Journal of Childbirth Education, 27*(4), 44–48.

Richards M., & Deary I. J. (2014). A life course approach to cognitive capability. In D. Kuh, R. Cooper, R. Hardy, M. Richards, & Y. Ben-Shlomo. (Eds.), *A life course approach to healthy ageing* (pp. 32–45). Oxford University Press.

Rivas-Drake, D., & Marchand, A. (2016). Academic socialization among Latino families: Exploring the compensatory role of cultural processes. *Research in Human Development, 13*(3), 225–240. https://doi.org/10.1080/15427609.2016.1194708

Rowland-Shea, J., Doshi, S., Edberg, S., & Fanger, R. (2020). *The nature gap: Confronting racial and economic disparities in the destruction and protection of nature in America.* Center for American Progress. https://www.americanprogress.org/article/the-nature-gap/

Ryff, C. D., & Singer, B. (2003). Flourishing under fire: Resilience as a prototype of challenged thriving. In C. L. M. Keyes & J. Haidt. (Eds.), *Flourishing: positive psychology and the life well-lived* (pp. 15–36). American Psychological Association.

Saleebey, D. (1992). *The strengths perspective in social work practice: Power in the people.* Longman.

Saleebey, D. (2012). *The strengths perspective in social work practice* (6th ed.). Pearson.

Scerra, N. (2012). Strengths-based practices: An overview of the evidence. *Developing Practice: The Child, Youth and Family Work Journal, 31*, 43–52.

Sellers, R. M., Smith, M. A., Shelton, J. N., Rowley, S. A. J., & Chavous, T. M. (1998). Multidimensional model of racial identity: A reconceptualization of African American racial identity. *Personality and Social Psychology Review, 2*(1), 18–39. https://doi.org/10.1207/s15327957pspr0201_2

Shambley-Ebron, D. Z., & Boyle, J. S. (2006). In our grandmother's footsteps: Perceptions of being strong in African American women with HIV/AIDS. *Advances in Nursing Science, 29*(3), 195–206.

Shen, Y., Kim, S. Y., & Wang, Y. (2016). Intergenerational transmission of educational attitudes in Chinese American families: Interplay of socioeconomic status and acculturation. *Child Development, 87*(5), 1601–1616. https://doi.org/10.1111/cdev.12545

Singh, A. A. (2016). Moving from affirmation to liberation in psychological practice with transgender and gender nonconforming clients. *American Psychologist, 71*, 755–762.

Singh, A. A., Appling, B., & Trepal, H. (2020). Using the multicultural and social justice counseling competencies to decolonize counseling practice: The important roles of theory, power, and action. *Journal of Counseling and Development, 98*(3), 261–271. https://doi.org/10.1002/jcad.12321

Singh, A. A., & Moss, L. (2016). Using relational-cultural theory in LGBTQQ counseling: Addressing heterosexism and enhancing relational competencies. *Journal of Counseling and Development, 94*(4), 398–404. https://doi.org/10.1002/jcad.12098

Sisco, S., Gross, A. L., Shih, R. A., Sachs, B. C., Glymour, M. M., Bangen, K. J., Benitez, A., Skinner, J., Schneider, B. C., & Manly, J. J. (2015). The role of early-life educational quality and literacy in explaining racial disparities in cognition in late life. *Journals of Gerontology Series B: Psychological Sciences and Social Sciences, 70*(4), 557–567.

Smock, P. J., & Schwartz, C. R. (2020). The demography of families: A review of patterns and change. *Journal of Marriage and Family, 82*(1), 9–34.

Stewart, P. (2008). Care provision for African American elders. *Journal of Intergenerational Relationships, 6*(1), 61–81. https://doi.org/10.1300/J194v06n01_05

Sue, D. W. (2003). *Overcoming our racism: The journey to liberation.* Jossey-Bass.

Sue, D. W., & Constantine, M. G. (2003). Optimal human functioning in people of color in the United States. In W. B. Walsh (Ed.), *Counseling psychology and optimal human functioning* (pp. 151–169). Lawrence Erlbaum.

Sutton, M. Y., & Parks, C. P. (2013). HIV/AIDS prevention, faith, and spirituality among Black/African American and Latino communities in the United States: Strengthening scientific faith-based efforts to shift the course of the epidemic and reduce HIV-related health disparities. *Journal of Religion and Health, 52*(2), 514–530.

Syed, M., & McLean, K. C. (2017, April 24). Erikson's Theory of Psychosocial Development. https://doi.org/10.4135/9781483392271.n178

Tate, K. A., Fallon, K. M., Casquarelli, E. J., & Marks, L. R. (2014). Opportunities for action: Traditionally marginalized populations and the economic crisis. *Professional Counselor, 4*(4), 285–302.

Taylor, R. J., Chatters, L. M., & Levin, J. (2004). *Religion in the lives of African-Americans*. SAGE Publishing.

Telles, E. (2018). Latinos, race, and the US Census. *The ANNALS of the American Academy of Political and Social Science, 677*(1), 153–164.

Triandis, H. C. (2001). Individualism-collectivism and personality. *Journal of Personality, 69*(6), 907–924.

van den Bosch, M. A., Ostergren, P.-O., Grahn, P., Skarbaeck, E., & Wahrborg, P. (2015). Moving to serene nature may prevent poor mental health: Results from a Swedish longitudinal cohort study. *Public Health, 12*, 7974–7989. https://doi.org/10.3390/ijerph120707974.

Vander Borght, M., & Wyns, C. (2018). Fertility and infertility: Definition and epidemiology. *Clinical Biochemistry, 62*, 2–10.

Willis, S., & Martin, M. (Eds.). (2005). *Middle adulthood: A lifespan perspective*. SAGE.

Wilson-Barnes, S. L., Lanham-New, S. A., & Lambert, H. (2022). Modifiable risk factors for bone health & fragility fractures. *Best Practice & Research Clinical Rheumatology, 36*(3), Article 101758.

World Health Organization. (2018). *The global network for age-friendly cities and communities: Looking back over the last decade, looking forward to the next*. https://apps.who.int/iris/handle/10665/278979

Yearby, R. (2018). Racial disparities in health status and access to healthcare: The continuation of inequality in the United States due to structural racism. *American Journal of Economics and Sociology, 77*(3–4), 1113–1152. https://doi.org/10.1111/ajes.12230

Yosso, T. J. (2005). Whose culture has capital? A critical race theory discussion of community cultural wealth. *Race, Ethnicity and Education, 8*(1), 69–91.

Zelazo, P. D., Carter, A., Reznick, J. S., & Frye, D. (1997). Early development of executive function: A problem-solving framework. *Review of General Psychology, 1*(2), 198–226.

Zhang, Z., Hayward, M. D., & Yu, Y. L. (2016). Life course pathways to racial disparities in cognitive impairment among older Americans. *Journal of Health and Social Behavior, 57*(2), 184–199.

Zhang, P., Liu, Y., Gu, X., & Chen, S. (2020). Toward active living: SES-and race-based disparities in knowledge and behaviors. *Journal of Racial and Ethnic Health Disparities, 7*(2), 374–382.

CREDITS

Fig. 9.1: Geoff Heinrich, David Leege, and Carrie Miller, "The CRS Integral Human Development Conceptual Framework," A User's Guide to Integral Human Development (IHD): Practical Guidance for CRS Staff and Partners, p. 5. Copyright © 2008 by Catholic Relief Services.

Fig. 9.2: Source: Adapted from https://www.brookings.edu/blog/brookings-now/2014/03/28/this-happiness-age-chart-will-leave-you-with-a-smile-literally/. Data Source: Gallup World Poll, 2013.

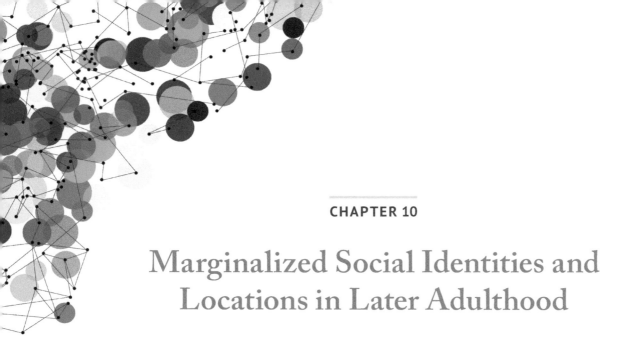

CHAPTER 10

Marginalized Social Identities and Locations in Later Adulthood

CHRISTINE D. HOLMES

Introduction

Today, 1 out of 6 people in the United States is age 65 or older. By 2040, this ratio will shrink to 1 out of every 5 people (Administration on Aging [AOA], 2021). These startling figures present a future in which the number of adults entering old age will drastically outnumber middle-aged adults, the age group primarily responsible for elder care. Given growth disparities between likely to face social isolation (i.e., the lack of social relationships and contact) than ever before. Older generations, older adults in the community are more adults are particularly vulnerable to the detrimental effects of social isolation through a multitude of age-related losses of functional autonomy and social support systems. In addition to the physical health risks that increase with social isolation, adults living on the margins of society face disruptions to their self-agency and social belonging that may be even more deleterious to their ability to survive and thrive in older age. Practitioners can help advance the well-being of older adults by recognizing signs of social isolation and loneliness during appointments with them; developing

LEARNING OBJECTIVES

1. Develop a nuanced understanding of the experiences and life transitions of older adults and their relationship to social health and well-being. (Competencies 2 and 3)

2. Distinguish between conceptualizations of social isolation and loneliness for older adults. (Competency 4)

3. Analyze historical, social, and structural factors that perpetuate the social isolation of older adults. (Competencies 2 and 3).

4. Learn skills of engagement, assessment, and intervention to advance the social health of older adults while prioritizing their individual worldviews, needs, and priorities. (Competencies 1, 6, 7, and 8).

awareness of the social, historical, and structural factors that impact social isolation; and partnering with older adults to develop an individualized care plan to reach their goals for social connection. This chapter will outline current conceptualizations of social connection, driving forces of social isolation within an older adult's multisystems context, and how to center older adults' perspectives and priorities in social health care planning.

Let's begin with a vignette that illustrates how a social worker confronts a case of social isolation in a nursing home.

VIGNETTE: SOCIAL DISCONNECTION

As I wandered the halls of a nursing home in search of my client, the odor of Lysol singed my nostrils with its burning yet familiar aroma. The spotless floors reflected the bright glares of the facility's fluorescent lights as the squeaking of my case manager's shoes echoed off of the pale pink walls. As I slowly made my way to the nursing station, an assemblage of nursing home residents quietly sat in the dayroom waiting for their midafternoon snack with the sound of the television buzzing in the background. Across the hall, a group of nurses were visibly hard at work flipping through medical records and running in and out of the nurses station as the ringing phone continued to go unanswered. I was undeniably in a nursing home.

While idling at the nurses station door, I managed to get the attention of a nurse rushing to respond to a call. Seizing this moment of opportunity, I introduced myself as a visitor from the court and presented a court order to conduct a routine investigation of my client's guardianship case. The investigation required a review of the client's medical records and interviews with those involved in the case to report concerns regarding her care. The nurse nodded in understanding and pointed to the client, "She's over there," before hastily moving on to her next destination. I steadily approached my client who was sitting at the edge of the dayroom facing the hall as if she was more interested in the passersby than anything

happening behind her in the dayroom. My client appeared to be a Black woman in her mid-60s, dressed in an all-blue tracksuit. Her hair was neatly wrapped in a bun at the top of her head. I knelt to make eye contact, introduced myself, and asked how she was doing and what she thought of the nursing home.

After the interview, I circled back to review my client's medical records at the nurses station, which was now occupied by only two nurses discussing the care of a resident. I asked for my client's medical book and sat beside the nurses as I skimmed the last year of medical appointment and visitor notes. The medical records dated back 5 years to the initiation of the guardianship case when the client was first diagnosed with dementia. A copy of the initial guardianship court order named my client's two daughters as coguardians. Based on my interview with the client and review of medical records, the coguardian sisters seemed to be meeting the state minimum legal requirements of guardianship care (e.g., visiting at least once a month, ensuring her safety and access to state benefits, etc.). To be certain, I turned to the nurses standing beside me and asked for their impressions of the daughters' care of my client. One nurse responded:

> Oh, them! Let's see ... yes, they call to check in about once a week before their mother has an appointment. If we ask them to bring clothes or something

(Continued)

like that, they'll do it. We don't have any problems with them. The only thing is ... they're her *daughters*. They only come once a month and when they do, they don't stay long. They're not affectionate either. They don't even hug her. If that was my mom, I would be here every day, especially if I was the only one visiting.

The nurse shook her head in disappointment, looking to the other nurse for validation.

After a brief interview with the nurses, I hurried back to court building to write my investigation report. Before typing up my handwritten notes, I skimmed the court database for the social history filed under my client's name. (I routinely waited to read social histories until after interviews to ensure I was listening openly with fewer assumptions about my client.) My eyes glided across the rows of words until I reached the following:

This Court Examiner found that the person recommended for guardianship lacks capacity for decision-making due to symptoms of alcohol-induced dementia. Her daughters reported that they were removed from their mother's care after she began abusing alcohol and were raised in the foster care system. Since the daughters are the only known family members in this case, they should be appointed temporary co-guardians over their mother's care until a long-term solution is identified.

A review of the family's history showed that the sisters had been raised in foster care separately from their mother due to her alcohol abuse. Decades later, the sisters reentered their mother's life when the nursing home filed a petition asking the court to appoint someone to help the mother make care decisions. Compounding the family's history of loss and trauma, the mother's alcohol abuse began after surviving domestic violence by the sisters' father. It is impossible to know whether my client would still have developed dementia without the use of alcohol to cope with memories of domestic violence. Regardless, the middle-aged sisters were now in a life stage to care for their mother despite the social and structural forces that disrupted their ability to bond, straining their relationship and capacity for a deeper social connection.

Social Isolation: An Overview

As mentioned previously, 20% of the U.S. population will be over age of 65 years old by 2030 (Roberts et al., 2018). As the world population ages, the well-being and social inclusion of older adults is of increasing concern. The prevalence of social isolation increased during COVID-19 lockdowns, quarantines, and other social distancing measures to prevent the transmission of the disease, especially amongst older and immunocompromised persons. Decades of research have documented the harmful consequences of social isolation that lead to increased risk of cardiovascular diseases, memory loss, psychological distress, and premature death (National Academies of Sciences, Engineering, and Medicine [NASEM], 2020). For adults living on the margins of society with lived experienced that predispose or present compounding factors for social isolation, such as those with disabilities, LGBTQIA+ individuals, and persons of color, a lack of self-agency and social belonging may be even more harmful to their ability to survive and thrive in older age (Brown & Munson, 2020).

Social Connection

While research has established the negative consequences of social isolation, general constructs of **social connection** (e.g., social isolation and loneliness), a system that embodies measures and concepts of social health (see Figure 10.1), are often conflated in the literature (NASEM, 2020; Brown & Munson, 2020). Where **social isolation** refers to the deficit of an active social support network, **loneliness** reflects a felt dissatisfaction with one's social connections (NASEM, 2020; Courtin & Knapp, 2015). Social isolation can be seen as a structural measure of social connection that is observed within the presence and intersection of social relationships and roles within one's social network. Structural features, such as marital status, social network size, and level of social integration, can indicate the existence and degree of social activity in an older adult's life (NASEM, 2020). In contrast, loneliness represents a sense of social support, a functional measure of social connection (see Figure 10.1). Functional dimensions of social connection reveal the various roles of one's social relationships as demonstrated by the kinds and degree of emotional and instrumental resources available within a social network (NASEM, 2020).

TABLE 10.1 Understanding Social Isolation Versus Loneliness

Social isolation	Loneliness
Definition: the objective state of having few social relationships or infrequent social contact with others (NASEM, 2020, p. 1).	**Definition**: a subjective feeling of being isolated (NASEM, 2020, p. 1); a discrepancy between the quantity and quality of relationships that people have versus what they want (Pinquart & Sörenson, 2001).
Role in social connection: a structural measure of social connection.	**Role in social connection**: a functional measure of social connection.
Relationship to loneliness: may exist with or independent of loneliness (e.g., personal satisfaction with living alone and leading a quiet life with limited social contact).	**Relationship to social isolation**: may exist with or independent of social isolation (e.g., having numerous social relationships with persons whom they lack emotional closeness).

The **discrepancy theory of loneliness** explains that loneliness is the difference between the number or quality of one's relationships and their desires for social connection (Peplau & Perlman, 1982, as cited in Pinquart & Sörenson, 2001). Cacioppo and Cacioppo (2018) theorized the relationship between social isolation and loneliness using the **theory of loneliness**, which describes social isolation and loneliness as mutually reinforcing. Older adults experiencing loneliness may retreat from social opportunities in response to the negative thoughts and feelings associated with their loneliness. However, even persons with larger social support networks can feel loneliness without isolation from social relationships (de Jong-Gierveld, 1987). Social isolation and loneliness are typically intertwined and are best understood when studied in conjunction (Newall & Menec, 2019). Similar to social isolation, loneliness is associated with poor health outcomes and early mortality in older adults. Research on its impacts is not as robust as the evidence between social isolation and the health and well-being of older adults (NASEM, 2020).

TABLE 10.2 Theoretical Perspectives on Loneliness

Theory	Definition
Cognitive discrepancy theory of loneliness (Perlman & Peplau, 1982, as cited in Pinquart & Sorenson, 2001)	Theory that loneliness is based on the difference between the number or quality of one's relationships and their desire for social connection.
Theory of loneliness (Cacioppo & Cacioppo, 2018)	Theory that loneliness compels a retreat from social opportunities in response to the negative thoughts and feelings associated with one's loneliness, mutually reinforcing the experience of social isolation and loneliness.

Older adults may face social isolation or loneliness, both, or, ideally, neither. Research estimates that 24% (NASEM, 2020) to 40% (Elder & Retrum, 2012) of older adults in the United States are socially isolated, while nearly half (43% over 60 years old) are experiencing loneliness (NASEM, 2020). For example, older adults experiencing loneliness may have numerous social relationships with persons whom they lack emotional closeness with, or they may only find belonging in certain relationships or social domains, such as with family or friends. Therefore, the perception of not having social support within a network of relationships may explain feelings of loneliness, leading to social disconnection. Conversely, an older adult may express satisfaction with living alone and leading a quiet life with limited social contact. While they are in relative social isolation, they may not feel a sense of social exclusion or loneliness. As separate concepts, social isolation is believed to precipitate a feeling of loneliness (ElSadr et al., 2009) or operate through distinguished pathways to impact on health (NASEM, 2020). To appropriately identify and address the needs of older adults, it is essential that practitioners differentiate aspects of social connection by understanding the nuances and variations of older adults' social lives.

TABLE 10.3 Understanding Observations of Social Disconnection

Observation	Implications for practice
Older adults experiencing loneliness due to a lack of emotional closeness within numerous social relationships.	Self-perception of not having social support within a network of relationships may explain feelings of loneliness.
Older adults only finding belonging in certain relationships or social domains.	
Older adults expressing satisfaction with living alone while leading a quiet life with limited social contact.	May not feel a sense of social exclusion of loneliness, despite being in relative social isolation.

Developmental Role of Social Connection in Old Age

Social connections are considered a potent driver of emotional and physical health that enable a greater ability to manage stress and can impact on the central nervous system to lessen the severity of social and physical pain (Eisenberger & Lieberman, 2004). We feel social connection in a number of ways: through the structure of social relationships, through functional **social support** (i.e., access to emotional or instrumental resources); and through the quality of social relationships (NASEM, 2020).

Due to common life transitions later in life, such as retirement, health issues, and bereavement, scholars have presumed that social isolation was integral to aging. Elaine Cumming and William Henry (as cited in Cornwell et al., 2008) attempted to theorize this myth in 1961 using **social disengagement**

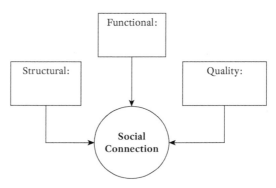

FIGURE 10.1 Conceptual Framework for Social Connection

Note: A multifactorial construct of social connection adapted from Holt-Lunstand (2018).

theory, which stated that social isolation of the aging was caused by the inescapable erosion of social roles and social relationships as the value of adults in society gradually degrades. The belief that social isolation is a characteristic of aging, however, is not supported by research, which has shown that social connectedness is quite possible in older age. Research focused on the generative potential of older adults, such as Glen Elder's **life course theory**, has emphasized the fortitude of older adults in the face of age-related changes to their social networks (George, 1993). Some researchers have theorized that even though the size of social networks typically shrink in older age, their quality can strengthen as casual relationships are relinquished (Frederickson & Carstensen, 1990) to center more supportive kinship relationships (Shaw et al., 2007). An older adult's support system may provide greater instrumental support as the adult's functional dependence increases and family members join to share in caregiving tasks to fulfill role expectations. For older adults, social connectedness is seen in their reciprocation of care with others and feeling valued within a group or community. Social connectedness correlates with the quality of their mental, emotional, and physical health and risk of suicidality (O'Rourke & Sidani, 2017). Cultivating a positive sense of social connectedness can also aid in buffering against stressors in late life (Suragarn et al., 2021).

Based on a scoping review of social connectedness for older adults, more is currently known about the outcomes of social connectedness than its determinants. Some determinants are influential in social connectedness but difficult to target for intervention: older age with its increased risk of cognitive decline and loss of social roles and a married marital status as a means to reciprocate interpersonal care (O'Rourke & Sidani, 2017). Social connection is also affected by other factors, such as technological access, in order to communicate and maintain relationships with others; the size and closeness of one's social network; and group affiliation and participation in meaningful pursuits that promote closeness. The authors' findings suggested that tangible and ambiguous losses suffered by older adults may have a stronger correlation with loneliness than social isolation (ElSadr, et al., 2009; Bekhet et al., 2008) and that more research is needed to understand determinants of social connection for clinical intervention (O'Rourke et al., 2017).

TABLE 10.4 Social Health in Older Age

Terms	Definitions
Social support	The actual or perceived availability of emotional and tangible resources from others (NASEM, 2020, p. 4).
Social connectedness	A feeling of interpersonal connection, different from objective social network features such as isolation or interpersonal contact, or the network function of social support (Ashida & Heaney, 2008).
Theories	
Social disengagement theory (Cumming & Henry, 1961, as cited in Cornwell et al., 2008)	The theory that aging is an inevitable, mutual withdrawal or disengagement between older adults and society, resulting in decreased interaction between the aging person and others in their social system (Cumming & Henry, 1961).
Life course theory (George, 1993)	The sociological perspective that refers to life course patterns that vary across time, space, and populations and focus on age-differentiated, socially recognized sequences of transitions with consequences that may be long term (George, 1993).

REFLECTION: CREATING A VISION FOR SOCIAL INCLUSION

Take a moment to reflect on the myths you have heard about the social lives of older adults. Where did these ideas originate? How might these beliefs promote or restrict the potential of older adults to experience social connection?

In the following sections, we will explore the structural factors that increase the risk of social isolation and approaches to expand the possibilities for the social participation of older adults.

Social Marginalization and Risk Factors for Social Disconnection

Although social connections are considered fundamental to the development of everyone, the role of social isolation across the lifespan has yet to be fully explored. For example, little is known about the long-term effects of social isolation in early development once a person reaches late adulthood. In addition to the absence of a developmental framework to understand social isolation, emerging research is just beginning to examine social isolation within a social justice framework (Brown & Munson, 2020). A social justice perspective enables practitioners to meditate on both the capabilities of the individual and their environment to promote a dignified life as well as society's responsibility to redistribute resources to the most subjugated communities. Research has also established a relationship between the mental and emotional well-being of older adults and their social connectedness, but the directionality of causation is unclear. Some scholars have suggested that the quality of an older adult's well-being may affect their ability to achieve social connectedness (ElSadr et al., 2009). Therefore, specific populations of marginalized older adults, such as those with disabilities, LGBTQIA+ individuals, and persons of color, with lived experiences that predispose or present compounding factors for social isolation require special consideration in addressing social isolation in practice (Brown & Munson, 2020).

Personal Risk Factors for Social Disconnection

A number of personal characteristics of older adults linked to social isolation can be understood through a structural lens. As an example, the social and economic marginalization of Black, Indigenous, and people of color (BIPOC) presents risk factors for social isolation: compromised health, low-income status, and limited access to resources and social support. Similarly, older adults with physical disabilities are less likely to have accumulated wealth or socially participate due to workforce and other societal exclusions. Older adults living with mental illness, particularly depression, and cognitive decline also face more social isolation either as an antecedent or result of social isolation. Although there has been minimal research on the developmental effects of social isolation and loneliness in children, studies have shown that abuse at earlier life stages is linked to a greater risk for depression and suicidality in older age, with depression and suicidal behaviors being correlates of social isolation and loneliness for the aging population (Leigh-Hunt et al., 2017). In addition, older adults have faced greater **ageism**, discrimination based on their age, since the onset of the COVID-19 pandemic. Older adults are among the subpopulations who were disproportionately impacted by COVID-19 due to preexisting health conditions and required additional public precautions, driving the devaluation and stereotype older adults as a societal burden (Cox, 2020).

TABLE 10.5 Personal Risk Factors for Social Disconnection

Personal characteristics	Associated risks
Old age	Age-based discrimination, leading to greater social marginalization. A recent example is the devaluation and stereotype of older adults as a societal burden during the pandemic due to their preexisting health conditions that required public precautions to mitigate COVID-19 transmission.
Race and ethnicity	Social and economic marginalization of BIPOC has led to compromised health, low-income status, and limited access to resources and social support.
Physical and cognitive disabilities	These individuals are less likely to accumulate wealth or engage in social participation due to workforce and other societal exclusions.
Psychiatric disabilities (e.g., mental illness, cognitive decline, etc.)	The individuals face more social isolation either as an antecedent or result of social isolation.
History of childhood abuse	These individuals have a greater risk of depression and suicidality in older age, with depression and suicidal behaviors being correlates of social isolation and loneliness amongst older adults.

Structural Risk Factors for Social Disconnection

An increasing number of older adults are living on their own in the community (Redfoot et al., 2013; National Alliance for Caregiving [NAC] & American Association of Retired Persons [AARP], 2020). A policy and intervention focus on "aging in place" has enabled older adults with disabilities to remain in their homes longer using community-based resources. Due to the risk of COVID-19 to older adults, older adults have avoided high-risk transmission settings, such as nursing homes and assisted living facilities, with the aim to be cared for by unpaid friends and family members delivering complex tasks typically done by trained professionals. The ability to age-in-place is a matter of affordability, and it can be more costly to be cared for at home than some higher care institutional settings, with home health aides costing an annual average of $61,776 versus a median of $54,000 for an assisted living facility in 2021 (Genworth, 2022).

In addition, the availability of in-home direct care workers, ranging from nurse aides to home-makers, is becoming increasingly inadequate as the number of young middle-aged adults grows at a much slower rate than those of older age cohorts. Older population growth combined with the shrinking of the middle-aged adult population is what public health scholars in the United States refer to as "the 2030 problem." In less than 10 years, the proportion of adults beyond 80 years old will expand by 79%, while the proportion of middle-aged adults will increase by 1%. By 2040, there will be only 2.9 middle-aged adults for every adult over 80 years old (Redfoot et al., 2013). The U.S. dependence on the home care workforce as essential workers during the pandemic stressed the significance of their role, despite their lack of professional training, health care benefits, and income. Health care policy advocacy is needed to increase the salaries, skills, and status of home health workers to address issues of professional burnout, worker–client COVID-19 transmission risk, the quality of care to older adults, and the risk of nursing home placement without adequate in-home support. Unless more action is taken to elevate the skills and benefits to home care workers (Cox, 2020), the United States will need to lean on other supports in the community, such as family members, to provide long-term support services.

In the United States, the likelihood of an older adult living alone is correlated with age, with community-based oldest adults (85+) most likely to live by themselves (NAC & AARP, 2020). Older adults who require functional assistance and lack assistive devices are more likely to experience social isolation, while those living in low-resource communities that inhibit accessibility and mobility report that higher crime rates or lack a health care infrastructure have constrained community and societal participation. Although an estimated 74% of older adults in the United States use technological devices on a daily basis to stay in touch with friends and family (Suragarn et al., 2021), older adults require the financial means to afford a technological infrastructure at home.

Social Connection of Racially Marginalized Older Adults

The literature on social isolation amongst older adults of color is quite sparse, as studies of social isolation have focused primarily on the well-being of older White adults (Taylor et al., 2019). Studies on the social connections of older adults that account for racial and ethnic differences

TABLE 10.6 Structural Risk Factors for Social Disconnection

Structural dimensions	Associated risks
Policy emphasis on aging in place without afford-able and accessible in-home care workforce	Increased risk of unmet health care needs and a lack of safety supervision while residing at home
Higher COVID-19 risks in institutional settings	
Disproportionately larger number of older adults compared to young middle-aged adults	
Low-resource communities	Limited accessibility and mobility (e.g., transit, sidewalks, and buildings)
	Higher crime rates and lack of health care infrastructure
	Constrained community and societal participation for social connection
	Inability to afford technological devices to stay in touch with friends and family
Conditions of institutional settings	Factors such as the behavior of facility staff can influence residents' level of social participation and ability to form quality relationships with other residents in long-term care.

tell different stories of social isolation and loneliness by race and ethnicity. For example, global studies on older migrant groups reflect that older migrants tend to experience greater loneliness than nonmigrants in their host country. Older migrants reported loneliness as a result of cultural differences, fewer social relationships, and discrimination by host country nationals (Victor et al., 2012).

In a study on the social isolation of an older adult subsample in a nationally representative survey (Taylor et al., 2019), older White adults were more likely to meet indicators of social isolation: living alone, not having adult children, and having minimal contact with a religious congregation. Taylor et al. (2019) explained that older White adults were more likely to never attend religious services and therefore may not be meaningfully impacted by a lack of contact with congregational networks. Furthermore, the researchers also suggested that alternative social networks of friends and extended relatives (versus kinship relationships) were sufficient instrumental support systems for older White adults. Black older adults are more likely to live with extended family members and friends, yet their network sizes tend to be smaller, which could limit opportunities for social connection. Their circumstances may be explained by sociostructural obstacles, such as having a low income, societal discrimination, and restricted mobility in their communities, and increasing dependence upon kinship relationships.

In another secondary analysis of a national survey of adults living in the community, researchers studied social isolation, loneliness, or what they referred to as "perceived isolation," and health outcomes across Latinx, Black, and White non-Hispanic older Americans (Miyawaki, 2015). While social isolation and loneliness had an inverse relationship with the physical and mental health of White older adults, social isolation was only correlated with mental health outcomes for Latinx elders. The author explained that social isolation's significant relationship with Latinx elders may be understood through age differences, as Latinx older adults were younger than the other groups and more likely to share a residence with their social network. For older Black adults, their mental health was overall poorer than White and Latinx older adults. Black elders are more likely to report a lack of friendship and feelings of social exclusion. Loneliness for Black older adults had a significant negative relationship with mental health, whereas social isolation was only related to their physical health outcomes (Miyawaki, 2015).

INDIVIDUAL LEARNING EXERCISE: THE CASE OF MR. P

Mr. P is a 74-year-old Black man residing in a nursing home in a densely populated, metropolitan city. He was originally referred to the nursing home for dementia care 4 years ago after being evicted from his apartment for missing rent payments. Little is known about Mr. P's social history. He speaks a West African French dialect. No staff at the nursing home speaks his dialect or has identified a translator to facilitate communication. The nursing home social worker reports difficulty finding information on whether Mr. P has relatives living in the area, as he receives no outside visitors. Since the staff has no way of communicating with Mr. P, a professional guardian is appointed by the court with the authority to make legal and health care decisions for him.

Discussion Questions

1. What factors may limit Mr. P's ability to achieve social connection at the nursing home?

2. To what degree is society responsible for promoting the social health and well-being of Mr. P?

3. Drawing from the conceptual framework for social connection (Figure 10.1), what may be some opportunities to enhance social connection for Mr. P?

Social Connection of LGBTQIA+ Older Adults

There will be an estimated five million LGBTQIA+ older adults in the United States by 2030 (Choi & Meyer, 2016). While 89% of elder care is currently provided by relatives in the general population (NAC & AARP, 2020), only 11% of elder care to LGBTQIA+ individuals is provided by a relative (Knauer, 2016). Due to a history of discrimination against LGBTQIA+ individuals, the natural support networks of LGBTQIA+ older adults are more likely to be comprised of "chosen family," or selected non-kin individuals who exchange emotional and instrumental support with the older adult (Kim et al., 2017; Orel & Coon, 2016). As we've discussed, discrimination and structural violence in early life has greatly affected LGBTQIA+ persons from fully participating in society. This has led to poorer mental and physical health outcomes, including social isolation and loneliness of LGBTQIA+ individuals in late life (Perone et al., 2020), and has also perpetuated a distrust of health care providers—putting LGBTQIA+ elders at even greater risk of social isolation (Services and Advocacy for Gay, Lesbian, Bisexual and Transgender Elders [SAGE] & National Center for Transgender Equality [NCTE], 2012).

LGBTQIA+ older adults who faced rejection from their family of origin were put in a position to find social and economic networks of their own across the life course. Older adults of this subgroup are less likely to have children or share their home with another person (Brown & Munson, 2020; Espinoza, 2011). As 48% of elder caregivers in the United States are adult children (NAC & AARP, 2020), almost one third of LGBTQIA+ elders are at least very concerned about being cared for in later life (versus only 16% of non-LGBTQIA+ older adults; SAGE, 2014). Transgender older adults also reported receiving less social support, despite carrying more expansive social networks (Witten, 2017, as cited in Perone et al., 2020). More than 3 out of 4 LGBTQIA+ older adults were worried about the availability of elder care support to them (SAGE, 2014). Since chosen family members are more likely to be of comparable age to the older adult (Butler, 2019), they are more likely to face health changes and bereavement concurrently as the network ages together.

Social Health Assessment and Intervention

The risk factors that inhibit older adults from a high degree of social contact in the community can pose obstacles in making their needs known to others, including health care and elder care providers (Molloy et al., 2010). In addition, there is a lack of scholarly agreement on how to assess and understand social isolation. Some scholars have proposed establishing a threshold for social isolation based on predetermined social concepts to be used to measure social isolation (Valtorta et al., 2016). While finding a uniform definition of social isolation may help standardize assessment protocols and identify avenues to intervene for greater social health (Newall & Menec, 2019), practitioners should also account for the heterogeneity of the older adult population in their assessment process. For example, in a qualitative study by Cloutier-Fisher and colleagues (2011), the authors found that the number of social relationships alone did not determine social connectedness, as social network sizes were explained by life course events, such as bereavement, or a personal preference for fewer relationships.

TABLE 10.7 Standardizing Social Health Assessments for Older Adults

Older adult population	Implications for practice
Older adults are a heterogeneous group, whose social and cultural contexts may shape their experience of social isolation.	Practitioners should account for the heterogeneity of the older adult population while seeking a standardized protocol and identifying avenues to intervene for greater social health.

Social Health Assessment

An assessment is a unique opportunity to actively listen to older adults to understand how they view their current social relationships, how they feel about those relationships, and what they wish to change. Assessments should be a teaching and learning exchange whereby the practitioner poses exploratory questions and a nonjudgmental disposition that enables older adults and those in their natural support networks to share and engage in deeper self-reflection through gentle probing and validation. By the end of an assessment, both the older adult and the provider should have a clearer understanding of the situation, including challenges and opportunities for the adult and their environment, and potential avenues to bolster social relationships, as needed.

Distinguishing Social Isolation from Loneliness

To optimize the potential for social connectedness of older adults, it is important to account for the discrepancy between their objective social isolation and the subjective experience of loneliness to gain a fuller picture of older adults' social health and implications for their care (Pinquart & Sorenson, 2001; Newall & Menec, 2019). Beginning with social isolation, practitioners should examine connections between the structure (e.g., social network size, types of relationships and closeness between network members); function (e.g., exchanges of social support within the network); and quality (the older adult's feelings about the positive and negative aspects of their social relationships) of social relationships. As importantly, practitioners should have a sense of the assets of the person's social landscape on multiple systems levels. These assets are to be incorporated and mobilized in planning to advance the older adult's efforts to reach their goals for social connectedness.

Despite societal misconceptions about the social value of older adults (Cornwell et al., 2008), older adults may have their own expectations of what social connection means to them. Practitioners should note that older adults may be experiencing variations of social isolation with loneliness: socially isolated and lonely; socially isolated but not lonely; lonely but not isolated; and neither socially isolated nor lonely (Newall & Menec, 2019). It is important to attend to risk factors, such as being single or widowed or living alone, and other structural factors that may impact the person's social participation in response to their marginalized social identities. Each grouping carries their own implications for intervention (Taylor, 2020). The timing of losses or changes within an older adult's life, such as an increase in functional dependence or loss of a loved one, may indicate how long a person has been experiencing social isolation and what interventions may be most effective (Taylor, 2020).

REFLECTION: CO-CONSTRUCTING A VISION FOR SOCIAL CONNECTION

The older adults we serve may be experiencing either social isolation or loneliness, both, or neither. How might you explore what social connectedness means to an older adult? What questions would you ask?

In the following sections, we will review assessment methods and approaches to partner with older adults in understanding the quality of their social health in their diverse contexts.

Social Health Assessment Methods

Providers working in health care settings may ask older adults questions to understand not only their degree of social participation but also their feelings and wishes to optimize the quality of their social connections. Questions should assess objective aspects of their social network (e.g., family, friends, and others in contact with them; frequency of contact; and the kind of support provided), as well as the subjective experience of their social lives (e.g., desire for more contact or social relationships with different people; see Tables 10.9 and 10.10 for sample questions). The information gleaned from social health instruments can illuminate areas for further exploration to understand the person's degree of social isolation (Taylor, 2020; Nicholson, 2012) and find ways to mobilize existing social network members in care planning or introduce new opportunities to promote social participation (Nicholson, 2012).

Measures of Social Isolation

The degree of one's social connectedness is most commonly measured using structural dimensions, such as network size and frequency of contact with other persons (Ong et al., 2016). Instruments to measure the social isolation of older adults, including the Lubben Social Network Scale (LSNS) or its other variations, the LSNS-R revised version or the LSNS-18 longer version, provide a brief impression of one's social network. The LSNS-6 is the short form version of the scale with six items measuring three dimensions of an older adult's social network: emotions, tangible, and network size. The LSNS-6 has good internal consistency ($a = 0.78$) and has increasingly been used by practitioners over the last decade to understand the degree of an individual's social isolation to follow up appropriately (Lubben & Gironda, 2003, as cited in Nicholson, 2012). When it is not feasible to provide the LSNS during an appointment with an older adult due to issues such as time constraints, the older adult may be asked to complete the questionnaire at home to discuss at the next meeting with the provider.

The LSNS is considered to be one of the most suitable social network measures of older adults based on its strong psychometric properties, brief administration time of 5–10 minutes, translatability to multiple languages, and adaptability across a range of settings (Siette et al., 2021). It is important to note that the LSNS is designed to examine one's social network, a structural component of social connection (see Figure 10.1) and does not include assessment of social support or aspects of social relationships that may be especially important in determining the social connectedness of certain subpopulations, including those living with depression or dementia who may further depend upon the available resources and quality of their social relationships (Siette et al., 2021) and older LGBTQIA+ adults who may require a broader definition of "family" that includes nonbiological connections in an assessment of their social health (Gabrielson & Holston, 2014). Practitioners who use the LSNS with older adults should account for the contextual factors that are most meaningful to an older adult's social well-being in their assessment.

Measures of Loneliness

Brief scales for loneliness are also available to reduce the time required by older adults to complete a questionnaire. For example, practitioners most commonly employ a global, single-item self-assessment question (e.g., "Do you sometimes feel lonely?") to measure feelings of lone-liness (Ong et al., 2016). Older adults may respond using a 4-point Likert scale ranging from 1 (*often*) to 4 (*never*) with a lower score indicating more loneliness. As a single-item measure of the complex concept of loneliness, this measure may be restricted in its ability to measure loneliness accurately and reliably (Drageset & Haugan, 2021). Practitioners should take additional steps to supplement measures using the guidance provided in the next subsection (Using Measures of Social Health in Practice).

Another widely used measure of loneliness is the Three-Item Loneliness Scale, which orig-inates from the 20-item UCLA Loneliness Scale developed by Russell, Peplau, and Cutrona (Hughes et al., 2004). The measure is administered by a trained interviewer who states, "The next questions are about how you feel about different aspects of your life. For each one, tell me how often you feel that way." The following questions are then asked: First, how often do you feel that lack companionship? How often do you feel left out? How often do you feel isolated from others? Participants can respond using a 3-point Likert scale ranging from 1 (*hardly ever*) to 3 (*often*). A higher mean score suggests a higher degree of loneliness. The Three-Item Loneliness Scale has demonstrated good internal consistency with a Cronbach's alpha of 0.72 (Hughes et al., 2004).

TABLE 10.8 Administering Measures of Social Health

Steps for administration	Purpose
1. **Prepare**: Persons who administer measures of social health should ensure they are trained to conduct personal interviews and/or be super-vised by an expert.	Ethically facilitate the assessment process and respond to questions from the interviewee.
2. **Assess**: Practitioners may use the tools pre-sented to identify social domains that require further exploration of older adults' experience of loneliness and social isolation (see Table 10.9).	Clarify how older adults understand and experience lone-liness as it intersects with or diverges from their objective state of social isolation.
3. **Contextualize**: Practitioners can develop a fuller picture of an older adult's social health by evaluating the clinical, social, and environmen-tal conditions of their social health.	Understand older adults' social health in context. For example, practitioners may consult caregivers and other close contacts to supplement social health assessments with observations of older adults, especially those with cognitive impairment like dementia.
	In addition, practitioners may be mindful of the social stigma of aging and being affiliated with other mar-ginalized groups that can inhibit older adults from self-disclosing their loneliness to providers (Drageset & Haugan, 2021).

Categories of Social Isolation and Loneliness

The assessment process reveals whether and how an older adult may be experiencing social isolation and loneliness with the aim of preventing and intervening to restrict

TABLE 10.9 Understanding Social Isolation and Loneliness

	Assessment Questions
Loneliness	Does the older adult sometimes feel lonely? To what extent is the older adult satisfied with their social relationships?
Structure	How many people does the older adult interact with regularly? What is their relationship to each person?
Function	To what extent do members of the older adult's social network reciprocate emotional and instrumental support?
Quality	What is the older adult's experience of the positive aspects and negative aspects of their social relationships?
Loss	For older adults who are lonely but not socially isolated, have they recently lost a person or relationship that was significant to them?
Environment	What barriers in the person's environment, such as their home or community, restrict their access to social interaction or participation?
Health	What is the role of the older adult's physical or mental health in their feeling of social connectedness?
Safety	Does the older adult with social isolation have an emergency response plan in case of an emergency, like falling at home?
Health	Would information on the health benefits of having a social network be helpful to an older adult facing social isolation?

the older adult's experience of either. How social isolation and loneliness are affecting the older adult are important considerations for social health care planning. In working with older adults, practitioners should first determine an older adult's social health goals, identify obstacles toward gaining social connection, and decide what programs may be beneficial to increase the adult's social participation as it aligns with their goals for social health.

Social Isolation with Loneliness

An older adult who is experiencing both social isolation (lack of social relationships and contact) and loneliness (a feeling of social dissatisfaction) may present with a combination of at-risk characteristics (e.g., living alone, older, low socioeconomic status, deteriorating health). This group of older adults are among the most difficult to reach, as they are isolated both physically and emotionally from social contacts that would otherwise aid in overseeing their well-being in the community. Practitioners who encounter adults in this group may wish to assess both the objective and subjective obstacles to social connection. As a correlate of loneliness, high degrees of social isolation may be perpetuated by structural causes, such as transportation access, physical health conditions, or occurrences of crime in the community. Loneliness may be compounded by other factors, such as mental health conditions or a history of losing meaningful relationships. The assessment process can be an opportunity to destigmatize the older adult's experience of isolation and loneliness while exploring their interest and readiness to seek more social contact and relationships. Fortunately, research suggests that older adults in this category are most receptive and responsive to a wide range of social interventions (Newall & Menec, 2019).

Social Isolation Without Loneliness

In contrast, some older adults experience relatively severe isolation but may not be happy with the quantity or quality of their relationships. These adults are likely to reside by themselves in remote areas, have conservative personalities (Newall & Menec, 2019), or not have children (Wenger & Burholt, 2004). Although small social networks are associated with loneliness for older adults, it is additionally important for practitioners to assess the degree to which an older adult feels they have a choice in the frequency in which they engage with network members. It is additionally important to understand the antecedents of their social isolation even when adults express satisfaction with current social connections. For example, adults who suffer a lifetime of social disconnection, lose a quality relationship through bereavement, or endure prolonged structural barriers to social connection, such as living in high-crime neighborhoods, might have adjusted their desire for social connectedness. Additionally, men also reportedly have a lower chance of expressing loneliness as a result of social stigma (Pinquart & Sörenson, 2001). Providers should gently explore social health history, along with the lonely adult's expectations for social connection, to decrease their risks of social isolation without impeding upon their desire for solitude.

Loneliness Without Social Isolation

Practitioners will likely encounter another group of older adults who are experiencing loneliness without social isolation. This experience is usually driven by a lack of satisfaction with the quality of relationships with members of an older adult's social network. Lonely adults with existing relationships may be engaged in higher intensity caregiving (Cloutier-Fisher et al., 2011) or exhibit greater dependence on their partners and hold high standards of them (Dykstra & Fokkema, 2007). To understand older adults expressing loneliness despite their large social network, practitioners should explore the older adult's expectations and features of their social relationships. As loneliness is more likely than social isolation to be associated with a personal history of loss, practitioners should also seek to understand recent changes to the most meaningful relationships within the older adult's network (Wenger et al., 1996). Practitioners can also inquire about their frequency of social contact, as fewer interactions with persons closest to the older adult can be a statistically significant correlate of loneliness compared to those with smaller social networks and low daily contact (Lee & Ko, 2017). Older adults in institutional settings, such as nursing homes or assisted living, may also belong to this group experiencing loneliness within a large social network. One study of nursing home residents with healthy cognitive functioning indicated that over half (56%) of older adults were experiencing loneliness at least sometimes, if not often (Drageset et al., 2011). Older adults who are not isolated but unsatisfied with their relationships may benefit from interventions that enhance their ability to improve upon their social relationships, including thoughts and beliefs about the relationships themselves (Masi et al., 2011).

TABLE 10.10 Sample Questions to Understand Loneliness Without Social Isolation

Loneliness	Do you sometimes feel lonely? How satisfied are you with your current relationships?
Loss	Have you recently lost a relationship that was important to you?
Structure	Who are you in contact with regularly? How often are you in contact?
Quality	What are the positive aspects of your current relationships? What are some of the negative aspects?
Expectations	What would you like to change about your relationships?

Social Health Care Planning

In planning for social health interventions, older adults' self-agency remains a priority. Their participation in care planning also increases the efficacy of interventions compared to planning solely done by the care provider. Interventions are also more effective when based on a theoretical model. Therefore, practitioners may use a theoretical perspective, such as the theory of loneliness (Cacioppo & Cacioppo, 2018), to conceptualize social isolation and use a theoretical underpinning for intervention (Dickens et al., 2011).

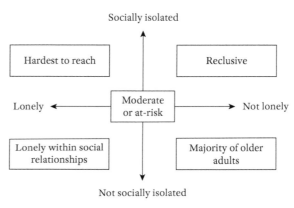

FIGURE 10.2 Social Isolation and Loneliness Categories for Older Adults

Note: Categories of social isolation and loneliness adapted from Newall and Menec (2019).

Based on an understanding of the older adult's social health history, social isolation, and alignment of social connectedness with social expectations, their intervention plan should be tailored to address both the objective and subjective aspects of their social connections (Taylor, 2020). As a subjective experience of social need, interventions can target any cognitions and behavior that may be driving an older adult's negative beliefs about their social connectedness. They can also address the quality of social contact with members of their social network. Although increasing social contact is not always the solution to address loneliness, social contact may be important to the older adult's well-being. Social isolation is correlated with physical health decline, and adults who are living alone with infrequent visits may receive delayed emergency assistance without a witness to initiate emergency response. Regardless of whether an adult expresses loneliness, it is important to coordinate with the older adult to develop a plan to increase home visits from someone they trust and a plan to respond to health emergencies. As the older adult should lead and determine their care, practitioners may implement interventions to the extent that is comfortable for the older adult. Interventions to address social isolation can and should be revisited regularly with the older adult for adjustments (Newall & Menec, 2019).

In the co-construction of social health planning with older adults, professionals should be mindful of the stigma associated with older adults expressing loneliness or social isolation, as it aligns with stereotypes about their vulnerabilities as an age group. Providers should clarify the potential value of interventions to an older adult while incorporating the strengths and coping strategies the older adult uses to manage social isolation into the plan. This partnership continues throughout the change process, as providers accompany and encourage socially isolated adults toward their goals for social connection (Taylor, 2020).

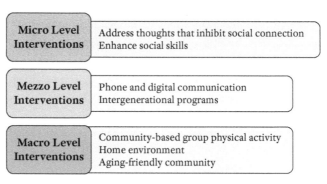

FIGURE 10.3 Micro- to Macro-Level Social Health Interventions for Older Adults

Note: Multisystem level interventions with older adults to promote social connectedness based on an integrative review of literature by Suragarn et al. (2021) and secondary analysis of the Health and Retirement Study, a longitudinal national survey of older adults in the United States, by Taylor (2020).

Interventions for Social Connection

Before implementing an intervention to alleviate social distress and enhance social connection, practitioners must sensitively engage in a teaching and learning assessment process (Finn, 2021) with older adults to co-construct an understanding of the structure and emotional influence of an older adult's social network and their goals for social connection. To develop a social health care plan, older adults and practitioners mobilize their new learning, including the strengths of the older adult's life, and identify additional opportunities to advance the older adult's goals. At the intervention stage, a personalized social health care plan of strategies to address social isolation and loneliness is implemented. Practitioners may find it appropriate to facilitate an older adult's access to resources that address immediate needs related to their health, safety, and mobility (Sellon, 2019).

For older adults, a social health care plan will likely include interventions on an individual level, as well as others, to address a combination of social isolation and loneliness, social isolation, or loneliness. Depending on the intensity and duration of social isolation and loneliness, it will be important for practitioners to emphasize the initiation of interventions that address their causes and risk factors. At the individual level, interventions are most likely to target factors related to loneliness, as it may accompany or exist separately from social isolation. In intervening upon loneliness, it is important to note that the degree to which an older adult feels social connectedness will have a stronger linkage to loneliness than the number of daily interactions with family and friends. Therefore, interventions for loneliness should be based on an understanding of the dimensions of social connection driving feelings of loneliness, the functional (social support) and quality (aspects of social relationships), while addressing the structure of social relationships (e.g., frequency of contact, social integration, etc.) as needed to achieve a greater sense of social satisfaction.

Cognitive and Behavioral Interventions

Some scholars of loneliness have reported efficacy in reducing the cognitions and behaviors that perpetuate loneliness. An older adult's initial impression that intimacy is inaccessible within their social relationships can trigger a focus on the negative aspects of social relationships, dysregulating their ability to register opportunities for connection other than a threat and reaffirm beliefs of rejection in subsequent social interactions. As mentioned earlier, Cacioppo and Cacioppo's (2018) theory of loneliness describes social isolation and loneliness as mutually reinforcing. Older adults experiencing loneliness may retreat from social opportunities in response to the negative thoughts and feelings associated with their loneliness. Therefore, cognitive behavioral strategies, social skill building, and positive health behaviors are used to decrease loneliness and increase feelings of social connection.

Although research suggests that cognitive interventions are the most effective in treating loneliness (Masi et al., 2011), it is important to consider age- and health-related factors that impact social cognitions when working with older adults. For example, an adult in a later life stage may experience reduced learning capacity due to poorer sleep quality. Older adults with conditions that alter cognitive functioning, such as dementia, grief, or depression, may also require special consideration to address loneliness. Some studies suggest that loneliness can even cause a loss of cognitive and functional performance, leading to more loneliness as social contact is restricted. Interventions that help older adults with cognitive impairment enhance memory (Winningham & Pike, 2007) or activate positive memories through sensory-based activities (Chiang et al., 2010) have been shown to increase social connectedness and may be a better fit for those managing memory loss. It is important for practitioners to be sensitive to the capacities of older adults with loneliness and the relationship between loneliness and the individual in their socioecological system.

TABLE 10.11 Cognitive and Behavioral Interventions for Social Connection

Age- and health-related factors that impact the social cognitions of older adults	
• Poorer sleep quality	Changes in mood and cognitive processes (e.g., learning capacity, memory retention, etc.)
• Mental health conditions (e.g., dementia, grief, depression, etc.)	
Cognitive interventions for older adults experiencing memory loss	
• Memory-enhancing interventions (Winningham & Pike, 2007)	Preserve memories of relationships, activate positive memories, and increase feelings of social connection.
• Sensory-based activities (Chiang et al., 2010)	

Social Skills

Similar to cognition-based interventions, promoting the development of social skills has been found to be more efficacious in treating loneliness than other social interventions. The literature also indicates that social skills interventions promote social skill-building while enhancing other dimensions of social connection, such as the social network size, exchanges of social support, and positive aspects of social relationships. Social skills interventions may also be provided on an individual or group level. In a meta-analysis of interventions to diminish loneliness (Masi et al., 2011), social skills intervention studies for loneliness used interventions focused on conversation by phone or in person, exchanging praise, non-verbal engagement, and establishing romantic relationships. Earlier studies of loneliness (McWhirter, 1990) demonstrated that social skills development in conjunction with cognitive behavioral therapy was efficacious for older adults with loneliness and social anxiety compared to either intervention on its own. Adults with disabilities, such as severe mental illness, are more likely to experience loneliness than persons without severe mental illness. Social skills enhancement for persons with severe mental illness has been found to be most effective in support group or mutual help group settings, which also improved upon their social support systems (Masi et al., 2011).

Communication Technologies for Social Connection

Although meta-analyses of digital technology intervention studies have produced mixed findings on the efficacy of technological interventions to reduce loneliness (Shah et al., 2021; Masi et al., 2011), a number of qualitative studies have demonstrated that supporting older adults using technological tools widens the reach of social engagement and participation. Technological interventions are particularly useful for older adults isolated by their residential location (e.g., rural areas, nursing homes, etc.) or those who belong to a geographically dispersed network or family and friends. Studies involving digital literacy have demonstrated the benefits in using technological devices to close the social and geographical gaps for older adults to develop or maintain social connections from a distance (Preston & Moore, 2019; Millard et al., 2018).

Telephone Buddy Programs

Qualitative research on telephone buddy programs have shown value in treating loneliness and social isolation in older adults. In Cattan et al.'s (2010) study on the use of telephone befriending for socially isolated older adults, a telephone befriending program was determined to be a low-cost intervention that participants reported improved their health outcomes, sense of inclusion, personal value, and loneliness. Other studies have found similar benefits to telephone communication as a befriending service to address loneliness in older adults. A study based on 42 semistructured interviews with older people who utilized a national phoneline found that the nonvisual format of services enabled participants to reach out for emotional support more readily despite the stigma of loneliness (Preston & Moore, 2019). Although some challenges were found in using the helpline, users reported the ability to confide in helpline providers without fear of judgement as with family or friends.

As discussed earlier in the Social Marginalization and Risk Factors for Social Disconnection section, LGBTQIA+ older adults are over 8 times more likely to be cared for by a nonrelative than the general population of older adults. Therefore, a pilot-friendly caller program of pairing members of the LGBTQIA+ individuals was found particularly beneficial to LGBTQIA+ older adult population in finding a sense of belonging. Perone et al. (2020) noted the following:

- Some participants of intersecting marginalized backgrounds (e.g., gender identity, income, incarceration, etc.) expressed interest in being paired with a service provider, or "member/caregiver" in this study, of a similar background with the exception of age.

- Members of the LGBTQIA+ community who provided the care were "quasi-members" who were at risk of personally experiencing social isolation and loneliness themselves.

- A service referral program component was created to maintain participants in the program, as they faced structural obstacles to continued participation.

This study demonstrated that social isolation and loneliness interventions to marginalized communities may require the provision of inclusive services that enable their participation.

Other Communication Technologies

Close to 3 out of 4 older adults in the United States use technological devices on a daily basis to maintain contact (Suragarn et al., 2021). Web-based communication and digital media platforms are most notable for their ability to help older adults maintain social contact, form new social relationships, or access information about the risks of social isolation. Technology was determined to be particularly beneficial in maintaining social contact between older adults and loved ones while social distancing during the COVID-19 pandemic (Suragarn et al., 2021). For older adults who may lack technological literacy or resources for web-based communication, some scholars have developed interventions, such as "internet cafes" to enable older adults to reciprocate care from a distance. In one study of digital participation of older migrants with minimal experience with digital communication technologies conducted by Millard et al. (2018), participants received home- and community-based education and support to develop skills in digital literacy. Researchers of this study found that participants' self-agency and social interactions increased in conjunction with their digital literacy.

TABLE 10.12 Communication Technologies for Social Connection

Benefits of using technology for social connection

- Increase social contact for older adults isolated by their residential location (e.g., rural areas, nursing homes, etc.).
- Maintain relationships with those who belong to a geographically dispersed network of family and friends.
- Provide an opportunity for older adults to develop digital literacy to establish or preserve social relationships from a distance.

Communication technology interventions

Telephone buddy programs	• A low-cost intervention that participants reported improved their health outcomes, sense of inclusion, personal value, and loneliness (Cattan et al., 2010) • Nonvisual format of services enabled participants to reach out for emotional support more readily despite the stigma of loneliness (Preston et al., 2019)

(Continued)

TABLE 10.12 Communication Technologies for Social Connection (*Continued*)

	• Ability to confide in helpline providers without fear of judgement as with family or friends (Preston et al., 2019)
	• Peer caller program particularly beneficial to LGBTQIA+ older adult population in finding a sense of belonging, with adjunctive services to address structural obstacles to their participation (Perone et al., 2020)
Other communication technologies	• Web-based communication and digital media platforms help maintain social contact, form new social relationships, or access information about the risks of social isolation (Elder & Retrum, 2012).
	• Web-based communication was beneficial in maintaining social contact while social distancing during the COVID-19 pandemic (Suragarn et al., 2021).
	• Internet cafes enabled older adults to develop technological literacy and access resources for web-based communication (Millard et al., 2018).

Intergenerational Programs

Intergenerational programs facilitate social interactions between older adults and younger persons within a formal infrastructure for social contact. Intergenerational programs enable persons across generations to exchange resources and support in community-based or residential settings. Studies of intergenerational programs include activities such as storytelling in classrooms, creating music, and cross-education through student practicums in residential aged care facilities (Suragarn et al., 2021). In the friendly caller program of LGBTQIA+ older adults, intergenerational matches between older adults and service providers enabled bonding through mutual interests, despite divergent social histories, and benefitted the younger providers who expressed interest in honoring the stories of older adults (Perone et al., 2020).

Community-Based Group Physical Activity

As group-based interventions have been found most effective in treating social isolation in older adults, studies on physical activity with older adults have demonstrated that older adults are more likely to participate in exercise programs to increase social relationships and contact. Participants of exercise programs with peers reported that these programs enabled them to develop new social relationships, participate in the community (Chiang et al., 2008), and connect with others in ways that created resonance of their younger selves while sharing an understanding of the physical changes to their bodies with peers of the same age An integrative review of the literature on social connection interventions for older adults also found gender to be an important aspect of physical activity groups for male-identified participants who expressed discomfort in mixed-gender groups and a preference for male-only programs that allowed them to relate to other men (Dunlop & Beauchamp, 2013). Therefore, practitioners referring older adults to physical activity groups should be mindful of gender amongst other considerations when identifying the most suitable programs to increase social connectedness in the community (Suragarn et al., 2021).

Home Environment

To address barriers to social connection in the older adult's environment, it is important for practitioners to be aware of such barriers and act as a broker to connect them to the appropriate resources that increase their functional autonomy, mobility, and safety to participate in their communities. Older adults managing social isolation and loneliness are more likely to see changes to their functional independence later in life and require greater functional assistance. In a study on older adults with mobility impairments, Greiman et al. (2018) found that the inability to bathe, dress, or care for one's own hygiene was associated with less social participation outside of the home. They explained that the cost and exertion of completing these activities of daily living impeded older adults' capacity for social participation. Personal assistance, assistive devices, and in-home modifications, especially in the bathroom, that ease the strain of caring for one's hygiene may reduce obstacles to social participation. Housing quality can also restrict older adult's capacity for social interaction (Greiman et al., 2018). Since less social isolation and loneliness is associated with more functional autonomy, practitioners should be attentive to the role of functional independence in an older adult's social life and the need for accommodations that enable accessibility in their socioecological environments.

Aging-Friendly Community

A community in which older adults are provided opportunities to find meaning through active social participation with neighbors and organizations can increase their ability to maintain significant connections in their community and prevent social isolation. Older adults who are low income and managing chronic health conditions are particularly vulnerable to social isolation due to factors in their physical environments, such as substance abuse and high crime. In addition, the conditions of streets and buildings may deter efforts to gather for social and recreational activities. Community-focused interventions can help attend to sociostructural issues that impede older adults' wishes for social integration. It is important for practitioners to understand the needs and assets of an older adult's community as it pertains to their social health, as well as the utility of community-based interventions.

Some aging-friendly community interventions have focused on mobilizing proximal supports and resources, such as the participant-driven "village model," in which villages are managed by participants and paid workers who assist older adults with in-home activities of daily living, as well as service referrals and coordination in the community (Graham et al., 2014). Other peer support approaches include a cohousing program that enabled social contact and mutual support in managing age-related obstacles (Glass & Vander Plaits, 2013). Older adults may access civic engagement or volunteer opportunities through social networks for religious institutions or community-based organizations. Intervention programs that facilitated community involvement through long-term volunteer work offered a renewed sense of purpose by assisting others (ten Bruggencate et al., 2019) and increased the quality of life and lifespans of participants by at least 5 years (Graham et al., 2017). The World Health Organization (2007) has published guidance to create "aging-friendly" cities that emphasizes the societal value of older adults and outlines how to promote access their mobility through the community's physical infrastructure (e.g., transportation, buildings, etc.) and other resources (e.g., health services, community centers, employers, etc.).

Case Study: The Story of Mrs. M.

Mrs. M. is a 55-year-old African American woman who lives with her only child, J., who is a 23-year-old African American man diagnosed with autism. Mrs. M. and J. share a two-bedroom apartment in an urban neighborhood with high crime but accessible, easy-to-use public transportation. Mrs. M.'s partner died in a car accident when J. was a young child. Mrs. M. is a former schoolteacher who retired early to care for her son full-time. There are no relatives, neighbors, or other informal caregivers assisting Mrs. M. with J. However, J. now receives part-time occupational and social development training and services through a government social services agency for adults with disabilities. Mrs. M. and J. are interested in J. eventually entering the workforce and living on his own through supported living services for adults with autism.

Mrs. M. believes she is moderately social but has only had contact with J.'s service providers in the last 2 weeks. She reports feeling lonely sometimes and wishes she could meet other parents who are also caring for an adult child. Mrs. M. was previously active with their local church and would participate in charitable events with the congregation. However, Mrs. M. gradually stopped participating in church after she retired to care for J. When J. goes out without her, she worries that J. is at risk of being harmed by community members because "he is a Black man who doesn't look like he has autism." In addition, Mrs. M. has elevated blood pressure, and her doctor has asked her to increase physical activity and eat a healthier diet to care for her cardiovascular health.

LEARNING ACTIVITY PART I: DEVELOP A SOCIAL HEALTH CARE PLAN FOR MRS. M.

Social Health Assessment

In this scenario, you are a case manager at J.'s social services agency for adults with disabilities. J.'s case manager has referred Mrs. M. to you with concerns regarding Mrs. M.'s well-being as the sole caregiver of J. You are meeting with Mrs. M. today to engage in a teaching-learning process of assessment in which you learn about her social environment, the needs and strengths of her situation, and what she wishes to change about her social relationships.

Based on the case study above, please answer the following questions to complete an assessment for social health care planning:

1. What is the role of race, ability, and socioeconomic status in this case study?

2. What are the relevant social and ecological risk factors and assets for Mrs. M.'s social health in this case study?

3. Is Mrs. M. experiencing social isolation and/or loneliness? What method(s) would you use to make this determination?

4. What else would you want to discuss with Mrs. M. to better understand her degree of social connectedness?

LEARNING ACTIVITY PART II: DEVELOP A SOCIAL HEALTH CARE PLAN FOR MRS. M.

Social Health Care Planning

Now that you have completed the assessment with Mrs. M., you are ready to develop a social health care plan based on what you learned and identify opportunities to advance Mrs. M.'s goals for social health. A personalized social health care plan should include strategies to decrease Mrs. M.'s social isolation and/or loneliness. If you identified urgent issues related to Mrs. M.'s health, safety, or mobility, you should prioritize service referrals to meet these time-sensitive needs.

Based on your assessment of the case study above, please answer the following questions to develop a social health care plan:

1. In what ways could social isolation and loneliness be a stigmatizing experience for Mrs. M.? What approaches would you take to help destigmatize Mrs. M.'s experience of social isolation and loneliness while working with her?

2. What issue(s) would you prioritize first when working with Mrs. M. to reduce social isolation and loneliness?

3. Which social and ecological assets or resources would be most important to include in Mrs. M.'s care plan?

4. Given that Mrs. M. appears to have a small–moderate social network size with infrequent social contact, which meso–macro level interventions may be the best fit for Mrs. M.'s interests and socioecological context?

5. What else would you want to know about Mrs. M. before implementing the care plan?

Assessment and Intervention

Mrs. M.'s case illustrates a gradual progression toward severe isolation and loneliness with opportunities to develop social connections within her social network. Addressing Mrs. M.'s social health requires a bird's eye view of her circumstances, including the personal history and sociostructural context of her social connections. In this case, Mrs. M. has expressed both social isolation and loneliness. Therefore, it is worth exploring the role of each in her social life. In response to the global item for loneliness—"Do you sometimes feel lonely?" (Drageset et al., 2011)—Mrs. M. indicates that she is sometimes lonely. According to the 6-item Lubben Social Network Scale (LSNS), which measures emotions, tangible, and network size, Mrs.

M.'s score of 10 indicates that she is at-risk for social isolation (Lubben & Gironda, 2003, as cited in Nicholson, 2012). The structure of her social network includes J., J.'s providers for disability services, and former church members and colleagues at the school from which she retired. Mrs. M. states that J. occasionally provides her with emotional support and assists with chores around the house, while disability services offer a great deal of instrumental support in assisting J. with life skills development. Despite the loss of Mrs. M.'s partner when J. was a young child, Mrs. M. is generally satisfied with the quality of her social relationships. However, she yearns to reconnect with former church members and meet other parents that understand her caregiving journey. Based on a co-constructed understanding of Mrs. M.'s social connections, Mrs. M. appears to be experiencing more social isolation than loneliness. Drawing from best practices in social health interventions and the theory of loneliness, interventions will primarily be group-based to increase the frequency of Mrs. M.'s social contact, network size, and degree of her social participation while monitoring her subjective experience of social connection.

Before proceeding to intervention, it is important to note the strengths and resources of Mrs. M.'s case. Mrs. M. and J. have navigated services in the community toward their shared goal of optimizing J.'s independence. J. is enrolled in an occupational training program where he has established his own relationships separate from life with his mother. Mrs. M. also brings the assets of a former schoolteacher to this situation. It is possible for her to draw from her educational knowledge, skills, and experience to facilitate her social engagement with the church or groups of parents who are also caring for an adult child with autism. Mrs. M.'s social network also contains latent relationships and resources that could be introduced into an intervention plan. For example, J.'s disability services agency may offer a peer support group for parents. If not, they may be receptive to initiating a peer support group with Mrs. M. It is also possible that Mrs. M.'s church offers a physical activity group where Mrs. M. could regularly meet with community members while engaging in physical activities. As community accessibility and safety is significant to Mrs. M.'s capacity for social connectedness, church members, disability services, or another resource may assist Mrs. M. in understanding how J. can reduce his risk of harm while navigating the community as an African American man with autism.

Implications for Practice

The experience of social isolation and loneliness can have a costly and catastrophic impact on the quality and longevity of the lives of older adults. As the population gaps widen between older adults and the rest of society (Redfoot et al., 2013), practitioners are well-positioned to eradicate social isolation by recognizing and proactively responding to the signs of social isolation and loneliness in the older adult population (Nicholson, 2012). Although definitions of "social isolation" and "loneliness" still lack uniformity, practitioners may incorporate social health care screenings into their routine assessments of older adults to determine when further assessment may be needed. Service providers who lack the time or resources for formal screenings may create brief checklists on the dimensions of social connections—social structure, function, and quality—with predetermined cutoffs to identify older adults who may require greater attention (Nicholson, 2012).

It is also of ethical importance that practitioners use a holistic approach to understand an older adult's experience of social disconnection within their sociostructural history and environment. Since older adults are a vast and diverse population (Newall & Menec, 2019), practitioners should co-create a shared understanding of how the older adult is experiencing social isolation before intervening (Finn, 2021). Practitioners should also recognize how an older adult's history of chronic isolation, losses, and marginalization may impact their reporting of social disconnection and should take steps to destigmatize social needs (e.g., avoiding negative labels) early on in the change process (Taylor, 2020; Perone et al., 2020). Older adults belonging to socially marginalized groups, such as persons of color, LGBTQIA+ persons, and persons with disabilities, may be at greater risk factors for social isolation as they age. Practitioners can take steps to understand how their social histories and current obstacles may perpetuate social exclusion and intervene upon recognition of these risk factors.

Lastly, research has established a significant relationship between social isolation and loneliness and all-cause premature death (NASEM, 2020; Newall & Menec, 2019). Although the majority of older adults do not experience social isolation or loneliness (Newall & Menec, 2019), practitioners should take a preventative approach to social health by routinely discussing the emotional and instrumental support structures in older adults' lives. Preventative education on the benefits of social connection may assist older adults in recognizing the warning signs of social isolation and adapting measures to safeguard their well-being and quality of life.

TABLE 10.13 Implications for Practice

Screening for social health care needs	Incorporate social health care screenings into routine assessments to determine when further assessment is needed.
	Create brief checklists on the dimensions of social connections—social structure, function, and quality—with predetermined cutoffs to identify older adults who may require more attention (Nicholson, 2012).
Teaching and learning assessments	Co-construct a shared understanding of how an older adult is experiencing social isolation before intervening (Finn, 2021).
	Recognize how an older adult's history of chronic isolation, losses, and marginalization can impact reports of social disconnection.
	Take steps to destigmatize an older adult's social needs and intervene upon risk factors.
Preventative approaches to social health	Routinely discuss the emotional and instrumental support structures in older adults' lives.
	Provide education on the benefits of social connection to assist older adults in recognizing the warning signs of social isolation and adapting measures to safeguard their well-being and quality of life.

CONCLUSION

The quality of older adults' social health will have widespread implications for the social, economic, and health systems of the United States (Taylor, 2020). As the population of older adults continues to increase and age in pace, practitioners will need to take a proactive approach to understand the compounding risks factors for older adults, who are more likely to be marginalized by age, health status, and other variables. The diversifying older adult population should also be considered so that practitioners understand the role of cultural factors and expectations in an older adult's experience of social disconnection. Practitioners should be aware of older adults' social ecosystem and social health resources within their sociostructural landscape. Although reducing the social isolation of older adults requires a coordinated, multisystems effort, practitioners have the collective potential to advance the social health of older adults from the frontlines of the health care workforce.

In the next chapter, we turn to the final stages of the lifespan.

KEY TERMS

- Ageism: discrimination against older adults based on their age.

- Discrepancy theory of loneliness: the difference between the number or quality of one's relationships and their desires for social connection.

- Life course theory: a sociological perspective that refers to life course patterns that vary across time, space and populations and focus on age-differentiated, socially recognized sequences of transitions with consequences that may be long-term.

- Loneliness: a subjective feeling of being isolated; a discrepancy between the quantity and quality of relationships that people have versus what they want.

- Social connection: the various structural, functional, and quality aspects of social relationships.

- Social connectedness: feeling interpersonal connection, different from objective social network features such as isolation or interpersonal contact, or the network function of social support.

- Social disengagement theory: a theory stating that aging is an inevitable, mutual withdrawal or disengagement, resulting in decreased interaction between the aging person and others in their social system.

- Social isolation: the objective state of having few social relationships or infrequent social contact with others.

- Social support: the actual or perceived availability of emotional or tangible resources from others.

- Theory of Loneliness: theory that loneliness compels a retreat from social opportunities in response to the negative thoughts and feelings associated with one's loneliness, mutually reinforcing social isolation and loneliness.

DISCUSSION QUESTIONS

1. Describe the difference between social isolation and loneliness in your own words. What are some of the concerns raised about recognizing social isolation and loneliness in older adults? With older adults of historically marginalized backgrounds?

2. Where have you encountered stereotypes about the social lives of older people? How might you address these stereotypes in your work with older adults?

3. What is the relationship between older adults' social health and their mobility at home or in their community? What interventions would you recommend to an older adult facing social disconnection due to the inaccessibility of their environment?

4. How would you go about assessing an older adult's level of social inclusion in their community–whether it be with neighbors, organizations, or members of their residential facility? What courses of action would you take to support their ability to become active community members?

5. Where do you see the possibilities for bringing social health knowledge and skills to your own practice?

REFERENCES

Administration on Aging. (2021). *2020 profile of older Americans*. U.S. Census Bureau. https://acl.gov/sites/default/files/Aging%20and%20Disability%20in%20America/2020ProfileOlderAmericans.Final_.pdf

Ashida, S., & Heaney, C. A. (2008). Differential associations of social support and social connectedness with structural features of social networks and the health status of older adults. *Journal of Aging and Health, 20*(7), 872–893. https://doi.org/10.1177/0898264308324626

Bekhet, A. B., Zauszniewski, J. A., & Nakhla, W. E. (2008). Loneliness: A concept analysis. *Nursing Forum, 43*(4), 207–213. https://doi.org /10.1111/j.1744-6198.2008.00114.x

Brown, S., & Munson, M. R. (2020). Introduction to the special issue on social isolation across the lifespan. *Clinical Social Work Journal, 48*(1), 1–5. https://doi.org/10.1007/s10615-020-00750-3

Butler, S. S. (2019). Social networks and social isolation among LGBT older adults. In L.W. Kaye (Ed.), *Social isolation of older adults: Strategies to bolster health and well-being* (pp. 181–196). Springer. https://doi.org/10.1891/9780826146991.0013

Cacioppo, J. T., & Cacioppo, S. (2018). Loneliness in the modern age: An evolutionary theory of loneliness (ETL). *Advances in Experimental Social Psychology, 58*, 127–197. https://doi.org/10.1016/bs.aesp.2018.03.003

Cattan, M., Kime, N., & Bagnall, A. (2010). The use of telephone befriending in low level support for socially isolated older people: An evaluation. *Wiley Online Library, 19*(2), 198–206. https://doi.org/10.1016/j.tics.2009.06.005

Chiang, K., Chu, H., Chang, H., Chung, M., Chen, C., Chiou, H., & Chou, K. (2010). The effects of reminiscence therapy on psychological well-being depression and loneliness among the institutionalized aged. *International Journal of Geriatric Psychiatry, 25*(4), 380–388. https://doi.org/10.1002/gps.2350

Chiang, K. C., Seman, L., Belza, B., & Tsai, J. H. (2008). "It is our exercise family": Experiences of ethnic older adults in a group-based exercise program. *Preventing Chronic Disease, 5*(1), 1–12. https://www.cdc.gov/pcd/issues/2008/jan/06_0170.htm

Choi, S. K., & Meyer, I. H. (2016). *LGBT aging: A review of research findings, needs, and policy implications.* The Williams Institute at UCLA School of Law. http://www.jstor.org/stable/resrep34905

Cloutier-Fisher, D., Kobayashi, K., & Smith, A. (2011). The subjective dimension of social isolation: A qualitative investigation of older adults' experiences in small social support networks. *Journal of Aging Studies, 25*(4), 407–414. https://doi.org/10.1016/j.jaging.2011.03.012

Cornwell, B., Laumann, E. O., & Schumm, L. P. (2008). The social connectedness of older adults: A national profile. *American Sociological Review, 73*(2), 185–203. http://www.jstor.org/stable/25472522

Courtin, E., & Knapp, M. (2017). Social isolation, loneliness and health in old age: A scoping review. *Health & Social Care in the Community, 25*(3), 799–812. https://doi.org/10.1111/hsc.12311

Cox, C. (2020). Older adults and COVID 19: Social justice, disparities, and social work practice. *Journal of Gerontological Social Work, 63*(6–7), 611–624. https://doi.org/10.1080/01634372.2020.1808141

de Jong-Gierveld, J. (1987). Developing and testing a model of loneliness. *Journal of Personality and Social Psychology, 53*(1), 119–128. https://doi.org/10.1037/0022-3514.53.1.119

Dickens, A.P., Richards, S.H., Greaves, C.J., & Campbell, J.L. (2011). Interventions targeting social isolation in older people: a systematic review. *BMC Public Health, 11*(647), 1–22. https://doi.org/10.1186/1471-2458-11-647

Drageset, J., Kirkevold, M., & Espehaug, B. (2011). Loneliness and social support among nursing home residents without cognitive impairment: A questionnaire survey. *International Journal of Nursing Studies, 48*(5), 611–619. https://doi.org/10.1016/j.ijnurstu.2010.09.008

Drageset, J., & Haugan, G. (2021). Associations between nurse-patient interaction and loneliness among cognitively intact nursing home residents: A questionnaire survey. *Geriatric Nursing, 42*(4), 828–832. https://doi.org/10.1016/j.gerinurse.2021.04.001

Dunlop, W. L., & Beauchamp, M. R. (2013). Birds of a feather stay active together: A case study of an all-male older adult exercise program. *Journal of Aging and Physical Activity the Official Journal of the International Society for Aging and Physical Activity, 21*(2), 222–232. https://doi.org/10.1123/japa.21.2.222

Dykstra, P. A., & Fokkema, T. (2007). Social and emotional loneliness among divorced and married men and women: Comparing the deficit and cognitive perspectives. *Basic and Applied Social Psychology, 29*(1), 1–12. https://doi.org/10.1080/01973530701330843

Eisenberger, N. I., & Lieberman, M. D. (2004). Why rejection hurts: A common neural alarm system for physical and social pain. *Trends in Cognitive Sciences, 8*(7), 294–300. https://doi.org/10.1016/j.tics.2004.05.010

Elder, K., & Retrum, J. (2012). *Framework for isolation in adults over 50.* AARP Foundation. https://www.aarp.org/content/dam/aarp/aarp_foundation/2012_PDFs/AARP-Foundation-Isolation-Framework-Report.pdf

ElSadr, C. B., Noureddine, S., & Kelley, J. (2009). Concept analysis of loneliness with implications for nursing diagnosis. *International Journal of Nursing Terminologies and Classification, 20*(1), 25–33. https://doi.org/10.1111/j.1744-618X.2008.01110.x

Espinoza, R. (2011). The diverse elders coalition and LGBT aging: Connecting communities, issues, and resources in a historic moment. *Public Policy & Aging Report, 21*(3), 8–12, https://doi.org/10.1093/ppar/21.3.8

Finn, J. L. (2021). *Just practice: A social justice approach to social work* (4th ed.). Oxford University Press.

Fredrickson, B. L., & Carstensen, L. L. (1990). Choosing social partners: How old age and anticipated endings make people more selective. *Psychology and Aging*, 5(3), 335–347. https://doi.org/10.1037/0882-7974.5.3.335

Gabrielson, M.L., & Holston, E.C. (2014). Broadening definitions of family for older lesbians: Modifying the Lubben Social Network Scale. *Journal of Gerontological Social Work,* 57(2–4), 198–217. https://doi.org/10.1080/01634372.2013.879683

Genworth. (2022). *Cost of care trends & insights.* https://www.genworth.com/aging-and-you/finances/cost-of-care/cost-of-care-trends-and-insights.html

George, L. K. (1993). Sociological perspectives on life transitions. *Annual Review of Sociology*, 19, 353–373. http://www.jstor.org/stable/2083392

Glass, A. P., & Vander Plaits, R. S. (2013). A conceptual model for aging better intentionally. *Journal of Aging Studies*, 27(4), 428–442. https://doi.org/10.1016/j.jaging.2013.10.001

Graham, C. L., Scharlach, A. E., & Price Wolf, J. (2014). The impact of the "village" model on health, well-Being, service access, and social engagement of older adults. *Health Education & Behavior*, 41(Suppl. 1), 91S–97S. https://doi.org/10.1177/1090198114532290

Graham, C.L., Scharlach, A.E. & Bradford, S. (2017). Impact of the Village Model: Results of a national survey. *Journal of Gerontological Social Work*, 60(5), 335–354. https://doi.org/10.1080/01634372.2017.1330299

Greiman, L., Fleming, S. P., Ward, B., Myers, A., & Ravesloot, C. (2018). Life starts at home: Bathing, exertion and participation for people with mobility impairment. *Archives of Physical Medicine and Rehabilitation*, 99(7), 1289–1294. https://doi.org/10.1016/j.apmr.2017.11.015

Holt-Lunstad, J. (2018). Why social relationships are important for physical health: A systems approach to understanding and modifying risk and protection. *Annual Review of Psychology*, 69(1), 437–458. https://doi.org/10.1146/annurev-psych-122216-011902

Hughes, M. E., Waite, L. J., Hawkley, L. C., & Cacioppo, J. T. (2004). A short scale for measuring loneliness in large surveys: Results from two population-based studies. *Research on Aging*, 26(6), 655–672. https://doi.org/10.1177/0164027504268574

Kim, H., Fredriksen-Goldsen, K. I., Bryan, A. E., & Muraco, A. (2017). Social network types and mental health among LGBT older adults. *The Gerontologist*, 57(Suppl. 1), S84–S94. https://doi.org/10.1093/geront/gnw169

Lee, Y., & Ko, Y. (2017). Feeling lonely when not socially isolated: Social isolation moderates the association between loneliness and daily social interaction. *Journal of Social and Personal Relationships*, 35(10), 1340–1355. https://doi.org/10.1177/0265407517712902

Leigh-Hunt, N., Bagguley, D., Bash, K., Turner, V., Turnbull, S., Valtorta, N., & Caan, W. (2017). An overview of systematic reviews on the public health consequences of social isolation and loneliness. *Public Health*, 152, 157–171. https://doi.org/10.1016/j.puhe.2017.07.035

Knauer, N. (2016). LGBT older adults, chosen family, and caregiving. *Journal of Law and Religion*, 31(2), 150–168. https://doi.org/10.1017/jlr.2016.23

Masi, C. M., Chen, H.-Y., Hawkley, L. C., & Cacioppo, J. T. (2011). A meta-analysis of interventions to reduce loneliness. *Personality and Social Psychology Review*, 15(3), 219–266. https://doi.org/10.1177/1088868310377394

McWhirter, B.T. (1990). Loneliness: A review of current literature, with implications for counseling and research. *Journal of counseling and development*, 68(4), 417–422. https://doi.org/10.1002/j.1556-6676.1990.tb02521.x

Millard, A., Baldassar, L., & Wilding, R. (2018). The significance of digital citizenship in the well-being of older migrants. *Public Health*, 158, 144–148. https://doi.org/10.1016/j.puhe.2018.03.005

Miyawaki, C. E. (2015). Association of social isolation and health across different racial and ethnic groups of older Americans. *Ageing and Society, 35*(10), 2201–2228. https://doi.org/10.1017/S0144686X14000890

Molloy, G.J., McGee, H.M., O'Neill, D., & Conroy, R.N. (2010). Loneliness and emergency and planned hospitalizations in a community sample of older adults. *Journal of the American Geriatrics Society, 58*(8), 1538–1541. https://doi-org.ezproxy.cul.columbia.edu/10.1111/j.1532-5415.2010.02960.x

National Academies of Sciences, Engineering, and Medicine. (2020). *Social isolation and loneliness in older adults: Opportunities for the health care system.* The National Academies Press. https://doi.org/10.17226/25663.

National Alliance for Caregiving & AARP. (2020). *Caregiving in the U.S. 2020: A focused look at family caregivers of adults age 50+.* https://doi.org/10.26419/ppi.00103.022

Newall, N. E. G., & Menec, V. H. (2019). Loneliness and social isolation of older adults: Why it is important to examine these social aspects together. *Journal of Social and Personal Relationships, 36*(3), 925–939. https://doi.org/10.1177/0265407517749045

Nicholson, N. R. (2012). A review of social isolation: an important but underassessed condition in older adults. *The Journal of Primary Prevention, 33*, 137–152. https://doi.org/10.1007/s10935-012-0271-2

Ong, A. D., Uchino, B. N., & Wethington, E. (2016). Loneliness and health in older adults: A mini-review and synthesis. *Gerontology, 62*, 443–449. https://doi.org/10.1159/000441651

Orel, N. A., & Coon, D. W. (2016). The challenges of change: How can we meet the care needs of the ever-Evolving LGBT family? *Generations: Journal of the American Society on Aging, 40*(2), 41–45. https://www.jstor.org/stable/26556199.

O'Rourke, H. M., & Sidani, S. (2017). Definition, determinants, and outcomes of social connectedness for older adults: A scoping review. *Journal of Gerontological Nursing, 43*(7), 43–52. http://doi.org/10.3928/00989134-20170223-03

Perone, A. K., Ingersoll-Dayton, B., & Watkins-Dukhie, K. (2020). Social isolation loneliness among LGBT older adults: Lessons learned from a pilot friendly caller program. *Clinical Social Work Journal, 48*, 126–139. https://doi.org/10.1007/s10615-019-00738-8

Pinquart, M., & Sörensen, S. (2001). Influences on loneliness in older adults: A meta-analysis. *Basic & Applied Social Psychology, 23*(4), 245–266. https://doi.org/10.1207/153248301753225702

Preston, C., & Moore, S. (2019). Ringing the changes: The role of telephone communication in a helpline and befriending service targeting loneliness in older people. *Ageing and Society, 39*(7), 1528–1551. https://doi.org/10.1017/S0144686X18000120

Redfoot, D., Feinberg, L. & Houser, A. (2013). *The aging of the baby boom and the growing care gap: A look at future declines in the availability of caregivers.* AARP Public Policy Institute. https://www.aarp.org/home-family/caregiving/info-08-2013/the-aging-of-the-baby-boom-and-the-growing-care-gap-AARP-ppi-ltc.html

Roberts, A. W., Ogunwole, S. U., Blakeslee, L., & Rabe, M. A. (2018). *The Population 65 Years and older in the United States: 2016.* U.S. Census Bureau. https://www.census.gov/library/publications/2018/acs/acs-38.html

Services and Advocacy for Gay, Lesbian, Bisexual and Transgender Elders (SAGE). (2014). *Out & visible: The experiences and attitudes of lesbian, gay, bisexual and transgender older adults, ages 45–75.* Retrieved from https://www.sageusa.org/wp-content/uploads/2018/05/sageusa-out-visible-lgbt-market-research-full-report.pdf

Services and Advocacy for Gay, Lesbian, Bisexual and Transgender Elders (SAGE) & National Center for Transgender Equality (NCTE). (2012). *Improving the lives of transgender older adults: Recommendations for policy and practice.* Retrieved from https://transequality.org/sites/default/files/docs/resources/TransAgingPolicyReportFull.pdf

Sellon, A. M. (2019). Eradicate social isolation. In S. Sanders, S. Kolomer, C. Waites Spellman, & V. Rizzo (Eds.), *Gerontological social work and the grand challenges*. Springer, Cham. https://doi.org/10.1007/978-3-030-26334-8_5

Services and Advocacy for Gay, Lesbian, Bisexual and Transgender Elders. (2014). *Out & visible: The experiences and attitudes of lesbian, gay, bisexual and transgender older adults, ages 45–75*. https://www.sageusa.org/wp-content/uploads/2018/05/sageusa-out-visible-lgbt-market-research-full-report.pdf

Shah, S. G., Nogueras, D., van Woerden, H. C., & Kiparoglou, V. (2021). Evaluation of the effectiveness of digital technology interventions to reduce loneliness in older adults: Systematic review and meta-analysis. *Journal of Medical Internet Research*, *23*(6). https://doi.org/10.2196/24712

Shaw, B.A., Krause, N., Laing, J., & Bennett, J. (2007). Tracking changes in social relations throughout late life. *The Journals of Gerontology*, *62*(2), 90–99. https://doi.org/10.1093/geronb/62.2.S90

Siette, J., Pomare, C., Dodds, L., Jorgensen, M., Harrigan, N., & Georgiou, A. (2021). A comprehensive overview of social network measures for older adults: A systematic review. *Archives of Gerontology and Geriatrics*, *97*, Article 104525. https://doi.org/10.1016/j.archger.2021.104525

Suragarn, U., Hain, D., & Pfaff, G. (2021). Approaches to enhance social connection in older adults: An integrative review of literature. *Aging and Health Research*, *1*(3). https://doi.org/10.1016/j.ahr.2021.100029.

Taylor, H.O. (2020). Social Isolation's influence on loneliness among older adults. *Clinical Social Work Journal, 48*(1), 140–151. https://doi.org/10.1007/s10615-019-00737-9

Taylor, R. J., Chatters, L. M., & Taylor, H. O. (2019). Race and objective social isolation: Older African Americans, Black Caribbeans and Non-Hispanic whites. *The Journals of Gerontology: Series B*, *74*(8), 1429–1440. https://doi.org/10.1093/geronb/gby114

ten Bruggencate, T., Lujikx, K. G., & Sturm, J. (2019). To meet, to matter and to have fun: The development, implementation and evaluation of an intervention to fulfill the social needs of older people. *International Journal of Environmental Research and Public Health*, *16*(13), 1–13. http://doi.org/10.3390/ijerph16132307

Valtorta, N. K., Kanaan, M., Gilbody, S., & Hanratty, B. (2016). Loneliness, social isolation and social relationships: What are we measuring? A novel framework for classifying and comparing tools. *BMJ Open*, *6*(4), Article e010799. https://doi.org/10.1136/bmjopen-2015-010799

Victor, C. R., Burholt, V., & Martin, W. (2012). Loneliness and ethnic minority elders in Great Britain: An exploratory study. *Journal of Cross-Cultural Gerontology*, *27*(1), 65–78. https://doi.org/10.1007/s10823-012-9161-6

Wenger, G.C., Davies, R., Shahtahmasebi, S., & Scott, A. (1996). Social isolation and loneliness in old age: Review and model refinement. *Ageing and Society, 16*(3), 333–358. https://doi.org/10.1017/S0144686X00003457

Wenger, G. C., & Burholt, V. (2004). Changes in levels of social isolation and loneliness among older people in a rural area: A twenty-year longitudinal study. *Canadian Journal on Aging/La Revue canadienne du vieillissement*, *23*(2), 115–127. https://doi.org/10.1353/cja.2004.0028

Winningham, R. G., & Pike, N. (2007). A cognitive intervention to enhance institutionalized older adults' social support networks and decrease loneliness. *Aging & Mental Health*, *11*(6), 716–721. https://doi.org/10.1080/13607860701366228

World Health Organization. (2007). *Global age-friendly cities: A guide*. http://www.who.int/ageing/publications/Global_age_friendly_cities_Guide_English.pdf

CREDIT

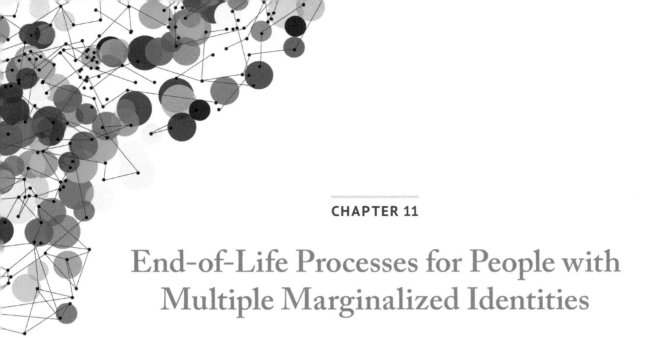

CHAPTER 11

End-of-Life Processes for People with Multiple Marginalized Identities

PABLO ARRIAZA

Introduction

The challenges faced by those at the end of life are myriad. Greater still are those challenges among marginalized populations. Social work can play a major role in mitigating the difficulties those facing imminent mortality experience. It helps, here, to see social work practice as both an art and a science: Both attributes must be present when addressing end-of-life care matters with people having multiple identities. The science part of social work connects with theories, evidence-based practices, and ethical interventions; these competencies are expected of all social work students. How the social worker interprets and delivers social work services then becomes the actual artistic aspect of the profession. As social workers addressing the end-of-life care needs of people with marginalized and multiple identities, we must consider and engage in services that are congruent with the dignity and worth of the person, unconditional acceptance and regard, ethical and effective interventions, and of course humility. These areas will be further discussed in the

LEARNING OBJECTIVES

1. Increase self-awareness, self-reflection, and critical thinking, and apply human behavior and the social environment knowledge to formulate ethical, person-centered, and culturally congruent interventions for and with people and families with multiple identities who are facing the end of life. (Competencies 1, 2, 3, 6, 7, 8, 9)

2. Explore and understand how end-of-life processes are shaped and reshaped by living with marginalization, multiple identities, and a hierarchical context. This chapter also builds upon earlier chapters by integrating trauma, interpersonal interactions, family processes, and social capital to explain the intergenerational transmission of marginalization experiences in families of origin and choice. (Competencies 2, 3, 6, 7, 8, 9).

next section. We will begin with an introduction to human behavior in a social environment (HBSE) in relation to social work practice with people with marginalized identities facing the end of life.

A "good death" is often reserved for people having financial resources, medical insurance, strong social support systems, and competent and inclusive medical service providers that include social workers, higher economic status, and those with higher education. These variables translate into privilege. In other words, it is a privilege to have a good death in the United States; it is not a right. The same can be said about grieving and bereavement processes, which are often not afforded to people with low socioeconomic status and otherwise living on the margins.

In my previous role as a hospice and bereavement social worker, I experienced various situations that required critical thinking and a strong sense of self-awareness. Unfortunately, as a new social worker, I was often challenged to think differently, especially in matters surrounding privilege and marginalization. The following brief vignette encapsulates the challenges to my self-awareness, personal sense of privilege, and listening skills.

VIGNETTE

"Grief? Grief? I don't have time to grieve the death of my husband. I wish I could stay home and grieve and cry and be angry at God, but I can't ... I have children to feed, bills to pay, and if I do not go to work, I will be fired." As a bicultural and bilingual social worker, I took it for granted that this person had all the necessary resources to "grieve" the death of her husband.

I never questioned my own cultural awareness, preparedness, judgments, biases, and education to fully engage in bicultural and bilingual social work practice. I am from Chile, and the family is from Venezuela. I assumed that because I was perceived as "Latino" I would understand the entirety of this family's wishes, beliefs, values, and practices. Looking back, I was not culturally sensitive and did not understand the family's priorities. The wife was experiencing deep regrets and guilt as a result of her husband's uncontrolled pain until the very end of his life. She regretted listening to her sister, who is a nurse, about enrolling in hospice. She was told that hospice would help with pain management and overall well-being.

As the social worker, I also felt guilty that I kept reinforcing, while the husband was alive, the hospice philosophy when what I needed to do was to enhance my listening and observational skills instead of reinforcing my personal beliefs. Later in supervision, I was able to explore my own personal marginalized identities, which to that point I had denied. This process was painful, and it took many years to accept the various diverse aspects of myself, including how acculturation and assimilation had shaped, in part, my sense of self, my values, and my sense of reality. I learned that the definition of social work at the end of life is not to take the pain, sorrow, anger, and anxiety away from the person facing the end of life but to listen, understand, and respect the dignity and worth of the person. Social work students are taught what to say and how to say things at the right time. We are taught to reflect, reframe, guide, support, and provide person-centered interventions. Listening, on the other hand, intersects all these competencies and may be taught but often not practiced enough in academic

(Continued)

social work programs, field practicum, and in supervision.

In supervision, I learned to use silence as an intervention. I learned that I felt uncomfortable with silence and would break that silence with hospice patients after only a few seconds. Regarding theories and models of practice, I believed I was confident and competent in using the generalist intervention model (GIM), but I was not. Although I understood this model of practice, I rushed to the first stage, engagement. I remember engaging in an internal dialogue to find the most appropriate thing to say, but I often struggled to do so. I had forgotten the main lesson I was taught in graduate school and reinforced frequently by many of my professors: The most important tool social workers have is themselves. If that is true, then using one's presence as an intervention can be extremely meaningful and essential when working in the realm of end-of-life care. My supervisor taught me that when we feel uncomfortable, we tend to fill the silence with words. This serves to assuage our own feelings but not those of the hospice patient or family. Also, my supervisor reflected on my commitment to the hospice agency, and although I did not understand the connection at first, I later became aware that my commitment to the agency was greater than my commitment to my hospice patients. Regrettably, I failed this family in exploring options for care, but most importantly, I failed to listen to the patient before his death and his wife during the death process and during my bereavement interview with her. I failed to understand how to use a systems approach to explore micro, meso, and macro barriers intersecting this family before and after the death of the husband. I had to embrace my deficiencies, my judgments, and my values. My supervisor helped me explore my identity and my assumptions surrounding the use of language and ethnic identity as proxies for establishing emotional safety, positive regard for the client and family, respect, and unconditional acceptance.

I mention the above scenario because that experience was the prelude for me to explore what is meant by a "good death" as well as my authentic self—two areas that will be explored in this chapter. My experiences in a hospice taught me to listen more and speak less. I learned that the patient was the expert in their lives, not me, and they oversaw their end-of-life care trajectory. The hospice patients taught me that there is no standard definition of a "good death." In fact, Corpora (2021) & Granda-Camerson., and Houldin (2012) mention that for many a good death means having adequate pain and symptom control, having loved ones present during the death process, having free will and volition, having effective and respectful conversations with health care providers, and dying where they want to die.

Conceptualizing Death and Dying

It seems simple to define the concepts of "death" and "dying." Most people believe that death happens when the body no longer is alive and when organs such as the lungs, kidneys, and heart stop working. Throughout the decades, there has been much controversy on exactly what we mean by these concepts. Some people believe that death happens when the heart stops beating, when breathing stops, and when there is no brain activity. We seem to have a conceptual definition or idea of the definition of "death" and "dying," but challenges exist in actual practice.

For example, if we believe that death happens when the heart stops beating, how long does the heart need to stop beating to make the decision that a person has died? And what is meant by "dying"? Related to this chapter, these definitions may be challenged or redefined by people living with marginalized identities and having different religious and spiritual beliefs.

Regarding myths and assumptions about death and dying, it might be helpful to consider some common misconceptions about these processes. Our understanding of life, death, and dying are deeply rooted in our lived personal and professional experiences, modeling from others, religious and spiritual practices, and of course society. Table 11.1 presents a beginning list of most common myths and assumptions about death and dying.

REFLECTION QUESTIONS

1. What are your definitions of these concepts (death and dying), and how do these definitions inform your social work practice?

2. Can you think of times when your definitions of these concepts may be contradicted or overridden?

3. What are some examples of when these definitions must be challenged in order to increase the dignity of the person and loved ones facing the end of life?

TABLE 11.1 Common Myths and Assumptions About Death and Dying

- Death is a painful event.
- People have a right to end their lives.
- People have a right to die with pain.
- The dying person does not have control over their care.
- People die alone.
- Grief and loss are only experienced by family and loved ones.
- Death is final.
- People have the right not to know they have a terminal illness.

These myths, assumptions, and misconceptions about death and dying are often reinforced by erroneous beliefs about death and dying, mainly by societal factors. For example, it is rare to witness the death of someone as it is portrayed in the movies. Aside from accidents where the person may be conscious at least part of the time before they die from internal bleeding, for example, death trajectories are experienced in similar ways. For example, most people dying from cancer will experience a systematic decline in physical functioning: sleeping more, eating less, and eventually falling into unconsciousness. Psychosocial and spiritual variables often influence this trajectory. While medical professionals may predict the possible physical trajectory for someone with a terminal illness, they are unable to predict how the person's psychosocial identities may prolong or hasten the death process. This is where hospice and palliative care social workers can play a significant role: understanding the person in their environment and familial dynamics, for example, to create, as much as possible, a death trajectory that is person- and family-centered.

Understanding Human Behavior and the Social Environment from the Lens of Diversity, Equity, and Inclusion

Specific to social work competencies at the end of life, the National Association of Social Workers (NASW, 2004) proposed standards for social workers to consider when delivering palliative and end-of-life care services. These competencies align with the Council on Social Work Education's (CSWE, 2022) core social work competencies found in their Educational Policy and Accreditation Standards (EPAS). For example, both the 2015 EPAS by CSWE and the NASW's standards mention the importance of having the knowledge, skills, and professional preparation to deliver social work services at the end of life. These guidelines by the CSWE and NASW will be discussed in greater detail later in the chapter. For now, consider and reflect on the various competencies required to deliver effective, ethical, and person-centered end-of-life care services to people who are marginalized and living with diverse identities. Although it can be overwhelming at first to answer these questions, it might be helpful to discuss the **person-in-environment (PIE)** perspective to scaffold your thoughts and professional social work practice.

The PIE perspective is central to the social work profession, as it guides social workers to understand the interdependent and bilateral connection between the person and their environment. This perspective, then, serves as a leading theoretical perspective for social workers to understand and effect change across all systems (micro, meso, and macro). Translating theory into social work practice requires ongoing education, training, self-reflection, and supervision. Such a translation process is ongoing, dynamic, and attentive to hierarchical, historical, and contemporary social issues. These are often embedded and exist within both external (society) and internal (personal) dynamics. Thus, to understand HBSE and the PIE perspective means understanding ourselves first across the various biopsychosocial, spiritual, and religious beliefs, our values, our biases, our judgments, our prejudices, and certainly our ability to understand and value differences in practice. This, as discussed later, is the prelude to ethical social work practice. Understanding others' challenges and struggles requires high levels of personal attributes such as empathy, unconditional acceptance, and respect, in addition to the professional attributes of social work assessment, intervention, and evaluation skills.

In relation to this chapter, social workers have an ethical responsibility to engage in self-reflection via supervision and life-long learning to challenge preconceived ideas about death, dying, and end-of-life care. Social workers begin this process of self-reflection in social work academic programs, but little is known about what takes place after graduation. To further enhance your awareness of these intricacies and complexities, consider these key questions:

1. How do we assess social workers' readiness to continue their work as social workers after graduation and licensing?

2. What mechanisms exist to provide a sense of accountability in relation to social work skills and competence?

Specific to end-of-life care, in 2004 the NASW released the *NASW Standards for Palliative and End-of-Life Care* (see Table 11.2) to "enhance social workers awareness of the skills, knowledge, values, methods, and sensitivities needed to work effectively with clients, families, health care providers, and the community when working in end of life situations" (p. 8).

TABLE 11.2 NASW (2004) Standards for Palliative and End-of-Life Care

Standard	Standard description
1	Ethics and values
2	Knowledge
3	Assessment
4	Intervention/treatment planning
5	Attitudes/self-awareness
6	Empowerment and advocacy
7	Documentation
8	Interdisciplinary teamwork
9	Cultural competence
10	Continuing education
11	Supervision, leadership, and training

While reading this chapter, keep in mind the NASW's Standards for Palliative and End of Life Care, and consider how they can support social workers' efforts in providing quality, ethical, culturally sensitive, and humanistic end-of-life care services to all people—and especially people living with different marginalized identities. It might be helpful to reference the case at the beginning of this chapter to reinforce these competencies.

One of the reasons for specifically highlighting CSWE's EPAS Competency 2 is that the definition of competency intersects with every aspect of this chapter. For instance, understanding someone's wishes as they face a terminal illness requires excellent assessment skills, which must consider all dimensions of diversity. Competency 2 guides social work students to consider and account for diversity across micro, meso, and macro systems. Competency 2 helps us understand the complexities of identity formation, which is created by internal and external forces, such as oppressive societal factors. As such, it becomes critical that social work students express an understanding of the need to challenge oppressive and hierarchical societal systems to support people who are marginalized and coping with death and dying. People living with marginalized identities and facing the end of life are vulnerable and in need of advocacy across all systems of social work practice.

Social workers providing end-of-life care services must work across systems by incorporating a systems approach to social work practice and understanding the roles that the environment plays in creating, shaping, and sustaining people's sense of identity and values. Consider the following case study:

> Marcelo is a bisexual, Latinx cisgender male with a trauma history. Born in Uruguay and raised as a Mormon in Salt Lake City, Marcelo left his home at

15 years old when he was shunned by his family after disclosing, he was bisexual. Marcelo is currently in the hospital in Gainesville, Florida, after suffering a heart attack while at work in a local supermarket. Unfortunately, Marcelo has been diagnosed with advanced heart disease, and unless he receives a heart transplant, his life expectancy is less than 6 months. Marcelo is 38 years old, is single and not dating, and is employed full time at a supermarket. He lives with three other roommates in a two-bedroom apartment. Marcelo is bilingual (English and Spanish) and prefers to communicate in Spanish. The hospice social worker has been consulted to explain hospice services, assess Marcelo's support system, and provide emotional support. Marcelo requested to have a Spanish-speaking social worker, but he was informed that none of the other social workers spoke Spanish. The social worker informed Marcelo that they could use the language phone line if he wished, but he declined. After spending some time with Marcelo, the social worker observed him to be increasingly anxious. The social worker realized that Marcelo was feeling overwhelmed and experiencing trauma-related symptoms. Marcelo reported he was dying and could not breathe. Marcelo was having a panic attack. The nurses were able to give him a sedative to help with the panic attack and increased anxiety. The social worker left his card and returned the next day to engage in discharge planning.

Critical Thinking Exercise

- What components of this case study are represented in EPAS Competency 2?

- What did the social worker do well?

- What did the social worker not do well?

- How does having a trauma history affect the shaping of one's identity? How is it portrayed in the case of Marcelo?

- What are the implications in not securing language services for Marcelo?

- Think about using a systems approach to understand this case. What are the potential interventions at the micro, meso, and macro levels?

- What aspects of the PIE perspective could be considered when identifying possible interventions with Marcelo?

Without a comprehensive understanding of the PIE perspective, social workers may find that interventions and solutions to biopsychosocial/spiritual/religious issues, especially when working with people at the end of life, may not be sustainable.

One of the reasons to underscore the importance of comprehensively understanding the efficacy of HBSE at the end of life is simply that people change, respond to, and evolve because of cultural experiences. These experiences are often shaped by contemporary social events and policies, and at times, these cultural experiences are generationally transmitted. Considering Marcelo's case study above, it becomes evident that his identity development has been a difficult trajectory and one shaped by traditional and contemporary social events. Being raised Mormon and later being shunned for being bisexual led to complete isolation from his parents, siblings, religious practices, and social support. Although he worked on this grief and has been at peace in living an authentic life, feelings of unresolved and unanticipated grief may emerge.

People develop their sense of personal and individual identity(ies) based on cultural and moral values that intersect acculturation and assimilation. One can certainly state, undoubtedly, that the world is a different place today compared to 10 years ago. In the most recent past in the United States, for example, people with marginalized identities have been further traumatized and marginalized because of shifting political views. These changes in politics opened the doors to shifting implicit discrimination, racism, and biases into explicit awareness. In other words, in the most recent past between 2016 and 2020, governmental entities have become vocal in giving permission to the country to be racist and discriminatory to anyone against their political views or their political agendas. For example, the ongoing marginalization and discrimination of African Americans, Asian Americans, Latinos, LGBTQA+ individuals, and people with disabilities gained much more attention and momentum by the previous presidency. Despite rallies, marches, and advocacy efforts against such discrimination and marginalization, the country became progressively more fragile, broken, and divided. Between 2016 and 2022, political rhetoric, for instance, served as a direct oppressive factor to people with marginalized identities, such as those belonging to or connected with the LGBTQA+ community, Native and Indigenous communities, immigrants (documented or undocumented), African Americans, Asian Americans, and people incarcerated, to name a few. The effects of such marginalization often result in delayed preventative health care services, leading to delayed procurement of end-of-life care services. With the increased marginalization of these groups, end-of-life care services, such as securing hospice services, are severely delayed, thus compromising the efficacy of hospice services. As discussed later in the chapter, most people facing the end of life enter hospice too late to take advantage of its benefits. People living with multiple identities, ethnically and racially marginalized, enter hospice much later in the disease process when compared to majority groups.

Matters of social justice, discrimination, racism, and marginalization quickly became endemic when the global COVID-19 pandemic started in December 2019. Matters surrounding death and dying became an expected topic of conversation as people were dying of COVID-19. Tracking the number of deaths and COVID-19 infections became a daily topic of discussion in mainstream media, communities, and governmental agencies, mainly because initially there were no vaccines and/or efficacious treatments. A paradigm shift happened almost instantly as people belonging to all races, ethnicities, and socioeconomic statuses and infected with COVID-19 became marginalized. What has transpired with COVID-19 parallels, historically, with the AIDS pandemic beginning in the late 1970s. We have learned that marginalizing people based on personal (not professional) values and practices increases mortality, delays seeking end-of-life care services, and has increased rates of mortality. Thus, with the AIDS pandemic and now with COVID-19, we can clearly see disparities in end-of-life care services among marginalized groups. These disparities often fall under the two categories of "worthy" and "unworthy." The underlying message here is to enhance awareness of these categories and, as social workers do, advocate for a just health care system for all people and especially those facing the end of life. The aim is for all people to have the opportunity to have a good death: one without pain and suffering, and with dignity and respect. This is a human rights issue and one that warrants social work advocacy and change.

For many, particularly in the first few waves of the pandemic, testing positive for COVID-19 meant the inevitable fact that they were going to die alone in an intensive care unit (ICU) without family present. Because family members were not allowed in the hospital, everyone died without a loved one next to them. As discussed then, the shaping of identities is often driven and dependent upon cultural variables and events. Whereas we have advocated for dignity at the end of life, the cultural phenomena of COVID-19 shifted such dignity and suspended the ability to be surrounded by people important to them for almost 2 years. People died in the hospital without family present and thus without hope. These cultural phenomena in conjunction with beliefs, morals, and personal values solidify such (marginalized) identities. Of course, one cannot ignore that marginalization is also transmitted through transgenerational familial and societal dynamics that are seldom explicit and overt. To further contextualize the impact of COVID-19 on end-of-life care processes, read the content in Table 11.3, which presents some of these negative outcomes specific to people with marginalized identities.

TABLE 11.3 The Impact of COVID-19 on End-of-Life Care Processes

1.	Patients dying alone in intensive care units without family or loved ones
2.	Increased anxiety, depression, and feelings of despair due to isolation and limited contact, if any, with family and health care providers
3.	Decreased sense of dignity
4.	Limited human touch and connection due to layers of gloves, face shields, and body gowns
5.	Increased death anxiety
6.	Financial hardships

Application of Knowledge: Mr. J.'s Case Study

Think of the case example of Mr. J. who is presenting to a social worker for feelings of anxiety, despair, and sadness due to being diagnosed with a terminal illness. The social worker supports Mr. J. and connects him to community resources that, unfortunately, are far from his home, and there is no public transportation. Due to Mr. J.'s declining health conditions and terminal illness, driving is not an option. Mr. J. expressed feelings of shame and embarrassment for reaching out to the social worker. He discussed being raised in a strict home with his father promoting and modeling that "men take care of themselves" and that "no one can help you but yourself." The social worker has the responsibility to address Mr. J.'s biopsychosocial and spiritual needs but also understand how his environment, such as his community, contributes to the lack of end-of-life care services in the vicinity. Furthermore, the social worker also has the responsibility to understand policies, either local or federal, that intersect the lack of end-of-life care services in Mr. J.'s community.

Now, let's consider the same case example above from a HBSE and PIE lens and incorporate Mr. J.'s intersecting identities to further understand the complexities of this case. Mr. J. self-identifies as a Black man who is gay and dying of AIDS. Mr. J.'s pronouns are "he, him, his." Mr. J. lives alone, is unemployed and uninsured, does not have any family support, has been living on his savings, which he will deplete in 2 weeks, and friends are far away. Mr. J.'s family rejected him when he disclosed (coming out) to them that he was gay 15 years ago. He has not spoken with his brother, sister, or parents in 15 years. His husband of 10 years died six months ago from AIDS; he was the driver in the relationship. His death caused Mr. J. to experience increased anxiety and panic attacks when interfacing with medical systems. He is learning how to take public transportation and is unsure of any city or county transportation support. He reports feelings of despair throughout the day and especially when reflecting on his husband's painful death. Mr. J.'s husband did not want to engage hospice until a few days before his death (worried about the cost) and thus died with uncontrolled pain and anxiety and conscious of his impending death.

Mr. J. reports that although they were both insured under his husband's policy, no one mentioned hospice services until a week before his death. Mr. J. lost his insurance benefits once his husband died. Mr. J. is also experiencing food insecurity and home insecurity. He disclosed that his landlord has asked him to vacate his property due to being 3 months late on his rent. Mr. J. was raised as Catholic, his church is not accepting of his sexual orientation, and he was asked to find another "more inclusive" church 3 months ago when he approached his priest for emotional support in coping with the death of his husband. Regarding social welfare benefits, he was informed by a Social Security officer over the phone that he did not qualify for services until he spent all his assets. Mr. J. believes he does not qualify for Obamacare because of the AIDS diagnosis and did not pursue coverage once he was informed that he did not qualify for Social Security benefits. Mr. J. was unsure if he was told that he did not qualify for Social Security or Social Security disability benefits. He reports receiving information about health care insurance, but the process has become too overwhelming for him, as his cognitive abilities have been affected by his current medical conditions—hence his increased anxiety, feelings of despair, and anticipated grief related to his own impending death.

REFLECTION QUESTIONS

Considering Mr. J.'s situation, as his social worker:

- What are the important aspects of this case leading to prioritizing his biopsychosocial and spiritual needs?

- What are the potential intervention points in this case?

- How would you proceed with Mr. J. and prioritize his needs? Are there theories or models that can help you in this process of prioritizing his needs?

- How can Mr. J.'s current biopsychosocial and spiritual/religious challenges be stabilized? What are the micro, meso, and macro needs, and who is best positioned to address these systemic needs?

- Which of the nine EPAS social work competencies from CSWE apply to this complex case?

- What are some ways that the PIE perspective can support you as the social worker to support Mr. J.?

Critical Thinking Exercise

- Reflecting on one's own mortality can cause feelings of despair, anxiety, and sadness. If this is true for you, what steps or actions can you take to enhance your capacity and competence when working with people facing the end of life?

- What are your definitions of "death" and "dying," and how/when did you learn these definitions?

- What is your comfort level in having end-of-life care discussions?

- What connections to CSWE's EPAS and the PIE perspective could be made to further enhance your capacity and competencies when working with people with marginalized identities at the end of life?

Language and Identity

Although the spoken language is often used as a proxy for acculturation and assimilation in the United States, we have yet to understand the evolution and trajectory of immigrants' identity development. Even more concerning is the fact that people belonging to minority-identified groups are at risk for complicated death processes, mainly due to service providers limited or lack of cultural humility and awareness (Rine, 2018). For instance, Latinx people's beliefs and attitudes about death are created by cultural heritage, religious practice, and family unit (University of Washington Medical Center, 2007; Catlin, 2001; Oltjenbruns, 1998). These attributes shared among most Latinx individuals also exist within other marginalized groups, such as African Americans, Asian Americans, people who are deaf, and LGBTQIA+ folks. Even with policies and standards created to enhance cultural and linguistic competence, such as the National Standards for Culturally and Linguistically Appropriate Services in Health Care (CLAS; U.S. Department of Health and Human Services, 2001) and the NASW's (2004) end-of-life care standards, there remains a vast gap in the research literature about cultural and linguistic competence (Arriaza et al., 2015; Chong, 2002). In fact, there seems to be a fallacy that learning to speak Spanish, for example, parallels language and cultural competence, but as my experience as related in the opening vignette suggests, social workers must strive toward a model of cultural awareness and sensitivity instead of cultural competence. This requires some rigorous self-assessment: What are your strengths and limitations surrounding cultural humility? What is your ontological perspective, or how do you understand reality? For example, do you need objective proof to understand reality (positivist), or do you have a more subjective understanding of the nature of reality (interpretivist) by focusing more on the social construction of knowledge and reality? How can you use this knowledge about how you see and understand social phenomena, such as death and dying, in your understanding of having a good death?

The next section on what constitutes a good death underscore what we have touched on in previous chapters: Many theoretical constructs employed in HBSE have served to implicitly marginalize individuals that are categorized as "non-White." Regarding HBSE traditional theories, such as psychosocial theory, psychodynamic theory, social systems theory, cognitive and behavioral theories, and attachment theories, have not, for the most part, included their relevance and/or application to and with people identified as non-White.

Self-Reflection and Critical Thinking Exercise

In summary, a global definition of "theory" includes how the specified theory helps to predict as well as interpret and evaluate situations, behaviors, and contexts. Such theories must account for such intersectionality and differences.

- What are the ethical challenges or dilemmas that coexist when applying or using a specific theory that excludes people's differences?

- To challenge this perspective even further, consider the word "Latinx." Who belongs to this category? If your answer pointed to people living in South America, Central America, Mexico, Spain, and the Caribbean, you may be pointing in the right direction. However, are all these people the same?

- Consider the implications of language. In Guatemala, for example, there are at least 25 languages spoken, and although Spanish is the primary language, there are approximately 22 Mayan languages along with other Indigenous languages. Can we conclude, then, that people from Guatemala are similar to people from Colombia or Argentina, for example?

- What role does language play at the end of life?

What Is a Good Death?

We have learned throughout the book that many research studies overrepresent people who self-identify as White, yet findings are often generalized to all people. In terms of understanding expected development and later death and dying from a non-White lens, we have just started the discussion. In fact, there is no global definition of a "good death," which presents challenges when creating applicable, meaningful, and culturally relevant end-of-life care services for all people but especially people from diverse cultural backgrounds and people with language challenges and differences (Barwise et al., 2019). Table 11.4 presents a few variables worth considering when attempting to understand what exactly qualifies as a good death (Ngabonziza et al., 2021).

TABLE 11.4 What Is a Good Death?

- Little to no pain
- Experiencing dignity and respect
- Feelings of comfort and acceptance
- Connection to loved ones
- Self-determination

These may seem self-evident to many of us. Yet it is crucial to understand that they are culturally weighted. The research on end-of-life care processes for people with marginalized identities has been scarce. Social workers can do better to generate and disseminate models of social work practices that represent everyone equally. Evidence-based practices are needed to support people living with marginalized identities who are coping with impending death. Other, perhaps less traditional theories, such as the theory of a peaceful death, the theory of self-transcendence, and the stages of grief theory, have been useful in discussing death trajectories and complexities. Table 11.5 presents some of these theories' usefulness and challenges when working with people with marginalized and multiple identities.

TABLE 11.5 Relevant End-of-Life Care Theories

Theory	Usefulness	Challenges
Psychosocial theory	• Provides expected psychosocial development across the lifespan • Incorporates social development	• Does not account for diversity, acculturation, assimilation, and/or cultural identity • Developed mostly with male children, thus has problematic generalizing • Strong emphasis on childhood development • Linear stage theory • Limited use with people facing the end of life who are also living with marginalized identities
Psychodynamic theory	• Promotes an understanding of unconscious drives • Attachment and early childhood development may explain cognitions, behaviors, and motivations for change.	• Defocuses biological development • Extremely deterministic in that the premise is that people have low or no volition
Social systems theory	• The whole is greater than the sum of its part. • Person functions within micro, meso, and macro systems • Opportunities to effect change across systems	• Minimizes or does not account for the need for psychological interventions • Challenges with evaluating one's practice effectiveness
Cognitive theory	• Explains how thought processes connect to behaviors	• Cognitive processes are not observable. • Does not account for social systemic influences
Behavioral theory	• Behavior can be learned or unlearned and maintained by various stimuli and rewards. • Aims to identify behavioral antecedents and consequences for the actual behavior, which is often seen and heard, and it is measurable and quantifiable	• Does not account for self-determination • Strong emphasis on external factors to behaviors and not accounting for psychological, spiritual, and social factors • Biological factors not considered • Learning is achieved in various ways. People have different ways to learn.

TABLE 11.5 Relevant End-of-Life Care Theories (*Continued*)

Theory	Usefulness	Challenges
Attachment theory	• Identity development is successful when primary needs of security, bonding, and safety are present during infancy. • Focuses on relationships between people • Successful attachment during infancy leads to healthy attachments as adults.	• Requires insight and motivation to revisit attachment trajectories, especially during infancy
Theory of self-transcendence	• The individual is at the center of creating increased well-being, especially when facing difficult life situations, such as coping with a terminal illness.	• Requires insight and contemplative skills • Meaning of transcendence may not be well-understood by younger individuals. • Open to providers' interpretation • Limited research on its efficacy
Stages of grief theory (also known as stages of death)	• Explains the five stages of grief (denial, anger, bargaining, depression, and acceptance) • Inclusive of diverse populations' beliefs, traditions, and religious/spiritual practices	• Assumptions that individuals must experience all five stages for positive well-being outcomes, including acceptance of mortality • Developed from case studies rather than empirical research • Grief is experienced differently among diverse groups. Social workers must account for cultural variables.
Theory of the peaceful end of life	• Provides guidelines for improving well-being for individuals facing the end of life • Primarily used in nursing by addressing pain control, bringing about feelings of comfort, promoting dignity and respect, increasing feelings of peacefulness, and promoting closeness with significant others	• Theory has not been evaluated empirically for its efficacy. • Some of the actions, such as "being at peace," have not been clearly defined. • Psychological support is not explicitly reinforced or considered.
Quality of life model	• Derived from Maslow's hierarchy of needs theory • Presents both subjective and objective quality-of-life indicators	• Quality of life changes frequently among people facing the end of life, requiring ongoing assessment and planning
Uncertainty in illness	• A nursing theory that focuses on antecedents, appraisal of uncertainty, and coping with uncertainty • Applicable with individuals facing the end of life • Aim is to return to earlier levels of functioning.	• Creating meaning at the end of life may not be perceived as a priority for people living with diverse identities.

(Continued)

TABLE 11.5 Relevant End-of-Life Care Theories (*Continued*)

Theory	Usefulness	Challenges
Watson's theory of human caring	• People are connected to micro, meso, and macro systems. • Focus is on the dyad between health care providers and individuals facing the end of life • Interdependence between health care provider and patient • Key aspects of the theory include aspects found in social work practice such as: inspiring faith and hope, trusting self and others, nurturing relationships, forgiveness, co-creating a healing environment, ministering physical, emotional, and spiritual human needs, being open to the mystery of death and dying, and allowing miracles to emerge.	• Requires flexibility, creativity, and joining in with the patient which may be problematic, ethically, if not done well • A nursing theory that may be challenging to translate into social work practice • Challenges with empirically testing the theory • Requires providers' interpretation of the theory, which may not be accurate • May alienate people who are atheists • Strong possibility for countertransference to emerge

HBSE theories that respond better to the needs of the dying person, especially people with different and often marginalized identities, are needed. These theories must explicitly address and be grounded in cultural humility models as well as humanistic approaches that account for and respect diversity and differences among all people.

Perhaps a global call is needed to identify applicable and more subjective models or theories of social work practice to center and focus on more qualitative and humanistic perspectives when addressing the needs of people coping with end-of-life issues and death and dying. For example, Murali (2020), considered Watson's theory of human caring (see Table 11.5 above for a greater explanation of Watson's theory) to discuss the process of end-of-life decision making from a subjective, patient-centered, and humanistic approach inclusive of all parties intersecting the person who is dying. Social scientists with a focus on death and dying, thanatologists, social workers, nurses, physicians, and other allied health professionals intersecting with people who are dying must explore theories of practice that align with the person's cultural beliefs, mores, and practices; biopsychosocial needs and strengths; spiritual and religious grounding; and personal preferences. Why is this important? It is important because a good death is a human rights matter: We only have one opportunity to experience a good death or a death with respect and congruent with our beliefs, practices, and end-of-life wishes. Social workers can play an important role in mediating quality-of-life outcomes for people living with marginalized identities. The work that is needed must be contextualized and understood from a systems perspective. In other words, macro- and meso-level interventions become central in sustaining micro-level interventions because policies, communities, and organizations intersecting with people at the end of life must have the necessary tools to support and empower those who are marginalized and oppressed and facing the end of life.

Interventions that should be considered include a local campaign to increase awareness on palliative and hospice care along with a simple explanation of advance directives. Social workers can support community agencies and nonprofit organizations to evaluate community capacity and even support the agency in grant writing to secure funds for these interventions. At the micro level, using the PIE perspective and an integrative theoretical approach can be useful when advocating for the needs of individuals at the end of life, including the procurement of home care hospice services; supporting individuals and families to apply for and secure Medicare services when applicable; exploring people's needs from an inclusive perspective free of bias, judgment, and honoring their worth; as well as engaging individuals at the end of life to participate in health care decisions.

THEORY ↔ PRACTICE

To effectively and sustainably respond to the end-of-life care needs of people with complex identities and cultural differences, social workers are encouraged to first understand the person who is dying and their loved ones from a multisystemic humanistic perspective in addition to other applicable theoretical perspectives that inform or direct the social worker to account for oppressive factors intersecting death and dying. Social workers may consider the following:

- Social workers need to have a level of cultural humility and awareness conducive to accepting differences and understanding the person in their environment from a holistic perspective. These differences sometimes may intersect ethical matters requiring effective supervision to intervene ethically and within the law.

- Understanding the client's belongingness to their community provides clarity on support systems that are available but not in use or may serve as a way to assess social support and identify new sources of support. Consider a client who is gay and Catholic wishing to receive communion. How would you advocate for this patient? How would you advocate for other gay, Catholic patients wishing to receive communion across the state and nationally?

- Using innovative assessment techniques to enhance social support, such as ecomaps, may be helpful. Consider how ecomaps could be used to evaluate your interventions.

- Understanding the efficacy and meaning of the humanistic concept of "accepting people with unconditional positive regard" is essential.

- Consider how to elevate end-of-life care awareness across communities and systems.

- Consider the power and influence of community collaboration and the power in numbers. We know that oftentimes policies are created by advocacy, qualitative and quantitative data, as well as contemporary movements, such as laws surrounding dying with dignity.

Barriers to Good Death for People Who Are Marginalized

These end-of-life care preferences or wishes, unfortunately, continue to be a challenge in the United States. Specifically, evidence shows that people with intersecting identities are not well-informed on advanced directives, hospice treatment, palliative care, and end-of-life care wishes. Similarly, it is unfortunate that the average length of stay for a new hospice patient is between a few days to several months. In fact, Harris and colleagues (2019) reported that over 50% of patients in their study died within 3 weeks, while Ornstein and colleagues (2020) reported an average length of hospice stay of fewer than 3 days for people who are Black. Although terminally ill patients must have a prognosis of fewer than 6 months to qualify for hospice services, they tend to remain in hospice for a short time. To fully engage and take advantage of the efficacy of the hospice philosophy, individuals qualifying for hospice must be identified much sooner in their disease progression. In fact, when patients enter hospice earlier than later, their health care and death outcomes are better than those admitted short term (Quinn et al., 2020; Connor et al., 2005; Brown et al., 2017). A recent study by Hughes and colleagues (2021) shows that one of the keys to increasing hospice use among community members, including people who are marginalized, is to "facilitate language translation, diversity in staffing, enhanced community outreach, and leadership and staff collaboration regarding inclusion" (p. 1).

People with marginalized identities and facing terminal illnesses are at risk of not being informed about care options, including hospice and palliative care. Researchers such as Griggs (2020) and Johnson (2013) discussed barriers, found in Table 11.6, to receiving, understanding, and deciding on end-of-life care options, choices, and services.

TABLE 11.6 Barriers to End-of-Life Care Options

- Language discordance
- Cultural barriers
- Isolation
- Living in rural towns
- Lack of medical insurance
- Having access to accurate information
- Intersecting identities
- Low socioeconomic status

Regarding advance directives (health care proxy form, living will, and power of attorney), for example, Portanova et al. (2017) have reported that people self-identifying as White overrepresent advance directives completion rates when compared to 18% for Hispanic and 15% for Black people. Information about palliative care, hospice care, bereavement care, and Medicare benefits are also incongruent when compared to different groups. People identified as White are once again overrepresented with higher rates of awareness about these services when compared to people identified as Black and Latinx. Researchers have been clear that effective and early hospice enrollment translates to better patient experiences and improved outcomes (Wright et al., 2016). More specifically as it relates to this chapter, researchers such as Tobin and colleagues (2022) have specifically discussed the inequities that exist in hospice care from a global lens. More people are dying in hospitals than in their homes as they have wished or planned. Consider the questions in the Critical Thinking Exercise to enhance your critical thinking on this important matter regarding why people are dying in hospitals instead of their homes, as usually preferred.

Critical Thinking Exercise

- What are possible explanations for the fact that most people die in hospitals instead of at home?

- What are possible underlying issues supporting this dynamic?

- What are the systemic and structural challenges mediating these outcomes for increased hospital deaths?

Social scientists have increased attention on utilization of hospice services, for instance, but the actual process of a good death or how to address these systemic and structural barriers to having a good death and dying process for people with marginalized identities has yet to be well-understood. Although a review of the literature chronicles the positive experiences of hospice patients when entering hospice care earlier in the disease process, we have limited information on efficacious interventions and especially with marginalized groups (Kleinpell et al., 2019). Regarding matters such as definitions of a "good death," which will be explored later in the chapter, using assessment models and theories, such as psychosocial theories to assess and evaluate death and dying outcomes, the literature falls short on guidance and explanation, and it becomes increasingly problematic when accounting for people living with marginalized identities. A recent systematic review by Maynard and Csikai (2020) presented the need to explicitly consider psychosocial and spiritual components to formulate a relevant and applicable definition of a "good death." This requires multiple social work skills and competencies (presented earlier in the chapter) that novice social workers may find overwhelming. For instance, in the case of Marcelo, understanding all of his biopsychosocial and spiritual factors may be extremely challenging for new social workers. Learning how to prioritize his needs and prepare for his impending death places much responsibility on the social worker, who is often pressured by hospitals to arrange for home care and discharge patients as soon as possible. Slowing the process down to integrate Marcelo's full understanding of his prognosis, securing social support systems, providing support to apply for Social Security disability, and securing a qualified interpreter may not be an option. Without a clear sense of personal and professional identity, knowing how to use theory or specific practice models accounting for diversity in terms of age, gender, sexual identity, language preference, acculturation, and assimilation may be a daunting task.

Furthermore, although we have made advances in hospice care and palliative care and end-of-life care discussions are increasing, communities of color remain significantly underserved (Gardner et al., 2018). What is needed is an understanding of how to infuse applicable theories to inform social work practice with diverse individuals facing the end of life. For example, Table 11.7 presents possible interventions, based on the presenting issue, at the end of life with individuals with marginalized identities. Note that many of the listed presenting issues are also present in both Mr. J. and Marcelo's case studies. Thus, this table may promote critical thinking as you consider possible interventions based on the applicable theory.

TABLE 11.7 Intersection of Theory with End-of-Life Care Interventions for Individuals with Marginalized Identities

Presenting issue	Applicable theory	What kinds of social work interventions could be used for each category?
Anticipatory grief	Stages of death	
Uncontrolled pain	Quality of life	
Uncontrolled anxiety	Watson's theory of human care	
Poor social support system	Social systems theory	
Denial regarding diagnosis and prognosis	Stages of death	

THEORY ↔ PRACTICE

The theories presented earlier, especially the stages of grief theory, quality of life model, uncertainty in illness model, stages of death model, and theory of a peaceful death, can provide a roadmap for social workers providing end-of-life care services to individuals and families with marginalized identities. The key is to acknowledge that there is no perfect theory, and thus social workers must understand how to apply aspects of a theory or theories to best support a good death, for example. Human behavior is a complex construct requiring a multisystemic approach to effect positive end-of-life care interventions. This requires being a good consumer of research and evidence and understanding the translation of theories into practice. Using theories to guide social work practice also serves as a grounding process for new social workers to identify and resolve "their own attitudes, moods, and reactions, which may result in ineffectiveness, inefficiency, and even harm clients" as quoted in Gentle-Genitty and colleagues (2014, p. 39).

Critical Thinking Exercise

From the list of theories presented earlier, identify two theories that could be used as guiding principles to supporting a good death trajectory for Mr. J.

- What are the similarities and differences between the two theories you have selected?

- Think about the intersection of the selected two theories and formulate a rationale for using aspects of these theories to support people with marginalized identities at the end of life—in this case, Mr. J.

SELF-REFLECTION
- What are some ideas on how social workers can view the world from an inclusive lens?

- How might you apply the knowledge in this chapter in your area of social work practice?

- What are some of the challenges that may emerge when working with people from different cultures, with different values and beliefs, and who are facing impending death?

- In your opinion, what is the most important skill or tool social workers have when working with people from different backgrounds, cultures, races, sexual identities, socioeconomic statuses, and abilities around end-of-life processes, death, and dying? Provide a rationale.

- At what point in the social worker–client relationships might social workers assess the client's understanding of death, dying, and end-of-life processes?

The Privilege of a Good Death

Although there has been increased interest among social scientists to understand the meaning and definition of a "good death," there remains uncertainty about translating an operational and conceptual definition of a "good death" into practice. While there has been research conducted to explore general definitions of a good death and experiences (Csikai & Maynard, 2020; Meier et al., 2016; Oliver & O'Connor, 2015; Lloyd-Williams et al., 2007), a good death is best understood and defined by each person facing the end of life, and social workers are well-positioned to support and guide the individual in creating a definition of a "good death" that respects their sense of dignity, wishes, values, and beliefs.

Using the skill of reframing to focus on a strength's perspective rather than the uncertainty of death and dying may be helpful. In other words, instead of exploring the meaning of a good death with some individuals with increased anxiety and some denial of prognosis, it might be worth exploring how to live life to the fullest until the end, for example. To avoid power differentials, social workers must consider a holistic approach to creating applicable "good death" or "live life to the fullest" definitions in tandem with individuals facing the end of life. Again, this may seem daunting at first, but here is where an integrative approach to theory application becomes crucial.

What seems to be needed to address the large gaps in hospice enrollment among minority groups and address the biopsychosocial and spiritual needs of people with marginalized identities at the end of life is to formulate plans to integrate aspects of theories that may apply to the individual facing death. This means evaluating these theories and using them as a menu to guide the intervention. Selecting some and not all aspects of a theory can be quite useful. I have engaged in this process by including the individual facing death and dying in the decision-making process about interventions. This was such a turning point in my clinical social work practice because I felt an alliance and partnership with the individual, and often the family, which reinforced inclusion and respect.

When thinking about dying a good death and living a good life until the end, we can begin to think about who these individuals are and, most importantly, who is excluded from this privilege. From the literature, one can ascertain that the privilege of a good death is often experienced mostly by people who are White, with stable socioeconomic status, and acculturated and assimilated into the values, beliefs, and norms of our society. We know, for example, that although we can wish for equitable end-of-life care experiences for all, access to death and dying and end-of-life care services congruent with one's wishes toward a good death is mediated by race, gender, class, and other social identities (Corpora, 2021). In other words, there are significant disparities in end-of-life care access and services for people who are often categorized as belonging to "minority" groups. Later we will discuss the implications of using the word "minorities" to describe people who are marginalized, oppressed, and living with different identities.

We know from research that people who are Black, for example, have much higher medical expenses at the end of life and are less likely to enroll in and use hospice services (Corpora, 2021). Consider Table 11.8, which presents prevalent disparities in the use of hospice care.

TABLE 11.8 Prevalent Disparities in the Use of Hospice Care by People Who Are Minorities

- Preference for aggressive treatment (especially among people with a cancer diagnosis)
- Mistrust of health care providers and systems
- Poor or no in-home care resources (especially having a live-in person responsible for the daily care)
- Miscommunication, misinterpretation, and misunderstanding of treatment options

In the past, this phenomenon has been partially explained by generational transmission of health care beliefs and values that have been based on gruesome violations of human rights, such as in the **Tuskegee Study**. There has been a strong argument for the lack of trust many minority groups have toward medical systems—again, all based on reality and factual events. However, it is also important to understand that people who are Black, Latinx, disabled, and others belonging to the LGBTQIA+ community experience disparities regarding medical services. For those who speak another language other than English, seeking medical services can be challenging, frustrating, and stigmatizing. The result is often a lack of engagement and follow-up with services. One example is attempting to explain the word "hospice" in Spanish. Most bilingual social workers use the word *hospicio*, which is the direct translation for "hospice," but for many Spanish-speaking people, "hospicio" means a hostel or hotel.

Living with multiple marginalized identities further complicates matters, as these groups of people are less likely to access and engage in end-of-life care services. They may not be aware that these services exist. The same may hold true for primary care physicians (PCPs) who are often at the center of the health care team. These PCPs may not be knowledgeable about palliative and hospice services and may be promoting more aggressive treatments and trips to emergency departments to stabilize the quality of life and functioning of people facing a terminal illness. Furthermore, asking people at every visit "Do you have an advance directive?" has served only to check off a box and not take the time to explore what these words mean and their relevance to the individual facing the end-of-life trajectory.

Social workers can use the information and research from this chapter to create interventions across systems. All social workers can immediately begin effecting change by including one question on their psychosocial assessments focused on advance directives, for example. Using a systems approach, social workers can evaluate the process for initiating and completing advanced directives, for example. Creating and translating a trifold in several languages mostly spoken in their community can be fruitful and inclusive. Social workers have the skills to disseminate important and relevant medical information to marginalized groups by creating focus groups to create printed materials that are inclusive and informative. Social workers are change agents, and such change often happens in communities. Thus, visiting local community centers and collaborating with other agencies to disseminate information about advance directives, palliative care, and hospice care can be extremely useful. For people who attend religious and spiritual events, collaborating with local religious leaders in increasing awareness of end-of-life care resources can be extremely helpful.

Such lack of access to information and services is particularly true among rural dwellers and is a topic that will be explored in another section. Because most people live within a family system, it is also important to acknowledge that this lack of privilege in having a good death is generationally transmitted. We learn to negotiate systems by observing and learning from our caregivers and family systems. When these systems are ill-informed about access to end-of-life care, such lack of information exists implicitly and is transmitted across generations. It is true that historical contexts, such as slavery and the Tuskegee Study between 1932 and 1972 with African American men, also play a role in our country's narrative of equity and inclusion. These narratives exist within the realm of explicit violation of human rights, trust, dignity, and worth of the person. Unsurprisingly, the ramifications of such blatant disregard for human life continue today. It has been well-established that many African Americans distrust medical systems, and again, such distrust is generationally transmitted. Such distrust is based on real-life events that have specifically targeted people of color and disregarded basic human rights.

From an intersectionality perspective, then, it is essential that we understand how to best support all people during the death and dying process by using theories from an integrated approach. There exist opportunities to effect change across micro, meso, and macro systems to enhance information dissemination about the rights of all people to have a death that is congruent with their wishes. For people with multiple marginalized identities, social work interventions must be systemically laden. At the micro level, explicit processes need to be created to have efficacious conversations about end-of-life care wishes. Knowing how to have these conversations with people with marginalized identities is essential. The intricacies of these conversations are also mediated by culture, experiences with health care systems, death and dying beliefs and misconceptions, society's beliefs about who is privileged to have their wishes respected at the end of life, and race, to name a few.

The Finality of Death

Philosophical aspects of death and dying often inform social work interventions at the end of life. These philosophical variables include questions presented in Table 11.9. These questions may be used as guiding principles when working with people with diverse and marginalized identities.

TABLE 11.9 Philosophical Aspects of Death and Dying

- What happens after we die?
- What is death and dying?
- Should death be hastened?
- What are the human rights of people when facing the end of life?
- How can social workers reinforce and consider the right to self-determination among people facing the end of life?
- What is a good death?

Thinking about death from a philosophical lens can help us understand and validate the finality of death. Death is inevitable. As such, death and dying requires an explicit understanding of the intricacies and complexities of the dying process. This discussion cannot be rushed and must be well-understood by social workers. It is important to underscore that as soon as an infant is born, they will one day die. Most commonly, infants will grow, become an adult, and eventually die. But we also know that death is experienced not only by adults but also by infants, children, adolescents, and young adults; it exists across the lifespan (CDC, 2021). We have been socialized to think about and perceive death and dying among people who are older and with chronic conditions. Perhaps this serves as a protective factor or defense mechanism to avoid or suppress the awareness that death is inevitable. As far as evidentiary proof, one can predict with much certainty that 130 years from now everyone currently alive will be dead.

Critical Thinking Exercise

To further bring into light the reality of mortality for all of us, write down the number 77 and subtract it from your age. For example, if you are 30 years old, subtract it from 77, which equals 47: your expected years to live. Next, consider the following self-reflective questions:

1. What feelings emerged for you when you found out the number of expected years you have left to live?

- What thoughts, including protective thoughts, quickly entered your thinking?

- How can you use this awareness to inform your social work practice?

- How does this awareness about mortality inform our understanding of humility and self-compassion in social work practice?

The approximate average age of life expectancy in the United States is roughly 77 years (CDC, 2022a) without considering variables such as race, gender, ethnicity, place of living (rural versus suburban and urban), and socioeconomic status. These mediating variables, when accounted for, may yield higher or lower life expectancy averages. Although there are discrepancies based on gender, race, ethnicity, and socioeconomic status, 77 is a fair prediction of life expectancy for most people. However, as previously stated, death exists among all age groups. For example, consider the report by the CDC (2020) found in Table 11.10.

TABLE 11.10 Number of Deaths for Different Age Groups

Age group	Number of deaths
Infants	19,582
1–4	3,529
5–14	5,623
15–19	12,278

These numbers elucidate the fact that social workers must be prepared to provide death and dying, end-of-life care, and grief-related services across the lifespan.

Social Determinants of Health

There are many reasons for considering **social determinants of health (SDOH)** in the discussion of current end-of-life care services and practices with people living with multiple identities. SDOH are the "conditions in the places where people live, learn, work, and play that affect a wide range of health and qualify-of-life risks and outcomes" (CDC, 2020, p. 1). The various SDOH help us understand how to improve population health and essentially intervene to lower health care spending. From a social work lens, it makes sense to understand these SDOH and engage in prevention to mediate the poor health outcomes at the end of life for people living with marginalized identities. Considering that most people enrolled in hospice and palliative care are White, gaps in hospice access and services are concerning. These inequities are extremely worrisome, as it becomes clear that one's environment plays a significant role in shaping people's identities and understanding of social systems and resources.

Rural Social Work Practice with People Marginalized at the End of Life

Rural areas experience many health-related challenges and certainly when creating and delivering end-of-life care services. Rural communities' challenges include (a) geographic isolation; (b) economic deprivation; and (c) poor medical infrastructure. Everyone should have equal access and opportunities to dying as they wish in urban, suburban, and rural communities. Unfortunately, people living in rural towns and living with multiple marginalized identities tend to use health care and preventative services far less often than people in urban areas. Geographic isolation, for example, poses significant challenges for people living in rural areas. Some of these challenges include infrequent or no access to public transportation, limited and often unreliable health care services, including end-of-life care services, and limited access to preventative interventions, such as screenings for colon and breast cancer, cancer therapies, and hospice services. When combined with lower economic standards (poverty) and limited or substandard medical infrastructures, geographic isolation decreases access to health care services.

Existing inequities in terms of end-of-life care services and access to such services among people living in rural places are supported, largely, by economic growth in larger cities. Such economic growth in urban places often shifts most of the resources to where the people live. Since it is obvious that more people live in urban and suburban towns, the allocation of economic resources to fund health care initiatives and services in rural towns is diminished or unfunded. From a business perspective, it seems to make sense to allocate services to towns with the most people. However, the lives of people are not a business, and thus we must acknowledge and respect the worth of each person no matter where they live. The focus needs to be on the inherited right to human dignity and respect, which are intrinsic values within the social work profession.

People living in rural areas often live in locations that are widely dispersed. Such diffuse living arrangements can lead to challenges in offering end-of-life care services, primarily due to the perceived expense of providing such services in rural towns (Friedman, 2003). It is important to acknowledge that people living in rural communities have a clearly marginalized identity intersected by other identities (e.g., low income, racial and cultural differences, and single parents). Friedman also points to the structural issue of low-income concerning access to care in general among rural residents. This inequity often results in rural citizens paying more for health care services or not having health care insurance. This has led to diminishing access to health and social resources in rural areas but increased spending for such resources in urban areas, which John Wheat (1994) coined the **urban undertow**.

Again, from a business perspective, it makes sense to direct resources to the people who will access and use them, which we know now exist primarily in urban and suburban towns and cities. However, from a human rights perspective, these inequities existing among rural residents do not align with a human rights and social justice perspective. This is a power differential that must be addressed to provide all people with the same opportunities to access and receive equitable end-of-life care services. Social workers are best positioned to address these power differentials by addressing the needs of rural citizens. Creating mechanisms to fund end-of-life care services in rural communities goes beyond the development of palliative care and hospice services.

What is needed is to address access to care in the first place. From a narrow lens, the argument can be made that it makes sense to fund services that people use and redirect funds from rural towns to urban and suburban towns. However, a critical view is needed such as understanding that access to care has been a significant variable for decades experienced by people with diverse identities in rural communities. The perpetuation of diminished end-of-life care services in rural towns can be contributed to factors such as impoverishment, family members and support systems relocating to urban and suburban towns where opportunities for employment and career advancements are disproportionately higher than in rural places, nonexistent or limited public transportation, lower levels of education and literacy, poorer physical and mental health, and a general lack of awareness about these services. Regarding race, Belisomo (2018) discussed how there are evident discrepancies in end-of-life care services for marginalized identities. Belisomo explains how some races are not educated efficiently on end-of-life care options, which results in marginalized communities falling further behind in terms of equity. African American people, specifically, are faced with structural racism within the health care system, and a call to address this public health crisis is needed.

Self-Reflection Exercise

Think about the community where you live and identify specific structural inequities existing at the end-of-life and across micro, meso, and macro systems.

- What can social workers do to address these structural inequities for people facing the end of life?

- What is the general responsibility of social workers as change agents attempting to effect change at the micro, meso, and macro levels?

- What is the first step to effecting change among people marginalized at the end of life?

Marginalized Identities at the End of Life

Although one could create a long list of different groups of people living with marginalized identities, this section will address a few of these groups in hopes of creating a roadmap to apply to any one person or group of people facing the end of life and living with marginal identities. As a result of the dearth of research in this area, social workers are charged and encouraged to contribute, generate, and disseminate evidence of best practices at the end of life for people living with marginalized identities. The first group that will be discussed will be LGBTQIA+ folks.

LGBTQIA+

People who identify with the LGBTQIA+ community have a long history of being denied multiple human rights due to being marginalized as a community (Javier, 2021). It is important that social workers understand the aspect of intersectionality among people who are LGBTQIA+. For example, a Black woman from Puerto Rico who is transgender can include the following marginalized identities: (a) being a woman; (b) being Latinx; (c) being transgender; and (d) being Black. Furthermore, we could also consider adding other marginalized identities, such as being an older adult, living alone, coping with pancreatic cancer, or receiving public assistance. Javier (2021) points to the daunting indicator that 53.6% of people who are LGBTQIA+ experience discrimination within hospice environments. Many people living with marginalized identities live with the trauma of family after "coming out," losing their primary support system, losing housing and food security, and losing the legacy of being part of a family. It is important that social workers and other health care workers understand the cultural frameworks that create and maintain marginalization, especially as they pertain to the provision of high-quality palliative care, hospice care, and end-of-life care for people who identify as LGBTQIA+. Not paying attention to these dynamics may translate into poor death outcomes and goes against the social work mission and vision.

Self-Reflection Exercise

Consider a couple of these intersecting identities and apply them in practice.

- If you were the hospice social worker, how would you identify a patient's and their support system's needs? How would you prioritize the needs?

- How would you establish rapport and emotional safety?

- Now, imagine the person above dying alone in a hospice unit with people unknown to them. What could you offer or do in order to facilitate a more inclusive good death process?

- Based on previous sections, select two intersecting identities for the patient above and discuss possible death and dying trajectories.

Racial and Ethnic Minority Groups

Despite discussing race and ethnicity in previous sections, it is essential to reiterate the various marginal identities that racial and ethnic minority groups experience at the end of life. The sad history of the United States in relation to enslaving people has not been forgotten and never should be. The robbing of human dignity, human worth, and a sense of well-being continue to be factors that across generations remain alive today. Racism and linguistic discrimination or predation is very much alive in the United States. The biopsychosocial and spiritual and religious implications of racism and linguistic discrimination or predation are vast and especially important within racial and ethnic minority groups at the end of life. As already established, every person has the inherited right to a good death, but barriers to a good death are considerable and significant. The unknown efficacy of medical health professionals' practices in facilitating discussions about death and dying with people with marginalized histories and identities adds to the deficiency in this area of health and mental health practice. Researchers have discussed the role that race and ethnicity play in relation to health outcomes; their outcomes are poorer when compared to their White counterparts.

Self-Reflection Exercise

- After reading this last section, what would you say are the similarities?

- Are there marginalized minority groups that are most at risk for not having their end-of-life care wishes upheld or addressed?

- From a strengths-based perspective, if you were the social worker of a patient belonging to one of these groups, how would you establish rapport, emotional safety, respect, and unconditional acceptance?

- What values do you bring into the social work profession that will support your cultural humility?

- What challenges do you foresee in your practice of social work with diverse and marginalized groups at the end of life?

- What are your privileges, and how can you use them effectively and ethically?

CONCLUSION

Social workers are well-equipped for the challenge of assessing, intervening, and evaluating end-of-life care services for people living with marginalized identities. This chapter has focused on increasing social workers' capacities and competencies to address the end-of-life care needs of vulnerable groups, such as people with multiple identities. Relevant literature, theories, and research have been presented to center and clarify social work roles and responsibilities across systems of practice. At the micro level, more research is needed to identify barriers to access palliative and hospice services for marginalized groups. Areas of immediate social work interventions include responding to the needs of people living in rural areas where access to medical care and services, including palliative care and hospice, may be limited or nonexistent. Prevalent themes of privilege, access to end-of-life care services, and decolonizing HBSE content were presented to increase students' curiosity and awareness for the need to address and question traditional theories and practices. These practices have historically ignored people living with multiple marginalized identities and are seldom represented in larger studies, leading to generalizing outcomes. The section on understanding the concept of a "good death" became a central and underlying theme, as it presented the importance of creating a feasible and applicable definition of a "good death" along with input and participation from the individual facing the end of life. Most importantly, the chapter presented various theoretical models and perspectives that can be used within an integrative approach to theory application with people who are marginalized and facing the end of life. Lastly, it is my hope that social workers develop sustainable professional development plans to continue increasing their skills and competence in this specialized practice area, but also the content of this chapter serves as a guiding force to all social workers, as death and dying exist across the lifespan. Competencies to practice social work must be enhanced and supported with effective and reflective supervision and consultation. Historically, social workers have advocated for the needs of marginalized, oppressed, discriminated against, disabled, and impoverished groups. Perhaps advocacy is the common thread that connects all social workers. With a long history of public service and advocacy for individuals, families, and communities, social work has proven to be capable of helping address end-of-life care inequities among people living with marginalized identities. Social workers add value to the profession when they challenge their own values, judgments, beliefs, myths, and misconceptions about end-of-life care and find equitable solutions to support all people facing the end of life, no matter their class, gender, race, ethnicity, abilities, sexual identity, sexual orientation, and religious/spiritual beliefs.

KEY TERMS

- **Person-in-environment (PIE):** The functioning interdependence and bidirectional relationship between an individual, or group of individuals, with their environment.

- **Good death:** According to Corpora (2021), a "good death" means having adequate pain and symptom control, having loved ones present during the death process, having free-will and volition, having effective and respectful conversations with healthcare providers, and dying where they want to die.

- **Tuskegee Study:** *The study initially involved 600 Black men–399 with syphilis, 201 who did not have the disease. Participants' informed consent was not collected. Researchers told the men they were being treated for "bad blood," a local term used to describe several ailments, including syphilis, anemia, and fatigue. In exchange for taking part in the study, the men received free medical exams, free meals, and burial insurance* (https://www.cdc.gov/tuskegee/timeline.htm)

- **Social determinants of health (SDOH):** *Social determinants of health (SDOH) are the conditions in the environments where people are born, live, learn, work, play, worship, and age that affect a wide range of health, functioning, and quality-of-life outcomes and risks* (https://health.gov/healthypeople/priority-areas/social-determinants-health).

Terms and Definitions

- **Acculturation:** There has been much controversy to the definition of "acculturation" as there is no standard definition that exists in the literature. In this dissertation, the word "acculturation" has been used to explain or depict the process and/or phenomena that emerge when an individual moves from one place (i.e., birth country) to another place where the culture may be different. Embedded within these process/phenomena are acquisition of language, cultural changes, adaptation of customs/rituals.

- **Advance Care Directives:** According to the National Institute on Aging, advance directives are legal documents that go into effect when a person is incapacitated or unable to make decisions such as being on life support. These documents (power of attorney, health care proxy, and living will) provides clarity on your personal wishes in the event of incapacitation or a terminal illness.

- **Assimilation:** Adapting the customs, rituals, and beliefs of a prevailing culture. People moving from one place to another may "acculturate" but never assimilate.

- **Cultural competence**: According to the National Association of Social Workers (NASW, 2022), cultural competence in social work practice implies a heightened consciousness of how culturally diverse populations experience their uniqueness and deal with their differences and similarities within a larger social context" (NASW, 2022).

- **Cultural Humility**: Cultural humility "refers to the attitude and practice of working with clients at the micro, mezzo, and macro levels with a presence of humility while learning, communicating, offering help, and making decisions in professional practice and settings. (NASW, 2016, p. 16).

- **Good Death:** According to Corpora (2021), a "good death" means having adequate pain and symptom control, having loved ones present during the death process, having free-will and volition, having effective and respectful conversations with healthcare providers, and dying where they want to die.

- **Hispanic:** The United States Federal Government's definition of "Hispanic" was used. Hispanic is "A person of Mexican, Puerto Rican, Cuban, Central or South American or other Spanish culture or origin regardless of race".

- **Hospice care:** According to NIA, "hospice care focuses on the care, comfort, and quality of a person with a serious illness who is approaching the end-of-life (NIA, 2022). Hospice is a type of healthcare for people with a terminal illness and a prognosis of less than six months of life. Hospice aims to address people's comfort, pain, social support, and spiritual care as they face the end of life. The main goals of hospice are to reduce pain and suffering.

- **Palliative Care:** According to the National Institute on Aging, "palliative care is specialized care for people living with a serious illness, such as cancer or heart failure.

Patients in palliative care may receive medical care for their symptoms, or palliative care, along with treatment intended to cure their serious illness. Palliative care is meant to enhance a person's current care by focusing on quality of life for them and their family" (NIA, 2022).

- **Provider Effects:** Healthcare providers', or other professionals, personal and professional attributes which may affect the therapeutic relationship. Usually seen in power-differential dynamics, provider effects correlate with healthcare outcomes.

- **Reflective Practice:** A model of supervision that centers the supervisee and the supervisor at the core of the change process. Reflective practice means constantly analyzing and questioning social work interventions as they intersect professional and personal beliefs and values. Questioning one's clinical decisions, for example, warrants introspection, vulnerability, and wisdom to determine what else needs to achieve and how to achieve it successfully.

- **Thanatologists:** Professionals who study death and dying.

- **Urban Undertow:** A term first proposed by Wheat in 1994 to describe the process and phenomenon of rural community resources being drawn to urban settings thereby affecting and undermining rural growth.

DISCUSSION QUESTIONS

1. Based on the content presented throughout this chapter and your opinion, what are the systemic needs (micro, meso, macro) of people at the end of life who are living with multiple identities?

2. Reflect on your values, perceptions, and feelings surrounding the end of life. Have your values, perceptions, and/or feelings changed after reading this chapter? If so, discuss how they have changed.

3. In your opinion, what is a "good death"? What are potential ethical dilemmas that may arise when your definition of a "good death" conflict with the patient's definition? How can these potential ethical challenges be resolved?

4. In your opinion, what are the tools social workers need to effect change when working in the realm of end of life care?

5. How can theories support your process of identifying applicable, available, and rigorous social work interventions when working with people with marginalized identities?

6. What has been the most significant awareness you have gained from reflecting on the content of this chapter?

REFERENCES

Arriaza, P., Nedjat-Haiem, F., Lee, H. Y., & Martin, S. S. (2015). Guidelines for conducting rigorous health care psychosocial cross-cultural/language qualitative research. *Social Work in Public Health, 30*(1), 75–87. https://doi.org/10.1080/19371918.2014.938394.

Barwise, A. K., Nyquist, C. A., Espinoza Suarez, N. R., Jaramillo, C., Thorsteinsdottir, B., Gajic, O., & Wilson, M. E. (2019). End-of-Life decision-making for ICU patients with limited English proficiency: A qualitative study of healthcare team insights. *Critical Care Medicine, 47*(10), 1380–1387. https://doi.org/10.1097/CCM.0000000000003920

Belisomo, R. (2018). Reversing racial inequities at the end-of-life: A call for health systems to create culturally competent advance care planning programs within African American communities. *Journal of Racial and Ethnic Health Disparities, 5*(1), 213–220. https://link.springer.com/article/10.1007/s40615-017-0360-2

Brown, J. M., Havener, D. J., & Byrne, J. T. (2017). *A systematic review: The effect of hospice and palliative care* (Honors research project). University of Akron. Retrieved March 18, 2022, from https://ideaexchange.uakron.edu/cgi/viewcontent.cgi?referer=&httpsredir=1&article=1488&context=honors_research_projects

Catlin, G. (2001). The role of culture in grief. *The Journal of Social Psychology, 133*(2), 173–184.

Centers for Disease Control and Prevention. (2021). *Underlying cause of death 1999–2020.* Retrieved July 3, 2022, from http://wonder.cdc.gov/ucd-icd10.html

Centers for Disease Control and Prevention. (2022a). *Mortality in the United States, 2020.* National Center for Health Statistics. https://www.cdc.gov/nchs/products/databriefs/db427.htm#Key_finding

Centers for Disease Control and Prevention. (2022b). *Social determinants of health: Know what affects health.* https://www.cdc.gov/socialdeterminants/index.htm

Chong, N. (2002). *The Latino patient: A cultural guide for health care providers.* Intercultural Press.

Connor, S. R., Horn, S. D., Smout, R. J., & Gassaway, J. (2005). The National Hospice Outcome Project: Development and implementation of a multi-site hospice outcomes study. *Journal of Pain and Symptom Management, 29*(3), 286–296. https://doi.org/10.1016/j.jpainsymman.2005.01.003

Corpora, M. (2021). The privilege of a good death: An intersectional perspective on dying a good death in America. *The Gerontologist, 62*(5), 773–779. https://doi.org/10.1093/geront/gnab130

Council on Social Work Education. (2022). *2022 educational policy and accreditation standards.* https://www.cswe.org/accreditation/standards/2022-epas/

Csikai, E., & Maynard, Q. (2020). What do older adults consider a good death? *Innovation in Aging, 4*(Suppl. 1), 420–421. https://doi.org/10.1093/geroni/igaa057.1357

Friedman, P. (2003). *Meeting the challenge of social service delivery in rural areas.* The Finance Project, *7(2),*Welfare Information Network. Washington, DC: The Finance Project.

Gardner D. S., Doherty M., Bates G., Koplow A., & Johnson S. (2018). Racial and ethnic disparities in palliative care: A systematic scoping review. *Families in Society, 99*(4), 301–316. https://doi.org/10.1177/1044389418809083

Gentle-Genitty, C., Chen, H., Karikari, I., & Barnett, C. (2014). Social work theory and application to practice: The students' perspectives. *Journal of Higher Education Theory and Practice, 14*(1), 36–47.

Granda-Cameron, C., & Houldin, A. (2012). Concept analysis of good death in terminally ill patients. *American Journal of Hospice & Palliative Care, 29*, 632–639.

Griggs J. J. (2020). Disparities in palliative care in patients with cancer. *Journal of Clinical Oncology, 38*(9), 974–979. https://doi.org/10.1200/JCO.19.02108.

Harris-Kojetin L., Sengupta M., Lendon J. P., Rome V., Valverde R., & Caffrey C. (2019). *Long-term care providers and services users in the United States, 2015–2016.* National Center for Health Statistics. https://www.cdc.gov/nchs/data/series/sr_03/sr03_43-508.pdf

Hughes, M. C., Vernon, E., Kowalczyk, M., & Basco-Rodillas, M. (2021). U.S. hospices' approach to racial/ethnic minority inclusion: A qualitative study. *BMJ Supportive & Palliative Care*. Advance online publication. https://doi.org/10.1136/bmjspcare-2020-002680

Javier, N. M. (2021). Palliative care needs, concerns, and affirmative strategies for the LGBTQ population. *Palliative Care & Social Practice, 1*, 1–17. https://doi.org/10.1177/26323524211039234

Johnson, K. S. (2013). Racial and ethnic disparities in palliative care. *Journal of Palliative Medicine, 16*(11), 1329–1334. https://doi.org/10.1089/jpm.2013.9468

Kleinpell, R., Vasilevskis, E. E., Fogg, L., & Ely, E.W . (2019). Exploring the association of hospice care on patient experience and outcomes of care. *BMJ Support Palliative Care, 9*(1), Article e13. https://doi.org/10.1136/bmjspcare-2015-001001

Lloyd-Williams, M., Kennedy, V., Sixsmith, A., & Sixsmith, J. (2007). The end of life: A qualitative study of the perceptions of people over the age of 80 on issues surrounding death and dying. *Journal of Pain & Symptom Management, 34*(1), 60–66.

Maynard, Q. R., & Csikai, E. (2020). The psychosocial and spiritual components of a good death. *Innovation in Aging, 4*(1), 420. https://doi.org/10.1093/geroni/igaa057.1355

Meier, E. A., Gallegos, J. V., Thomas, L. P., Depp, C. A., Irwin, S. A., & Jeste, D. V. (2016). Defining a good death (successful dying): Literature review and a call for research and public dialogue. *The American Journal Of Geriatric Psychiatry: Official Journal of the American Association for Geriatric Psychiatry, 24*(4), 261–271. https://doi.org/10.1016/j.jagp.2016.01.135

Murali, K.P. (2019). End of life decision making: Watson's theory of human caring. Nursing *Science Quarterly, 33*(1), 73–78.

National Association of Social Workers. (2004). *NASW standards for social work practice in palliative & end-of-life care.* www.socialworkers.org/practice/bereavement/standards/default.asp

National Association of Social Workers. (2006). *Social work speaks: NASW policy statements, 2006–2009.* http://www.naswdc.org/resources/abstracts/abstracts/rural.asp

Ngaboniza, S., Murekatete, M. C., Nyiringango, G., & Musabwasoni, S. M. G. (2021). Peaceful end of life theory: A critical analysis of its use to improve nursing practice. *Rwanda Journal of Medicine and Health Sciences, 4*(3), 412–417. https://doi.org/10.4314/rjmhs.v4i3.11

Oliver T., & O'Connor S. J. (2015). Perceptions of a "good death" in acute hospitals. *Nursing Times, 111*, 24–27.

Oltjenbruns, K. A. (1998). Ethnicity and the grief response: Mexican American versus Anglo American college students. *Death Studies, 22*(2), 141–155.

Ornstein, K. A., Roth, D. L., Huang, J., Levitan, E. B., Rhodes, D., Fabius, C. D., Safford, M. M., & Sheehan, O. C. (2020). Evaluation of racial disparities in hospice use and end-of-life treatment intensity in the REGARDS cohort. *JAMA Network Open, 3*(8), Article e2014639. https://doi.org/10.1001/jamanetworkopen.2020.14639

Quinn, K. L., Stukel, T., Stall, N. S., Huang, A., Isenberg, S., Tanuseputro, P., Goldman, R., Cram, P., Kavalieratos, D., Detsky, A. S., & Bell, M. B. (2020). Association between palliative care and healthcare outcomes among adults with terminal non-cancer illness: Population-based matched cohort study. *British Medical Journal, 370*, Article m2257. https://doi.org/10.1136/bmj.m2257

Portanova, J., Ailshire, J., Perez, J., Rahman, A., & Enguidanos, S. (2017). Ethnic differences in advance directive completion and care preferences: What has changed in a decade? *Journal of the American Geriatrics Society, 65*(6), 1352–1357. https://doi.org/10.1111/jgs.14800

Rine, C. M. (2018). Is social work prepared for diversity in hospice and palliative Care? *Health & Social Work, 43*(1), 41–50. https://doi.org/10.1093/hsw/hlx048

Tobin, J., Rogers, A., Winterburn, I., Tullie, S., Kalyanasundearam, A., Kuhn, I., & Barclay, S. (2022). Hospice care access inequalities: A systematic review and narrative synthesis. *BMJ Supportive & Palliative Care, 12*(2). https://doi.org/10.1136/bmjspcare-2020-002719

University of Washington Medical Center. (2007). *End-of-life care: The Latino culture.* https://ogg.osu. edu/media/documents/sunset/End%20of%20Life%20Care-Latino.pdf

U.S. Department of Health and Human Services, OPHS Office of Minority Health. (2001). *National standards for culturally and linguistically appropriate services in health care: Executive summary.* https:// minorityhealth.hhs.gov/assets/pdf/checked/executive.pdf

Wheat, J. R. (1994). Strategy to outcome urban undertow: An obstacle to rural health development. *Journal of Agromedicine, 1*(3), 59–67.

Wright, A. A., Keating, N. L., Ayanian, J. Z., Chrischilles, E. A., Kahn, K. L., Ritchie, C. S., Weeks, J. C., Earle, C. C., & Landrum, M. B. (2016). Family perspectives on aggressive cancer care near the end-of-life. *JAMA, 315*(3), 284–292.

Index

About the Contributors

Beverly Araújo Dawson is an Afro-Latinx professor in the School of Social Work at Adelphi University and the inaugural program director of the online MSW program. She received her doctoral and master's degrees from the University of Michigan and a bachelor's in psychology from Hunter College. Her research focuses on social work pedagogy in online learning environments and the impact of discrimination and cultural protective factors on health outcomes and identity development among first- and second-generation Latinx individuals.

Dr. Pablo Arriaza is a tenured social work associate professor, practitioner, researcher, and consultant. Currently, he is the program director and chair of the Undergraduate Social Work Program at the West Chester University of Pennsylvania. His research interests include (a) bilingual social work practice; (b) the professional and academic needs of bilingual social workers; and (c) end-of-life care. Dr. Arriaza is independently licensed as a clinical social worker and has practiced social work for the past 30 years with 19 years providing direct services to military families both in the United States and abroad. He has published and presented with national and international leaders in the field of social work and nursing. Dr. Arriaza is a consulting editor for various professional high-impact journals.

Dr. Autumn Asher BlackDeer is a queer decolonial scholar-activist from the Southern Cheyenne Nation and serves as an assistant professor in the Graduate School of Social Work at the University of Denver. Her scholarship illuminates the impact of structural violence on American Indian and Alaska Native communities. Dr. BlackDeer centers Indigenous voices throughout her research by using quantitative approaches and big data as tools for responsible storytelling. Dr. BlackDeer is a racial equity scholar with an emphasis on Indigenous tribal sovereignty and is deeply committed to furthering decolonial and abolitionist work.

Flora Cohen, LMSW, is a doctoral candidate at the George Warren Brown School of Social Work, Washington University in St. Louis. Her research centers on decolonized approaches to mental health service implementation in low-resource settings. She has worked in low- and middle-income countries for more than 12 years. She also has 7 years of experience as a clinical social worker with populations who have experienced significant psychological distress, primarily children and families. Flora received a Bachelor of Social Work degree from Temple University and a Master of Social Work degree from Columbia University. In her free time, she enjoys playing with her dog and doing home renovations.

Tanika Eaves, PhD, LCSW, IMH-E, is an assistant professor of social work at the Egan School of Nursing and Health Studies at Fairfield University. Tanika has been a licensed clinical social worker in Connecticut for over 20 years and holds the CT Association for Infant Mental Health Endorsement as an infant mental health specialist. Her clinical and research interests include reflective supervision and other workplace supports promoting workforce well-being, culturally responsive parent–infant psychotherapeutic interventions, and achieving equity in maternal–infant health and mental health outcomes.

Braveheart Gillani is an engineer and a social worker. After spending a decade working on offshore engineering rigs, Braveheart earned his master's in social work with a concentration in mental health and domestic social and economic development and a specialization in system dynamics from the Brown School of Social Work. Braveheart's research and advocacy are focused on sexual and gender minorities, healthy masculinity, health disparities, along with issues of racial equity and social justice. He is interested in using system sciences and system dynamics to understand wicked social problems, identifying integrated interventions and leverage points toward collective healing.

Christine D. Holmes, MSW, DSW, is the founder and counselor of Hand in Hand Caregiver Counseling, supporting individuals and families through caregiving, loss, and racial and cultural distress. Having been born to a multicultural family in Japan, Dr. Holmes's interests bridge elder care and international social work. Dr. Holmes earned her doctorate in clinical social work from the University of Pennsylvania, where her research focused on the burden of long-distance parent caregivers of the international workforce. She received the Dr. Ram Cnaan Award for merit. Her Master of ofSocial Work degree is from Columbia School of Social Work, where she enjoys teaching decolonizing social work courses as an adjunct lecturer. Dr. Holmes would like to give special thanks to editor Dr. Beth Counselman-Carpenter for shining a light on the path to publishing and supporting her contribution to this text.

Gio Iacono is an assistant professor at the University of Connecticut School of Social Work. He completed his MSW and PhD from the University of Toronto Factor-Inwentash Faculty of Social Work. His areas of practice and research specialization are LGBTQIA+ youth mental health, youth resilience, promoting diversity and inclusion within social work education, and mindfulness-based treatment approaches. Gio primarily focuses on intervention and community-based participatory research. He has worked as a psychotherapist, clinical social worker, educator, community organizer, and researcher in a variety of health and community-based settings for over 15 years. His community development work has been focused on promoting the mental and sexual health of diverse and excluded communities. Gio has also been a mindfulness meditation practitioner for many years and integrates mindfulness in his work as an educator, researcher, and clinician.

Dr. Mayra Lopez-Humphreys is an associate professor at the Silberman School of Social Work at Hunter College. Her research focuses on restorative approaches with justice-involved individuals. Currently, she serves as the principal investigator on a research project with Exodus Transitional Community; the study examines interventions with returning citizens and their transition to noncongregate hotel settings. Additionally, her interest in justice, equity, diversity, inclusion, and belonging (JEDIB) research has focused on community-led interventions and pedagogical approaches in social work education. Her work has appeared in *Social Work*, *Social*

Work Education, and *Urban Social Work*. She has taught undergraduate and graduate courses in JEDI, social welfare policy, and macro practice. Dr. Humphreys has 20+ years of nonprofit leadership experience in asset-based community development and program evaluation. She is dedicated to using a liberation ethic to address societal transformation and has co-led the development of participatory program designs and academic community partnerships that endeavor to center the lives of people who experience social and economic marginalization.

Melissa Mendez, LCSW, IMH-E, is a licensed clinical social worker and child development specialist who has been working with young children and their families for over 20 years. Her work has primarily targeted young children and families with challenging life circumstances, such as poverty, abuse and neglect, and traumatic childhood experiences. Melissa works with early childhood professionals in the United States and internationally to provide training, support, and consultation for organizations that serve young children and families throughout Mexico and other Latin American countries. She is a part-time instructor of clinical practice with children and families at Southern Connecticut State University and teaches courses in human development and family sciences at the University of Connecticut Stamford.

Jamali Moses, LCSW, is a first-generation Trinidadian American. She is a native Brooklynite and has worked as a school social worker for the New York Department of Education for almost 20 years. Her specialty as a school social worker includes building restorative justice practices and offering evidence-based clinical interventions. She also has a private practice with a specialty of helping woman of the African diaspora heal from generation and societal trauma. Jamali has one beautiful daughter, Autumn, whom she considers her magnum opus and is expected to graduate in the Spring of 2024 as a Doctor of Social Work.

Amelia Ortega, LCSW, currently works as a somatic psychotherapist, organizational consultant, and professor of social work practice. As a nonbinary, mixed Chicanx-identified clinician, Amelia's work focuses on healing from racial trauma and gender-based violence. Amelia specializes in trauma-conscious facilitation and trauma-informed classroom pedagogies through their role as a senior lecturer at the Columbia University School of Social Work and as an organizational consultant. Amelia's clinical and teaching practices engage healing generational trauma through use of feminist psychotherapy, EMDR, and their training in the Trauma-Conscious Yoga Method. In 2019 Amelia was named by Negocios Now as one of "NYC's 40 Latinos under 40" for their trauma therapy work with the LGBTQIA+ Latinx community.

Rose M. Perez, an associate professor at Fordham University's Graduate School of Social Service, migrated from Cuba as a child. Her migration experience inspired her to seek further studies focusing on Latino acculturation and well-being. Dr. Perez holds a master's degree in Latin American studies, a master's and doctorate in social work from the University of Chicago, and an MBA from the University of Michigan. She has taught human behavior and immigrant and refugee adaptation to the United States—the same topics that drive her research. Her current research explores the experience of ambiguous loss of homeland with Spanish-speaking immigrants to the United States.

Dr. Laura Quiros joined Montclair State University's Department of Social Work and Child Advocacy as an associate professor on September 1, 2022. This move situated Dr. Quiros in her community of Montclair, NJ, where she continues to lead and be involved in anti-oppression work within the academy, her daughters' school system, and the wider community. Her research and scholarly interests focus trauma-informed care through a social justice lens and the social construction of racial and ethnic identity. As a woman of color from a multicultural background, Dr. Quiros leverages her experiences, relationship building, and clinical skills to foster connections, inclusion, and empathic accountability. Having to negotiate her own identity required her to create brave and safe spaces to survive and thrive and helped her develop tools that allow her to relate to various experiences that impact diverse groups. Dr. Quiros's latest book focuses on incorporating diversity and inclusion into trauma-informed social work (https://www.lauraqc.com/book).

Lisa Werkmeister Rozas is a first-generation Peruvian American and professor at the University of Connecticut School of Social Work. She began her career as a clinical social worker at a community-based agency with Latin@ individuals and families. After receiving her PhD in social work, she completed a postdoctoral fellowship at Yale University Department of Psychiatry before joining the UConn in 2004. She has served as the director of the BSW program and the Puerto Rican/Latin@ Studies Project at the UConn School of Social Work. Her research and teaching interests focus on the examination of coloniality, White supremacy, implicit bias, and their effects on intersectional identities and the importance of critical consciousness on advocacy and allyship. Her interests also include centering Indigenous knowledge within higher education and the environmental justice movement. She is the coauthor of the 3rd edition of *Racism in the United States: Implications for the Helping Professions* (2021).

Soma Sen is a professor at the School of Social Work, San Jose State University, California. She teaches research and theory courses in the graduate program. She has master's degrees in economics, community and regional planning, and social work and a PhD in social work. Her primary areas of research are social epidemiology of HIV/AIDS and theory building and application. She disseminates her research through publications and other opportunities at local, national, and global levels. She serves as advisory board member for a consortium of international scholars working on health and well-being and serves as editorial board member for their journal, *International Journal of Health Wellness, and Society.*